ALL-TIME GREATS

A Golden Hands book

Marshall Cavendish, London

Edited by Phil Soar and Martin Tyler

Published by Marshall Cavendish Publications Limited,
58 Old Compton Street,
London W1V 5PA

©Marshall Cavendish Limited 1971-72-73-74

Most of this material was first published
by Marshall Cavendish Limited
in the partwork *Book of Football*

This volume first published 1974

Printed by Morrison and Gibb, Edinburgh, Scotland

ISBN 0 85685 055 1

This volume is not to be sold in
the USA, Canada or the Philippines

INTRODUCTION

Football is about footballers; great football is about great footballers. These are the men this book is devoted to.

Great, flowing so easily off the tongue and typewriter, is as overused an expression as any in the game. Such is the nature of football that many players are capable of performing feats worthy of that adjective. But to be deservedly so described there must be a degree of consistency.

That is the criterion of this collection of 'All-Time Greats'. As always, it will be a selection that provokes argument, not only about those who are included but about those who are missing. It is a selection not restricted by time—there are forwards from Steve Bloomer and G O Smith through to Martin Chivers and George Best—or by geography—included are Eusebio from Africa, Pele from South America, Yashin from the heart of Russia and stars from all over Western Europe.

Over the years the game has completely altered its shape. Even today there are widely differing tactical styles in different continents. But wherever and whenever men play the game there will be outstanding individuals. They are what football—and 'All-Time Greats'—is all about.

CONTENTS

THE GOALKEEPERS

Gordon Banks	8
Peter Bonetti	12
Pat Jennings	14
Lev Yashin	16

THE DEFENDERS

Bob Crompton and Jesse Pennington	20
Eddie Hapgood and George Male	22
Joe Mercer	24
Alf Ramsey	26
Johnny Carey	29
Bobby Evans and George Young	30
Billy Wright	32
Neil Franklin	34
Franz Beckenbauer	35
George Cohen and Ray Wilson	38
Bobby Moore	40
Jack Charlton	44

THE MIDDLE-MEN

Charlie Buchan and Len Shackleton	48
Clem Stephenson	51
Alex James	52
Raich Carter, Peter Doherty and Wilf Mannion	54
Danny Blanchflower	58
Alfredo di Stefano	60
Bobby Charlton	63
Duncan Edwards	68
Johnny Haynes	70
John White	72
Martin Peters	74

Jim Baxter	77
Billy Bremner and Johnny Giles	80
Gunter Netzer	84
Alan Ball	86

THE WINGERS

Billy Meredith	90
Alan Morton	92
Cliff Bastin and Joe Hulme	94
Tom Finney	96
Stanley Matthews	98

THE GOALSCORERS

Steve Bloomer	102
Gilbert Smith and Vivian Woodward	104
Hughie Gallacher	106
Dixie Dean and Tommy Lawton	108
Jackie Milburn	112
Stanley Mortensen	114
Nat Lofthouse	116
Ferenc Puskas	118
John Charles	121
Eusebio	124
Jimmy McGrory	127
Jimmy Greaves	128
Pele	130
Ron Davies	135
Martin Chivers	139
Denis Law	142
Geoff Hurst	146
Gerd Muller	150
Johan Cruyff	153
George Best	156

PART 1
THE GOALKEEPERS

Why Banks is best

THE GOALKEEPERS

Goals are what football is all about. And the great ones, like great occasions, live long in the memory, stored away in the mind to be re-lived and re-told again and again.

But if there is one facet of the game which captivates the onlooker as much, it is 'the great save'. The ball speeds goalwards but, in the very moment that the roar reaches a crescendo, a palm or a finger-tip stretches to divert it away. And, in that moment, one hero replaces another.

Joy changes sides as grateful defenders pump the keeper's hand. Disappointment creases the faces of the attackers. And the game goes on.

Every goalkeeper has his day but few can stretch that day into weeks, into months, and into years. One man has, and his name is Gordon Banks. They say he was the greatest in the world, and when 'they' means Pele, Greaves, Charlton, Hurst and many more, who would dare to disagree?

In 1972, England's football writers elected 'Banksy' as their Footballer of the Year. Why 1972? Did they have to wait until he was on the winning side in a Wembley final? If Banks ever reacted so belatedly in his profession he would be struggling for his place in a Sunday morning side.

Perhaps it was because he has never played for a fashionable club. Perhaps it was because goalkeepers, as they sit at the back of the class, are too often regarded as part of the furniture. Only one other had ever been Footballer of the Year, and that was Bert Trautmann of Manchester City in 1956.

In 1956, when he was 18 and just starting on a career in professional football with the first of his unfashionable clubs, Chesterfield, Banks used to imagine he was Trautmann. When he was elected by the FWA he was 34. He had been at the top for nearly ten years and, like all immortals, he looked as good as new. In a country where the standard of goalkeeping in the First Division is probably higher than anywhere in the world Banks was number one—even to the ambitious young men burning their hearts out to take his place in the England side.

'He's brilliantly professional,' said Chelsea's Peter Bonetti, 'a model goalkeeper'; 'I've watched him on television at every opportunity and he's always been my idol,' says Liverpool's Ray Clemence; 'He's the best goalkeeper in the world and he could have played for England for years,' says Leicester City's Peter Shilton.

For a decade from 1963 Banks kept the international appearances of some fine keepers down to a handful. Peter Springett, Tony Waiters, Alex Stepney, Gordon West, Bonetti and Shilton were players who, in most countries, would have been regular choices. Another band of hopefuls including Peter Grummitt and Jim Montgomery never even had a look in.

It was ironic that Shilton should have replaced Banks in the Leicester City side in 1967. The door opened when Leicester transferred Banks to Stoke City for £52,000 on April 17—move which Danny Blanchflower described as 'the bargain buy of the century.'

'People are paying £200,000 for strikers in 1972,' commented Stoke chairman Albert Henshall, 'yet this fellow destroys strikers with saves that are out this world.'

Why, then, did Leicester sell? Their manager at the time was Matt Gillies: 'I was placed in a most unenviable situation,' he explains. 'Banks was firmly established as England's number one but Leicester also had Shilton, a local boy with tremendous potential and ambition. Shilton was 17 and Banks 28. One had to go.

'Arsenal were keen on Shilton and he wanted first-team football. With the future in mind I decided to keep the younger man. I didn't want an auction so I decided on what I thought was a fair price and Stoke were the first club to put that price in writing.' The interest of Bill Shankly had not been shared in the Liverpool boardroom, so Banks went to the Victoria Ground and not to Anfield.

Although Banks and Leicester had not seen eye to eye on more than one occasion, the goalkeeper was not exactly enthralled about the move. 'I was hurt that Leicester were ready to part with me and keep Shilton. It was all too soon after the World Cup.'

Banks had been voted the best goalkeeper in the 1966 World Cup finals in England when he conceded only three goals in six games, including one penalty.

'I worried about my career at that point in 1967,' he says. 'But then I recalled that three of the world's best goalkeepers, Russia's Yashin, Scotland's Simpson and Mexico's Carbajal, were

p left Over the years Banks has had a broken wrist, dislocated thumbs and ctured fingers, but remained free of serious damage on the field.

set Banks adjusts his dress during the game with Greece in Athens in 1971. had conceded only 53 goals in his 69 England matches by that time.

p The brilliant save, seen by millions, that reinforced Banks' position as the rld's best goalkeeper, made against Brazil in the 1970 World Cup match at uadalajara. Banks, coming across from the near post, had been sure nobody

would reach the cross. But Pele's header was a bullet, aimed for the corner, bouncing awkwardly; the England keeper, sprinting across his line, still had to stretch full-length and, as the ball was almost over the line, scoop it up. Banks' recollection is rather too modest: 'The ball landed just in front of me and to be sure of saving it I flicked it away.' Pele's reaction? 'At that moment I hated Gordon Banks. I just couldn't believe it . . . It was the greatest save I had ever seen.'
Above Banks in First Division action for Stoke at Crystal Palace in 1969.

all older men.'

Stoke manager Tony Waddington had no inhibitions. 'We had tried to buy Gordon 18 months before when Leicester wouldn't sell at any price. He'd always played brilliantly against us.'

The Stoke players were soon to become the observers of Banks' amazing pre-match loosening-up ritual: a combination of ballet movements and the stretching actions of a cat. The effect is not only a relaxation of the nervous system but a toning up of every muscle in readiness for the action ahead.

Banks has always believed in practice, and more practice. The young Shilton, studying him at Leicester, was amazed at his dedication, at the hours he put into perfecting some facet of his game. Shilton admits he was fortunate. 'If you've got the England goalkeeper at your club you know how good you have to be to get to the top.'

Though his position invites exhibitionism, Banks has never been showy. The continentals may play to the gallery with tumbling routines and exaggerated gestures. It is easy to give the illusion of greatness; it is not easy to maintain it. Yet the two really memorable saves of the many Banks has made needed no artificial dressing. They needed only genius.

The first was against Brazil in the blazing heat and high altitude of Mexico and the 1970 World Cup. England, the holders, and Brazil, the favourites, had been playing for 18 minutes in Guadalajara when the South Americans launched an attack on the right.

Jairzinho sped down the wing and cut inside; his cross seemed to hang in the air as Pele climbed to meet it. Banks takes up the story: 'I'd been covering the near post but as Jairzinho chipped the ball over I started back across the goal. Halfway across I was sure the ball was too high for anyone to reach but then I saw Pele. He seemed to climb higher and higher until he got the ball on his forehead, putting everything behind it. The ball landed just

in front of me and to be sure of saving it I flicked it away. Never at any point did I think I was beaten, but I'm prepared to admit it was the save of my career.'

Pele was aghast. 'At that moment I hated Banks more than any man in football. I just couldn't believe it. But when I cooled down I had to applaud him with my heart. It was the greatest save I had ever seen.'

Pele's comments conveyed the greatness of that save more so than Banks' modest recollections. The header was low and fast, heading for the corner, the bounce was awkward; Banks, sprinting across his line, still had to stretch full-length and, as the ball was almost over the line, scoop it up; and up it went, in a tense parabola over the bar. The whole stadium, on its feet in anticipation of a goal, sat down in disbelief.

'Everybody has bad games and I'm no exception to the rule'

The other really great save could easily have been over-dramatized for the simple reason that it changed history. Whereas Brazil went on to win against England, Stoke, who had won nothing in 109 years until they triumphed in the Football League Cup final of 1972, would have had to wait at least another season if Banks had been beaten by a Geoff Hurst penalty three minutes from the end of extra time during the second leg of the semi-final against West Ham at Upton Park.

Stoke had lost the first leg 2-1 but had drawn level on aggregate with a goal from John Ritchie after 72 minutes of the return. But the hearts of their supporters sank when Banks impeded West Ham's Harry Redknapp in a furious scramble for the ball in the goalmouth. Hurst had beaten Banks from the spot in the first leg and there was no surer striker of a ball.

The two England men faced each oth enemies now. Hurst shot fiercely to Banks' ri —just as he had done at Stoke. Banks follov the right way, but his anticipation was almost good: the shot was straighter than at Sto Banks, at full stretch, wrenched himself in m air, got his two arms up in line—and, as Mexico, the ball curved up over the bar.

Hurst just stood there gaping in disbel the Stoke players ran at Banks and smothe him in gratitude. He came out of the clin bawling and gesticulating angrily in that nerv fashion of all goalkeepers when they are tryi to hide the embarrassment of having achiev something extraordinary.

What does Banks remember of that save? 'I v concentrating so much that the rest of field was completely shut out of my mind. I could see was the ball and Geoff. I decid to go right but I'm not prepared to say why. was certainly the most vital penalty I've ev saved.'

'Of course I like to make special sav he continues, 'but the greatest compliment I c be paid is when a player says, "that was an ea game, Gordon." I may know differently.'

Banks talked to himself during matches, coa ing and cajoling himself to maintain his conce tration. But he was not invincible.

'Everybody has bad games and I'm no exce tion,' he said. West Bromwich Albion put five pa him in August 1970 at The Hawthorns—the sar ground where he had once conceded another n hand with Leicester. 'As England's goalkeep I have a high standard to maintain but you c never take things for granted, whatever yo reputation. I had a bad night against Albion.'

After a game against Everton Banks was on criticized by their manager Harry Catteric 'Gordon seems a bit susceptible to the b crossed to the near post. This is a weakness most goalkeepers. 'You can't be everywhere once,' retorted Banks. 'I don't make a habit conceding these kind of goals.'

That was the thing about Banks. He had lapses, like anyone else; but he had no *consistent* weakness, though his distribution, sometimes erratic, was suspect.

His temperament was good—though he got irritable when he knew he was in the right and was penalised. He was booked against Crystal Palace for showing dissent after he had been penalised for handling outside the area. Banks claimed that 'for ten years I've cleared balls from the edge of the area by throwing the ball up inside the area and kicking it outside. This way I can use the area to the full.' On occasions like this the famous Fernandel grin disappears and Banks stands with feet rooted to the spot and his arm beating up and down like a railway signal. But these occasions are few and far between.

The greatest tribute to Banks is the respect he has won from others. 'With most goalkeepers I used to approach them with the ball and wonder which side to put it,' says Jimmy Greaves. 'With Gordon I used to ask myself "how can I beat this man?"'

'This man can sell forwards the dummy,' said Stoke manager Tony Waddington. 'He reserves this trick for suicidal occasions, when a forward is clean through. He deliberately leaves a gap to invite a shot and then, somehow, jack-knifes back to make a save. It doesn't always work but I've never seen a goalkeeper confronted with so many impossible situations and overcome them with such professionalism, positioning and anticipation.'

With the attendant physical risks of keeping goal, it was ironic as well as tragic that it should all end for Banks in an off-the-field accident. An accident which would not have happened but for his professionalism.

On Sunday 22 October 1972, he elected to drive to a friend's house to watch the televised highlights of Stoke's game at Liverpool the previous afternoon—a match that was not being broadcast in his home television region. He didn't have to go, but a foul awarded against him had cost Stoke a goal, and he badly wanted to see if he had transgressed.

He never got there. His car was involved in a crash, and glass from the shattered windscreen reached his eyes. For Stoke, for England, for football, it was a stunning blow. The damage to one eye was extensive.

Typically, he did not give up his career without a fight. After a period of recuperation, he returned to Stoke City. He began to train, and earned himself a game or two in the reserve side. Sir Alf Ramsey, with characteristic loyalty, summoned him for a minor representative appearance. But in August 1973, he retired.

'Had I been an outfield player, I could have played on, I'm sure,' he admitted. 'But I don't want to have to play in lower football, so I think I must stop.' The loss to Stoke's first team was their youngsters' gain, as he accepted a coaching position. And they are the lucky ones, being taught by a man whose respect in the football world remains total.

Top left The save that kept Stoke in the 1972 League Cup. With the scores tied Banks faced a spot-kick Hurst penalty in extra time of the semi-final second leg at Upton Park; Hurst had beaten Banks from the right from the spot in the first leg and Banks went to that side. But he almost went too far: the shot was straighter this time and he had to twist back to deflect the ball up and over the bar.
Top Banks receives the adulation usually reserved for goalscorers after the save. Stoke went on to

the final—after two more struggles with West Ham—and there beat Chelsea to gain the first major honour in their 109-year history.
Above For Banks, especially, it was a happy occasion. Although he had been part of England's World Cup triumph at Wembley in 1966, he had twice known disappointment in finals at club level—with Leicester in 1961 and 1963. The following month he was voted Footballer of the Year, the first goalkeeper since 1956.

Gordon BANKS

Honours: World Cup winners medal 1966
FA Cup runners-up medal 1961, 1963
League Cup winners medal 1964, 1972
League Cup runners-up medal 1965
Footballer of the Year 1972

Club	Season	League	Int'nls
Chesterfield	1958-59	23	
Leicester City	1959-60	32	
	1960-61	40	
	1961-62	41	
	1962-63	38	4
	1963-64	36	9
	1964-65	38	6
	1965-66	32	14
	1966-67	36	4
Stoke City	1966-67	4	
	1967-68	39	8
	1968-69	30	7
	1969-70	38	10
	1970-71	40	5
	1971-72	36	6
	1972-73	8	
Total		511	73

POPPERFOTO

SYNDICATION INTERNATIONAL

THE GOALKEEPERS

Sour cream for 'The Cat'

'The three greatest goalkeepers I have seen are Gordon Banks, Lev Yashin and Peter Bonetti.' That is not the casual opinion of a journalist, a spectator or an amateur player. It comes from Pele.

If Bonetti has so impressed a player of such standing, then it seems grossly unfair that, for the world and most Englishmen, the instant recollection of him is his one nightmare game—England's defeat by West Germany in the quarter finals of the 1970 World Cup.

It is, however, somewhat inevitable. England, 2-0 up with only 20 minutes to play, eventually lost to their great rivals by 3-2 in extra time. And it was Bonetti who bore the brunt of the criticism. Ramsey had been outpointed by Schoen in the tactical use of substitutes, but Bonetti was the more immediate target for blame.

Just as a string of the fine keepers had waited on Bonetti at Chelsea, so Bonetti had waited on Banks. Before Mexico he had played in six full internationals in four years, been on the winning side every time, and had conceded only one goal, to Spain in Madrid. Then, at Leon, came the unexpected seventh call.

'The day before the match Gordon Banks went down with the stomach bug, but by the morning he'd recovered so well that he was in the team talk and I was all set to take my place on the substitutes' bench. Then just an hour before kick-off Sir Alf came to me, smiled and said "You'll be playing. Gordon's not right. Good luck".'

'I was too choked to put more than two words together: "Sorry Alf".'

'In six weeks since injuring a knee in the Cup Final replay against Leeds I'd played only one game—a friendly in Ecuador three weeks before that quarter-final at Leon. But the fact that I'd not had any other match practice to help me get used to the extra speed the ball travels in the atmosphere out there hardly seemed to matter when England went two goals up. Then came Beckenbauer's goal that put West Germany back in the game. His diagonal shot hit the ground, kept low and I was beaten by pace. Seeler's equalizer I'll always regard as a freak. He had his back to goal when Schnellinger floated a high one into our box, and I'm sure he went up more in hope than expectation. His back-header was so high I thought it must go over the bar, but the ball dropped inside the post. I couldn't believe it. I don't think Gordon Banks would have been able to do much about Muller's winner from close range in extra time. What he might have done about the first two no-one will ever know.

'In the dressing-room afterwards Sir Alf moved from one dejected player to another, trying to give a few consoling words. We all felt sick. As I pulled off the yellow jersey I was too choked to put more than two words together. I just said "Sorry Alf." He managed five: "Don't let it worry you," he said.

'I didn't. What was done could never be undone, and if I'd dwelt on it I might as well have packed up the game right then. In my disappointment I grasped for something I'd learned very early in my career—a lesson that said simply "Forget the bad days. Try and learn from them, but don't let them get you down".'

Certainly there was one collection of people

who felt that it was not his fault—the Chelsea fans who had watched and admired his skill and agility for ten years, and were looking forward to enjoying it for many more. At the start of the 1972-73 season Bonetti already held the club records for first-team appearances (555) and League matches (444) and, though his England career had probably evaporated for ever on that hot day in Leon, he had not, at 31, yet reached the peak age for a goalkeeper.

Ever since Bonetti took over from England international Reg Matthews and made his debut in April 1960 the most unrewarding role at Stamford Bridge has been that of his understudy. Some fine names have played second fiddle to him—England amateur Mike Pinner, Jim Barron, Alex Stepney, Tommy Hughes and John Phillips among them—and in all those years only one man has gladly handed back the jersey without feeling it might be a long time before he was in the Chelsea side again. That was defender Dave Webb, after he was pressed into emergency service at home to Ipswich in December 1971.

In September the following year, with Bonetti again in fine form, Phillips (signed from Aston Villa for £25,000) asked for a transfer. 'I feel sorry for John,' said Bonetti as the request was turned down. 'I would have done the same in his position at his age. He's a first class keeper in his own right and has pushed me more than anyone. It's an awful problem, this reserve goalkeeper business. You can juggle with all the other shirts but there's only one green jersey.'

Style, grace and the quickest reflexes earned from his team-mates the nickname of 'The Cat' that has been his from the time he came into the first team. But Bonetti's talents are recognized far beyond Stamford Bridge.

'He's a master of the reflex save and more agile than I am,' says Banks. 'I'm too big to fling myself about at the speed Peter does and have to make up for that with positioning.' Bob Wilson, of Arsenal and Scotland, claims that 'When I was a struggling goalkeeper trying to improve my game, Peter Bonetti was the player I watched more closely than anyone. Agility is one of his outstanding qualities, and his immaculate handling and timing have helped him to overcome his lack of inches (Bonetti stands 5ft 10½in). But what has always impressed me most is his superb judgment in leaving his line and plucking the ball amid a mass of bodies in the penalty-area. Bonetti is one of the game's entertainers, and at an important stage of my career with Arsenal he showed me much about the art of top-level goalkeeping.'

Bonetti was the quiet and unsung hero of Chelsea's cup successes

If his presence has baulked the progress of all other 'keepers at Stamford Bridge, his daring and spectacular play has thrilled the crowds and been a decisive factor in the cup triumphs of the modern Chelsea. In the 1970 FA Cup Final at Wembley he touched world class in extra time to deny Leeds United the victory their superiority merited; and in the replay at Old Trafford Bonetti allied bravery to brilliance to bring Chelsea back from the brink of disaster after being knocked to the ground in the mid-air collision with Mick Jones.

With his left knee outrageously swol[len] Bonetti played for the remaining hour of nor[mal] time and through the torture of the extra per[iod] The injury had left him unable to take off the shot with which Jones put Leeds into lead, but the turning point came at 1-1, w[hen] twice in a minute he dived to save fierce sh[ots] from left-back Terry Cooper. Without s[uch] courage the Cup would never have gone Chelsea for the first time that night . . . without that victory there could have been European Cup Winners Cup triumph in Ath[ens] a year later.

It was touch-and-go whether Bonetti pla[yed] there in the final against Real Madrid, beca[use] pneumonia had kept him out of the quarter-[and] semi-finals, in which Phillips proved an admir[able] deputy. But in Athens manager Dave Sex[ton] went for experience—and it paid off.

There, after Chelsea had been shocked [by] Zoco's 89th minute equalizer, Bonetti produ[ced] three superb extra-time saves and Chelsea li[ved] to fight again two nights later. In the rep[lay] they led by a comfortable 2-0 with 15 min[utes] left, but a goal by Fleitas revived Real, and [the] closing minutes belonged to Bonetti. Twice [he] was off his line to block shots by Amancio, [and] seconds from time came one of his greatest-e[ver] saves when he sprang to the left and clutch[ed] Zoco's point-blank header. In the drama of th[ese] two Athens finals Bonetti's experience un[der] pressure was decisive.

'With Banksie around I'm lucky to have played seven times for England'

Bonetti's future in professional football w[as] shaped before he left school—on the day in 19[xx] when his mother wrote to Ted Drake, th[en] manager of Chelsea, and asked if he would giv[e a] trial to her son who 'might make you a use[ful] goalkeeper'. He had that trial in January 19[xx] joined the Stamford Bridge groundstaff [some] months later, signed professional forms in A[pril] 1959, and made his senior debut at home [to] Manchester City on 2 April 1960.

From then on he was always first choice. [In] 1962-63 he helped Chelsea to promotion, in 19[62-] 65 he was in goal when they won the League C[up] and in 1967 (the season he was voted Chelse[a's] first 'player of the year') he made his first appe[ar]ance at Wembley, when Spurs beat them in [the] FA Cup Final. Then, in 1970 and 1971, came [the] FA Cup and European successes. In 1972 he w[as] back at Wembley, though when Stoke beat Chel[sea] 2-1 in the League Cup final it meant that he h[ad] appeared in three club games at the Stadium—a[nd] never finished on the winning side.

The ability, dedication and loyalty of t[he] model clubman were rewarded in May 1971 w[ith] Chelsea's record testimonial—some £12,000, p[lus] a pair of gold cuff-links presented after [an] impromptu whip-round by Chelsea's notori[ous] Shed.

Only once did he ever want to leave Stamf[ord] Bridge: in 1966 when, unable to see eye to eye w[ith] Tommy Docherty, he asked for a transfer. 'Wh[en] Tommy went and signed Alex Stepney fr[om] Millwall I clapped my hands,' explains Peter. [It] seemed I was on my way, and there was a lot of t[alk] about West Ham at the time. Instead, Alex mov[ed] on after playing only one game for Chelsea. I w[as] never more surprised. But in the end everythi[ng] worked out for the best for me.'

In nearly one third of his first-team appe[ar]ances Bonetti has kept his goal intact; in tw[o] thirds of them he has given away only one goal [or] none; and in a poll conducted in the club p[ro]gramme in April 1969 he was voted Chelse[a's] greatest ever player.

How long will he go on? 'No-one can predi[ct] is his answer. 'I feel I'm as fit and have be[en] playing as well as ever and I'd like to thi[nk] I can keep right on in the way keepers l[ike] Hopkinson, Hodgkinson and now Gordon Ban[ks] have done. Banksie was a shining example to us a[ll] To be honest, with him as a contemporary I cou[ld]

elf fortunate to have played seven times for
land. I've often thought to myself "he's bound
ave an off-day some time," but he never does.
sistency stands highest among all his qualities.
nakes the fewest mistakes and to me that's how
keepers must be measured.'
.way from football Bonetti is both family man
businessman. He and his wife Frances have
e daughters and a son, and Peter is a director
flourishing wholesale sports goods company
Mitcham in south London. He has already
ded that he will not be looking for a living
n football when his playing days are over.
ere's only a limited number of jobs as pro-
ional coaches and too much anxiety about
g a manager for my peace of mind. Anyway,
manager who does his job properly has next to
nome life, and that's not for me. But I won't
myself off entirely from the game. I enjoy
ching, but it will be with some schoolboy or
teur team, not among professionals. That way
be able to put back something into the game
's been so good to me.'

Peter BONETTI

Honours: European Cup Winners Cup medal 1971
FA Cup winners medal 1970
FA Cup runners-up medal 1967
League Cup winners medal 1965
League Cup runners-up medal 1972

Club	Season	League Mtchs	Int'nls Mtchs
Chelsea	1959-60	6	
	1960-61	36	
	1961-62	33	
	1962-63	39	
	1963-64	35	
	1964-65	41	
	1965-66	38	1
	1966-67	38	2
	1967-68	40	1
	1968-69	41	
	1969-70	36	3
	1970-71	28	
	1971-72	33	
	1972-73	23	
Total		467	7

Left Peter Bonetti gives out the orders for Chelsea
in 1972. He had been doing it for 12 years as a
succession of talented understudies came and went,
and had established club records for both League
appearances (444 at the start of 1972-73) and first
team matches (555). He was unlucky to have Gordon
Banks as a contemporary—though he could have
played for Switzerland via his father's birth—
and even unluckier to have one of his rare off days
in the disastrous defeat by West Germany in the
1970 World Cup quarter-final at Leon.
Below Bonetti displays the agility which quickly
earned him the nickname of 'The Cat'—this time
during the FA Cup semi-final against Liverpool at
Villa Park in 1965. He was to wait another two
years for his first Wembley appearance, and another
five for his Cup winners medal—after a heroic
performance against Leeds in the replay at Old
Trafford, when he played most of the game
with a crippling knee injury.

Pat Jennings —with apologies for excellence

Pat Jennings, Spurs and Northern Ireland keeper—during a quiet moment and taking the knocks.

It is an irony of football that the position which allows most scope for flamboyant exhibitionists should so often be filled by efficient introverts.

Gordon Banks springs instantly to mind as one who stripped his game of dramatic effect and unnecessary gesture and Peter Shilton, quite deliberately, chose the same path. Pat Jennings almost seems ready to apologize for the excellence of his goalkeeping.

In many ways Jennings is the most interesting case, for he plies his trade in London. If a sports star has no great love for personal publicity, then Stoke and Leicester are places in which the national spotlight may be avoided. But London is different; it is the place where most of the media men operate. People become magnified.

Yet Jennings, an important member of the most expensive team in the history of British football, opted for near-anonymity. And, despite a level of performance which placed him among the best half-dozen keepers in the world, he secured his privacy.

Quiet and unassuming—'I think the last word he spoke was "goodbye" to his parents in Ireland,' said Bill McGarry, once his boss at Watford—Jennings made his quest for peace and seclusion a lot easier by constantly changing his ex-directory telephone number.

He established the basis of his ability in a sport which has only the most tenuous links with soccer. A native of Newry in County Down, he acquired a reputation as a first-class Gaelic footballer in his early teens, and was to look back with gratitude on that peculiarly Irish mixture of rugby and football. 'It taught me to accept hard knocks,' he explains. 'The physical contact was tremendous and the result is that if I get a few cuts and bruises these days they don't worry me.'

Jennings brought the Gaelic disregard for injury to his early attempts at goalkeeping—'I just enjoyed throwing myself about'—and as his talent developed he earned a place in the Northern Ireland youth team.

In 1963 that side reached the final of the 'Little World Cup' at Wembley, with Jennings in goal. They were beaten by an England team captained by Chelsea's Ron Harris, but Jennings performed well enough to make a move to an English club almost inevitable. That move came just a week after the end of the tournament.

Former Spurs captain Ron Burgess, then managing Watford, was urgently seeking a goalkeeper, and the big Irishman's confident handling was worth a gamble at £6,000. Jennings left Newry, went straight into the Watford first team, and within a few months won the first of his many full Northern Ireland caps. Then only 18, he was developing rapidly both in technique sheer size. Plainly he would not remain too l at Third Division Watford.

In the event he remained for just 15 mon before Bill Nicholson made his play. Nichol was in the process of rebuilding his Tottenh side: Alan Mullery and Cyril Knowles had b acquired for some £120,000, and Alan Gilz was to follow for £72,000 later that ye Jennings' fee was £27,500 and the deal w Watford was to prove as important as Nicholson brought off.

The presence of Bill Brown, a stalwart of double side, stood between Jennings and a regu first-team place on his arrival at White H Lane. But within two years he had made position his own, and over the next seven seas he was to miss only seven League games.

It is difficult to calculate his contribut to Tottenham's development over that peri A team forced to play in the shadow of a gr side and often criticized by an unsympathe public desperately needed players of certain men whose performances were dependable, alm invariable. They had one in Dave Mackay, anotl —as his total of goals verified—in Jim Greaves. And they found a third in Jennings.

Certainly he was one of the major reas behind the FA Cup win in 1967. The side v far from the best Spurs have produced, they worked for their rewards and in Jennin they could look to accomplished insurar when things were going wrong.

The first Spurs keeper to see his name on the club's scoring list

His size was an obvious asset. There is som thing enormously assuring in a goalkeeper w can dominate his area with his bulk, accepti the physical challenges from big strikers a making his weight tell when forced to battle the brink of his six-yard box to take out dang ous crosses. But size is nothing without agil and technique—and Jennings worked solidly those aspects of his game.

The essential purpose of goalkeeping, af all, is to prevent goals, and the keeper there to make things as difficult as possible f the forward. Jennings, like all the best go keepers, reduced this objective to a matter angles through impeccable positioning and fa aggressive advances on the man with the b Having forced a decision on the forward, he wou then gamble on his agility and bravery to co plete the save.

If that courage owed much to his experien of the Gaelic game, then his kicking owed ev more to the Irish sport. Jennings could co fortably drop the ball around the fringe of t opposing penalty area and, with strikers Al Gilzean and Martin Chivers in pursuit, t frequently proved an asset for Tottenham.

Its most spectacular reward came during t FA Charity Shield match with Manchester Unit at Old Trafford in 1967. Aided by the wind, l kick soared deep into the United box; A Stepney misjudged the bounce and Jennin became the first Spurs goalkeeper to find

Pat JENNINGS

Honours: FA Cup winners medal 1967
League Cup winners medal 1971, 1973
EUFA Cup winners medal 1972
Footballer of the Year 1973

Club	Season	League	Int'nls
Watford	1962-63	2	
	1963-64	46	2
Tottenham	1964-65	23	6
Hotspur	1965-66	22	5
	1966-67	41	2
	1967-68	42	3
	1968-69	42	6
	1969-70	41	4
	1970-71	40	5
	1971-72	41	5
	1972-73	40	6
Total		380	44

ame in the list of scorers. Typically, Pat nnings looked acutely embarrassed.

Such has been his reticence that his voice mained virtually unknown to the public until, surpassing his own high standards of excellence 1972-73, he became a prime target for television's most persistent interviewers.

In that year his magnificent consistency irned him the Footballer of the Year award, ppropriately as successor to Gordon Banks. lost players would be delighted to be so onoured, but not the quiet Irishman. Any feel-ig of elation was quickly quashed when he alised that a speech was expected of him in ont of an audience of around 700 at the ootball Writers' Dinner.

He clinched the award one memorable day in larch in front of the most appreciative crowd England at Anfield. With Liverpool surging towards the Championship, Jennings' brilliance cost them a valuable point. Not only was there a string of acrobatic stops, but he utterly demoralised the home side with two breath-taking penalty saves.

The first denied Kevin Keegan and then when Tommy Smith stepped forward late in the game, ostensibly to shoot his team's winner, the Spurs keeper dived—and came up with the ball. For once his massive calm was shattered. As he rose to his feet, the ball clasped in one giant hand, he raised the other arm, the fist clenched in gladiatorial salute.

The following season, he continued in the same athletic vein, as Spurs sought a fourth successive trophy after their League Cup wins of 1971 and 1973 which sandwiched the UEFA Cup successes of 1972.

He reserved one of his finest performances for Europe, continually thwarting Grasshoppers of Zurich in the first leg of a UEFA Cup tie. Spurs won 5-1, but the score could have been easily reversed had it not been for his razored reflexes. The only time he was beaten was from the penalty spot, and even that disappointed him: 'I should have saved that penalty. I got my hands to it,' he said after the game with such a rueful shake of the head that one could have been forgiven for thinking he had cost his team the tie.

For his country, Pat Jennings has often stood between defeat and total rout. And it is one of the periodic tragedies of football that Wales and Northern Ireland throw up talents that can never find their true stage in the centre of world football. Pat Jennings' gifts are of that calibre. In 1974 he stood as arguably the best goalkeeper in the world.

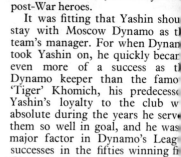

Lev Yashin—the reluctant goalkeeper

THE GOALKEEPERS

Below *Lev Yashin, in his famous black strip, gathers the ball during the 1968 USSR Championship final. Yashin, Moscow Dynamo's world-class goalkeeper, played a large part in their spate of League successes during the fifties, but was unable to prevent them losing on this occasion.*

Bottom *Yashin proudly displays the Russian Cup which Moscow Dynamo won in 1969. The cup only assumed importance in the USSR when it was realized that the winners gained entry into European competition.*

Konstantin Beskov, one of Dynamo post-War heroes.

It was fitting that Yashin shou stay with Moscow Dynamo as t team's manager. For when Dynan took Yashin on, he quickly becan even more of a success as t Dynamo keeper than the famo 'Tiger' Khomich, his predecesso Yashin's loyalty to the club w absolute during the years he serve them so well in goal, and he was major factor in Dynamo's Leag successes in the fifties winning fi Championship medals.

Yashin almost always played in I famous black jersey, which made hi appear taller than his six feet. O of Yashin's finest games—or ha game—was one that he remembe best, and one where, curious Yashin was not in his customa black. This was at Wembley in 19 when Yashin kept goal for the R of the World team against England

At Wembley, 1963 Yashin makes a remarkable save

the FA Centenary match. For minutes, until he was replaced Yugoslavia's Soskic, he brilliant held the English forwards at b with his seemingly telescopic arr his courage, judgement, and maste of angles.

Yashin capped that memoral display of goalkeeping at its fin with an effortless save right on ha time. At the exact moment t referee's whistle sounded for ha time, a shot flew towards Yashi goal. He met the ball with I clenched fist, and almost casua gave it a short-arm punch which so the ball flying, first bounce, to t halfway line. When it hit the grou Yashin was picking up his cap fro the back of his goal, while the cro were applauding his remarkal confident save.

Lev Yashin was born in 1929, a when he first went to school at t age of seven, he stood a head high than any of his classmates, w called him 'Eiffel Tower'. Young L did not like being described as steel-built Paris landmark, and tr to make the point with his fis Unfortunately he was not only strikingly unsuccessful fighter, I because of his height and his lack manoeuvrability, he was not ve good at games either.

But Yashin hated losing, and father was always teaching him try harder at sport. 'The big thin he told Yashin, 'is willpower. you've got willpower, you can over defeat and disappointme We've all got willpower, but you ha to develop it. Try to get throug whole day without getting angry pulling the girls' hair—that's r willpower training!'

Yashin says of his schoolda 'I ran, did the high jump, put shot, threw the discus, took fenc lessons, had a go at boxing, divi wrestling, skating, tried basket-b played ice-hockey, waterpolo, football. I spent my winters on s and skates, and in the summer I v playing basketball and football.

'In the winter of 1943, just bef my fourteenth birthday, I went work at the aircraft factory wh

Lev Yashin is probably the only world-class footballer who has neither written his own life story nor had it written for him. The pity is that Yashin's is such an interesting story: the lanky schoolboy big enough, but not good enough to be a fighter, trying almost every other sport and failing, later managing to get into his factory's football team at outside-left, then being pushed back through the side until there was nowhere to go but into goal, eventually becoming one of the best ever goalkeepers.

When Yashin was in England with Moscow Dynamo in 1970, he was asked, just before Dynamo's friendly

with Leicester, why he had never written a book or found a ghost writer. His answer was that as he began playing for Dynamo in 1951 and Russia's first entry into post-War international competition was in the 1952 Helsinki Olympics, his life story is really the story of Soviet football. And, he said, 'you know that story for yourself. Sometimes it's better to wait a few years so that we can look back at everything in an historical perspective. There are plenty of things I could write about, but I always think', said Yashin, 'that memoirs never give a complete picture.'

Six months after that game with

Leicester, Yashin was at a far grander occasion—his testimonial in the Lenin stadium in Moscow, where before a crowd of more than a hundred thousand, Moscow Dynamo faced a Rest of the World side. It was a tribute to Yashin's standing in the game that so many of the famous names in world football, Bobby Charlton amongst them, travelled to Moscow to play in that game.

At half-time Dynamo were two-nil up. After eight minutes of the second half Yashin left the field, and so retired unbeaten on his last appearance in big-time football. The next day, Yashin was appointed Dynamo's manager, to work with trainer

ht *Yashin's consistently fine goal-*
ing won him 78 caps. Here he stops
filippe scoring for Argentina.
ow right *Yashin, for the Rest of*
World, saves from England's Bobby
th during the FA Centenary match.
tom left *and* **right** *West Ger-*
y put Russia out of the 1966 World
despite Yashin's usual safe goal-
ing. Here he dives bravely at Uwe
er's feet and turns a shot away.

UNITED PRESS INTERNATIONAL

mother and father had jobs.
.es were hard then and I had to
get about football. I started as an
rentice and then I became a fitter.
the time the War was almost over
t into the factory youth football
n. I wanted to be a forward—I
always dreaming about hitting
ls—but gradually I got moved
k and back until I became a
keeper.

I'll never forget the time in 1945
n I crouched over the radio
ening to the commentary of the
ch in London between Dynamo
Chelsea. I almost became Alexei
omich, the Dynamo goalkeeper.
en he finally came out evens with
mmy Lawton, and Dynamo drew
, I was leaping about and scream-
for joy. Three years later I was

The English
give Yashin his
famous nickname

ASSOCIATED PRESS

ed up. I began playing hockey
ile I was in the army, and after a
r I got a place in the Dynamo
th hockey team.'

Once he had started playing for
namo—though only hockey—
shin followed Khomich's career
y closely. And although he won a
key champion's medal in 1953,
shin says that football was always
most important thing in his life.
few months later, Yashin won a
ond gold medal in the USSR
ampionships, but this time play-
football for Dynamo.

The English have a great gift for
ding nicknames for footballers,'
s Yashin. 'They called Khomich
iger". When I left hockey I began
study "Tiger's" style very closely.
at might be why English sports-
ters began to call me "Panther"—
another big cat.'

Yashin made his debut in mid-
son, 1951, when Khomich was
ured. Yashin remembers that
ne somewhat unhappily. 'Beskov
t me on as a substitute, and I
my first goal through minutes
er. It wasn't a good beginning.'
d the worst goal Yashin ever con-
ed? 'Well, there was a time when I
the opposing keeper score from a
arance. . . .'

Every player makes mistakes, but
shin, in a position where mistakes
ariably get the most publicity, has
bably made fewer than most.
deed, his consistent reliability in
al earned him 78 international
s, a total only ever bettered by
o other goalkeepers, Grosics of
ingary and Brazil's Gilmar.
shin's agility and daring have
ned him other honours too: in
63 he was named European
otballer of the Year, the only goal-
eper to win the award, and he has
en the Russian Footballer of the
ar several times. His country has

TOPIX

ASSOCIATED PRESS

also conferred on Yashin two notable
distinctions: he is a member of the
Order of Lenin and an Honoured
Master of Sport.

Yashin's first international success
came in the 1956 Melbourne Olympics, when the Soviet football team,
with Yashin its keeper, won a gold
medal. Yashin's 1956 gold was not
only his first major honour in international football, it was the first,
and so far the last, Olympic medal
for Soviet football—at Tokyo and
Mexico they failed to qualify.

In his modest two-roomed flat,
Lev Yashin has a small glass-fronted
cupboard where he keeps his medals

and trophies. There is his Olympic
gold medal, several USSR Champions' medals, and gold and silver
European Nations Cup medals.

Yashin is always—rightly—
regarded as an international star. But
he never thinks of himself in those
terms; Yashin is a very modest man.
Despite the fact that he played for
Dynamo, the KGB team, as a serving
member of the Soviet internal
security police, he never even became
an officer—he ended up as a sergeant.

A Soviet football star's life can
be monotonous. The Soviet football
bosses believe that pre-season training should last at least ten weeks.

So a year in the life of a top Soviet
footballer like Yashin is pretty full.
The season finishes at the end of
October, but in 1971, for example,

Stars complain
of 'prison camp
for free men'

the championship final did not take
place until 5 December. At the end of
the season, the players have a chance
to rest, but once the New Year is in,
the teams are recalled for training.
They all go down to the Black Sea
coast where the weather is not

Above *Yashin prepares to deal with a corner kick from Moscow Spartak, Dynamo's fierce rivals, in the course of the 1968 Russian Championship final.* **Left** *Yashin faces the cameras with the famous names who travelled to Moscow to play in his testimonial in 1971.*

quite as fiercely-cold as it is inland. Referees are obliged to start training at the same time.

This minimum of ten weeks' pre-season training is unpopular with the players. They have repeatedly said that nothing ever comes of this kind of schedule. Indeed, some top stars have gone as far as describing the pre-season training as a 'prison camp for free men'. The players live in sports centres while they play on neutral grounds on the Black Sea coast. The USSR Cup has not always been rated as highly as the FA Cup has always been in England. But since the European cups started and national cup-winning teams had a chance of entering European competition, Soviet football has taken its cup as seriously as other European countries.

Indeed, any chance of honours at a national level is taken seriously. The Soviet national team has always had first call on any Soviet footballer. The national team manager has an absolute right to demand any player from any team at any time and for as long as he is needed.

The Soviet team's greatest success in the World Cup was in England in 1966 when they got to the semi-finals. They were beaten 2-1 by Portugal in the match for third place. Yashin's typically reliable goal-keeping played a large part in

Russia's winning through to the last four.

Top Russian footballers do not, of course, make the kind of money British and European players earn. When he was at his peak Lev Yashin was officially paid around 200 roubles a month (something less than £100). That is no more than the average wage for a University teacher, but it was enough for Yashin to keep himself and his family quite comfortably in his Moscow flat, though he did not acquire a car of his own until 1971.

A team whose players don't know who employs them!

In the Soviet Union there is no professionalism—at least, not professionalism as understood in the West. Every athlete, footballers included, is either a student or has a job. A footballer's wages depend on where he works—Yashin, for example, was paid as a KGB sergeant and drew a grant as a student of physical education. That at least is the official story. Unofficially, footballers are paid colossal sums for 'overtime'. In the Second Division of the League there is actually a team whose players do not even know who they work for because the factory

that nominally employs them is engaged in the manufacture of secret military equipment, and the players receive their 'salaries' through the post!

When a Russian footballer travels abroad to play, he is paid about £7 per match. However, there are exceptions. For the World Cup in 1966, Morozov, the Soviet team manager, promised his team—and lived up to the promise—that they would be paid £30 for the first win, £60 for the second, £120 for the third, and so on. The Soviet team won four matches before losing to West Germany in the semi-finals. Morozov was also able to arrange for official visas for the players' wives who came to England as tourists.

Immediately after the 1966 World Cup, Morozov resigned and Yakushin took charge of the Soviet team. Soviet football then began to develop the North Koreans' system —building a winning team by keeping the players together. Yakushin brought thirty players together, organized a world-wide tour and, in so doing, destroyed the Soviet Championship by commandeering the top players. Consequently, the idea of the isolated national team caused total chaos and Yakushin was fired. Once again, top Russian players were able to turn out for their clubs.

Lev Yashin had this to say on the

subject: 'Once again I could se[e] family, talk to the press, and [play] for Dynamo. It's all very well [play]ing abroad. It's great fun for a w[hile] you see the sights, you live in [good] hotels, but on the whole it gets p[retty] boring. Hotel, airport, stadium, [the] match, and back to training. . . .

'Moscow isn't merely my h[ome] town—it's the town where [my] friends live. Our trainer, Konsta[ntin] Beskov, is married to an actress a[t the] arts theatre. Several of us [at] Dynamo quite often drop in [on] Beskov. We know all the ac[tors,] seeing we go to the theatre on[ce a] week, and I know quite a l[ot of] writers. In the dressing-room yo[u're] just as likely to find us talking a[bout] the latest production of Ibse[n or] Shaw as about football.'

Once someone asked Yashin [what] the main problem was in produ[cing] top-class young footballers in Ru[ssia.] He said: 'The kids can't get ho[ld of] the right size of boots!' That[, of] course, was not meant as a ser[ious] answer to what was intended [as a] serious question. In general, the[se] league clubs do not produce t[heir] own young players, they ten[d to] recruit them from lower divisi[ons.] Spartak, for example, has 30 re[gis]tered players of whom only five w[ere] born in Moscow, and none of t[hem] were spotted by the club in the [first] place. The army team has only [ten] players who have always been [with] the club.

The top clubs are [only] allowed to take the best players

Where do the first-class pla[yers] come from? From the Second [and] Third Divisions. As soon as a pla[yer] begins to show good form h[e is] immediately 'transferred' into a F[irst] Division side.

Second Division trainers natur[ally] complain about this. They ask [why] they should be expected to spot [and] develop young players, when t[hey] are immediately taken over by [the] big clubs. In Russia, any player h[e feels] right for the purpose of perfect[ing] his skills to transfer from the low[er] divisions to the highest. Before [a] Moscow Dynamo—Leicester C[ity] friendly, Yashin and some of [the] other Soviet players could [not] understand how Frank O'Far[rell,] then manager of Leicester, was a[ble] to hold Peter Shilton down in [the] Second Division. In the So[viet] Union, they said, even if a pla[yer] wants to stay in the Second Divisi[on,] he is not allowed to. The top cl[ubs] will grab him anyway.

But if this unorthodox syst[em] means that the USSR will give wo[rld] football more stars of the calibr[e of] Lev Yashin, there will be few co[m]plaints outside Russia. For Yas[hin] was arguably the best footballer p[ro]duced by his country, and [was] certainly the most popular.

Lev YASHIN

Honours: European Nations Cup winners medal, 1960
European Nations Cup runners-up medal, 1964
Olympic gold medal, 1956
Russian League Championship medal, 1954, 1955, 1957, 1959, 1964
Russian Cup winners medal, 1953, 1969
European Footballer of the Year, 1963
Member of the Order of Lenin, Honoured Master of Sport
Internationals: 78

PART 2
THE DEFENDERS

Crompton and Pennington: players and gentlemen

Until full-backs began to follow the very recent trend of contributing their special skills to planned team tactics instead of working in partnership, the great ones were better remembered as pairs rather than as individuals. In nearly every instance they were backs of different build and styles and the contrasts made each an ideal foil for the other.

Among the most celebrated for England were the Old Carthusian brothers A M and P M Walters, Robert Howarth and Bob Holmes of the Preston side who won the League and Cup double in 1889, Roy Goodall and Ernie Blenkinsop, Arsenal's pair of George Male and Eddie Hapgood, Laurie Scott and George Hardwick, and Jimmy Armfield and Ray Wilson. Often the pattern was one full-back of the solid, shrewd, non-roaming variety, the other sharp, assertive, more adventurous and less powerfully built.

Above all, perhaps, there were Bob Crompton and Jesse Pennington, partners in 23 of England's 31 internationals between 1907 and 1914. On 13 occasions they were joined by Harry Hibbs, the Liverpool and Aston Villa goalkeeper, in one of England's finest defensive trios.

Footballer and writer Ivan Sharpe, who knew the game from both sides of the touchline before the First World War, later headed his choice of the top ten full-backs he had seen with the majestic, rather awe-inspiring Crompton, who had a fine manly figure of 5ft 10in and 13 stone, and also included the crisp-tackling Pennington, the rapier to Crompton's broadsword.

Both players were born in a town widely known by the name of its League team, in each case one with an impressive football history, and both served only that club after emerging early from the junior ranks. Crompton spent over 23 years and seven months as a player with Blackburn Rovers and was the team's inspiring captain throughout the latter period of his career. He held the long service record with a single club until the fifties, when Ted Sagar the Everton goalkeeper beat it by six months, and his 41 caps was an England record until Billy Wright

passed it in 1952, 38 years later.

Crompton began playing football for the Moss Street Board school team. Though he became an apprentice plumber he was ultimately persuaded to join Rovers as a professional but, at first, unwilling to jeopardize his amateur status as a swimmer and water-polo player, he remained unpaid, and it was two seasons before he signed professional forms.

A reliable account of Crompton's League appearances was never kept, but they must have exceeded 500. The first was in April 1897 against Stoke at Ewood Park, the last in the spring of 1920, when he had turned 40. He continued his active association with the club as a director and, a few years later, as honorary team manager. Indeed Rovers, aided by Crompton's experience, won the FA Cup for the sixth time in 1928 but, as with Pennington, it was always a matter of deep personal regret that while he had gained most of the game's honours he had missed a Cup winners' medal.

Pennington, born at West Bromwich in August 1884, made his League debut against Liverpool at The Hawthorns a month after his 19th birthday, and was a regular member of the side until the end of the 1921-22 season. During his 19 years' service he played in 455 League matches, the happiest being those which ensured a Second Division championship medal in 1910-11 and a League title medal in 1919-20.

It was said of him after his first League game: 'Young Pennington has every qualification for making a first class back.' Like Crompton, his heart had certainly been in football from boyhood. His great ambition was to captain West Bromwich Albion—his father was one of the supporters whose subscriptions helped to found the club—and he was encouraged to play football by his schoolmaster, one R L James. Pennington's love of the game resulted in his starting a local club, which did not last long, so he played in other Midlands junior teams, including Dudley, and represented Birmingham Juniors against Scottish Juniors at Parkhead.

Bob CROMPTON

Honours: League Championship medal 1911-1912, 1913-14

Club	Season	League Mtchs	Int'nls Mtchs	Gls
Blackburn Rovers	1897-98	*		
	1898-99	*		
	1899-1900	*		
	1900-01	24		
	1901-02	31	3	
	1902-03	28	2	
	1903-04	32	3	
	1904-05	27		
	1905-06	36	3	
	1906-07	28	3	
	1907-08	33	7	2
	1908-09	31	6	2
	1909-10	25	2	
	1910-11	31	3	
	1911-12	33	3	
	1912-13	31	3	
	1913-14	33	3	
	1914-15	34		
	1919-20	2		

*Statistics for seasons before 1900-01 are not available

Top left and right *Bob Crompton of Blackburn Rovers. His long service record for a single club and his record 41 England caps both stood until the fifties.*

Aston Villa, who once registered him as an amateur, were to have reason to rue their subsequent loss of interest. It was skill and speed in positioning and interception rather than size that brought Pennington to the fore. His height was 5ft 8in and he weighed only 11½ stones, but 37 League appearances when Albion won the League Championship in 1919-20 proved that, even at 36, there was still plenty of stamina in his compact frame. The same season he won his last cap, figuring in the 5-4 win over Scotland at Sheffield.

Stocky and strong, Bob Crompton had size in his favour from boyhood. Already earmarked by Rovers and signed by them before any rival club could move in, the well-built, determined lad did not disappoint. He promised well in the reserves and was taken on a tour with older players at 17, making a start in the senior side (at centre-half) towards the end of the 1897-98 season. The following week he was in the Blackburn team against Aston Villa, holders of the League and Cup double, for the first match at the Villa Park ground, and from then on he was a regular choice. He increased in stature in both ability and physique, becoming burly and dominant, and had a preference for playing against men his own size—because he enjoyed the old-fashioned shoulder charge and did not care to flatten smaller players.

An entirely mistaken impression of Crompton, gained from his natural commanding style, was that arrogance was part of his make up. He was in fact the quiet type, unassuming off the field, the kind of player who could be found in a corner seat with a book on train journeys.

Crompton made an auspicious England debut in 1902 and played well enough to keep his place. 'Crompton was the back of the season,' wrote one journalist, 'a hard worker all the time but thoughtful and resourceful. He kicks well with either foot but prefers right-back, and his tackling has greatly improved. His only fault is a little lack of pace.' That last remark perhaps explains why he restricted his operations to a limited orbit, and when he eventually found his true partner (in 1907), Pennington's anticipation and speed made up for this deficiency. Both had good judgement and they developed a superb understanding. Crompton's three caps in his first season had increased to an England record of 41 when the outbreak of War ended his international career. From 1908 he was captain and he played in all but five games from 1902 to 1914.

In June 1911 the FA presented him with a framed photograph of himself in recognition of having played in more internationals than any other English player—then 32, including seven against foreign teams. England lost only six games when he was playing.

In his reminiscences 'Wickets and Goals', J A M Catton ('Tityrus' of the old *Athletic News*) wrote this of Crompton: 'As a right back he never had an equal from 1902 until 1914, when he as good as retired from the game he had adorned. He was a brave tackler, but fair and honest in his charges. He preferred to meet big and heavy men, and Scotland always had an eye during his supremacy to build a left wing that could 'bump' Bob Crompton. Nothing ever seemed to amuse the Scottish crowd as much as 'big Bob' being hurled to mother earth. It was in an Inter-League match that George Livingstone and James Quinn were once chosen as a left wing in order that Crompton might not have all his own way. But Crompton never troubled himself—the bigger the better for him. But not for worlds would I have anyone who never saw the great Crompton imagine that his game was merely charging. He played the best and purest football, was a perfect kicker, a choice player, and the finest man at screwing a ball from the touchline into the middle that I ever saw. Not for him the line of least resistance. He scorned to put the ball into touch. He was a grand player and a fine personality, for he was a quiet, a courteous and hearty fellow who, above all things, hated publicity. His idea of bliss off the field was serenity and comfort. He deserved every honour he gained, and if any man doubts the real modesty of Robert Crompton let me add that no money would tempt him to write his recollections. His quiet but firm answer was "I don't like publicity. I have had my day as a player—and let it end at that." He was content with having been an international back.'

Yet, unlike most of his contemporaries, he shrewdly combined football with his former trade—with such success that, as early as 1906, a critic remarked how Crompton was 'now accustomed to drive down to his training at Ewood Park in his own motor-car'; a status symbol indeed at that time, and one that reflected his early rise to prominence.

A so-called 'professional' foul might have won Jesse Pennington the FA Cup medal for which he yearned, but he was not the sort to commit calculated, deliberate trips. In the 1912 replayed Final at Bramall Lane, Sheffield (where the crowd was, because of a railway strike, heavily pro-Barnsley) he was true to his scruples. A relentless replay was one of seven matches that West Bromwich Albion had to squeeze into the season's last ten days—and it ran to extra time. The deciding goal was brilliantly scored by Fred Tufnell, with Pennington on his heels. He could have tripped the Barnsley player outside the penalty area but, too chivalrous to do it, he vainly tried to dispossess Tufnell—who settled the issue with almost the last kick of the match.

Jesse PENNINGTON

Honours: League Championship medal 1919-20
FA Cup runners up medal 1912

Club	Season	Matches	
		League	Int'nls
West Bromwich	1903-04	20	
Albion	1904-05	23	
	1905-06	31	
	1906-07	33	2
	1907-08	35	4
	1908-09	35	5
	1909-10	24	2
	1910-11	33	3
	1911-12	29	3
	1912-13	31	2
	1913-14	32	2
	1914-15	30	
	1919-20	37	2
	1920-21	33	
	1921-22	29	
		455	25

Left Three views of Jesse Pennington: as an England player, as captain of West Bromwich Albion (sitting, left of ball), and in action late in his long career. With Crompton he formed one of England's finest full-back pairings, and they played together in 23 of the 31 internationals between 1907 and 1914. Pennington led West Bromwich to the championship in the first post-War season.

21

The rear Gunners

Between 1933 and the outbreak of War in 1939, the full-back partnership of George Male and Eddie Hapgood was the most famous of its day— unbreakable in club football with Arsenal, and a steady feature of the England team from November 1934. Like so many of life's successful partnerships, this one was based on temperaments which at once contrasted with and complemented each other.

Male, an East Londoner from West Ham, was powerful, steady, quiet, a rock of a player, stern but fair in the tackle, with few frills or flourishes. Hapgood, by contrast, was a volatile Bristolian, overflowing with ambition and self-confidence, an elegant, graceful player who prevailed through technique and intelligence. At the same time, he had an almost boyish vulnerability and innocence which was perhaps a drawback when he was no longer cushioned by the family atmosphere of football and, more specifically, of Arsenal.

Both men owed much to Herbert Chapman, Arsenal's celebrated manager of that period, and each readily admitted it. For Hapgood, Chapman was nothing less than a father figure: a man who showed him how to live, 'who taught you how to dress, who told you how to comb your hair'.

In Male's case, he was instrumental in turning him from a moderate left-half into a splendid right-back, a remarkable piece of clairvoyance. It was in the autumn of 1933 that Chapman decided he needed a new right-back in his conquering team. Tom Parker, the excellent skipper whom he had bought from Southampton, was now a veteran. Who should take his place? Perhaps if the tall, young Leslie Compton had been a little quicker he could have been the man—and he would not have had to wait another 14 years before becoming a regular League player.

As it was Chapman sent for his left-half George Male, gave him one of his famous and mesmerically convincing pep talks, and made him feel, by the time he left the office 'not only that I could play right-back, but that I could be the best right-back in the world'. It was not long before Male was arguably just that.

Many years later as an Arsenal coach, reminiscing about those days, Male wondered whether Chapman's near-dictatorial methods would have worked so well in the present; a reflection one could never imagine coming from Hapgood. Those, as Male sensibly emphasized, were the days of the Depression. Today, he suggested, 'a player might say, "Well, I'm not staying here for that".'

Yet Chapman and the exuberant, sometimes impulsive, Hapgood never clashed, and the other man at Highbury whom Hapgood worshipped was the trainer and future manager, Tom Whittaker. He, too, with his powerful, effective hands, his soothing personality, had a great influence over Hapgood, but it was said that, in later years, certain tensions and misunderstandings grew between them. Whittaker seemed to feel menaced by the presence and prestige of Hapgood, perhaps believing him a possible rival for the Arsenal managerial job; though in fact Hapgood was willing to go back to Highbury in a far less exalted capacity.

This, in turn, led to tensions and misunderstandings between Hapgood and the club to which he has remained so emotionally bound. There was a distressing episode in 1956 when Hapgood wrote to the club, after losing his managerial job at Bath City, asking for a retro-spective benefit, and was disappointed by Arsenal's offer of a small cash payment instead.

Intriguingly, Hapgood scarcely played football at school in Bristol, and it was only some years after he had left and was driving a horse-drawn milk cart for his brother-in-law that he began to play seriously. It seems remarkable in these days of 'factory farming' of young footballers that he was 18 before Bristol Rovers spotted him, gave him a trial, and offered him professional terms. Hapgood turned them down because, although they offered him £8 a week in season, they wanted him to drive a coal cart in the summer! A milk float, he thought, was one thing, a coal cart decidedly another.

So, with all the great clubs sleeping the days away, he was signed by the non-League club, Kettering, at £4 a week in season, £3 out of it— and the right to work summers at his dairy.

After little more than a dozen games, Herbert Chapman turned up in Kettering's office, asked Hapgood whether he smoke or drank and, on being assured he did neither, signed him for

Arsenal. That was in 1927. On the way up to London he lost his signing-on fee of £10 to a gang working the three-card trick on the train.

At this time he was physically so fragile that he regularly used to faint after heading a heavy ball, so Arsenal saw to it that he built himself up on steaks. He made his League debut in 1928, and the following year replaced Horace Cope in the First Division side. He went on to make 393 League appearances, for five Championship medals, plus Cup winners' medals in 1930 and 1936, and

another Cup Final appearance in 1932. That w the game, lost on the 'over the line' goal to N castle United, when George Male was pitch-for into the side for his very first Cup tie, at left-h after Alex James' injury.

Were it not for the War, Hapgood's reco would have been still more impressive. So would Male's, though he actually went on u 1948, when Arsenal's 8-0 win at home to Grims Town represented his 285th appearance. display in the 1936 Cup Final, when he gained only winners' medal, was one of the most imma late he ever gave.

Male had joined Arsenal from the Isthm League club Clapton as a half-back. He eventua won four Championship medals and, like H good, served during the War with the Royal Force.

Though Male, the younger man, outlas Hapgood as an Arsenal player by several yea he dropped out of the England team at the o break of war, while Hapgood went on captaini England till the end of 1943. Altogether he m 43 appearances for England, 34 of them captain—if one counts the unofficial warti games. If you do not, then he won 30 caps, Male's 19. The first of them was in Rome agai Italy in May 1933, and it was in the ill-omen return the next year, when he had his n smashed by an Italian's elbow, that he fi captained his country.

An immaculate sportsman whose chivalro standards seem almost archaic by contrast wi today's 'professionalism', he even controll himself at the banquet that evening when assailant on the field looked at him across t table and laughed in his face.

Some regarded Hapgood, in his playing da as egocentric, but the quiet Cliff Bastin, colleague in the England team on so many occ sions, was at pains to deny this: 'I couldn't ha wished for a pleasanter or more modest travelli companion,' he wrote in passing while pay tribute to Hapgood's perfect timing, skil jockeying of the winger, admirable kicking w both feet, and splendid fighting spirit. 'A f given against him,' he added, 'was a rarity.'

Hapgood and Male, perhaps the greatest of the full-back pairs

Hapgood got on less well with Chapma successor, George Allison, as the Arsenal manag and was particularly distressed when, in 194 Allison readily agreed to lend him to Luton To as a guest player. Later he played as a guest Chelsea, but at the very end there was a ra prochement when he played for Arsenal once mo George Male—who was ultimately posted India, but arrived back just in time to play Arsenal in their second leg of the FA Cup against West Ham in 1946—spent much of th years at left-half. He succeeded Eddie Hapgo as captain of the side just as, for a brief spell 1937, he had succeeded him as England's captai and he skippered the Arsenal team which thrash Charlton Athletic 7-1 in the League South C final of 1943 at Wembley.

When Hapgood retired in 1945, it was to becom manager of Blackburn Rovers, and after a sho spell at Ewood Park, he took over the managersh of Watford, then in the Third Division South. neither club was his record a poor one, but impulsive honesty was perhaps a handicap dealing with directors. Used for so long to bein star, cosseted by Chapman and Whittaker, Ha good was simply too straightforward and ou spoken to play politics or to assuage other eg So both his jobs in League football ended u happily, with his losing them. He then had good years in his native West Country as manag of Bath City in the Southern League, twi taking them to the second round of the FA Cu and winning that League's 'Manager of the Ye award in 1952-53. Here too, however, it end badly, with Hapgood being forced out.

Male stayed on at Highbury. At first

Eddie HAPGOOD

Honours: League Championship medal 1930-31, 1932-33, 1933-34, 1934-35, 1937-38
FA Cup winners medal 1930, 1936
FA Cup runners-up medal 1932

Club	Season	League		Int'nls
		Mtchs	Gls	Mtchs
Arsenal	1927-28	3		
	1928-29	17		
	1929-30	38		
	1930-31	38		
	1931-32	41		
	1932-33	38		2
	1933-34	40		5
	1934-35	34	1	5
	1935-36	33		6
	1936-37	32	1	1
	1937-38	41		4
	1938-39	38		7
Total		393	2	30

George MALE

Honours: League Championship medal 1932-33, 1933-34, 1934-35, 1937-38
FA Cup winners medal 1936
FA Cup runners-up medal 1932

Club	Season	League	Int'nls
		Mtchs	Mtchs
Arsenal	1930-31	3	
	1931-32	9	
	1932-33	35	
	1933-34	42	
	1934-35	39	4
	1935-36	35	6
	1936-37	37	6
	1937-38	34	
	1938-39	28	3
	1946-47	15	
	1947-48	8	
Total		285	19

looked after the third team in the Eastern Counties League, down at Hendon. He was a calm, benign figure—he had gone bald at an early age, and this now lent him a certain avuncularity. He has stayed at Highbury ever since, later taking charge of the reserve side.

Hapgood, whose heart remained at Highbury, became estranged from it, and dropped out of football altogether after the episode at Bath. For some years he was a tennis coach. He took a job as warden of an Atomic Energy Authority hostel for 60 apprentices, at Weymouth, but felt hurt, bitter and bewildered by his inability to find a job in football. In 1970 he left the hostel when it closed and sadly died in 1972. He and George Male were to be found at Arsenal's celebration banquet after they had won the 1971 Cup final; and with it the double which had always eluded their Arsenal team.

Hapgood was very much a product of his time, an idealist who believed that the game was the thing, and who put material rewards a very distant second. He has said, with a certain pride, that unions in his day were regarded as 'tin-pot', which is really to say that a footballer, earning £8 a week when most men were on the dole and glad to get 30 shillings when they were not, thought only of the present.

Captaincy was something which he took very seriously—again by contrast with the present day, when managers and coaches leave players with little scope to do much more than toss up and choose an end. Hapgood inspired his men, and perhaps never more so than in the famous Scotland-England game at Hampden Park in April 1939, when England put an end to a 12-year sequence of failure by winning 2-1. Hapgood had a magnificent match, and at the end still had the energy to dance around, congratulating his weary and victorious team.

Famous captain of both club and country, but later so estranged

Male's first cap came in the 1934 'Battle of Highbury' against Italy, the day Hapgood first captained England, when Tom Cooper, the first choice, dropped out. All in all, there were seven Arsenal men in that side, and Male played well enough to keep Cooper out of the team. Though Hapgood continued to captain England (with the brief break of 1937-38), he did not finally become captain of Arsenal until the retirement of Alex James in 1937.

One thing Hapgood always prided himself on was his ability to blot out the finest outside-right of his time, Stanley Matthews. There seemed, here, an element of competitiveness, as if Hapgood instinctively felt that there was a rival for his pre-eminence.

Hapgood's bitterness in later years should be seen as the obverse of his great idealism. He expected everybody to be enthusiastic, as honest, as straightforward and as sincere as himself. Alas, they were not. George Male, clearly expecting less, at least managed to stay in the game from which Hapgood felt himself so cruelly estranged.

Left Eddie Hapgood on the defence at Highbury.
Below George Male is equally solicitous for England. They played together for Arsenal through the thirties and regularly appeared in the same England team. In 1934 they were two of the seven Arsenal men to appear against Italy.

PRESS ASSOCIATION

Joe Mercer – the smiling tiger

For a few long minutes, on a spring afternoon at Highbury in 1954, with 33,000 people in the ground, there was complete dead silence. It was a rare and disturbing feeling. The players stood in groups of three or four, and everyone's eyes were fixed on the only moving figures—the stretcher-bearers in their dark uniforms walking steadily towards the dressing-room tunnel.

On the stretcher, with his broken left leg hastily bound in splints and his long pale face screwed up in pain, lay Joe Mercer, Arsenal captain, 22 years in football, nearly 40 years old. As the stretcher passed the stand he opened his eyes, worked one arm free from the blankets, smiled, and waved goodbye. A light sound of clapping began, spread round the ground as those on the far side picked out the bare arm, strengthened, and Mercer went down the tunnel to an ovation. That was the end of Mercer's career as a player. Everyone knew it, and there was respect and affection in the applause.

It had been quite a career. Despite a six-year gap because of war he won three League Championship medals—one with Everton and two with Arsenal—and captained Arsenal to two Cup Finals, taking the trophy in one of them. He led England and played in 27 internationals. Mercer was a first-class left-half, but he was more than that. He had spirit, courage and determination; he was never half-hearted, never gave up.

Above all Mercer had the gift of breathing these qualities into other players. His example drove them and shamed them into giving all they had. 'You might be just about ready to drop,' says Denis Compton, 'but you never did—not with Joe behind you.'

Two things about Mercer were unforgettable—his smile and his legs. The smile *was* Joe. It was not a handsome boy smile or a big star smile; there was no affectation in it; it was natural, humorous and warm. It twisted his mouth sideways on his lean face, and the creases of it almost closed his blue, close-set eyes. As for his legs, he had to listen to jokes about them from the day he joined Everton as a boy of 16 and stripped for the first time in the dressing-room. 'Look at them,' said Dixie Dean, 'they wouldn't last the postman for a morning.' The legs were shaped like a pair of brackets, the left rather more bent than the right. He walked with a sagging, plodding motion and they gave slightly outwards at each step.

His appearance was deceptive. He weighed only 11 stone, and was 5ft 10½in, but his tackling was strong, determined and technically sound, his body lean, sinewy and tireless. The man he

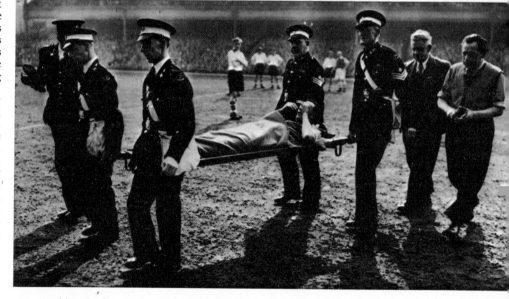

was marking had no rest. The inside-forward who slipped him had better not slow down or take a moment to consider his pass. If he did, Joe was on him again. He was sometimes beaten, but never done with.

Mercer began his football, like many other good players, in the square piece of Cheshire that juts out between the mouths of the Mersey and the Dee—the Wirral. Both his father and his grandfather had been footballers, and he himself grew up in good company. When he played for Cheshire schoolboys there were two other half-backs in the side who would later appear with him for England—Stan Cullis and Frank Soo.

'Look at this,' said Whittaker. 'You've been playing against ten men'

He was still a schoolboy when Everton spotted him, and he signed as a professional with them at 17—for £5 a week. In return he gave them not only his skill but enormous enthusiasm, energy, hard work—and loyalty, staying at Goodison for 15 years, from 1931 to 1946. By 1939, when the War began, he had reached his peak. He was the best left-half in the country, had won a League Championship medal and five international caps, and was unlucky that precisely at that point the War was to take a six-year slice

from his playing career.

Though he regrets it, Mercer is grateful for the fact that, during that time, he had the chance of playing with so many great footballers. The wartime and victory internationals were not to be classified as full internationals, yet the men who played in them (Mercer appeared in 22) can compare with any generation of England players.

By 1946, when he was 31, one would have thought that Mercer was a reasonably contented footballer, but with only three or four good seasons ahead of him. Neither was true: 1946 was probably the lowest point of his career as far as hope was concerned, though those who could only read the papers would never have guessed it. In the England-Scotland match that year his knee had been damaged and he had an operation to remove the cartilage. Later in the season when Everton visited Highbury, he went to the Arsenal dressing-room after the game to show the knee to Tom Whittaker. 'Look at this, lads,' said Whittaker. 'You've been playing against ten men.' The knee was swollen and inflamed, the leg muscles wasted.

Worse than this, Everton and Mercer were losing confidence in each other. He lost his place in the first team and, almost unbelievably, he of all people was losing confidence in himself. At this low point Arsenal bought him from Everton for £7,000—his first and only transfer—in one of the best buys a club ever made.

FOX PHOTOS

KEYSTONE

COLORSPORT

Far left top Joe Mercer is chaired after Arsenal's FA Cup victory over Liverpool in 1950.

Far left bottom Highbury still and silent as Mercer, suffering a broken left leg, waves farewell to the applauding crowd in 1954. Both they and he knew his fine career was at an end.

Centre left Mercer clears a Burnley attack in 1950. He arrived at Highbury in 1946 when, at 31, Everton let him go for only £7,000. It was to be one of football's great bargains, for he played another eight seasons, leading Arsenal to two League titles and two Wembley Finals.

Left Mercer with a characteristic tackle on Les Medley of Spurs.

Below left With Malcolm Allison (right) as team manager, Mercer took Manchester City to promotion and four major honours in five seasons.

ship, the crowd stayed behind at Highbury to call for a speech from Joe. 'This has been the most splendid day of my life,' he said, 'but I am sorry to have to tell you that it has been my last game for Arsenal. I'm retiring from football.' When the elation of the occasion had worn off he signed on for another season—his last, ended in spite of himself by the broken leg.

Of course he did not leave football, though it was once again rumoured how he was going to retire into the grocery business. He took the job as manager of Sheffield United in 1955, too late to save them from relegation, and in 1958, half-way through the season, was called on to do another salvage operation for Aston Villa, bottom of the First Division. Again it was too late, but he brought them back to the First Division the following year. Then in 1964, under the pressure of overwork, his health broke down. The directors of a struggling club waited until he was over the worst effects of his stroke—and then fired him.

In 1965, after a year off, Mercer was offered the manager's job at Manchester City. His wife and his friends were convinced that, if he accepted, it would kill him. He did accept, but had the sense to know he could not do it alone. He sent for the help of a man he had described as the best coach in the world—Malcolm Allison, also unemployed since he had been sacked by Plymouth Argyle. Never was there such a contrast of temperaments, and many believed the partnership would never work. But it did—and that's an understatement. Allison was team manager, Mercer club manager and partner. In their first season together City were promoted; in their third they were League Champions. The following season they won the Cup, the next year they won the League Cup and the European Cup Winners Cup. It was a record that spoke for itself.

In 1971 Mercer became general manager and the following year the partnership split up as he left for Coventry. There his benevolent air, in such contrast to his tigerish play, once again proved the inspiration for success.

Arsenal needed some luck then as much as [Me]rcer. The War had brought a great period to [an] end—nine seasons in which the club had never [bee]n lower than sixth in the First Division and [wo]n the Championship five times. Now they [we]re £20,000 in debt, the ground had been [dam]aged by bombs, they were second from [bot]tom of the table, and the side had developed [a d]epressing habit of running out of spirit in the [sec]ond-half. They bought Mercer for his experi[enc]e and solidity, to see them over the bad spell. [Th]ey reckoned two or three seasons would do it— [as] much as could be expected from a man of [his] age.

'Everton told me I was a bad player. Arsenal [t]old me I was a good one'

[I]n the most literal sense they bought more [tha]n they bargained for. 'Everton told me I was a [bad] player,' he said, 'Arsenal told me I was a [goo]d one.' He knew he was needed, his confidence [cam]e back, and it flowed from him into the rest [of] the team. Under his captaincy, Arsenal won [the] Championship the following season. (1947-48) [and], still led by him, won it again in 1952-53. In [195]0 they won the Cup, and in 1952 reached the [fin]al.

[B]esides his renewed confidence there was

another reason why Mercer's extraordinary legs did not now give way under the drive of his undefeatable temperament. He had become a different kind of player. He had always been a storming wing-half, well up behind his forwards, sometimes over-running them, counting on his ability to get back the length of the field into defence when the game switched. This would not do for Arsenal. To fit Whittaker's team plan Mercer had to make himself into a defensive half-back. His business was to break up attacks, win the ball, push it upfield to his forwards, and let them get on with it. He was intelligent enough to make the adjustment, and the discipline he imposed on himself made him an even better player.

Mercer was no longer burning up his energy covering every square yard of the field. He was measuring his strength. It was not his speed that was seen now, but his quickness. He had a little more time to think, and his thinking was of a shrewd and calculating kind. His tackling was all the more deadly now that it was combined with his mature and controlled watchfulness. He could not be tempted into striking too soon, but when the moment was right he moved like a whiplash. He came out of the tackle with his foot and leg crooked securely behind the ball, his head and shoulders well over it, his arms spread and high as he carried it on in his wide-legged stride.

In 1953, after Arsenal had won the Champion-

Joe MERCER

Honours: League Championship medal 1938-39, 1947-48, 1952-53
FA Cup winners medal 1950
FA Cup runners-up medal 1952
Footballer of the Year 1950

Club	Season	League		Int'nls
		Mtchs	Gls	Mtchs
Everton	1932-33	1		
	1933-34			
	1934-35	8		
	1935-36	33	1	
	1936-37	39		
	1937-38	36		
	1938-39	41		5
	1946-47	12		
Arsenal	1946-47	25		
	1947-48	40		
	1948-49	33		
	1949-50	35		
	1950-51	31		
	1951-52	36		
	1952-53	28	2	
	1953-54	19		
Total		417	3	5

THE
DEFENDERS

Alf Ramsey – the single-minded

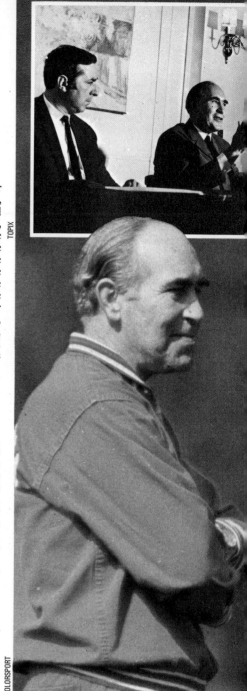

Passionate and enigmatic, an inspiring right-back who became an inspiring club and international manager, winner of England's only World Cup to date, Sir Alf Ramsey is now a man of controversy. Though nothing and no one can take away from him the triumph of 1966 which, as a tearful Nobby Stiles assured him after the World Cup final, might well have been impossible without him, his methods and attitudes have been criticized as often as they have been praised.

His admirers praise him for his single-mindedness, his vast professionalism, his power to care about his players and to make them believe in him, his ability to make a silk purse out of a sow's ear, to weld modest talent into a highly successful side. His detractors say that he is narrow, xenophobic, stubbornly conservative; that like the Bourbons, he learned nothing and forgot nothing after the 1966 World Cup. They believe that his tactics are inflexible and sometimes downright silly—as in the 1972 home leg of the Nations Cup tie with the West Germans. And they believe that his antipathy towards the press touches on the irrational.

Alf Ramsey was born in 1920 in Dagenham, then a little township in Essex, not yet inundated by the Ford Motor Company and overspill from London's East End. His father was a smallholder, and while his older brothers taught him football, his own, avowed ambition was to be a successful grocer. Ramsey has always seemed over-sensitive about his background. Once, when being interviewed on the radio, he was asked: 'Are your parents still alive, Mr Ramsey?' 'Oh yes,' he replied. 'Where do they live?' 'In Dagenham, I believe.'

He was an extraordinarily late developer as a player, and perhaps if it had not been for the War, might never have become a professional at all. Called up in 1940, he was posted on the south coast and began to play for Southampton, at first in the forward line. Gradually he was turned into a right-back, in which position he was eventually partnered by Bill Rochford, Portsmouth's left-back in their winning Cup Final team of 1939, and a useful influence.

He turned professional, and in December 1948, was good enough to be called up to play for a depleted England team against Switzerland, at Highbury. England won 6-0, but it was a strange season for Ramsey, who lost his Southampton place at right-back to the young Bill Ellerington. By the end of the season Ellerington was in the England team, and that summer, Ramsey joined Tottenham Hotspur for the equivalent of £21,000, Welsh international winger Ernie Jones moving to The Dell.

It was the start of the great period in Ramsey's playing career, and of his immensely fruitful relationship with Arthur Rowe, who had just left Chelmsford to become manager of his old club, Spurs. Rowe wanted his team to play the short passing, push-and-run game. In Ramsey, though he did not make him captain, he saw and found the perfect player to exert a benign, constructive influence over the lively team. The two men were temperamentally poles apart, but complemented each other superbly. Ramsey was taciturn, outwardly inhibited, inwardly as passionate and vulnerable as the Cockney, ebullient Rowe himself.

By the seventies, and the all-purpose, overlapping full-back, Ramsey's style seemed quaint and old-fashioned. He was far too heavy and deliberate—a strongly built, squarely muscular man—to be a volatile attacker. What he was, par excellence, was a constructive full-back. Cruel critics said that Bill Nicholson, then right-half, did his tackling for him, and Sonny Walters, the right-winger, did his running for him, but the fact was that Tottenham never looked the same without Ramsey. His kicking, practised in the past for hours on end, was superb, his use of the ball splendidly intelligent. If it was true that he was vulnerable to quite different types of winger—two Scots, the direct and forceful Billy Liddell, and the sinuously dribbling Bobby Mitchell, usually ran circles round him—his positional sense was admirable. And all the time he was learning from the gifted, imaginative Rowe.

Ramsey's penalty kick preserves England's unbeaten home record

Spurs won the Second Division Championship that season, the First Division title the season afterwards. Ramsey himself consolidated his place in the England team with whom he went to the 1950 World Cup, taking part in all three games, including the sadly unforgettable 1-0 defeat by the United States at Belo Horizonte. Ramsey was also famous for his deadly penalties. One of them, taken with characteristic coolness, saved England's unbeaten home record against FIFA, at Wembley, in the closing minutes of the celebration match of October, 1953. A month later, Ramsey scored another penalty goal; England's third and last when Hungary demolished them 6-3. That was Ramsey's last game for England.

One of his penchants with Tottenham was for the carefully, sometimes impertinently made back pass to his excellent goalkeeper, Ted Ditchburn. It cost Spurs a place in the 1953 Cup Final when Jackie Mudie of Blackpool, at Villa Park, nipped in to score. Ramsey was bitterly taken to task by the Spurs directors after that but maintained, with typically bitter pride, that he had done the right thing.

On retirement, he was persuaded to become manager of Ipswich Town, then a Third Division South club with no history; they had reached the Football League only in 1938. Behind them were the patrician Cobbold family. For Ramsey, with his sense of social unease, his carefully elocuted accent, being brought into contact with them was a new and perhaps radical experience. John Cobbold, the Ipswich chairman, loyal and exuberant, calmed Ramsey down on the various, early occasions when he wanted to resign. Scott Duncan, his long-serving predecessor at Portman Road, had stayed on as secretary of the club and it was not a very happy arrangement. But in due course Ramsey got his team into Division Two, a fine achievement in itself.

It was more remarkable still to lift them into the First Division in 1960-61, and quite astonishing to win the First Division Championship against all the big battalions the very next season. For Ramsey spent merely peanuts. His was a team built with superb skill out of virtual flotsam and jetsam, the highest transfer fee Ramsey paid being a mere £12,500. Rehabilitated players like the fragile ex-Chelsea and Brighton veteran Jimmy Leadbetter at outside-left, centre-half Andy Nelson from West Ham, and Ray Crawford from Portsmouth, did wonders for him.

Insert left The job Ramsey finds the most diffic[ult] —explaining himself to the press.
Insert right One of Ramsey's reliable penalti[es] against Hungary in his very last international.
Above Ramsey jokes with Norman Hunter.
Below right Definitive Ramsey: 'while all arou[nd] are losing their heads' at the final whistle in t[he] World Cup final.

Sir Alf RAMSEY

THE MANAGER (with England)
Honours: World Cup 1966

Honours: (with Ipswich Town)
League Championship 1962,
Second Division 1961,
Third Division South 1957

THE PLAYER
Honours: League Championship medal 1951

Club	Season	League		Int'nls	
		Mtchs	Gls	Mtchs	Gls
Southampton	1946-47	23	1		
	1947-48	42	5		
	1948-49	25	2	1	
Tottenham Hotspur	1949-50	41	4	7	
	1950-51	40	4	6	
	1951-52	38	5	8	1
	1952-53	37	6	8	
	1953-54	37	2	2	2
	1954-55	33	3		
Total		316	32	32	3

It was a triumph of mind over matter. The double spearhead of Crawford and the tall, lean Ted Phillips, a local man, struck terror into other defences. But by 1962, when Ramsey accepted the managership of the England team, the side had virtually blown up, and it was not much more than a shell that Ramsey could leave to his successor, Jackie Milburn.

It is said that when Ipswich had just won the Championship and were joyfully celebrating in champagne, Ramsey, absent, was found at last sitting in the stand watching a junior game. To the invitation to join the party, he allegedly and classically replied, 'I'm working.' This is a companion story to that told of his demeanour the day after England won the World Cup, when two journalists always loyal to him went up to congratulate him. 'This is my day off,' he said.

Ramsey was not the first choice for the England job; he was only considered after Burnley's Jimmy Adamson, but he was probably the best. He made it clear from the first that he was not going to be obstructed by amateurs. At a stroke, he had the selection committee abolished, the selectors reduced to a mere, irrelevant Senior International Committee. He is said to have once informed one of them that so far as he was concerned, he would gladly substitute them with extra players in tour parties, but at least they could save him from attending cocktail parties.

'If Stiles goes, I go', says Ramsey, and the pair of them stay

His contempt for the amateur administrator was never so strongly shown as when, after England had played France in the World Cup, officials insisted he drop Nobby Stiles from the team after a foul on Jacky Simon of France in front of the Royal Box. Ramsey replied that if Stiles went, he went. They both stayed.

A further, slightly bizarre, example of his single-mindedness was given in his Tottenham days when he had just married his pleasant wife, who brought with her from a previous marriage his step-daughter. Sunk in thought after a match, he was just leaving the cold corridor outside the dressing-rooms when someone called, 'Hey, Alf, you've forgotten your wife!' In his absorption, he had walked right past her.

What mattered most, however, when Ramsey took over the England managership and boldly promised that he would win the World Cup of 1966, was that he was a professional and a players' man. His predecessor, the highly academic Walter Winterbottom, had been, for all his virtues, a hierarchical figure, very much the protege of the secretary, Sir Stanley Rous. In all his 16 years at Lancaster Gate, he had never even managed to get a team doctor appointed. Ramsey chose the forceful, gifted specialist, Dr Alan Bass, and their partnership was exceedingly successful and harmonious.

Though England badly lost their first game under his tutelage, 5-2 to France in Paris in the Nations Cup, early in 1963, he had licked them into shape by the time it came to his summer tour. Making excellent use of wingers in a 4-2-4 formation, working smoothly with a press to whom he carefully explained what he was doing, he won all three games, against the Czechs, the East Germans and the Swiss.

But by the 1966 World Cup his policy of using wingers to go round the back of a massed defence had lapsed. To this day nobody can be quite sure whether it was a question of abstract policy or a mere response to the sheer lack of decent wingers. Ramsey himself has given both views. Be that as it may, policy was what it became, turning eventually into the 4-4-2 formation which failed in Mexico, putting so heavy a burden in the heat on its overlapping full-backs.

Hard running and hard work was the essence of Ramsey's philosophy and because the players utterly accepted and believed in him, he was able to apply it. He was never at ease with the unorthodox, brilliant player, such as Jimmy

Ramsey happily concedes a goal. The picture would tell a vastly different story of course if it was not merely an England training session, for Ramsey drills his teams best in the art of defence.

Greaves, the little Cockney Spurs inside-forward. Indeed, Ramsey's first great battle with the press came in Gothenburg in 1965 when he omitted Greaves from the team against Sweden, said that every player was fit, then resented it when the papers said that Greaves had been dropped. But it was characteristic of the man's fundamental largeness that he later admitted being wrong.

With his players, Ramsey could be relaxed, cheerful, even jolly, wholly belying the image of tense suspicion with which he confronted the world at large, foreigners and the press in particular. Ramsey, of course, does not seek to conceal this attitude. A South American journalist —the awful combination, foreigner and press man —once asked Sir Alf cheerily by way of introduction, 'I don't know if you remember me . . .' 'Yes,' Alf is supposed to have said, 'you're a pest.' But any strangers, indeed any strange situation, showed him at his least beguiling. There was the moment in 1962 when he was cheerfully greeted at San Siro, before a Milan-Ipswich European Cup tie, by the then Torino centre-forward, Gerry Hitchens. 'Oh, yes,' said Ramsey, coldly. 'You're playing in these parts.' But to players he knew and who knew him, it was another, warmer story.

One surprising aspect of his managership was, as has been intimated, his penchant for the hard men; Nobby Stiles, Norman Hunter, later Peter Storey. Always ready to condemn rough play against England, he could be curiously blind to physical violence by his own team. But he was certainly a hundred times justified when, after the 1966 quarter-final against Argentina, he made his famous stricture, accusing the Argentinians of 'acting as animals'. FIFA rebuked him and he later apologized, but provocation had been immense, not merely on the field, with the callous fouling, the expulsion of Rattin, but afterwards outside the dressing-rooms when Argentinians had spat and even urinated. In Latin America, however, he had still to be forgiven, as would be seen in the 1970 World Cup.

In any event he was proved right in his belief that England's best football would come against a team which wanted to play really well itself. In the semi-final and final, his hitherto plodding side came to life. Bobby Charlton, whom he had converted from a fluent left-winger into a midfield player, was superb against the Portuguese; Geoff Hurst, the powerful West Ham player he had chosen instead of Greaves got three against West Germany in the World Cup final.

Smitten by a last-minute equalizer in a World Cup final they seemed to have in their pockets, England's team were roused to new exertions by Ramsey who told them, 'You've won it once; now you must win it again.' And they did. Throughout the series he only once gave the players a dressing-down, and that was after the French match, when he felt they had sinned with presumption. The whole country delighted in the knighthood with which Ramsey was rewarded.

He stayed on at Lancaster Gate, though admitting it was a lonely job, in which he missed the day-to-day contacts of club football. He was also dismayed and frustrated by the uncooperative attitudes of certain leading clubs and their blatant unwillingness to release players if there was the slightest inconvenience to their plans.

In the years that followed the 1966 victory, he was more and more sharply criticized for the negativity of his tactics, his preference for the hard worker over the artist, his sometimes naive tactics and substitutions. He maintained that it would be easier for England in the 1970 World Cup than in 1966, when there was so much pressure on them, but his own lack of diplomacy and strategies helped to bring about his team's failure in Mexico. Unlike the Brazilians, who seduced the public of Guadalajara, Ramsey made no concessions, and the end product was the siege of the England team's Guadalajara Hilton Hotel the night before their vital game against Brazil.

If Gordon Banks had been fit to play against West Germany instead of the vulnerable Peter

Bonetti, it is more than probable that Engl would have reached the final to play Brazil ag but as it was, Ramsey's substitutions at I against West Germany were bewildering ineffective, while his full-backs were run into ground with finally catastrophic results.

A hero of both World Cups, however, unquestionably the England left-half and capt Bobby Moore; a fact which represented ano triumph for Ramsey. On the 1964 tour of Americas, Moore had led a brief and ea quelled revolt by certain England pla against training. Ramsey's way of bringing to heel was curiously characteristic. He refu until the very last moment to confirm Bo Moore's captaincy of the England team aga Northern Ireland in Belfast, the follow October.

The 1970 World Cup over, Ramsey still did return to club management, as some had fel would. There had been subtle changes in attitudes. Thus, after turning down a £10, offer for his memoirs in 1966, he had wri them, in ghosted collaboration, for a pop Sunday newspaper in 1970. He was critic by certain players for the high-handed way which he had allocated the running of their 1 World Cup pool to the Huddersfield agent, Stanley, who had been in charge of the ra disappointing 1970 version, and he came un fire again for the way he dropped Geoff H from his squad in May 1972; not least beca Hurst had been one of his most loyal and effec players, running himself to the point of exhaust in Mexico.

Hurst hears from Ron Greenwood that Ramsey has dropped him

After Hurst had been rather humiliatin pulled off and substituted in the disastr Nations Cup quarter-final against West Germ at Wembley in April, Ramsey picked his play for the return match and the British Champi ship, without Hurst. Far from telling Hu personally and in advance, he did not commu cate with him at all, so that the West H forward heard at second hand from his c manager, Ron Greenwood, who was under legitimate assumption that Hurst must b been told already.

The match against West Germany wa tactical disaster, for England took the field w out a single genuine wing-half capable countering Germany's tremendous power midfield, especially the skills of the blond Gur Netzer. Worse still, Ramsey had called up ideal man for the job, Alan Mullery of Sp and left him on the bench. So Ramsey had one blow weakened England and demorali Mullery, who said he was no longer willing play for his country.

Ridiculed in midfield, giving the Germ superabundant space, England were beaten at Wembley. Ramsey, reportedly deeply woun and affected by press criticism, picked for return game in Berlin a highly defensive te with a midfield packed with destructive play forcing a useless 0-0 draw. Criticism soared to peak, the press being polarized among those w felt that Ramsey and his concepts were ho lessly out of date, those who argued that talent just was not there to be picked, and th who felt there was no one capable of taking place. So far had the pendulum swung in hal dozen years.

But the attitude of his players did not chan After Germany, as after Mexico, the play declared themselves unreservedly for Alf. A failure, they insisted, was theirs, not his. A perhaps they still claimed that even after most traumatic game the English had witnes in twenty years—the 1-1 draw against Poland 17 October 1973. In seven years Ramsey, fr the man who won the World Cup, had beco the man who presided over her first ever fail to qualify for the finals. A sad fate indeed.

THE DEFENDERS

The versatile Johnny Carey

...st of those who are contenders for a place in ... list of great footballers have one, perhaps ..., claims for their inclusion. Johnny Carey is ...ong the few who had more.

...irst, he was a supreme all-rounder, making his ...est impact at full-back but at home in any ...ition, in any company; second, he was an ...piring captain—of Manchester United, of Eire, ...l of Europe; third, he was dual international, ...ying for both Irish football associations and, ...1947, finding himself available for selection ... both sides in the famous match between Great ...tain and the Rest of Europe; fourth, he was a ...nager not without successes, taking two clubs ... to the First Division and enabling another ...enjoy a brilliant, if brief, revival. Add to this ... fact that United found him almost by chance, ...ight him at a bargain price, and the ingredients ... the story are complete.

...Carey's contemporaries were, and still are, ... of praise. 'He was a credit to football,' says ...ow Irishman Peter Doherty. 'No more honest ...n ever pulled on boots. And few will match his ...dership.'

...Jackie Milburn chooses to single out his play. ...ere were some wonderful full-backs around in ...nny's time, but he was the best of them all. ...e best adjectives in football have been associa-...l with his name . . . stylish, studious, skilful.'

...Carey was discovered, almost by accident, after ...nchester United scout Louis Rocca had gone to ...land in pursuit of another player. 'Having ...sted days I decided to stay the weekend and ... to find some other talent,' recalled Rocca later. ...chose a bad game but in one team, St James' ...te, there was a useful inside-forward. It didn't ...ke me long to realize he was a brilliant prospect.'

... November 1936 Carey joined Manchester ...ited—for £250.

...Carey's first-team debut came on 23 September ...37, at inside-forward. 'Those who saw the ...me,' wrote a local reporter, were unanimous ... their view that he has the makings of a valuable ...yer. His footwork at times would have done ...dit to an experienced man.'

...Only six weeks later Carey played his first ...me for the Republic of Ireland, figuring at ...ide-left in the 3-3 draw with Norway in the ...rld Cup qualifying match in Dublin. That ...son he helped United back to the First Division ...d, when War brought official football to an end ...1939, he was firmly established for both club ...d country.

...Carey did not return to the Republic. 'A coun-...' that gives me my living is worth fighting for,' ... explained, and he joined the British Army. His ...ties took him to Italy and there, nicknamed ...ario' by the local fans, he found time to play ...h considerable success for several Italian pro-...sional clubs.

...After the War he duly resumed his place in ... United side—at wing-half—and in the (North-...1) Ireland and Eire teams. His post-War inter-...tional career began, in fact, with two games ...inst England in three days; for Ireland in ...lfast on 28 September 1946 and for the Repub-...on 30 September in Dublin. The irony of his ...sition was emphasised the following May ...en, after four more games for Eire and two for ...rthern Ireland, he was chosen to captain the ...st of Europe against Great Britain at Hampden ...rk. He could easily have been selected for ...tain. Though his side lost 6-1, Carey impressed ...eryone that day. 'If ever I admired the play of

the strong Irishman I did that day,' said Spurs' Ronnie Burgess, left-half for Britain at Hampden. 'Although he was unable to hold much conversa-tion with his team-mates he led them with wonder-ful skill, setting a superb example.'

In 1948 Carey led United to Wembley, and it was his chat in the dressing-room at half-time, when Blackpool were leading 2-1, that lifted his side to a magnificent 4-2 win. His Championship medal, however, was a lot longer in coming. In three consecutive seasons (1946-1949) and again in 1950-51, United knew the disappointment of finishing second. They eventually made it in 1951-52, by four points from Spurs.

Carey, who had been voted Footballer of the Year in 1949, had by now settled at full-back. There he played an intelligent, constructive game, his skill augmented by an excellent physique. In style, technique and authority he was comparable to Alf Ramsey, who in the same period exerted a similar influence at Tottenham.

Carey continued playing admirably until 1953 when, at the age of 34, he turned to football management with Blackburn. His new career was not to be without success—or drama.

In 1958, after several seasons of threatening promotion, Blackburn returned to the First Division, and the team Carey built was to reach the Cup Final two years later. Carey, meanwhile, had moved to Everton in the summer of 1958 on a five-year contract. He took some fine players to Goodison, including Alex Young and Jimmy Gabriel, and by April 1961 had lifted Everton to fifth place—their best position since the War.

Carey is sacked as manager of Everton— in a London taxi

Then he and the new club chairman, Little-woods millionaire John Moores, attended a Foot-ball League meeting in London. As they left the session in a taxi, Moores told him he was sacked. 'I was at Everton before Mr Moores arrived, and he wanted a man appointed by him,' explained the redundant Carey. 'And I think he wanted a tough manager, someone to crack the whip. I'm afraid that's not for me.'

The following day Carey sat in the directors' box at Goodison while Everton beat Cardiff 5-1. The cheers from the crowd on his appearance told Moores what the fans thought. 'I know in my own mind that I was never a failure,' he said. But on Monday Harry Catterick took over.

Carey, in time, took over an £80,000 side at Orient—and promptly took them up to the First Division. In 1963 he joined Nottingham Forest and, while also managing the Republic of Ireland team for a time, made Forest into a fine side. The peak came in 1966-67, when they finished second in the League and reached the last four of the FA Cup. That, apparently, was not enough: and, after Forest had dropped into the relegation zone, the club committee fired the manager. In January 1969 Carey, with no big offers, returned to Blackburn, now struggling at the foot of the Second Division, as co-manager to Eddie Quigley. Then in June 1971, after Rovers had dropped to Division III for the first time in their history, both managers were sacked.

It might appear that, considering his consider-able success, Carey had a rough deal in manage-ment. The reasons, however, are not difficult to find. He was never a manager in the style of Revie, Docherty or Clough: he was, in a sense, a 'front man', the genial father who presented the right image for a club, perhaps surviving more on respect than on ability.

It would, of course, be grossly unfair to remember Johnny Carey in this light. It would be more just, and far more satisfying, to recall the fine player and inspiring captain. But it works both ways: in 1972 Carey was a representative for a tile company, and he did not seem to miss the game to which he had given 35 years of his life. His wife put it like this: 'I think John has been to only one football match since he finished with manage-ment.'

Top Manchester United right-back Johnny Carey is chaired after leading his side to their 4-2 win over Blackpool in the 1948 Cup Final. This was the peak of his best years: the previous season he had cap-tained Europe against Britain at Hampden, and in 1949 he was to be voted Footballer of the Year.
Above Carey in a tense aerial battle with Reg Lewis of Arsenal at Highbury in 1947.

Johnny CAREY

Honours: League Championship medal 1951-52
FA Cup winners medal 1948

| Club | Season | League | | Int'nls | | |
		Mtchs	Gls	*Mtchs	*Gls	†Mtchs
Man-chester United	1937-38	16	3	3		
	1938-39	32	6	5	2	
	1946-47	31		5		3
	1947-48	37	1	1		1
	1948-49	41	1	5		3
	1949-50	38	1	4		
	1950-51	39		3	1	
	1951-52	38	3			
	1952-53	32	1	2		
Total		304	16	*28	*3	†7

*Republic of Ireland   †Northern Ireland

Scotland's greatest defenders

THE DEFENDERS

Below Bobby Evans (left) leads out Scotland at Wembley in 1959 for Billy Wright's 100th England international. It was Evans' 38th. He had replaced George 'Corky' Young as his country's centre-half and captain two years before. **Right** Evans in the hooped shirt of Raith Rovers in 1967. The empty terraces were a far cry from days in the fifties when he won all the honours with Celtic.

UNITED PRESS INTERNATIONAL

The fact that George Young and Bobby Evans are Scotland's most capped players almost automatically justifies their inclusion in a list of the great British players—if only because, with that country's fickle selectors, it is testimony to their obvious consistency.

Between them they won 101 caps—not many compared to the totals of Billy Wright (105) and Bobby Charlton (106)—but only eight of the 88 sides chosen between November 1947 and June 1960 took the field without either of them. Young, in fact, missed only 11 Scotland games during his long international career.

There are striking similarities of both men's careers with that of Wright. Like the Wolves captain, both are remembered as the outstanding defender in a fine club side of its day—Young with the Rangers of the late forties and early fifties and Evans with the Celtic of a few years later. Like the England captain, both are best remembered as centre-halves, though they started and won recognition elsewhere on the field: Young gained nearly two-thirds of his caps at right-back, Evans exactly a half of his at wing-half.

Of the three, perhaps, Evans is the odd man out. For one thing, he was not a one-club man; he did stay at Parkhead for a decade and a half, but then tried his luck elsewhere. Wright and Young, for different reasons, retired not much past their peaks. Evans, too, differed in build and style. While the dominating figures of Wright and Young were renowned for their dependability and professionalism, the sort of player any defender would like to have covering him, the shorter, chunky Evans was essentially a player of energy and attacking flair.

Though George Young had five appearances at

centre-half for Scotland in 1948 (during which Evans made his debut), it was not until 1955, after more than 30 further appearances at right-back, that he moved there again. Much as Wright plugged the gap after England had struggled with different players following the loss of Neil Franklin, so Young came to the rescue after Scotland had used five number 5s in 18 matches since the end of Willie Woodburn's international career.

Young was dropped after 53 internationals—but with no explanation

During the time Young and Woodburn did play together they formed the core of what became known as Rangers' 'iron curtain'. That was one of Scotland's first post-War attempts to break the positional redundancy of the prevalent 3-4-3 system. This tended, in Scotland at least, to rely on a slow build-up with short passes from centre-half to full-back to wing-half and then forward. Rangers attempted to change all this with a policy of first-time defence—either from the backs or the goalkeeper: the 60-yard punt upfield soon became one of Young's trademarks.

Detractors criticised the emergence of a 'mid-field desert'; supporters rather unconvincingly tried to suggest that Rangers' backs, and Young in particular, were so accurate that it was a constructive rather than pragmatic measure. But such argument counted for little. What mattered was that it worked. And while Wright and his Wolves were working on the simple premise that the quicker and more often the ball reached the penalty-area the more likely they were to score,

so Young and Rangers were proving the sa north of the border. Out would come the long b to Waddell, over went the cross to Thornto Williamson or Duncanson. Ibrox saw the Cha pionship six times between 1947 and 1957, t Cup four times and the League Cup twice. A that run included the first ever treble, in 1948-4

With Sammy Cox and Woodburn, Young pr vided the real strength of those Rangers team He often appeared with both in the nation team—where his less disparaged talents we more often in evidence. 'They say that You could only boot it clear,' said Willie Waddell, la to manage Rangers, 'but it just wasn't true. I could play it on the ground as well as anyone.'

Perhaps that is a slight overstatement. You was probably too big to ever be a ball-player. S feet two inches tall and over fifteen stone f much of his career, his very bulk was suited Rangers style of play and his role in it. But th mere battering rams do not win 53 caps.

Young's introduction to the club he was lead for so long was a little fortuitous. He w born in Grangemouth in 1922 and played for while for a local club. A friend, an aspiring box as it happened, was training at Falkirk's grou at the time and found he so liked football th he became a goalkeeper and eventually signed f Rangers junior club, Kirkintilloch Rob Roy. I told his new club about Young ... 'a big strappi left-back'. They had a look, signed him, pass him on to Rangers in 1941, and within 18 mont he had been converted into Scotland's centre-ha for a Wartime international against England.

He was always a versatile player. He scor two penalties in the 1949 Cup final again Clyde and, in 1953, played in goal to earn a dra

30

obby EVANS

nours: Scottish League Championship medal
153-54
ottish Cup winners medal 1951, 1954
ottish Cup runners-up medal 1955, 1956
ottish League Cup winners medal 1957, 1958

ub	Season	League Mtchs	Gls	Int'nls Mtchs
ltic	1946-47	21	4	
	1947-48	27	3	
	1948-49	24		4
	1949-50	27	2	4
	1950-51	28		2
	1951-52	25		1
	1952-53	30		1
	1953-54	29		5
	1954-55	30	1	5
	1955-56	31		4
	1956-57	31		2
	1957-58	33		9
	1958-59	19		4
	1959-60	30		7
elsea	1960-61	32		
ewport County	1961-62	31		
orton	1962-63	31		
	1963-64			
ird Lanark	1964-65	7	1	
ith Rovers	1965-66	36		
	1966-67	38		
	1967-68	4		
tal		564	11	48

eorge YOUNG

nours: Scottish League Championship medal
I46-47, 1948-49, 1949-50, 1952-53, 1955-56,
I56-57
ottish Cup winners medal 1948, 1949, 1950,
I53
ottish League Cup winners medal 1946-47,
I48-49
ottish League Cup runners-up medal 1945-46,
I51-52

ub	Season	League Mtchs	Gls	Int'nls Mtchs
angers	1946-47	28	4	4
	1947-48	15	1	5
	1948-49	28	3	4
	1949-50	30	3	6
	1950-51	30	1	8
	1951-52	28	3	6
	1952-53	29	5	4
	1953-54	20		2
	1954-55	28	1	4
	1955-56	29		4
	1956-57	28	1	6
tal		293	22	53

Below George Young looks on as Tom Finney's shot beats Tommy Younger but goes over the Scottish crossbar at Hampden in April 1956. The following year, after a record 53 caps, 'Corky' was suddenly dropped without explanation—and he retired the same season. He had captained Rangers through some of their greatest years, winning six League Championship and four Cup winners' medals during an illustrious career.

a successful replay against Aberdeen.

Known to all as 'Corky'—because he always ried the cork from the champagne bottle with ich Rangers celebrated their 1948 Scottish p win over Morton—Young rates the highlight his career, like most Scottish internationals, e a defeat of England.

That was at Wembley in 1949. 'When we came my eyes caught the scoreboard with just two rds on it: ENGLAND SCOTLAND. And I nember thinking: "What's it going to say at the ish?" And I never thought about it again until oked up in the second half and saw ENGLAND SCOTLAND 3. I'd seen Jimmy Mason, Billy el and Lawrie Reilly score their goals, but it s only when I saw the figures that it really vned.' England got one back, but it remains a nous victory.

After 53 full internationals Young was sudly dropped from the Scottish team before the al qualifying match before the 1958 World p. There was, according to reports, no word of lanation or sympathy. Young was understandy upset and he retired soon afterwards. He was t 35, and could have gone on at club level for east two more seasons.

After a brief spell managing Third Lanark he ired to take over a hotel, keeping in touch h the sport via the odd newspaper piece. No bt it was a welcome break for a man who had ken his nose three times, his fingers once and I his leg in plaster on six occasions.

The man who replaced him in the national side s Bobby Evans, recalled after a short absence. had played centre-half for Scotland twice ore, in 1955, and now he settled down to a long n in that position.

Evans had moved there for Celtic in 1955, when an ankle injury put an end to the playing career of Jock Stein. His skill in compensating for lack of height with mobility and anticipation was not lost on the selectors.

Evans had taken some time to establish himself at Celtic after joining them from a Glasgow junior club, St Anthony's, in 1944. He was smallish, and had not yet developed the powerful physique that later enabled him to be such a hard-running wing-half. He was then an inside-forward, tenacious and energetic but short in the forward skills. It was not until he was dropped back to the half-back line that he developed his full potential. In that position his tireless running had a great destructive effect on opposing attacks, and this was backed with hard, sure tackling.

After 16 years with Celtic Evans moves: and plays for 8 more years

The hard little red-headed man with the florid complexion found the partners he needed when he was joined by Bertie Peacock and Jock Stein to form what was one of Celtic's best ever half-back lines.

Evans was the hard running tackler, always involved in the play; Stein was the composed static defender, wonderfully cool and sure in the air; Peacock was a subtle player, the creator, an excellent passer of the ball.

Celtic won the League and Cup double in 1954 —their first for 40 years—with a team which had during the previous close season won the Corona-

tion Cup, the tough competition in which Arsenal, Manchester United, Spurs and Newcastle had represented England and Rangers, Hibs, Aberdeen and Celtic had played for Scotland.

Evans was the lively inspiration in the middle of the team who beat Arsenal 1-0 and then Manchester United 2-1. By the time the final was played the strength of the half-back line had encouraged the forwards—among whom were Bobby Collins, Neil Mochan and Charlie Tully— and Hibs were beaten 1-0. All except Stein also figured in the side which thrashed Rangers 7-1 in the 1957-58 League Cup final.

The highest tribute paid to Bobby Evans at that time was that he never played a poor game. He was indeed a player who was never off colour, who always had abundant energy. Evans played in all the three World Cup matches for Scotland in Sweden in 1958, but perhaps his most satisfying match was at Wembley in 1959. It had been eight years since he had played in the stadium and he was back for Billy Wright's hundredth appearance for England. He was then challenging Young as Scotland's most capped player.

In 1960, however, he decided to follow Bobby Collins and move south—not long after what was to prove his last international, an ignominious 4-2 defeat by Turkey in Ankara. He went to Chelsea, then Newport, and then back to Scotland with Morton. Despite a back injury—one that had troubled him since 1958—he continued to play into his forties, having a brief spell at Third Lanark and then playing a major part in Raith Rovers' return to the First Division in 1967. But it was still rather sad to see a career built on loyalty to a great club dissipated in a trek round a set of lesser clubs for a season or two at a time.

Wright for Wolves, wrong for Arsenal

Fate cheated fiction when it gave William Ambrose Wright to football. It endowed Wright with the kind of qualities, character and career pattern one normally finds in the world of make-believe; and it did the job so thoroughly that now a writer bent on a story about a traditional football folk-hero will be sore-pressed to avoid the charge that he has simply added a little tinsel to the real life story of Billy Wright.

Any thumb-nail synopsis of the Wright story would have to run something like this: Shropshire lad, son of iron-foundry worker, joins famous local First Division club . . . ogre-manager tells him he is too small to be a footballer . . . given second chance . . . breaks ankle and is told he is finished . . . stays with club for 21 years, wins three League Championship medals and FA Cup winners medal . . . captain of club and country . . . wins record 105 England caps, the first man ever to play in 100 internationals . . . travels all over world . . . awarded CBE . . . marries well-known singer . . . manages world-renowned London club . . . becomes television personality and executive.

To all this would have to be added a few personal details: blond hair, broad forehead, open face and crinkly smile, medium height and powerful build, and a modest, helpful, honest and conscientious personality.

Wright rarely excited; he just did the obvious thing superbly well

A publisher offered a story-line like this might be forgiven for suggesting the central character be reconstructed along more mortal lines. Super-humans are one thing but nobody yet has come down from Olympus to play football for a living.

But this *was* Billy Wright. In the unremarkable age before football's new deal and its recognition as an acceptable culture by middle-class intellectuals, Wright was one of a select handful of players who stood for something special. His image, manner and permanency helped give the game a sheen it did not always deserve.

Inevitably, perhaps, his true worth as a player is sometimes questioned. He admits that if he had been born 20 years earlier (than in February 1924) or even 20 years later, he would not have won 100 caps. An earlier arrival would have seen him competing with Joe Mercer, Stan Cullis and Cliff Britton and a career hit by the War; a later arrival would have run him into the era of Bobby Moore and Jack Charlton.

In the first major phase of his career he was a wing-half, essentially a defensive player—safe, economical, utterly consistent. His play rarely raised a howl or the temperature. He did the obvious superbly well, avoiding risks but relishing conflict.

His tackling was hard and positive, his speed into the tackle devastating. He read the game well enough to make interceptions appear both easy and obvious, a mere break of the ball in his direction. He covered selflessly and re-covered quickly; and in the air his anticipation, bounce and timing gave him a regular edge over much taller opponents.

Wright was also a first class team man, prepared to dovetail into any format and happy to provide a springboard for greater talents around him. As Stan Mortensen puts it: 'Billy was always a

player we wanted in our side . . . particularly when the going was sticky.'

His early weakness as a wing-half, much emphasized both then and later, was said to be an inclination to be drawn too far upfield. He would lose contact at moments like this with the man he was marking, leaving space and responsibility behind him. This was, perhaps, inevitable: Wright's involvement with every moment of every game was so total that he was sometimes drawn irresistibly into forward areas.

It was, in any case, a problem that experience taught him to overcome, and a problem that

ceased to exist when, with time beginning to his wings, he switched to centre-half. This during the 1954 World Cup in Switzerl the second of the three series in which he pla Behind him were 59 appearances for Engl ahead of him another 46. Since the departur Bogota of Neil Franklin four seasons ea England had used no less than 11 different pla in a vain attempt to replace his talent. Now problem was solved.

There can be no reservations about Wrig worth as a centre-half. This was a job—wit more precisely defined area of responsibility marginally lesser demands on mobility imagination—that suited him down to ground. His club followed his country in gi him the number five shirt and, though he init had doubts about the wisdom of changing role, he accepted it uncomplainingly bec this was where he was most needed.

Wright was fortunate in having Stan C as his club manager. A great manager before that, a fine centre-half, Cullis's advic Wright on evaluating opposing centre-forwa dictating the direction of play, and holding defence together, was priceless.

Even after he changed roles, however, t remained criticism of Wright's captaincy. He

example, magnificently, but for some this was enough: they wanted a more obvious captain, a man who shouted and bullied and waved his hands, a martinet who pushed rather than led. But this was foreign to Wright's character, and if this was what England team manager Walter Winterbottom had wanted he would have had to have looked elsewhere.

But Winterbottom was always one of Wright's greatest admirers, and he was more aware than anyone of the influence that Wright's example and enthusiasm had on the players around him.

Wright captained England on 90 occasions. The first time, at the age of 24, was against Ireland in Belfast in 1948, with an England team that contained the previous captain Frank Swift—a goalkeeper, Swift had admitted, 'should never be captain'—Stanley Matthews, Tom Finney, Stan Mortensen and Neil Franklin. 'I decided early on,' says Wright, 'that captaincy is the art of leadership, not dictatorship. Respect is the hardest thing for a captain to come by and the easiest to lose. I never changed my mind about this.'

There were one or two other things about which Wright never changed his mind. From his first full cap—against Ireland in Belfast on 28 September 1946 (England won 7-2) to his last,

against the United States in Los Angeles on 28 May 1959 (England won 8-1)—he regarded playing for his country as the highest honour his chosen profession could give him. He always accepted that during any week of any season another player might present better credentials than his for a place in the England team; but, this much admitted, Wright always convinced himself that when he was chosen it was because he was the very best man for the job. It was a happy philosophy that never let him down.

England lost only 21 of the 105 games in which he played, while during his years with Wolves he achieved just about everything a club footballer could do in those days. The beginning, it is true, was a little uncertain: Wolves manager Major Frank Buckley, a forceful and far-sighted celebrity, told the 15-year-old Wright that he had better go home. Buckley thought he was too small, even for his age, and not really much of a footballer. Young Wright fled the scene, only for a reprieve to be announced 20 minutes later: it had been hinted to Buckley that Wright was useful with a broom.

It was a remarkable start to a remarkable career. Wright was captain of the Wolves side that won the Cup in 1949, beating Leicester City 3-1, captain of the side that won Wolves their first League Championship in 1954 and, again, in 1958 and 1959. Then, too, he led Wolves in the memorable floodlit matches against Moscow Spartak and Honved of Budapest in 1954—matches important in themselves but also prime factors in the inauguration of European competition. Wolves won both matches dramatically, with that against Honved the more significant of the two. This was the Honved of Zoltan Czibor, Sandor Kocsis and Ferenc Puskas, members of the immortal Hungarian side that only a year before had torn the heart out of English football. Wolves' victory helped the wound to heal.

Wright gets excited, even now, at the memory of that night. But if one match more than another can be described as the climax of his career, then that match was England against Scotland at Wembley on 11 April 1959—the match that gave him his 100th cap, and made him the first man in the history of football to pass this milestone. To Wright, however, it was more than just a line for the statisticans.

The previous year, just after the World Cup in Sweden, Wright had married Joy Beverley of the internationally-known Beverley Sisters. It was then a marvellous match between the worlds of sport and show-business that filled the women's magazines: Billy, captain of England, one of football's most eligible bachelors . . . Joy, a star in her own right, blonde and vivacious. They

married at Poole—a 'secret' wedding that attracted about 6,000 people to the scene. The following April their first child was born and, on the same day, Wright was selected for his 100th international. The three sisters—Joy, Teddy and Babs—were there at Wembley on the day. The sisters wore white, like England, and as Wright led his team out into the sunshine he spotted them immediately, just to the right of the royal box.

Wright decided to retire as a player just before the start of the next season—quietly and while he was still at the top. He was 35, and though he could have held his own for another season he knew, in his heart, that the pace was beginning to tell. The outcome was that Wright's last game for Wolves was not a glittering command performance, a major occasion, but the club's annual pre-season trial game, held on 8 August 1959. It was a measure of the esteem in which he was held by the town that 20,000 people turned up at that fixture to say goodbye. Cheers, handshakes, telegrams, telephone calls . . . and it was all over.

There were immediate offers. Wolves wanted to groom him as Cullis's successor, and clubs in Birmingham and London would have liked him. He became team manager of England's Under-23 and Youth sides (the heir-apparent to Walter Winterbottom), an FA staff coach, a TV personality and disc jockey, a regular contributor to newspapers and magazines, and a players' agent.

Why did a man with so much experience fail as Arsenal's manager?

Then came the one offer Wright could not resist. Arsenal, the club he had idolized before he joined Wolves, invited him to become their manager. He accepted gladly, even though he knew the size of the task. His predecessor, George Swindin, had not been a failure: his crime was simply that he was only a modest success while up the road Tottenham had been doing such intolerable things as winning the League and Cup double.

Wright took over at Arsenal at the start of the 1962-63 season, armed with a three-year contract. In his first season Arsenal were seventh, a promising start. But the next season they were 8th, the next 13th and the season after that, his last, 14th. He never led them beyond the fifth round in the FA Cup and in his third season they even went out to Third Division Peterborough.

Something was missing . . . but what? He bought well—altogether he spent £270,000 and took to the club such players as Frank McLintock and Don Howe—he had a vast playing experience to call on, and he treated his players with warmth and consideration. That was, perhaps, his fault; he was too nice. He would always have a good word for everyone; he was not ruthless enough when the occasion demanded it. As a result he was liked but, within the context of the tough world of First Division football, he was sometimes not sufficiently respected.

Perhaps all he needed was time; perhaps he would have been better advised to hurry more slowly and to have started with a smaller club—like all strangers he found Arsenal's glorious past irritating and pervasive. Whatever the reason Wright was bitterly hurt when Arsenal informed him in the middle of England's World Cup summer that 'the board had decided that results justified a change of management.'

Wright felt, with some justification, that he had done the ploughing and planting and that, given a little longer, he could have done some reaping.

But there were to be compensations. He joined ATV, the Midland television company, as a front man, later became their head of sport, and would not return to football management 'whatever the offer, whatever the club.' He was involved with sport, people and a challenging medium. 'It provides me' he says, 'with complete fulfilment.' A lucky man, perhaps, but then a man who brought great distinction to his sport.

PRESS ASSOCIATION

Billy WRIGHT

Honours: League Championship medal 1953-54, 1957-58, 1958-59
FA Cup winners medal 1949
Footballer of the Year 1952

Club	Season	League		Int'nls	
		Mtchs	Gls	Mtchs	Gls
Wolverhampton	1946-47	34	1	8	
Wanderers	1947-48	39	5	6	
	1948-49	35	2	8	1
	1949-50	35	3	10	1
	1950-51	38		3	1
	1951-52	39		8	
	1952-53	38	1	8	
	1953-54	39		10	
	1954-55	39	1	7	
	1955-56	37		9	
	1956-57	40		8	
	1957-58	38		11	
	1958-59	39		9	
Total		490	13	105	3

Far left Billy Wright leads out England against Scotland at Wembley in 1959: his 100th cap.

Left Nine months before, in July 1958, Wright had married Joy of The Beverley Sisters.

Left below The man who captained England 90 times had less success as Arsenal's manager.

Below Wright during his 100th international. He retired four months and five caps later.

Neil Franklin leads out Stoke for a Cup tie in 1949. The following year his fine career was ruined by his decision to play in Colombia.

THE DEFENDERS

Better off in Bogota?

The story of Neil Franklin is a sad and an anti-climatic one; blemished and completely changed by one wrong decision. Five splendid years in the England team as the best all-round centre-half since Stan Cullis came sharply to an end in May 1950, when he was persuaded to jump his contract with Stoke City, turn his back on England's first World Cup, and fly to Bogota to play for the unaffiliated Santa Fe club in the rebel Colombian League.

Within weeks he was back again, to be ostracised by his fellow professionals at Stoke and given a mercifully light suspension by the Football Association—until February 1951. It was still a traumatic experience. Though he was transferred to Second Division Hull City for £20,000, Franklin would never again be the same, elegant player. His career petered out in anti-climax, and England did not find another decent centre-half (they went through 11) until the combative but much less elegant Billy Wright moved there during the 1954 World Cup. It is reasonable to speculate whether Franklin himself would have been gracing it, had it not been for his mistaken trip to Bogota.

Born in Stoke, Franklin joined Stoke City as a right-half. He then became a centre-half and made his name during the war in RAF football, winning a place in that powerful representative team, then, early in 1945, in the English team. Five feet 11 inches tall but weighing little more than 11 stones, he was a change from the big, muscular stoppers who dominated the position at this time and was heaven sent to an England side who had badly missed the gifted Cullis since Army service took him abroad the previous year.

Neil FRANKLIN

Club	Season	League		Int'nls
		Mtchs	Gls	Mtchs
Stoke City	1946–47	37		8
	1947–48	35		6
	1948–49	36		8
	1949–50	34		5
Hull City	1950–51	14		
	1951–52	34		
	1952–53	13		
	1953–54	8		
	1954–55	38		
	1955–56	7		
Crewe Alexandra	1955–56	13	3	
	1956–57	39	1	
	1957–58	12		
Stockport County	1957–58	20		
Total		321	4	27

By the time official internationals were resum in 1946 Franklin was a poised and experienc international England player, consistent to degree, and he retained his England pla unchallenged for 27 matches.

Shortly before the 1950 World Cup was due be played in Brazil, Franklin wrote to the Engla selectors, asking permission to miss it because wife was having a baby. At that time, when players jumped at the chance of playing England, and when the adventure of a World C in distant South America was something new was odd that the request caused so little surpri The Football Association readily granted Fran lin's request, which turned out, in the event, to a little disingenuous. There is, perhaps, anotl way of looking at it, for if Franklin gave no su warning to Stoke—how, in the circumstanc could he?—at least he gave the English select the time to look for another centre-half.

In May 1950 Franklin, still only 27, and Stoke City colleague, outside-right George Mou ford, flew by Transatlantic Clipper to New Y en route to Bogota. His wife and his six-year-son also went. It was announced that the t players would be paid the then spectacular sum £50 a week—the Football League player's c tract still limited him to a skinflint maximum £12. Stoke City then revealed, through th manager Bob McGrory, that Franklin a Mountford had in fact asked permission to go coaches to Bogota during the summer, but t this had been refused.

Tempted to earn ten years' wages in twelve months

The position of Colombian football was the very special one. Their federation had left FI which meant their major clubs were free to po players from wherever they wished, without be fit of transfer fee. Up to this time the poach had been confined to Argentina, where there been a virtual haemorrhage of famous play pouring into Colombia to take advantage of better terms, among them Pedernera, Rossi the young di Stefano. Most of these had gone to Millionarios club of Bogota, but Santa Fe, who signed Franklin and Mountford, also had th own quota of Argentinians. The two Stoke n would not find it easy to harmonize with them.

It was soon announced from Bogota t Franklin and Mountford were there to play; an stay. 'British clubs could learn a lesson here,' s Franklin in this honeymoon period. 'St City could have sold me at any time for £30,0 but I'd still get only £10. At home we played ten years to earn £5,000, and half of it was tax In Colombia we've been promised that amount year.' A spokesman for the Santa Fe club said t the players were getting: 'About £2,000 paid i the bank, £120 a month salary, premiums of ab £20 for a win (in England it was £2) and f compensation for away matches.'

In an interview with an English Sunday ne paper Franklin insisted that his excuse to Football Association over the World Cup been quite genuine; in Bogota, his wife wo be treated for the nervous condition caused her pregnancy: 'The one and only reason I wr reluctantly to the Football Association on, begg them to release me.' But the honeymoon was sh indeed. A couple of months later, to the fury Luis Robledo, the Santa Fe director who plan the coup in London, Franklin accompanied wife to New York; and then impulsively flew ho

It was all over. Mountford also came back, only Manchester United's Charlie Mitten, slipp over to Bogota just when the whole affair see closed, stayed, made money, and came back in own good time.

'I'm not too happy about football conditi here,' explained Franklin at the time. 'A lo Argentinians are in the team and some are di cult to play with.' So to his suspension, to a de for Hull on which he gave away a goal, and sadly swift oblivion.

'Kaiser Franz'

...s, perhaps, a fair gauge of the ...re that Franz Beckenbauer had ...ved in 1972 that when an ...ish commentator was grasping ... superlative to describe a fine ... of play by Derby's Colin Todd, ...ould do no more than venture ...'even Beckenbauer would have ...proud of that'.

...the time of the 1966 World Cup ...that comment would have been ...inkable. As if frightened of ...and's potential, the Germans ...then been happy to sacrifice ...enbauer in the unfulfilled hope ...he would mark Bobby Charlton ...of the game. By the time of the ... European Championship, the ...s had been comprehensively ...ed. Now it was Beckenbauer ...was the man to be watched, ...England player who had to do ...watching. Beckenbauer's play ...enly was the standard by which ...round him were judged.

...rhaps the key to understanding ...z Beckenbauer is to know that ...is a Bavarian. Bavarians are ...rent from other Germans. They ...more akin to the Austrians than ...compatriots to the North, and ...carefree ways are far removed ... the image of the stereotyped ...nan. Given that he is a German, ...enbauer's style, with all its ...nce and seeming nonchalance, ...d only be that of a Southerner.

...is manner may be that of his ...but his talents are unique. ...enbauer's skills allow him to ...in any of the outfield positions ...international level. He is as ...ble of leading the attack as ...cting the defence, but his prefer- ...is for the role of sweeper.

...ractically all his past and ...ent coaches recognize that this ...e position which suits Becken- ...r best. In Italian football, where ...oots lie, the role of the sweeper ...ntirely defensive. Beckenbauer ...turned it into a kind of launching ... for attack. He is, perhaps, as ...h the first line in attack as the ... line in defence. His remarkable ...ing intelligence and range of ...n enable him to select exactly ... right moment for a counter- ...ck. With either a long, accurate ... to a colleague already running ... space through the middle, or by ...g a cross-field ball to start a ...ement along the wings, Becken- ...er will at a stroke direct the ...ck where his opponents suspect ...ast. Combining and interchang- ...with Gunter Netzer in the 1972 ...opean Championship, Becken- ...er seemed to hold the reins of a ...r unstoppable footballing force.

...No sweeper can ever have been so ...enturous as Beckenbauer. At ...ry opportunity he will move for- ...d into attack. His skill on the ball

and the inventiveness of his quick reverse and double passes would do credit to any South American virtuoso.

Beckenbauer's ability was clear from the start, but perhaps the most interesting facet of his early career is the number of positions he has played in. Then as now he was astonishingly versatile. It was his exploits as a centre-forward in his school team, for whom he once scored 100 goals in a season, that convinced his club, Bayern Munich, of his potential. He played regularly in the Bayern youth teams as a centre-forward, but it was on the left-wing that he made his first team debut in 1964.

Beckenbauer's family background did much to help him in these early days. His father, a postal worker, had been a footballer and his older brother played for and later managed 1860 Munich. Football in Germany was then still largely amateur so, after leaving school, Beckenbauer had to learn a profession.

'Charlton knew Hurst's shot never crossed the line'

He first trained as an insurance salesman and later spent 18 months as a supervisor of a clothing store. In February 1964, a year after the formation of the professional Bundesliga, Beckenbauer signed a professional contract with Bayern Munich at the age of 18.

Now able to devote himself entirely to football, he completed his soccer education under the guidance of junior coach Rudi Weiss, then Bayern managers Zlatko Cajkovski, Branco Zebec and Udo Lattek.

Just three months after taking over from Sepp Herberger as the manager of the national team, Helmut Schoen called up the 19-year-old Beckenbauer for the preparations for the 1966 World Cup. He gained his first full cap in a vital World Cup qualifying game in Stockholm against Sweden. In March he scored his first goal for the national team, getting two in a 4-2 win over Holland at Rotterdam, and by June he was a certainty for a place in the World Cup team.

In England, he faced the first truly great test of his career, when West Germany met England in the World Cup final at Wembley. Beckenbauer, whose role in the previous matches had always been a creative one, was now detailed to the restrictive task of closemarking

'Franz is so smart, he could be playing for Germany when he's 40 . . .'

SYNDICATION INTERNATIONAL

Franz BECKENBAUER

Honours: European Championship winners medal 1972
World Cup runners-up medal 1966
European Cup Winners Cup medal 1967
European Footballer of the Year 1972
West German Footballer of the Year 1966, 1968
West German League Championship medal 1969, 1972
West German League Championship runners-up medal 1970, 1971
West German Cup winners medal 1966, 1967, 1969, 1971
International caps: 69 (at 1 Sept 1973)

Above *Perfectly balanced, Beckenbauer shoots for goal in the 1972 Europ Championship final. His position as a sweeper gives him ample scope to n forward to support the midfield and attack.*
Above right *Beckenbauer gives chase to Colin Bell in the quarter-final c World Cup in Mexico. Beckenbauer's second half goal was the first sig the recovery with which Germany pulled back two goals to win 3-2.*
Below left *Beckenbauer in training for the 1972 European Championship f The game confirmed Germany's place as one of the leading soccer powers.*
Below right *With the European Championship at their feet, Beckenbauer (and his team were already firm favourites for Munich in 1974.*

Bobby Charlton. Years later Schoen still insisted that his decision to make Beckenbauer do this was correct, that Germany's best chance of victory lay in cutting Bobby Charlton out of the game, but for many it seemed a cruel waste of so much talent. Beckenbauer prevented his adversary from scoring, but even he was powerless as Germany went down to that disputed third

goal credited to Geoff Hurst. Beckenbauer is emphatic that the goal should never have been allowed: 'I was 12 yards away, and that ball never crossed the line. Even Bobby Charlton patted me on the back, saying, "Sorry, Franz". He too must have known that it was not a goal.'

While England were content to rest on the laurels of their triumph, the Germans were reappraising their whole attitude to the game. The emphasis came to be placed on skill on the ball rather than hard running off it, and where skill was at a premium, Beckenbauer was in his element.

The culmination of this development was not to come until the 1972 European Championship, but in the meantime Germany got their revenge for that defeat in 1966, winning a friendly in Hanover by the only goal and eliminating England from the World Cup in Mexico. In both games Beckenbauer scored an excellent and crucial goal.

Despite his ability, Beckenbauer, like all great players, has his critics. They point to his often lazy-looking, casual approach and

nonchalance, sometimes even depicted as arrogance. Perhaps the best answer to this came from Sepp Herberger, Schoen's predecessor as national team manager: 'Franz is so smart, intelligent and mature that he could be playing for Germany when he's forty. So many players today are like clockwork toys. They run themselves silly and then stop. But Franz knows how to conserve his energy, and that is vital for anyone who is going to have a long playing career.' In fact Beckenbauer is far from a lazy player. As Herberger says he is simply intelligent enough to avoid the senseless expenditure of energy that cuts short the careers of so many others.

In Munich, where they still enjoy royal titles in nostalgic reminiscences of the nineteenth century, they call Beckenbauer 'Kaiser Franz'. It is the Olympian calm and unperturbed manner which the nickname suggests that makes Beckenbauer one of the cleanest and fairest of players—he has never been sent off the field.

Off the field Beckenbauer is always co-operative and diplomatic. On his visit to Britain for the 1972 European Championship he wanted

to be rid of an English journa but rather than be rude to the r Beckenbauer declined the interv by saying that he was on an exclu contract to a German paper. It w white lie, but one which avoided ill-feeling.

For all his immense popularit his own country, Beckenbauer frequently been jeered by hostile at away matches. His majestic c posure, the almost contemptu manner in which he leaves oppon stranded, often invites the e even malice, of opponents and t more partisan support.

The last of the great attacking centre-halves?

Their disenchantment is shared by those with more knowle of the game. Beckenbauer has been pursued by numerous for clubs ready to offer fabulous fees trimmings for his services.

As far back as 1966, AC M reputedly offered £250,000 Bayern. Because of the ban imports of foreign players, the

SYNDICATION INTERNATIONAL

through. Nowadays, only the
[Du]tch giants like Ajax Amsterdam or
[Fe]yenoord Rotterdam are in a posi-
[tion]—legally and financially—to
[mee]t the sum that Beckenbauer's
[sign]ature would command. But in any
[cas]e he is unlikely to move from
[Mu]nich where he lives comfortably
[wit]h his wife Brigitte, whom he met at
[a s]ports training centre, and their
[thr]ee sons.

Together with Bayern's technical
[dir]ector Robert Schwan, who has
[bec]ome his closest friend and adviser,
[Bec]kenbauer has founded an
[ins]urance agency to provide for his
[fam]ily when he leaves the game.
[Th]at will be the day he stops playing,
[for] he has no desire to stay on in
[foot]ball as a manager. 'Not at any
[pri]ce,' he has often said. Throughout
[his] playing career he has watched the
[tri]als and tribulations of soccer
[coa]ches in Germany, where, since
[the] formation of the Bundesliga, an
[ave]rage of five managers a year have
[bee]n sacked. Such a risk holds no
[app]eal for Beckenbauer.

[One] who has enjoyed a bit more
[sec]urity than most is the man at the
[top], the national manager Helmut
[Sch]oen, whom Beckenbauer regards

as a great psychologist and outstanding tactician. Perhaps that is why he
has been so patient, having toiled
through 26 internationals in the
midfield position which he dislikes,
before being allowed to occupy his
favourite role of sweeper, in which,
ironically, he can find more freedom
to express his creative talents.

Beckenbauer is no ordinary
defender. For comparisons one has to
turn to the past. In some respects he
is in the tradition of the great
attacking centre-halves of an earlier
era, especially the last of that
exclusive breed, the unforgettable
Ernst Ocwirk of the Austrian side
of the late forties and fifties.

Beckenbauer's boyhood idol was
another of the great players of those
times, Fritz Walter, captain of
the German side that won the World
Cup in 1954. By the time of the
Munich tournament, twenty years
would have passed since Walter and
his team beat Hungary to win the
cup for their country. After their
brilliant performances in the 1972
European Championship, who would
deny that it was Beckenbauer's influence which had brought Germany
to the top of the international pile.

COLORSPORT

THE DEFENDERS

The quick and the deft

England's outstanding and consistent full-back pairings can be counted on the fingers of one hand —Crompton and Pennington, Goodall and Blenkinsop, Hapgood and Male, and Cohen and Wilson. And though, with the advent of the back four, the linking of full-backs had become a little unrealistic, there is a strong case for maintaining that Cohen and Wilson, with their attacking approach in England's World Cup winning saga, were the finest of the lot.

The memories of the bustling, busy Cohen and the reliable, skilful Wilson stand the test of time even though, after finishing playing, both have chosen careers far removed from the game that brought them together.

Cohen is a land buyer with Brickland Builders in Tunbridge Wells and a director of an off-shoot firm; Wilson is a funeral director in his father-in-law's business in Huddersfield, though he still plays as an amateur in a Sunday league.

They have been as opposite in choice of profession as they were in style during an England link-up which ran as smoothly as any traditional family business.

Cohen and Wilson played together as if born to it, as if they had kicked a ball side by side from the playground and, strangely in an age of planning and strategy, never discussing a tactic.

'We never talked things over before a match,' says Cohen. 'During games we occasionally helped each other by making the odd suggestion to assist covering or something. Cursed one another, too, on the odd occasion. Every pro does that at times.'

'I'd often finish by banging the ball into the crowd. Not Ray . . .'

'We were a natural partnership, Ray and I, and we didn't even have to be extra close off the field to achieve that. I didn't mix much with any of the England players particularly in the camp, come to that, although I got on well with all of them. Alf used to switch us a lot in hotel pairings so that we got to know one another better.'

Cohen was the more spectacular player, an instant crowd pleaser, not least because he tried to give fuller interpretation to the modern back's invitation to overlap, as did Jimmy Armfield, an England captain and Wilson's previous partner in over 20 internationals.

But Cohen is honest enough to admit: 'Although I was more powerful physically than Ray, he was more accurate than I was. When I went off upfield I'd often finish by banging the ball into the crowd or into the goalkeeper's hands. Not Ray. He usually made sure every ball was placed spot on. A real pro.'

Armfield, later to become manager of Bolton, says: 'Ray had pace and superb positional sense, but also greater ball skills than the majority appreciated. He seldom wasted a ball.'

Cohen's first full cap and his initial tie up with Wilson was against Uruguay in May 1964 (when Wilson already had 24 caps) and his World Cup debut came against the same country at Wembley two years later.

They played together in the six games England needed at Wembley—against Uruguay, Mexico, France, Argentina, Portugal and West Germany—to lift the trophy for the first time.

'Ray was such a predictably reliable player,' says Cohen, 'that a mistake he made in the final against the Germans somehow stuck in the mind. It was the only serious error I ever saw him make. That's how good he was.'

One report of the dramatic final recorded: 'The West Germans led after 13 minutes when Ray Wilson, most untypically, headed a cross weakly down to Haller, who scored.'

Wilson resumed, unshaken, and returned to the monumental efficiency that won him 63 England caps, the most won by a left-back, and a reputation, once Brazil's Nilton Santos had retired, as the world's best in that position.

Neutral judges put him ahead of Italy's Facchetti (another who exploited the over-lap) through his sounder defensive play. Facchetti, though, scored far more goals. Wilson's significant tally in a League career of 405 matches with Huddersfield, Everton, Oldham and Bradford City was five goals. Cohen could claim only one more, in three more appearances.

Wilson was good enough as a Second Division player with Huddersfield to command a regular England place under Walter Winterbottom, predecessor to Ramsey. Bill Shankly, one of his managers at Huddersfield, called him, in typical Shankly fashion, 'the best left-back in the business,' and Denis Law, who as a 16-year-old came up against Wilson in Huddersfield practice matches, described him (and still does) as 'the most difficult defender to pass I've ever faced'.

Although the name of Garrincha twice appeared on the score sheet against England in the 1962 World Cup quarter-final in Vina del Mar, Chile, the famous Brazilian winger would no doubt give support to Law's high rating of Wilson.

'We contained the Brazil forwards well that day,' says Armfield, right-back on that occasion. 'Ray did a good job on Garrincha, and he was compelled to wander to get the room he wanted. His goals were with a header from the centre and a swerve free-kick.'

Wilson, born in Shirebrook, Derbyshire, in 1935, left Huddersfield later than expected. Shankly persuaded the Town board to reject offers from First Division clubs, most of them from Chelsea when Joe Mears was chairman.

It was one of football's many coincidences that, nearly five years after Shankly had taken over as manager of Liverpool, Wilson arrived on Merseyside to be an Everton rival, at a cost of £40,000.

Although he was nudging 29, Wilson was not too late to revive dulled ambitions at club level, and he twice went to a familiar ground for him—Wembley—to collect an FA Cup winner's and runners-up medal in the space of three seasons.

He had gone to Goodison Park a year after manager Harry Catterick's first League Championship win, and left just before the second—this time on a free transfer after knee trouble.

Wilson spent only a season at Oldham before another free transfer took him to Bradford City as a player-coach. When he was eventually offered the team manager's post he turned his back on football—apart from the Sunday excursions—and chose the unusual profession of undertaking. 'He's turned out to be an excellent funeral director,' says his father-in-law, Ed Lumb.

Cohen, whose playing career was killed by a knee injury when he was still the right side of 30, also took on the challenge of coaching—in charge of Fulham's youth side under Bill Dodgin's

Ray WILSON

Honours: World Cup winners medal 1966
FA Cup winners medal 1966
FA Cup runners-up medal 1968

Club	Season	League		Int'nls
		Mtchs	Gls	Mtchs
Huddersfield Town	1955-56	6		
	1956-57	13		
	1957-58	31		
	1959-59	42	2	
	1959-60	41	1	4
	1960-61	32		
	1961-62	36		11
	1962-63	33	1	6
	1963-64	28	1	9
Everton	1964-65	17		5
	1965-66	35		16
	1966-67	31		5
	1967-68	28		7
	1968-69	5		
Oldham Athletic	1969-70	25		
Bradford City	1970-71	2		
Total		405	5	63

managership—but finally left the club for the wider scope he felt building offered him.

'I had to realize that, much as I loved the game, there had to be other things in life,' he explains. 'For example, I made my debut in Fulham's first team when I was 16, but I didn't sign professional forms for them until I was several months past 17 because I wanted to stay on for 'O' levels.

'I got one of them in engineering and drawing because I happened to be able to draw lines very well. I now realize its full value when I have to read complicated builders' plans.'

Born four years later than Wilson in West Kensington, Cohen had a lucrative testimonial at Fulham and, like his England partner, has no complaints about football.

But the pain, mental as well as physical, of that fateful injury against Liverpool remains forever vivid in his mind.

'I was off the ground at the time,' he recalls. 'I tried to play the ball away. I didn't connect properly and there was an extraordinary rotation in the right knee. I've never known such terrible pain. I was really finished with the game at that moment, although there were futile attempts to get it right for the next 15 months when I lost two cartilages into the bargain. It was all a terrible legacy from such a harmless jump.'

Cohen, who also won eight Under-23 caps for England, went into that Fulham side managed by

SYNDICATION INTERNATIONAL

RAY GREEN

lford Jezzard and enriched by characters like die Lowe, Arthur Stevens, Jimmy Hill, Roy ntley and Jim Langley.

It was a team headed for an FA Cup semi-final k against Munich-shattered Manchester ited in 1958, promotion to the First Division the next season and then a series of relegation apes before dropping back into the Second vision around the time of his exit as a player.

Like many Fulham loyalists, Cohen suffered frustrations silently. He and Johnny Haynes, wever, stayed to the death. 'Johnny was the t player I've ever seen. More accurate than bby Charlton, who was the midfield director of gland during most of my internationals.' Two rs separated the international careers of hen and Haynes, whose own finished in 1962.

'They wanted me to be manager, but I wasn't happy in the work'

At Fulham, Cohen was impressed by the thods of Vic Buckingham, 'a manager more phisticated in ideas than most'.

Buckingham made him captain over Haynes, d Allan Clarke, later to leave for Leicester and eds, says of Cohen the skipper: 'A wonderful ample to a young player such as I was in those

days at Fulham. He never stopped encouraging me on the field and helping me off it. He made my days at Craven Cottage.'

Wilson almost stayed in the game. 'I was tempted to stay in football as a manager. Bradford City had made me assistant manager, and when Jimmy Wheeler left the number one seat about six weeks after the season had started, I took charge until Christmas. They wanted me to take the job and the money was attractive, but I wasn't entirely happy in the work, so I went to join the family business instead.'

Wilson compromises when asked which of Armfield and Cohen he preferred playing along-side in a great England career. 'They were both so similar in style that it was marginal. The main difference really was that when I played with Jimmy the tactics were for a back to pivot on the centre-half so you had more of a partnership with the other back; whereas when George came along the game had changed a little defensively.

'I was then more concerned linking up with the left of the two centre-backs. I didn't realize I played 25 with Jimmy and 28 with George.'

In those 28 internationals, Wilson and Cohen successfully defended England's flanks against the attacking forces of the world, and in the end added their contribution to an effort which made their country, for a time, the most potent there was.

Left above George Cohen holds off Siggy Held during the 1966 World Cup final. It was Cohen's 30th cap and the 21st time he had partnered Ray Wilson in the full-back positions. The two played together, in fact, throughout the successful run of six World Cup matches.

Left below Time for celebration after the final as Ray Wilson adopts an unusual style of headgear. Cohen, unusually, takes a more subdued role, partly hidden by Jack Charlton.

Above After retirement, less strenuous efforts for Wilson and son at home in Huddersfield.

George COHEN

Honours: World Cup winners medal 1966

Club	Season	League		Int'nls
		Mtchs	Gls	Mtchs
Fulham	1956-57	1		
	1957-58	26		
	1958-59	41	1	
	1959-60	42		
	1960-61	41		
	1961-62	41	1	
	1962-63	38		
	1963-64	41	1	5
	1964-65	40	2	9
	1965-66	39		16
	1966-67	35	1	5
	1967-68	17		2
	1968-69	6		
Total		408	6	37

Bobby Moore—the footballer who has everything. As a player he took the World Cup as captain of England, and is the most consistent member of his club West Ham. As a man he has a contented home life, thriving businesses—and a reputation for honesty which made the Bogota accusation laughable.

40

A captain designed by a computer

...of the surest ways of obtaining an insight ...the ambiguous relationship which exists ...ween Bobby Moore and his public is to watch ...in action outside London.

...he very sight of Moore trotting onto a pitch ...say Nottingham or Newcastle ignites an ...ant, collective reaction which is a fascinating ...pound of hostility, envy, scorn and respect.

...he fact that these are precisely the emotions ...ch the provinces feel for the capital is no ...dent, for Moore is pre-eminently a Londoner, ...a all that implies. But the causes of the reaction ...broader than that ancient enmity.

...Moore is the one footballer who makes the ...ase 'Golden Boy' seem something more than a ...., facile tag. If you asked a computer to ...te up with an idealized version of the captain ...England's football team in 1971, it would ...duce a blond six-footer, rich and tolerably ...dsome with an attractive wife, two children— ...oy and a girl—an equable temperament and ...ability to do his job better than anyone ...in the world. The Order of the British ...pire and the Freedom of the City of London ...ild be useful optional extras.

...obby Moore, of course, is and has all these ...igs and the vague, undefined feeling of the pro-...ial crowd is that it seems all too easy.

When the curt command means more than the brandished fist

...is on-field character heightens this impres-...n. There is no passion about his game. One ...s that he long ago thought it through and ...ided that emotion would impair effectiveness, ...s it was discarded. His one outstanding gift, ...t of reading a game more quickly and com-...hensively than any other defender, enables ...to reduce frantic chasing and desperate tack-...; to the minimum, so he is rarely seen in any ...sical distress. And his preference for the ...t command rather than the brandished fist ...gests that he is not putting too much sweat into ...captaincy.

...t all seems too easy, particularly when you ...nk of the salary he draws. Estimates of foot-...lers' earnings are about as reliable as estimates ...casualties in modern warfare. In other words ...y can be doubled or halved depending on what ...t want to believe. But there is good reason to ...ieve that after the 1970 World Cup Moore was ...ning around £11,000 a year from football alone ...t perhaps £25,000 yearly from all sources.

...There is a dark, Puritan corner hidden away ...the heart of most Englishmen which insists ...t it is somehow wrong for a man to earn that ...d of money merely because he can play football. ...e more the money, the greater the resentment ...nd, with the sole exception of George Best, ...ody earns more than Bobby Moore.

...Those are the kind of thoughts which seem ...provoke the crowd into derisive whistling and ...ing when Moore makes his entrance on a pro-...cial pitch, but beyond it all there is a strong ...l undeniable respect. Nobody wins a record ...nber of caps without being an exceptional ...tballer. And there is no question that he *is* a ...y exceptional footballer.

...orn in Barking, East London, in 1941 he ...nded the Tom Hood school, Leyton, and ...rished the ambition common to most kids in East London. At first it seemed he would be disappointed: 'I was choked when the time came for me to leave school,' he recalls. 'All my mates had gone off for trials with clubs around London but nobody seemed to want me. I thought I'd missed out . . . then West Ham called me up for a trial.'

The development was steady. He played a record 18 times for England Youth, turned professional in June 1958 and followed the conventional route towards the international team with eight Under-23 caps and an international debut in Peru in May 1962.

The maximum wage had been abolished a year earlier and, for the purposes of Moore's pocket, the timing of its abolition could scarcely have been bettered.

As a 20-year-old international, his earning potential—both inside and outside the game— was considerable. But when, after 17 caps, he was made England's youngest-ever captain for the match against Czechoslovakia in May 1963, that potential became enormous.

The comparison between Moore and another blond defender who himself had been England's youngest-ever captain is itself a comparison between football's past and present. Billy Wright's international career had yielded him 105 caps, and while the 105th was being won his weekly wage was around £20. Moore was about to establish a new pattern.

In 1964 he began to be aware of the limitations of his club. 'Homely' was the adjective most frequently used to describe West Ham in those days. It was a friendly club, packed with amiable, civilized people. It had risen from the Second Division in 1958, and was mightily pleased to sit among the elite. But it did not look like winning anything.

Spurs, on the other hand, were the side by which other teams measured themselves. The memory of the Cup and League double was still fresh and, with the talent available at White Hart Lane, there were still things to achieve. But Dave Mackay had broken a leg and Spurs were searching for a top-class replacement. Moore, in a newspaper interview, admitted that he would not mind a move to a bigger club. Only a successful West Ham team, it seemed, could change his mind.

Captain in the greatest performance by a British side in Europe

Then West Ham became successful. They worked their way to the FA Cup Final, improving all the time. They won the Final, beating Preston, and Moore was elected Footballer of the Year.

Cup victory sent West Ham into Europe. The team just kept on getting better and, on a warm spring evening at Wembley, they produced what many people still regard as the finest performance by a British side in Europe to take the European Cup Winners Cup by beating Munich 1860.

Moore grew immeasurably during those two seasons. His leadership of West Ham had established his place as one of the most influential people in the British game and the pace at which other West Ham players, notably Geoff Hurst and Martin Peters, were progressing was eloquent tribute both to the influence of Moore and the stewardship and brilliant coaching of West

Ham's manager, Ron Greenwood.

Moore's own talent had passed from precocity to maturity. He was now in the front rank of international defenders, his natural ability refined by Greenwood and his England manager, Alf Ramsey, his temperament steeled by seasons of world-class competition.

The business interests were developing apace. By August 1965 he owned a sports shop opposite West Ham's ground, he appeared in hair cream and anti-smoking advertisements ('I wouldn't lend my name to anything unless I really believed in it,' he said), and he was a director of Bobby Moore Ltd, a company formed to exploit his name which, among other things, purchased land, constructed buildings and acquired inventions.

But the big test was ahead, the World Cup of 1966 when he was to lead an England team with the finest chance of winning the trophy any English side had ever possessed.

Yet three months before the competition began, Moore stunned West Ham with another transfer request. He had, by now, played more than 250 games for the club; he had led them to another Cup Winners Cup semi-final. But, just a few days before that important match was to be played, he asked for a move for the reason he had cited two years before . . . he wanted a bigger club.

'If the West Ham image doesn't suit him, then he knows what to do'

Greenwood reacted angrily. He took the club captaincy from Moore and announced: 'If the West Ham image does not suit him, then he is better off where the image does suit him.' But that storm, like the previous one, blew itself out within a couple of months and, freed from distracting considerations, Moore was able to work and worry about the series of matches which were to secure his reputation and ensure his fortune.

His form before that 1966 World Cup fell far below the standards he had set himself—indeed, there was talk in some quarters of Leeds' Norman Hunter taking over Moore's England shirt and George Cohen assuming the captaincy.

If Ramsey was aware of such speculation he made no move towards vindicating it. Close observers of the England organization in the late sixties and early seventies tend to agree that Ramsey and his captain are something less than bosom friends. That is not to say that there is antagonism, but they have their own distinctive ideas and attitudes, and there is not the warm, personal friendship which exists between, say, Busby and Charlton or Bremner and Revie.

But they share a strong belief in the futility of finishing second. They are winners; and they recognized that they needed each other if victory were to be achieved. They were, of course, absolutely right.

A year before the World Cup of 1966, a football writer was asking Ron Greenwood what he thought England's chances were of winning. Greenwood just pointed across the pitch to where Bobby Moore was practising with a ball. 'We're going to win,' he said, 'and that man's the reason why. He can already see in his mind's eye a picture of himself holding up the World Cup, and he's calculated down to the last detail just what that will mean to him and to his career.'

If the England side of 1966 was steeped in the dogma of Ramsey then it was inspired by the example of Moore. Over six matches he was as near impeccable as anyone can be in a team game. 'Bobby Moore is my representative on the field. He is responsible for seeing that the plans we have worked on are carried out,' said Ramsey.

Moore fulfilled that role with distinction, but he embellished it with the finest football of his career. As the competition wore on he became more of a presence than a player, hugely capable, massively comforting, totally assured.

He won the Player of Players award at the end of the tournament, and such was the calibre of his performance that a competition which had featured all the world's finest players could come up with no conceivable alternative.

The indirect financial rewards for World Cup success were prodigious, and Moore began to capitalize on his fame with a shrewdness and single-mindedness which impressed even the experienced businessmen with whom he worked.

'Football has obviously opened a lot of doors to Bobby,' said one business associate. 'But he'd have made money if his name had been Fred Bloggs and he'd never kicked a ball. He's got this East End shrewdness, he knows what he wants and he's prepared to work to get it. He'll never starve.'

As a further precaution against starvation, Moore became a partner in a suede-leather manufacturers producing expensive and high-quality coats for men. He discovered that he had a flair for design and this was put to useful effect in the business. And all the time he obeyed Henry Ford's dictum: 'Money is like an arm or a leg . . . use it or lose it!'

But always he was at pains to insist that no amount of business involvement would be allowed to interfere with his football, the root of his wealth. And certainly his football—particularly when playing for England—betrayed precious few signs of outside preoccupation.

By now, of course, one of the more popular pastimes among Football League managers was to discover a weakness in Moore's game. The discussions usually boiled down to three facets of his play: his pace, his heading and his tackling.

Moore himself would admit that he is not the fastest defender in the League—or even in East London! He is inclined to be one-paced, and only a brave man would back him against some of the fliers in the First Division. But you could count on one hand the number of times in a season Moore allows himself to be drawn into these situations of direct conflict. Similarly with his heading. He may win only an average share of aerial challenges, but his anticipation secures him far more than his share of deflections.

The myth that he can't tackle has long since been exploded

The myth that he cannot tackle he has long since exploded. Again, he prefers to decline direct confrontation, but he tackles to win the ball, and both West Ham and England have cause to be grateful for a number of goals which had their origins in Moore winning a tackle around the fringe of his own area and setting up a situation with a fast, 30-yard pass.

If anything, he actually became a better player in the seasons which followed his 1966 triumph. West Ham started to fall on relatively hard times, but Moore's own game was completely unaffected. At the end of one trying season, Greenwood (who singles out individuals as reluctantly as Ramsey) was heard to say: 'I think we all take Bobby too much for granted. His level of performance is so high that people only notice him when he makes a mistake. I've never seen a player put together so many good games as this fellow does.'

His life-style attracted a growing number of sneers. An indifferent performance would inspire a quota of tedious, carping articles about the Moores' French maid, and their gardener, and their daily, and their lavish £20,000-plus home in Chigwell, and Tina's television advertising, and Bobby's two dozen hand-made suits, and his three dozen hand-made shirts and his West End manicures.

Their effect upon his composure was rather less than nil. Yet nobody really knew how ingrained was that composure until in May 1970 there occurred a distasteful episode which was to make 'Bogota' a dirty word in the vocabulary of English sport.

It happened in the last few weeks before the start of the World Cup finals in Mexico. The English planning, under Sir Alf Ramsey, had been immaculate in its detail and as part of the attempt to accustom players to altitude it was decided to play matches in Bogota, Colombia and Quito,

Ecuador.

Colombia were beaten 4-0 and Ecuador were defeated with similar ease. The confidence of the English team—led, of course, by Moore—was at an encouraging peak when they returned to Bogota on the way back to Mexico City.

Five hours later, when the team's plane set off for Mexico, Moore was left behind in Bogota, under house arrest, accused of stealing a £625 emerald and diamond bracelet from a boutique at the luxury Tequendama Hotel a few days earlier.

His accusers were a shop assistant and a witness, produced a week after the incident, who claimed to have seen Moore slip the bracelet into his pocket while two other English players distracted the shop-girl.

It was the biggest sports story in years; the world champions deprived of their captain only a few days before they began the defence of their trophy; the bizarre pantomime of South American justice involving dramatic reconstructions of the 'crime' with large and noisy crowds and hundreds of reporters and television cameramen; the conflicting stories of the prosecution; the background of Latin resentment to England's triumph in 1966; the fact that similar charges had been laid against other sports stars in previous years at the same shop; the appeal for urgent justice by Prime Minister Harold Wilson . . . and in the middle of it all the figure of Moore, looking just as he looks when West Ham are victims of a bad decision and saying simply: 'I am innocent. All I want to do is go to Mexico. I don't know why they picked on me.'

His colleagues in the England party were furious but conscious of the need to watch words until their captain was freed. Sir Alf described the whole affair as 'a sick joke', saying: 'I should have thought the integrity of the man would be answer enough for these charges.' Alan Mullery was scornful: 'Steal a bracelet? With Bob's money he could have bought the shop! It's ridiculous.' And that was the conclusion at which the judge arrived when he decided that there was no real evidence against Moore.

The England team, now established in their headquarters in Guadalajara, gave him a hero's welcome on his return four days later, and Moore himself said he wanted to forget the whole thing with the first match only days away.

But perhaps the most perceptive comment on the whole affair came from Joe Mercer, manager of Manchester City and a television commentator for the World Cup: 'If they had to do it to any of our players then I'm glad they picked Bobby,' said Mercer. 'All the others would let it get to them, upset them. The only reaction of this fellow will be to punish them on the field for the things they said in court.'

And what lasting impression did the whole affair have on Moore? 'You find yourself looking in jewellers' windows with your hands stuck in your pockets, pointing at things with your nose,' he was to say, months later.

Mercer, of course, was right. Moore performed in the matches with Rumania, Czechoslovakia and even in the losing game with Brazil in the same magisterial manner he had exhibited in England four years earlier. But the results were not to follow the same pattern.

Pele, the player for whom Moore has a great and abiding respect, named England's captain the finest defender in the world after their epic battle in Guadalajara. The football world eagerly waited for the return duel between the two men which was to have been in the final in Mexico City. But things went catastrophically wrong for England against West Germany when a two-goal lead was squandered and an extra-time defeat was inflicted.

One might have thought that the tension of the Bogota affair and the anguish of World Cup defeat would have sent Moore away for a long, relaxing holiday before the start of the new season. But his business head decreed otherwise. He took his holiday, but not before joining a television company to comment on the semi-final and final of the Mexico tournament.

Odious though the whole South American affair must have been to Moore, the publicity he received at home—both for his conduct in Bogota and his playing performances in Mexico—was entirely favourable.

The fans were behind Greenwood's heavy penalty on Bobby Moore

The only wholly bad publicity Bobby Moore has received in his whole career lay six months ahead. In November 1970 West Ham played Celtic in a testimonial match for Moore; the game raised £10,000. Two months later, on the eve of a third-round Cup tie with Blackpool, Moore and three other players were spotted in a Blackpool night-club. West Ham lost the Cup tie 4-0, and Moore had a wretched match.

The contrast between the lavish testimonial and the late, late night was too brutal even for the East Enders who had followed his career with loyalty and pride from the earliest days, and there is little doubt that the mass of fans were behind Greenwood's action in handing out a hefty fine and keeping him out of the side for five weeks.

Ramsey, too, punished the indiscretion and left his captain out of one international. But for club and country the set-back was a short one, and he resumed for both with that almost inhuman consistency.

But one slip, sadly proving his mortality, could not have come at a worse time. In Poland, in the World Cup on a summer's evening in June, he allowed Lubanski to purloin the ball from him to shoot a match-clinching goal—a goal which severely threatened England's chances of reaching the finals.

That match was his 105th international. Within eight days he had added two further caps to break Bobby Charlton's England record. But at the start of the 1973-74 season, his place in Ramsey's plans became unclear.

Unsettled at West Ham, because of their lack of success, he was left out of one match. Less than a fortnight later, Ramsey only chose him as substitute against Austria and, later, Poland. And with England's World Cup demise, a great career was nearing its end.

left Prophetically, perhaps, Bobby Moore finds [him]self behind a row of soldiers in Ecuador 1970 [...] only a few days later, he was to be arrested [on a] charge of theft in Bogota, Colombia.
[ab]ove left Moore holds high the Jules Rimet trophy [at] Wembley in 1966. Not only was it a team and [per]sonal triumph, but it also ensured him a com-[fort]able future.
[lef]t When Moore was arrested on the dubious charge [of] stealing a bracelet in Bogota, he conducted [him]self with dignity and did not allow it to affect his [per]formances in the World Cup.
[belo]w Concentration shows on Bobby Moore's face as [he] moves forward to head a ball against Wales.
[below] right The authority of a captain—Moore [dre]ams at his West Ham team-mates, pointing out [wha]t they should have been doing.
[ab]ove Moore rises in the air in a match against [Ma]nchester United. In 1966, those responsible for [selec]ting a Player of Players could find no possible [alte]rnative to the captain of England.

Bobby MOORE

Honours: World Cup winners medal, 1966;
European Cup Winners Cup winners medal, 1965;
FA Cup Winners medal, 1964;
Footballer of the Year, 1964

Club	Season	League		Int'nls	
		Mtchs	Gls	Mtchs	Gls
West Ham	1958–59	5			
United	1959–60	13			
	1960–61	38	1		
	1961–62	41	3	5	
	1962–63	41	3	9	
	1963–64	38	2	10	
	1964–65	28	1	7	
	1965–66	37		16	2
	1966–67	40	2	6	
	1967–68	40	4	10	
	1968–69	41	2	9	
	1969–70	40		12	
	1970–71	40	2	5	
	1971–72	40		7	
	1972–73	42	3	11	
Total		524	23	107	2

43

THE DEFENDERS

The not-so-gentle giant

On the eve of the new season in August 1972, after a lot of thought and personal agony, Leeds United manager Don Revie declared that he was going to phase 37-year-old Jack Charlton out of the game as a player. 'There hasn't been a better centre-half in the world over the last ten years,' he said. 'And to have to tell a player like Jack that you're going to replace him is terribly hard.'

Just over ten years earlier the player had given the manager a different kind of agony. Then Revie had told Charlton he wasn't his kind of centre-half, that he could go the moment someone made a reasonable offer.

In the decade between those contradictory statements Revie built one of the finest teams in the world, with Charlton becoming not only the key figure in Leeds' success, but also in England's World Cup triumph at Wembley in 1966.

The articulate Charlton has also become as famous for his forthright comments as for his distinctive build and style. But though he has often appeared to be displaying his honesty like a red badge of courage, he has always been an earthy, uncomplicated man who simply believes in saying whatever is on his mind.

'Big Jack' must be the prime example of a player whose rewards come late in his career. He had been at Leeds for a dozen years and had made over 300 League appearances for them when, following their promotion to the First

Division, he became England's centre-half and a world figure.

Yet he had been in no rush to enter professional football, and did so virtually as a third choice career. While kid brother Bobby was still at school dreaming of becoming a footballer (like his uncles in the Milburn family), Jack was enjoying life as a ticket laddie in the weigh-cabin at the mine where his father worked in Ashington, Northumberland. At 15 he was asked to go for a trial with Leeds United—where Jimmy Milburn was the left-back—but Jack wasn't happy with the idea of leaving home and declined.

A spell down the pit quickly prompted him to apply to become a police cadet at Morpeth, but Leeds asked him to go for another trial the day the police told him to turn up for an interview. He decided to go to Leeds.

Life as a 'Buckley Boy' at Elland Road proved hard. While the first team trained in the morning the groundstaff boys weeded the field, cleaned the toilets, cleaned the boots and cleaned out the baths.

'The first team was something miles away,' Charlton remembers. 'You never went into their dressing-room unless you knocked on the door. Often when I walked in without knocking they'd put me in a bath and throw a bucket of water over me.'

It was the John Charles era at Elland Road,

and a year after his arrival at Leeds (as a back) Charlton was tried at centre-half in practice match and told to mark the g Welshman. 'I must have impressed them, recalls, 'because from then on I played centre and made my first team debut there at 17.'

After one League appearance, howe Charlton was called away for his two y National Service with the Horse Guards—hel them win the Cavalry Cup in Germany for the time in their history. He got little chance to off and play for Leeds during his Army days after demob, he soon regained his place an his first season back they won promotion u the managership of Raich Carter.

With Charles dominating nearly everyt Leeds did they were often considered a one-team. Charlton argued that this was unfair, when Charles was sold to Juventus for £65 in April 1957 the side quickly crumbled.

As Leeds slipped back into the Second Div Charlton became increasingly aware of position as a senior player, and with his uncon able urge to speak out against anything suggested injustice he soon became an off union leader in the dressing-room.

Carter went and Bill Lambton took ove manager and he and the truculent Charlton row after row. 'I fell out with him many ti recalls Jack, 'not only over what I was d but over things affecting the others. If som moaned about something I tended to say, "I'll a word with him for you".'

One incident indicates the position. After match in London, Charlton tried to get s relatives a lift back to the station on the t coach, but was refused. He was angry, remained silent, accepting because it was a rule. A couple of weeks later Leeds played a in London and Charlton exploded when s hotel waiters were offered a lift in their co after the match. 'If my people can't get on, y people can't get on,' he stormed, refusing to on the coach until the waiters had been tur off.

Charlton became known as a one-man awkw

Far left Jack Charlton puts his point of view to John Radford of Arsenal in the 1972 Cup Final. Though he had quietened down over the years, he retained the same rebellious and outspoken attitude that had jeopardized his career at Leeds on more than one occasion.

Left Charlton's long legs managed to rescue Leeds for a long time: Everton's Royle (left) was only two years old when 'Big Jack' made his League debut.

Above The tall, awkwardly built centre-half, renowned for causing havoc in opposing goalmouths at set pieces, beats Peter Bonetti to convert Eddie Gray's corner and give Leeds the lead against Chelsea in the 1970 Cup Final. In the end, however, the game was another disappointment.

ad. 'Other people might have been too weak too spineless to get up and say what they nted to say. But I was honest enough to say at I felt.'

On another trip Charlton asked for melon fore his soup and was told by the manager that body ate melon before soup in decent taurants. Charlton told the manager to stick meal and walked out.

When Don Revie moved from Sunderland to eds as a player in 1959 he and Charlton kept ir distance. 'He was never really a player's yer,' explains the big man. 'He played for eds United but he was never really part of eds United. He came as an older player and ver mixed socially with any of the lads. He ined and then left and I was never particularly endly with him. We got on all right, but he was some ways unapproachable.'

'If I was manager,' said Revie, 'I wouldn't play you in practice matches'

Charlton liked to lark about in practice tches, starting at centre-half but usually nning out of position so that he could keep volved. One day Revie snapped at him: 'You piss out so much that if I was manager I wouldn't ay you in practice matches at all. You spoil em for everybody else.'

Charlton remembered that clash in training d anticipated trouble when Jack Taylor (who d followed Lambton as manager) departed and vie was put in charge. 'Don had to make a oice between myself and Freddie Goodwin, cause Freddie and I had very different ideas on e way defences should play. He chose Freddie centre-half and moved me to centre-forward— d then dropped me.'

Revie called Charlton to his office and told m: 'I'm putting you on the transfer list because u're not my type of centre-half.'

'Let's be fair,' countered Charlton, 'I've been aying centre-forward for you.'

'Yes, but you're not the type of centre-half I want, so I'm putting you on the list.'

But as Leeds edged closer to the Third Division, Charlton was recalled at centre-half—and after a couple of good results he was again summoned to the manager's office.

'I want you to come off the list,' said Revie. 'The way you've been playing, if you keep it up and get the attitude right, there's no reason why you shouldn't play for England. You know you've got the ability, it's only a case of putting your mind to it and doing the job.'

Charlton promised he would do his best. He shook hands with coach Syd Owen, whom he had threatened to punch a couple of times, and made his peace with first-team trainer Les Cocker and one or two other people with whom he had argued. He kept his first team place and Leeds avoided relegation.

The remarkable success story master-minded by Revie had started to take shape. Promoted in 1964, Leeds were to be consistently in the chase for domestic and international honours. Charlton was the king-pin of their defence, but he would also lope up for corners and free-kicks, his awkward, 6ft 1½in frame causing severe problems on the goal-line for opposing keepers.

After a run-out with the Football League team, Charlton made his international debut, lining up with brother Bobby (already the owner of 57 caps) in the England-Scotland match at Wembley in April 1965.

Nobody was happier than Revie over Jack's England call. 'I said that if you did the job right you'd get a cap,' he told the big fellow. 'You've worked well and you deserve it.'

Charlton couldn't resist adding a touch of bravado. 'Once I'm in I'm going to be in a long time,' he told Revie. 'There's no way that I'll get in and come straight out again.'

A year later Jack and brother Bobby collapsed in each others arms on the Wembley turf as delirious England fans danced around them in celebration of the World Cup final win over West Germany.

With England almost home and dry in the final

the Germans made it 2-2 with barely two minutes remaining, a hotly disputed free-kick conceded by Jack Charlton leading to the equalizer. He felt guilty about that free-kick, but never doubted that England would win. Geoff Hurst made it 3-2 in extra time, and after that Jack remembers:

'I was absolutely shattered at the end. I was at the back when Bobby Moore got the ball down and as I ran round behind him he hit a long ball to Geoff on the half-way line.

'Geoff started to run and what with watching him and the referee, who'd been looking at his watch a long time, it seemed to take ages for Geoff to reach their box. We'd done the same sort of thing so many times in extra time and when he lashed the ball into the top of the net it came as a surprise.

'I ran the length of Wembley flat out but missed Geoff when I got up there because he'd run in the other direction. I turned and chased after him and got hold of him about the half-way line.

'Then I gave our kid a hug and I think we were both knackered. We sort of ran into each other and collapsed.'

Altogether Charlton was capped 35 times by his country, but he had drifted out of the England team by the time they went to Mexico to defend the World Cup in 1970. He was in the Mexico party but played only once, against Czechoslovakia.

In the season leading up to the World Cup, Leeds finished runners-up in both the League and FA Cup and reached the semi-finals of the European Cup. Because of this Charlton set off with England 'honed down to the bone' and was disappointed when Sir Alf Ramsey retained Brian Labone as the first choice centre-half.

England again clashed with Germany, this time in the quarter-finals, and the Germans got their revenge, the match once more going to extra time. With England leading 2-0, Beckenbauer made a goal out of nothing to force the Germans back into a match which had seemed settled. Charlton, not liking his role as a spectator, could stand no more and, leaving the

45

stadium to drink coffee in a nearby cafe, he began to fear the worst.

He had hoped it would all be over when he got back, but he returned to see Germany get the deciding goal in extra time. He said he had never felt so sick at the end of a football match in all his life, and that night he got stoned with the rest of the England party.

On the way home he went to Sir Alf at the back of the plane and tried to tell him he wouldn't be available again for England. 'I felt I'd done my bit,' he recalls. 'I was sick of the bloody travelling. And especially sick of the travelling when I wasn't playing. I tried to tell this to Alf. He sort of understood and said, "Well, I probably wouldn't call you up again anyway".'

There was talk of Ramsey recalling Charlton during the 1971-72 season. 'I would have loved to have been called up—but only for my own ego. It would have been a step backwards for Alf to have done that.'

The October after England had lost the World Cup, Charlton's candour for once, in the opinion of some, went a little too far. During a television interview he said, with an impish look on his face, that he kept a little black book with the names of two players in it and that if he got the chance he would 'do 'em'. He would, he said, kick a man back; and if he was chasing a yard behind a player in an international and thought he couldn't catch him he would flatten him.

Below Charlie George beats Charlton in the air— a rare lapse by a man whose height, timing and positioning kept him among the world's best stoppers for a decade.
Below bottom Facing younger brother Bobby. Between them they played 141 times for England, with 26 appearances in the same side—including the 1966 triumphant World Cup final.
Right While colleagues celebrate, Jack looks at the medal he thought he would never win: an FA Cup winners medal after the 1972 Final.

Brother Bobby was reported as saying that Jack's remarks had destroyed a lot of hard work to improve the image of the professional footballer. The big fellow was rebuked by the FA and by an army of commentators—most of whom rushed into print without listening to the interview so they could at least judge the spirit in which it was given.

If he had been too old for England in Mexico, Charlton was far from finished with Leeds. And though many tried to suggest he was going over the top he continued to be a vital figure in the side as they finished runners-up to Arsenal in the League, then won the FA Cup the following season while coming within one desperate goal of the double.

He could not hide his disappointment when Revie announced that he was being phased out, and said he intended to fight like hell to get his first team place back.

After their stormy early days together, Revie never again had to threaten Charlton with a transfer. 'If he felt my game wasn't good enough or I wasn't concentrating enough he'd call me in and tell me so,' admits Charlton.

'He's jolted me like this every now and again over the years. Usually he had his little chat around September or October, but for the last two or three years it didn't happen until January. So it must have been sinking in a little bit.

'I was never a bad lad really. I'd take the mickey and have a bit of fun. Maybe throw a bucket of water over somebody. People would say "You silly bugger. Why don't you grow up". But I'm still like that today. I still like to carry on with the lads. I still shout up when things are wrong, and they'll say "For God's sake, shut up. Once you start you get the whole bloody lot involved.".'

Charlton has a wonderful ability as a coach for the FA, his passion for the game coming through in everything he does. Joe Mercer has long been convinced he will make a great manager. But Charlton is not too sure.

'I've got to stay in football when I'm finis playing, but I'm not over enamoured with professional game and the way managers treated. I'm not really interested in look after a football club, only a team.'

But the lure of professional football pro too strong, and when he finally turned his b on Leeds in 1973 he moved into the manag office at Middlesbrough.

Never one to do things by halves, he scou the club for failings, in both playing and adm stration. And within two months of his managerial appointment, Middlesbrough led Second Division. The not-so-gentle giant treading another road to success.

Jack CHARLTON

Honours: World Cup winners medal 1966
Fairs Cup winners medal 1968, 1971
Fairs Cup runners-up medal 1967
League Championship medal 1968-69
FA Cup winners medal 1972
FA Cup runners-up medal 1965, 1970
League Cup winners medal 1968
Footballer of the Year 1967

Club	Season	League		Int'nls	
		Mtchs	Gls	Mtchs	G
Leeds United	1952-53	1			
	1953-54				
	1954-55	1			
	1955-56	34			
	1956-57	21			
	1957-58	40			
	1958-59	39	1		
	1959-60	41	3		
	1960-61	41	7		
	1961-62	34	9		
	1962-63	38	2		
	1963-64	25	3		
	1964-65	39	9	5	
	1965-66	40	6	17	
	1966-67	29	4	4	
	1967-68	34	6	2	
	1968-69	41	3	4	
	1969-70	32	3		
	1970-71	40	6		
	1971-72	41	5		
	1972-73	18	3		
Total		629	70	35	

PART 3
THE MIDDLE-men

THE MIDDLE–MEN

Two good for England

It is usually a negative exercise to compare two footballers, particularly when those two players belong to different generations. But, in the case of Charlie Buchan and Len Shackleton, the factual similarities are too tempting to ignore. Each, for instance, was an outstanding inside-forward for Sunderland; each was renowned for being so talented and original as not to fit easily into the plans of representative teams, and received only a handful of England caps where lesser players won so many; each, as a youth, was allowed to slip through the fingers of Arsenal without signing as a professional—though Buchan did go back to Highbury in the famous 'hundred pounds a goal' transfer 14 long years after he had left them over a question of 11 shillings expenses; each had their early careers restricted by war; each became a successful journalist.

It should further be said that however many caps they may or may not have won, each bulks large in the history of the game. And not only on Wearside. Far larger, indeed, than those less dazzling footballers who won a great many more caps because their faces fitted.

Shackleton, it may be added, achieved all this without so much as ever winning a Cup Final or Championship medal. Buchan did rather better. The Sunderland team in which he played before the First World War was indeed a 'team of all the talents', he himself forming a splendid triangle with winger Jackie Mordue and right-half Frank Cuggy, and a fine partnership with that other powerful inside-forward whom he so much admired, George Holley.

The backgrounds of Buchan and Shackleton, however, were as different as their characters. Shackleton not inappropriately took as the title of his lively autobiography *Clown Prince of Football*, since he possessed an impish and anarchic humour. Buchan, for all his other virtues, had virtually none. Shackleton was something of an anarchist but, while Buchan went his own way, he was at heart a traditionalist and an establishment man, a schoolmaster who had gladly used the cane, a brave soldier in the First World War. Later he was what one might be called an anti-broadcaster and journalist, one who made his very failings work for him.

That ugly, monotonous London voice, that reach-me-down newspaper style, were in a sense guarantees of sincerity. You could not imagine him doing what Shackleton whimsically did in his book—devoting a complete, blank page to the chapter he called 'The Average Director's Knowledge of Soccer'. By the same token, Buchan had it in him to be the great captain that he was at Arsenal, the great innovator who is said to have conceived the third-back game and changed the course of football. Shackleton was too much the lone wolf, the solitary man, for anything like that.

Buchan was one of four brothers—three of whom became professional footballers—the son of an Aberdonian colour-sergeant who became a blacksmith in the Woolwich Arsenal: hence Buchan's South-East London birth and background. 'Shack' was born in Bradford and spotted as a boy by Arsenal, by that time the aristocrats of the Football League.

Arsenal seem to have shown a rare lack of tact and percipience in dealing with both these brilliant players. In November 1909 Buchan, a 17-year-old still attending the Woolwich Polytechnic and playing for Woolwich Arsenal reserves, put in an expense account for shillings. George Morrell, the club manager, hi handedly refused to pay it. Buchan left and, aft spell with the amateurs Northfleet, turned pro sional with Leyton in the Southern League. March 1911, following a splendid game aga Southampton, he joined Sunderland.

Like Buchan, Shackleton was small and f as a youth. Later Buchan grew to over six fee rawboned, powerful man, but Shackleton always chunky enough. When he came fr Yorkshire to play for the Arsenal nursery tea Enfield, however, he seemed very fragile. Jus Charlie Paynter, for so many years with W Ham, looked at Buchan as a schoolboy and m no approach because he thought him too small Arsenal decided to get rid of Shackleton.

George Allison, Arsenal's manager, a sonor broadcaster and publicist, called the yo Shackleton into his office at Highbury to him the shattering news. Then, in a gesture t Shackleton would never forget, a well-me but tactless attempt at sugaring the pill, took the lad to see a television set in his offic television sets then being as rare as Arse defeats. Shackleton interpreted it as an effor placate the country bumpkin. He was not placat

He went home to sign for Bradford P Avenue and spent the War in the mines, play for Bradford and building an impressive rep tion. Like Buchan he was a marvellous ball pla but where Buchan's style—or the lack of it— a sort of triumph of mind over matter, an u duckling performing like a swan, Shackle arms akimbo, was fluent and elegant. Both pas superbly, Buchan's theory being that timing still more important than accuracy, that a pass struck at the right moment could still damage.

Buchan, a true Londoner, did not even kn where Sunderland was when they signed him 1911. His success in the team was not immedi For one thing he was still growing fast, shoot from 5ft 9½in in August to 6ft 0½in by the end November, when he still weighed only 10 stone 5 After each training sesssion he was too weak do anything but lie on his couch in vacant a pensive mood. The Roker Park crowd began get at him and he asked to be dropped, l manager Bob Kyle stoutly refused.

The club trainer, Billy Williams, looked af him loyally, and even made him give cigarettes through the expedience of present him with a pipe—the pipe which later became familiar an aspect of his public image.

Scotland, no doubt going by his name, asl Sunderland if they would release him to p against England at the beginning of 1912, which time his strength and form had mu improved. The answer, of course, was that he v English born—parentage not counting in th days. His first England cap came on 15 Febru 1913, against Ireland in Belfast, with Mordue his side and Cuggy behind him. It was a disastr game for England, Ireland beating them for first time ever, by 2-1. Buchan, however, hea the English goal after ten minutes.

His debut was also marred by hot words of the game with a linesman who criticized right-wing pair in his hearing—and turned to be an England selector—and another involv a dispute over expenses. This time, the mig

PRESS ASSOCIATION

otball Association were unwilling to pay for the
ab which took him from Sunderland station to his
ame. Why not a tram, he was asked. Buchan
ainted out that the trams did not run in
underland on a Sunday morning...

Shackleton's international debut was also
unfortunate: the victory game against Scotland
at Hampden Park in April 1946. For years
England had dominated Scotland in the unofficial
wartime matches—especially at Hampden Park,
where they were in the habit of scoring half a
dozen goals a game. Not this time, however.
Scotland played well and won 1-0.

Both great players were continually ignored by the England selectors

Shackleton was still more of a dissident than
Buchan. The story is told that before one international match the England players were in
training on the spacious Bank of England grounds
out at Roehampton under their team manager,
Walter Winterbottom. At one point he asked the
forwards to run up and down the field, inter-
passing, and finish by shooting into the empty net.
Shackleton looked up at him: 'Which *side* of the
net, Mr Winterbottom?' he wryly enquired.

The three Sunderland players, including
Buchan, were dropped after the Irish match in
1913—despite the fact that the club came within
an ace of the double that season. They finished
four points ahead of Aston Villa to win the
League, setting a new League record of 56 points
from 38 games, and also reached the Cup Final, a
hectic and sometimes violent affair in which Villa

*Top Charlie Buchan leads out Arsenal against
Spurs in 1925, a few months after joining them
for £2,000 plus £100 for every goal he scored
that season. Ironically Buchan had left the club
14 years earlier over a triviality.*

*Centre Buchan (second left) takes on the Bolton
defence at Highbury in October 1925.*

*Right Len Shackleton at the same ground as an
apprentice 13 years later. He left soon after,
having been told he was 'too small'.*

*Opposite page Shackleton in 1957 during his last
days with Sunderland, the club with whom he
won his five England caps.*

Chapter 9

*The average director's knowledge of football.**

* *Publisher's note:* This chapter has deliberately been left blank in accordance with the author's wishes.

This page from Shackleton's book 'Clown Prince of Soccer' illustrates the author's anarchic and rebellious nature. Buchan, in contrast, became something of an establishment figure.

beat them 1-0.

Buchan never did get a Cup winners' medal. He was to play in one more Final, 14 years later with Arsenal, at Wembley—the day when Cardiff took the Cup out of England for the only time. When the Great War came Buchan went into the Grenadier Guards; and four vital years were cut out of his career. He was an NCO in the trenches, brought back in 1918 to take a commission. As for Sunderland, they closed down Roker Park for the duration. On his return to England and football he played his victory game against Wales,

partnered on the wing by the great Middlesex cricketer Patsy Hendren. He went on teaching for a time, found it a strain, opened a sports outfitters, and went on playing for Sunderland until the summer of 1925. In 1920-21 England capped him as a centre-forward—hardly his ideal position, though like Shackleton he could be scorer as well as schemer. Unlike Shack, he could make use of his height to head many a good goal.

Buchan went on getting occasional caps, but the great pre-War Sunderland team had disintegrated and, in May 1925, he was distressed when they agreed to sell him to Arsenal. The

remarkable Yorkshireman Herbert Chapman just taken over as manager at Highbury, Buchan was the man he wanted as his lieuten even though he was now 33. Buchan did not w to go, but Chapman was as persuasive as alw The end of it was that Arsenal agreed to pa initial £2,000 for Buchan, plus £100 for e goal he scored during his first season. Sunderl reckoned he would maintain his post-War aver of some 20 a season. Their calculation surprisingly close, for Buchan scored 19 g in the League and another two in the Cup. M important, however, was his alleged pioneerin the third-back game with Herbert Chapman.

The offside law had just been changed restrict the number of defenders needed to k a player onside from three to two. Buchan is to have suggested a stopper centre-half and inside-forward playing deep in midfield durin tactical discussion after a 7-0 defeat at Newca: Buchan expected to play this inside-forward himself. But Chapman kept him upfield and use third team player called Andy Neil in the posit: The first game with the new formation wa: Upton Park, and the result was a 4-0 win Arsenal with Buchan scoring two of the go Arsenal continued to flourish, had an excell season, and the following year reached the C Final under Buchan's captaincy.

Buchan became a sports writer on the D News, later the *News Chronicle*, where ultimately died in harness. He was also a fam BBC radio broadcaster, noted above all for 7.25 evening summaries of the Saturday's p It is pleasant to record that he publicly expres admiration for the gifts of Shackleton, o describing him as 'a ball artist who could drit round a threepenny piece . . . the brilli Sunderland inside-forward.'

The most concrete of Shackleton's achie ments, however, was helping Newcastle Unite gain promotion from the Second Division 1946-47—after joining them from Bradford sensational transfer halfway through the seas He cost the then huge fee of £13,000, celebrated by scoring six goals in his first gam St James' Park, against Newport. With Bentley, later the Chelsea and England cent forward, and Charlie Wayman making up splendid inside-forward trio, he also hel Newcastle reach the semi-final of the Cup bef they were surprisingly routed by Charl Athletic. The following season, after much t of crisis and bad blood at St James' Pa Newcastle most suprisingly allowed him to g their local rivals, Sunderland, at a £7,050 pro In retrospect, he was extraordinarily cheap at price, spending the rest of his career on Wears and striking up a memorable partnership w another fine inside-forward in Ivor Broadis, w arrived from Carlisle United in 1948-49.

Shack's Sunderland, an expensive team inde was never so successful as Buchan's. Nor was th the happy harmony of Buchan's era. The tensi between Shack and the big Welsh internatio centre-forward Trevor Ford were well kno and the legend went on Wearside that Shackle would carefully and cunningly bias his pas to Ford to make them as difficult as possible control. It is certainly on record that, in o friendly game in Holland, Shackleton dribb superbly round the whole of the baffled Du defence, including the goalkeeper, paused the empty goal, then rolled the ball back Ford, standing on the edge of the penalty a with a cry of, 'Here you are! Don't say I ne give you a pass!'

What he might have achieved had he play regularly for England was suggested in a brilli appearance against West Germany at Wembley December 1954, when for once England thr caution to the winds and picked a team of gif ball players. He responded with a supe performance and a dazzling goal—chipping ball over the keeper's head. Perhaps it only c firmed the long-held opinion that the select had of both he and, at an earlier time, Bucha 'Too clever to play for England'. Shackleton v never again selected for his country.

Charlie BUCHAN

Honours: League Championship medal 1912-13
FA Cup runners-up medal 1913, 1927

| Club | Season | League | | Int'nls | |
		Mtchs	Gls	Mtchs	Gls
Sunderland	1910-11	6	1		
	1911-12	31	6		
	1912-13	36	27	1	1
	1913-14	36	14		
	1914-15	37	23		
	1919-20	36	22		
	1920-21	39	27	2	2
	1921-22	40	21		
	1922-23	41	30	1	1
	1923-24	39	26	1	
	1924-25	39	12		
Arsenal	1925-26	39	19		
	1926-27	33	14		
	1927-28	30	16		
Total		482	258	5	4

Len SHACKLETON

| Club | Season | League | | Int'nls | |
		Mtchs	Gls	Mtchs	Gls
Bradford PA	1946-47	7	4		
Newcastle United	1946-47	32	19		
	1947-48	25	6		
Sunderland	1947-48	14	4		
	1948-49	39	8	2	
	1949-50	40	14	1	
	1950-51	30	6		
	1951-52	41	22		
	1952-53	31	6		
	1953-54	38	14		
	1954-55	32	8	2	1
	1955-56	28	7		
	1956-57	26	8		
	1957-58	1			
Total		384	126	5	1

Crystal gazer at the Palace

is still one of football's minor mysteries why m Stephenson, a man with a brilliant record club level over nearly 20 years, won only one, agre, grudging England cap. The foremost ics of the day, such as Charlie Buchan, who so en played against him, and Ivan Sharpe, the gland amateur, praised him to the skies as one he greatest constructive inside-forwards of his . He was not only the heart and soul of the ndid Aston Villa team immediately prior to the st World War, but also, when it was over, and ryone but the extraordinary Herbert Chapman ught he was finished, he enjoyed a superb umn with Huddersfield Town, captaining them heir three consecutive League titles.

t is baffling that he should win just that solitary for England—against Wales in the 1923-24 son. Whatever the competition for inside for-d places before the War, the England teams of early twenties were anything but consistently cessful. It would have been thought that phenson was a natural choice, with his utifully economical play and, still more, splendid combination with Billy 'Tantoby' ith, the outside-left he so often sent flying away wn the wing at Leeds Road. Charlie Buchan's ark on the subject is uncompromisingly to the nt: 'Every week, Stephenson produced his t form. Yet he never stood out like an Alex nes. Despite his great work, he played for gland only once during his career. He should e had a houseful of caps.'

He played for Aston Villa a dozen years before his first cap

Stephenson was born at Seaton Delaval, in rthumberland. But it was Aston Villa, a great ce in the land in those days, who found him, ting him initially with their nursery club at urbridge, who played in the Birmingham ague. He was finally taken to Villa Park—and first-team place, in 1911—a dozen years before first cap.

One of the strangest stories of his career cerns the 1913 FA Cup Final, played at the ystal Palace between Villa and another great m of the era, Sunderland. To this day it remains only Cup Final ever played between the clubs t finished first and second in the League. on after the game began, at a throw-in, phenson informed Charlie Buchan, the nderland inside-right, 'Charlie, we're going to t you by a goal to nothing.' When Buchan ed why he thought so, Stephenson replied, dreamt it last night. And that Tom Barber's ng to score the winning goal.' So he did: from a kicked corner by Charlie Wallace which flew ist high across the goal. It was the only goal of game—though Villa should have taken the d after 15 minutes when Stephenson was ught down but Wallace missed the penalty.

Perhaps if the War had not intervened Clem ephenson would have inspired Aston Villa to the t of success he later caused at Huddersfield. In 3-14, the season after they won the Cup, Villa re again runners-up in the League and reached semi-final of the Cup.

After the War, Stephenson performed the usual feat of winning a Cup winner's medal h for and against Huddersfield within three sons. He was Villa's inside-left, partnering

Dorrell, when the club won the Cup, again by 1-0, again by another odd goal from a corner—the ball hit Kirton on the back of the neck—at Stamford Bridge in 1920. Two years later, again on the Chelsea ground, he was inside-left to Billy Smith, whose penalty won the Cup for Hudders-field against Preston. There was still another Final to come, in 1928; and it proved to be the only one he lost of his four. Blackburn Rovers defeated Huddersfield Town by 3-1.

Perhaps one of the reasons Stephenson was overlooked by the selectors was that for all his many gifts, he was not fast. He was a classical player; shrewd, poised and accurate, weighing and judging his passes admirably, unselfish to a degree rare in any generation.

Stephenson's long career at Villa Park was not always a happy one. Like several Villa players he did not live in Birmingham and after he and Frank Barson missed the opening game of the season against Bolton in 1920 they were both suspended for 14 days.

At Huddersfield, where he became less of a scorer and more of a general, he was also a fine captain. No doubt this was one of the things that Herbert Chapman saw in him at a time when Villa were mistakenly convinced that he had had his day.

After he was 'finished' he led Huddersfield to three League titles

It is impossible to conceive Huddersfield's magnificent run of success without him. When Chapman bought him in 1921, the club were over-shadowed by the local rugby league side, yet so deeply and quickly did he influence the whole team that the three successive League titles came in 1924, 1925 and 1926. It is interesting to note that many years afterwards, Stephenson would pick two of that Huddersfield team in his best-ever side; Sam Wadsworth, the left-back, and his winger, Billy Smith.

Ivan Sharpe had Stephenson in *his* best ever team: 'A greater club player and team maker I have never known,' he wrote. 'A greater failure by England's selectors I have never known. For here, at this time, they had a heaven-sent left-wing in Stephenson and long-legged, loping Smith, W H, from Tantoby, and failed even once to choose them.'

Stephenson became, for a spell, manager of Huddersfield Town in 1929, but did not have the same success he had achieved as a player. 'I am sure the general standard of League football has declined,' he observed over two decades later. 'I think one of the main causes of the deterioration is cinema.

'The boys don't go to the playing fields as we did. They would rather go to the pictures. In order to make a success of football or of most games, one has to start young.' Goodness knows what he would have thought about the impact of television.

Clem STEPHENSON

Honours: League Championship medal 1923-24, 1924-25, 1925-26
FA Cup winners medal 1913, 1920, 1922
FA Cup runners-up medal 1928

Club	Season	League		Int'nls
		Mtchs	Gls	Mtchs
Aston Villa	1910-11	5	3	
	1911-12	20	10	
	1912-13	35	13	
	1913-14	33	12	
	1914-15	37	11	
	1919-20	39	28	
	1920-21	21	8	
Huddersfield Town	1920-21	9	1	
	1921-22	39	9	
	1922-23	27	1	
	1923-24	40	11	1
	1924-25	29	5	
	1925-26	36	4	
	1926-27	25	5	
	1927-28	31	2	
	1928-29	12	4	
Total		438	127	1

COLORSPORT

The legendary Alex James

If it is a true test of fame that a man should be remembered even by those who never saw him, then Alex James was truly famous. James had finished playing before the Second World War, yet fans born since 1939 still unthinkingly use his name in their arguments as the standard by which other forwards should be judged. The legendary skills of the baggy-shorted Scot left so vivid an image that the absurdity of the comparison is seldom questioned.

James died in 1953 at the age of 51, having worked for some time as a match reporter for Sunday newspapers and then Arsenal coach.

The obituary notice which perhaps most fittingly summed up the little wizard and his ways was written by the late Don Davies, 'An Old International' of *The Guardian*, who lost his life in Manchester United's Munich air tragedy:

'Once the pride of Preston and Arsenal . . . he was regarded by many as the shrewdest tactician of his day. It was around him that the late Herbert Chapman built an Arsenal side capable of winning four First Division Championships in five years, the last three in a row, with the FA Cup thrown in for good measure. A team of the talents, and James was its master-mind. You might have suspected, when you saw him shuffle on to the field for the first time, that there was one who might lay claim to genius . . .

'Some held that James' slovenly appearance was natural; others said it was a pose; but if it was a pose, it was in sharp contrast to one of the tidiest minds in football. James hated waste, particularly wasted effort. To him it was the surest mark of inadequate technique. "Let the ball do the work" was his motto, and how miraculously it could work when guided by his touches . . .

'In his Arsenal days James developed a taste for strategy. The policy was to pass the ball to him whenever possible and leave it to the baggy-trousered Napoleon to direct offensive moves as he thought fit. How well he did so is part of the Arsenal saga.'

True enough, and Don Davies, in likening James to Len Shackleton, did not overlook the natural comic streak which made the pawky Scot one of the beloved characters of football. During the four seasons he spent at Deepdale before his transfer to Highbury in June 1929, Preston followers saw vastly more of James the entertainer and comedian that he was permitted to show the Arsenal crowds. Periodically he indulged the Londoners with endearing glimpses of the *gamin* aspect of his make-up, but it was serious business now for James: Arsenal were bent on winning honours and prizes. Soon after his arrival—and he was not an immediate success—Herbert Chapman tactfully advised him to 'cut out the circus tricks until we're winning 3-0.'

James duly blossomed as a masterly player in a forward line of specialists hand-picked from the few available for their rare gifts. He readily acknowledged he had to raise his game and take it more seriously than during his sojourn at Preston in order to fulfil Chapman's conception of him as the mainspring of a penetrative and deadly attack. All his Preston football had been played in the Second Division and James, in his role of individual entertainer, had seemed content to shine in a capable team at or near the top until the spring, when their promotion hopes invariably faded.

Now it was different. Chapman, the enterprising and inventive visionary, demanded the best results without any nonsense, and took pains to make a reluctantly serious James aware that he was an integral part of the plan to achieve them. It meant the sacrifice to some extent of a captivating personality, though he soon began to express it through team-work in a more effective manner. It also called for a deeper role and a curb on his fondness for scoring spectacular solo goals. His infrequent goals for Arsenal tended to be regarded as a joke, whereas with Preston he averaged rather more than one every three games.

It cannot really be true that James, as is generally thought, played his best football with Preston, because he subsequently made himself a star in a much finer team playing a better brand at top level in the First Division over a period of years. But what is true is that he enjoyed his football more when with Preston because he was a natural showman who was encouraged to entertain, and that is what he loved to do. Perhaps this explains the two versions of his abbreviated christian name, always the affectionate Alec at Preston, Alex during his later years of glory and triumph. He was proud enough of Alexander 'as long as ye shorten it to Alec, which is ma fancy, or Alex.'

There were contrasts, too, in his style and appearance from when he first crossed the border to his more sedate maturity at Highbury. Deepdale's first sight of him, before he donned the long floppy pants which were a cartoonist's joy, was of a short sturdy figure wearing even baggier golfing plus fours with sports jacket, pullover and thick gaudy stockings to match this odd but fashionable garb. A chubby youthful face and eyes twinkling with fun were crowned by fair hair cropped short back and sides but allowed to grow straight up from the scalp about an inch high. There was no sign here of the smart clothes and immaculate parting down the middle of well-groomed hair when he had become the idol of Arsenal's legion of followers.

James, the crowd magnet and star turn with his bewildering tricks in a clever Preston team—when there were so many Scots on the staff that the place resounded with 'och, ayes'—readily confessed that Second Division football was, to him, light-hearted stuff. It pleased him that players could enjoy their game and put the result second. Not so at Highbury, where he had to accept that each match had to be won possible, and treated like a Cup tie. He firm believed that the widespread imitation of 'win at all costs' complex would bring a sur of negative football. He would never acc the time-honoured view of each succeed generation that 'the footballers of today not as good as their predecessors'. He arg that the modern players were not inferior ball-work, positional play and the other arts crafts; the trouble was they were not allowed play football, which, as he saw it, me displaying their skills and individual styles.

While he was certainly the joker in the p at Deepdale it would be a fallacy to assu that the Preston directors paid Raith Rovers high sum of £3,250 (in September 1925) to a showpiece. First Division football had b played at Deepdale for 28 of the previous League seasons; they had now just been relega and their desire to regain their rightful pl at the first attempt was intense.

James himself was no raw-boned novice. A 23, he was in his fourth season with Raith on the fringe of Scotland's team. A first was not long delayed, and there would have b many more than the eventual total of eight for his ways, which needed team-work a familiarity to be match-winning assets in international side. How could Scotland, ho international champions with six points in 19 change a forward line comprising Jackson, Du

Alex JAMES

Honours: League Championship medal 1930-31, 1932-33, 1933-34, 1934-35
FA Cup winners medal 1930, 1936

Club	Season	League		Int'nls	
		Mtchs	Gls	Mtchs	Gls
Raith Rovers	1922-23	25	5		
	1923-24	34	11		
	1924-25	37	11		
	1925-26	4			
Preston North End	1925-26	34	14	1	
	1926-27	39	11		
	1927-28	38	18	1	2
	1928-29	36	10	2	
Arsenal	1929-30	31	6	3	1
	1930-31	40	5		
	1931-32	32	2		
	1932-33	40	3	1	
	1933-34	22	3		
	1934-35	30	4		
	1935-36	17	2		
	1936-37	19	1		
Total		478	106	8	3

Top left Alex James leads out Arsenal in August 1936. A few months before (left) James had captained them to victory at Wembley. Above The expressions on the faces of the three beaten Manchester City players tell their own story. Below The 1933 Tom Webster cartoon: after that the shorts became even longer. Top right On 8 August 1938 James visited Highbury to say his final farewell. He had been the inspiration behind four League Championships and two FA Cup wins. Right James pictured at the opening of a shop next to the Arsenal ground in 1935.

Gallacher, Cairns and Morton? They did, but only to replace Dunn with Russell for one match.

Preston, who had been on James' trail for months, showed much shrewdness in beating several competitors for his signature. He was taken by car to Middlesbrough for an evening debut in English football on a dry, bumpy pitch. He and Hughie Gallacher, both of Bellshill, Glasgow, had learned their adeptness and tricks, as poor boys did, practising in the streets dribbling and passing a rubber ball. But, on this occasion, James was scarcely seen. His laconic comment after Preston had lost 5-1 was: 'Ye'd better by gieing me a ticket back home! I canna play fitba' wi' the baw up in the air most of the time.' James' home bow was delayed by two more away matches—and two more defeats.

There was much pessimistic talk about 'buying a pig in a poke' and throwing good money after bad. James dispelled it with tantalizingly brilliant displays in two big home wins, and was the talk of the town by scoring six goals after only six games. The crowds flocked from near and far to be mesmerised or bewitched. He was the cleverest, most artful ball player and schemer Preston had possessed for years, a finished craftsman whose strategy and passing, long or short, were an education, as were his bafflingly deceptive solo touches and capacity to size up a situation instantly. If not always accurate with his powerful shooting, he scored several remarkable goals, two or three times

walking the ball through in making himself leading scorer with 14.

But Preston were still in the Second Division and the reason was the team's indifference in away matches: they won only one and drew five of 21. At home they won 17.

The following season they made their best start for 23 years but, after losing their last five matches, finished sixth. In a more determined promotion bid in 1927-28 they rubbed shoulders with Manchester City, the eventual champions, for most of the season. In February James was offered a cap against Ireland but agreed to forego the honour owing to the vital character of an away match with City. There Alec played one of the games of his life in a 2-2 draw, and jinked through to score a superb solo goal.

Once more, however, Preston faltered and finished fourth. And if they had been as tactful in October 1928 about an invitation to release James for an international as they had been the previous season they might have held him longer. They were furtive and kept quiet. The truth leaked out. James was deeply hurt. He showed his sense of injustice by strolling through the next home game with indifference, cutting out all his tricks. He was duly reprimanded by the board, but weeks passed before he was his customary entertaining self.

The parting of the ways for James and Preston became increasingly apparent and several big clubs, including Arsenal, put out feelers.

A record £15,000 offer was refused. During a three-day wonder in March 1929 terms were agreed with Manchester City but James, ever contrary, declined to go after having a look round Maine Road and at houses in Manchester. Exactly a month after his last match for Preston, and a few hours after the League's annual meeting, he was transferred to Arsenal at the Euston Hotel for the surprisingly low fee of £8,750.

James scored 53 goals in 146 appearances for Preston North End and missed only 22 of 168 League games. His 26 First Division goals, of course, are incidental compared with his vast contribution towards making that Arsenal attacking machine—which at first comprised Hulme, Jack, Lambert, James and Bastin—so wonderfully effective. The pass inside the back to the goal-scoring Bastin, the through ball to Lambert, the long crossfield pass to Hulme—these were the tools of his trade. He was also a great dribbler, picking the ball up from defence (in a space he had found or created) and taking it past several players before putting in the telling pass.

The 1932 Cup Final is a pointer to the vitality of James' presence. There, his injury led to a major reshuffle of the Arsenal side, and he was sorely missed. Whether Arsenal would have had their magnificent heyday if James had not gone to Highbury remains an unanswerable question. Those who saw him, however, have no doubts about the truth.

Left *Peter Doherty puts Derby 2-1 up during e* time *in the 1946 Cup Final against Charlton.*
Left below *Doherty takes over at Bristol C in January 1958, the same month he gu Northern Ireland to the finals of the World Cup.*
Right top *Wilf Mannion is carried off during game against Scotland in 1951, when he gained last but one of his 26 England caps.*
Right centre *Mannion climbs in vain at Sp*
Right below *A kick around with some local in 1952. Despite some wrangles Mannion rema a Middlesbrough player all his career.*

The shy, red-headed boy was hustled into dressing-room and told to put on a jersey beca the right-winger had missed his train. He did receive one pass throughout the first h. nobody spoke to him at half-time, and when Ly the winger, did eventually appear, the substit was ordered to give up his shirt. 'Even now', wr Doherty long afterwards, 'when my mind g back to that dreadful afternoon I find it diffic not to shudder.'

Remarkable as it may seem by the standa of later, scout-ridden days, he actually spent best part of a year playing junior footb. taking odd jobs to earn a living, until proprietor of the local sweetshop recommen him back to Coleraine. He was now 16, and t time did well in his trial, ultimately be offered a signing-on fee of £24 and £2 10s a w wages—which the club later tried to reduce to

Mannion had a rather easier beginning. B near Middlesbrough, at South Bank, he was outstanding schoolboy player, turned out South Bank St Peter's, and went professional w Middlesbrough in September 1936. The follow year he was already playing in their First Divisi side, at the age of 17, and when War broke out made his first appearances for England—until was drafted abroad with the Green Howards 1943.

This, in turn, gave Raich Carter the cha to regain and consolidate the place in the Engla team which he had failed to hold since his f caps—won no less than nine years earlier.

Shapers of an era

THE MIDDLE-MEN

Raich Carter, Peter Doherty and Wilf Mannion: names that tingle the memory of anyone who followed football in the thirties and forties, players who personified the complete inside-forward of the era, at once schemer and scorer.

Carter and Doherty enjoyed a brilliant if brief partnership with Derby County, one which found its crescendo in the Cup Final of 1946. Carter and Mannion played memorably together in England's first seven internationals after the Second World War. The link between Doherty and Mannion, if not so tangible, was equally important: the careers of both reflected and exemplified the injust treatment and impotent position of professional footballers in that period.

Sadly, none was centrally involved in the game of the seventies. Carter, who was sacked as manager of Leeds United and Middlesbrough, had long since drifted out of football. Mannion, who had a spell as manager of Cambridge, had been reduced to working on construction sites. Doherty, always a stormy petrel, a trade unionist before his time, had a splendid run in charge of the Irish international side of the late fifties but, after giving up the managership of Bristol City, he opted out of the game for years before taking minor roles at Notts County, Villa and Preston.

The careers of Mannion and Doherty have a common theme in their many brushes with authority and the establishment caused by their disagreement with the treatment of the professional footballers of their day. Doherty, too proud and independent to put up with the way players were then exploited, went from one club to another in a persistent flurry of resentment and dispute. Mannion spent months out of the game without wages when he refused to re-sign for Middlesbrough, and was suspended by the Football League for refusing to give chapter and verse about alleged illegal payments.

Doherty was perhaps the most winning and intriguing figure of the three, partly because he was so far ahead of his time in his scorn for the system—a time when players were so pleased to be off the dole that they put up with the iniquities of the game—and partly because he became so successful as an international team manager.

Born at Coleraine in Northern Ireland, he was barely 15 when the local Irish League club watched him playing junior football for Station United and invited him for a trial. What happened that Saturday was a trailer for Doherty's whole turbulent career.

Carter—'the finest inside-forward of his generation'

Born in Sunderland and an excellent all-rou athlete, Carter had appeared in the same dist guished England schoolboys team as Len Gould and Cliff Bastin. The odd thing was that it w Leicester City, not Sunderland, who first secur him, but in 1931 they inexplicably let him go ba to his local club, where he was to stay for the ne 14 years.

Carter, like Doherty an inside-left when began his League career, had moved swiftly a smoothly into the Sunderland first team and early as April 1934 was awarded his first c for England, at inside-right. Scotland were t opposition at Wembley, and Carter played his pa in a 3-0 win to keep his place for the Europe tour.

This was less well augured. He played in t opening match against Hungary, on a hot d and a hard ground in Budapest, made little impa in a 2-1 defeat (only England's third by forei opposition) and was dropped.

The brilliance of Carter's performances f Sunderland, where he became a very young ca tain, were such that he was spasmodically recall to the national colours, playing against Germa in 1935, Hungary (a 6-2 win) and Ireland 1936, and Scotland in 1937. But the magisteri skills he showed with Sunderland—the elega control, the defence-splitting passes, the position flair—all of which moved his great Sunderla predecessor, Charlie Buchan, to call him 't finest inside-forward of his generation'—we never quite there for his country.

Carter was a splendidly unexpected playe alike with his passing, his stealing into space and his tremendous shooting, particularly with left foot. In his early days the dark hair w

Wilf MANNION

Club	Season	League		Int'nls	
		Mtchs	Gls	Mtchs	Gls
Middlesbrough	1936-37	2			
	1937-38	22	4		
	1938-39	38	14		
	1946-47	37	18	8	7
	1947-48	35	1	5	1
	1948-49	17	4	2	
	1949-50	38	6	6	2
	1950-51	35	13	4	1
	1951-52	39	11	1	
	1952-53	41	19		
	1953-54	37	9		
Hull City	1954-55	16	1		
Total		357	100	26	11

Peter DOHERTY

Honours: League Championship medal 1936-37
FA Cup winners medal 1946

Club	Season	League		Int'nls	
		Mtchs	Gls	Mtchs	Gls
Blackpool	1933-34	19	4		
	1934-35	37	13	2	
	1935-36	27	11	2	
Manchester City	1935-36	9	4		
	1936-37	41	30	2	
	1937-38	41	23	2	1
	1938-39	28	17	2	
Derby County	1946-47	15	7	1	
Huddersfield Town	1946-47	19	7	1	1
	1947-48	38	13	2	1
	1948-49	26	13	1	
Doncaster Rovers	1949-50	35	26		
	1950-51	23	14	1	
	1951-52	16	6		
	1952-53	29	9		
Total		403	197	16	3

parted down the middle in the fashion of the times. Later it was to turn a premature and distinguished silver, first contrasting with Doherty's appropriate red in the Derby County attack, then giving him the proper senatorial appearance when he was player-manager of Hull City.

Between 1935 and 1937 Carter's skilful Sunderland team won both League and Cup. In the 1937 Cup Final things were going badly against Preston in the first half, and Sunderland crossed over a goal behind. But in the second-half Carter and his cleverly varied passes began to call the tune; Sunderland equalized, Carter put them ahead, and eventually his side won 3-1.

When the War came both Carter and Doherty joined the RAF and found themselves working at the rehabilitation centre for wounded pilots at Loughborough. This enabled them to play as guests, under the Wartime dispensation, for Derby County, and to strike up a surprisingly fruitful partnership.

Surprising because here were two great egos, both used to running affairs. Doherty, sold to Blackpool by Glentoran for £2,000 in 1933, and then to Manchester City in 1935—'I might as well have been a bale of merchandise'—had developed into an astonishing, all-purpose forward. His speed, his stamina, his versatility, his ability both to score spectacular goals and help out his defence, were all remarkable. Yet he and Carter struck up a fine combination from the first. Each made his own unique contribution in an inside-forward partnership that must have been one of the finest of all time.

Doherty was on poor terms with Manchester City—partly through failing to arrive in time for a War Cup-tie—when they agreed to transfer him. It was rather more of a surprise that Sunderland should have been ready to sell Carter, who had gained new lustre during the War years.

This was the consequence of a splendid right-wing partnership with Stanley Matthews, a notoriously difficult winger to play with despite (or perhaps because of) his brilliance. Before he went abroad Mannion had been one of the many who had tried, with variable success. Now, in 1943, it was the turn of Carter. Matthews, like he and Doherty, was playing in the RAF representative side, and again this may have helped. Certainly Carter showed an exquisite comprehension of just how and when Matthews needed the ball and a necessarily limitless patience about getting it back. Matthews, for his part, made Carter some notable goals. The England forward-line of the time, completed by Tommy Lawton, Jimmy Hagan and Denis Compton, was indeed a formidable one.

If Carter and Sunderland had won the Championship in 1935-36, then Doherty and Manchester City had taken it in 1936-37—and were promptly relegated a year later. Doherty, with his marvellous swerve, acceleration and shot (he scored 30 that season) had been the principal architect of the success. A goal he hooked home against Arsenal at Maine Road, almost from the goal-line, was characteristic of his feats of individual virtuosity.

At the same time he found playing for Ireland a bitter experience, turning up at the last moment to meet a crowd of virtual strangers, with no chance to work out tactics, and barely the chance to get to know one another. These experiences would breed the radical transformation which occurred during the fifties under his aegis.

Doherty—with his marvellous swerve, acceleration and shot

Mannion may have been slightly less overwhelming a player than the other two, but he was just as influential and versatile in his way. Standing a mere 5ft 5in (to Carter's 5ft 8in and Doherty's 5ft 10in) and sturdily built, Mannion was a beautifully balanced player with immaculate close control, a dangerous burst of speed, and the ability to weave his team expertly together—even if some criticized him for an excessive use of the square pass.

His service in the Middle East and Italy seemed not to have affected his game in any way, for he returned to the England team in Belfast as soon as official internationals were resumed in 1946, scoring a hat-trick in a 7-2 win.

In May 1947 his magnificent performance at Glasgow against the Rest of Europe established him beyond doubt as a great player. Playing at inside-right, he scored the first goal, then another, and would have had a third had Lawton not touched one of his shots as it was crossing the line. He darted irresistibly all over the field, pulling the hapless European defence to pieces, giving Matthews a fine service, plying Lawton with the sort of passes on which he thrived. It was a marvellous exhibition.

The partnership of Doherty and Carter had

Top left Raich Carter, then with Derby, up against Arsenal's Joe Mercer. In 1946 he had, with Peter Doherty, inspired them to an FA Cup win.
Bottom left Having led Sunderland to victory in the 1937 Cup Final, and scored the vital goal, Carter heads north by train with the trophy.
Top right Carter scores in the 1-1 draw with Scotland in April 1947. He won only two more caps.
Bottom right Carter as boss at Leeds. Sadly his managerial ability never equalled his play.

meanwhile reached its peak the year before, in the 1946 Cup Final, when Derby beat Charlton at Wembley after extra time. Ironically it was Doherty's leg which deflected Bert Turner's free-kick into the Derby goal to give Charlton the equalizer and make the extra period necessary. Derby restored their lead within a minute when Jack Stamps' centre was pushed out by Bartram and Doherty scored. He and Carter then worked their wiles, and Stamps added two more goals to make it 4-1.

Later that year Doherty had the almost inevitable quarrel with Derby, who refused to let him open a pub, and moved on to Huddersfield Town, then struggling at the foot of the First Division. His rangy, exuberant play galvanized them to survival, and made Vic Metcalfe, in time, an England outside-left. Then, with his job done at Leeds Road, he stayed in Yorkshire to become

player-manager of Doncaster Rovers, juggle w[...] players' shirt numbers just to be different, [...] take them out of the Third Division in his f[...] season, helping out with 26 goals.

Carter stayed longer than Doherty with De[...] County, leaving them in 1948 for Hull City wh[...] with imperious foot often on the ball, shout[...] players into position, he helped them g[...] promotion from that same Third Division sect[...] (the North) in 1949. The first official post-V[...] season had seen the edge go from his game at [...] highest level and the much younger Stan Mor[...] sen had joined Mannion as England's other insi[...] forward.

After his success with Hull and a spell w[...] Cork Athletic, Carter became manager of Le[...] United, but his authoritative approach seemed [...] productive off the field than on it, and there w[...] times when players were rubbed the wrong way[...]

Raich CARTER

Honours: League Championship medal 1935-36
FA Cup winners medal 1937, 1946
FA of Ireland Cup winners medal 1953

Club	Season	League		Int'nls	
		Mtchs	Gls	Mtchs	Gls
Sunderland	1932-33	24	6		
	1933-34	36	23	2	
	1934-35	38	11		
	1935-36	39	31	1	
	1936-37	37	26	3	2
	1937-38	39	13		
	1938-39	39	14		
Derby County	1946-47	33	19	7	5
	1947-48	30	15		
Hull City	1947-48	4			
	1948-49	39	14		
	1949-50	39	16		
	1950-51	32	19		
	1951-52	22	9		
Total		451	216	13	7

DERBY EVENING TELEGRAPH

RADIO TIMES HULTON PICTURE LIBRARY

gh he was moderately successful with Leeds, themselves had never been more than that in ious years. Carter then had a managerial spell lansfield and another, nearer his home town, Middlesbrough, which lasted until the dle sixties. Again he did not take over Middles- igh at an easy period, and there was no nion to whip the team into life.

lannion himself had endured a bitter row with ame club in 1948, when he refused to re-sign. a time he took a demonstrating job outside ball, but in those days the clubs held all the and Mannion was forced to return to the e with Boro—having lost a good deal of money vages and missed six internationals. After ats by Scotland and Sweden, however, he ined his place in the England side and went laying until the first match of season 1951-52, aw with France.

Those were the days when it was practically impossible, even for as fine a player as Mannion, to put aside much of a nest egg—the more so as those players who did make money usually made it under the counter when they were transferred—and Mannion spent his whole League career with Middlesbrough.

He did become player-manager of one of the Cambridge clubs, but could not hold the job. After that the illness of his wife and, perhaps, his own gambling instincts, led to sad anti-climax. Where Carter and Doherty remained inside the game, at least for some years, Mannion, who had known nothing else since boyhood (apart from his years in the Army) was out in the cold. He ultimately went back to his native Teesside, but there was nothing for him there, and menial jobs were a pathetic coda to so brilliant a career in football— especially as around him far less gifted players

were to be seen making far more money.

If Mannion was betrayed by a certain lack of purpose and direction, and Doherty by a Celtic restlessness, a rightful discontent, then Carter's enemy was perhaps a certain abrasiveness. On or off the field, he was never one to suffer fools gladly. Thus, for all Carter's success at Hull, Peter Doherty was the most gifted of the three as a manager, and it was sad that he should ultimately give up the game in disgust when he left Bristol City, going instead into bookmaking.

Northern Ireland had never employed a team manager when Doherty took them over in the late fifties, and had certainly never even begun to generate the atmosphere of comradeship and dedication he achieved. He was obviously fortunate to have two admirable lieutenants in Spurs' Danny Blanchflower, as captain and right-half, and Jimmy McIlroy of Burnley, as the scheming inside-forward. Both were rational, gifted and intelligent footballers, just as he had been.

The three of them planned the tactics and cut their coat according to their cloth. The first high point was reached in November 1957, when Northern Ireland at long last won in England— and at Wembley. The following year even this was surpassed when, after drawing 2-2 with Italy at Belfast in a match that was friendly only in name (the Hungarian referee of what was meant to be a World Cup match had been fog-bound), the Irishmen proceeded to beat them 2-1 and qualify for the World Cup finals in Sweden.

There, too, they excelled themselves, beating Czechoslovakia, holding West Germany to a draw and in the end beating the Czechs in a play-off to reach the quarter-finals, where their tired and depleted team lost to a rampant France. But even the inspiration and the tactical wisdom of Doherty could not make up for ill-fortune, including the loss the previous February of the team's gifted centre-half Jackie Blanchflower, shaken by the experience of Manchester United's tragic air crash at Munich.

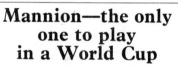

Mannion—the only one to play in a World Cup

Doherty returned to England to go on managing Bristol City. He did so efficiently enough, but his chief flair and brilliance were to be seen as an international team manager, fulfilling all the special demands which that task makes. Above all he could create the atmosphere of psychological well-being in which matches can be won.

Doherty himself had won 16 international caps —all before Ireland played against foreign opposition—the first as a Blackpool player in 1935, the last with Doncaster Rovers in 1951. Mannion played in 26 full and four Wartime matches, and was the only one of the three to play in a World Cup, while Carter was capped 13 times in official games, plus 13 more Wartime matches and three victory internationals.

Of the three, Doherty was the only specialist penalty-taker, with a knack of sending the keeper the wrong way. He was also by far the best header of the ball, and never scored a better goal than the diving header which helped Ireland to a 2-2 draw with England at Goodison Park in 1947 —the first time the Irish had avoided defeat in the fixture for 20 years.

In the same match Mannion both missed a penalty and equalized Ireland's first goal. But Doherty, that day, had the last word, and it is tempting to wonder what heights he would have attained had he played in more illustrious international company.

It seems unlikely that these three fine players would not have succeeded in the harder, sharper, and more realistic game of later years. Their characters and careers, their originality and dissent, these too were more in keeping with the more personalized and controversial environment of the seventies. They were in many respects 20 years ahead of their time—both on the field and off it.

**THE
MIDDLE-MEN**

'This is your Life –Danny Blanchflower'

yards, but it appears that most of his skill derived from his mother, a former centre-for in a women's team.

As a boy Danny played football in the st with his younger brother Jackie, later Manchester United centre-half; and at sch playing on the wing or at inside-right attracted the early interest of Glentoran.

He studied at St Andrews Universit Scotland for a year before joining the RAF starting aircrew training—actor Richard Bu was a hut-mate for a while—but the War e before he could become properly airborne ar returned to Belfast and a new career.

Glentoran paid him £50 to sign and £3 a m Blanchflower never really forgave them. 'I young at the game and very naive,' he says, they were not slow to take advantage of it.'

In his very first season Blanchflower selected to play at right-half for the Irish Le against the Football League at Goodison and, two years later, Angus Seed signed hi Barnsley, then in the Second Division, for £6,0

In October 1949 he won his first cap Northern Ireland, against Scotland at Win Park. But it was a dark day for the Irish, who 8-2, and a dark one for Blanchflower, who little hint of what was to come.

'Too many captains di no more than carry the ball and call "heads"'

He was happy enough to start with at Barn but there was too much of the free-thinker i man for him to remain that way for long. Trai at Oakwell concentrated on conditioning, when Blanchflower wanted to do more practice he met with a blank response.

'They told me it was traditional,' he expl 'It had been good enough for Alex James Charlie Buchan so who the hell was I to ch it? I was only a player. Why didn't I forget a the ball and get on with the business of ge fit? So that's what I had to do.'

In March 1951 Blanchflower and Barn parted company, with the Irishman movin First Division Aston Villa for £15,000. circumstances of the transfer did nothin enhance his opinion of football's administr for, while Barnsley chairman Joe Richards ducted his negotiations in the dining-room Derby hotel, the central figure was eating i kitchen quarters. 'It might well have embarrassing for Mr Richards to sell me lunch while I sat at the same table. But then I c have sat at another, couldn't I?'

Blanchflower, at heart a city boy, cert preferred Birmingham to Barnsley. He liked big stands and the big crowds. But the rebel of him inevitably collided with the club's linge traditions. He realized that they were still l in the past.

While touring Canada with a Northern Ire team in the summer of 1953, Blanchflower pl in Montreal against a Swiss side using a defe system that was new to him.

On his return to Villa Park for the new se he talked about this at length. 'The mo thought of it,' he said, 'the more I was vinced that it would suit Villa to adopt a 3 system . . . that is, to play three full-backs, t half-backs and four forwards.' But the talk, fo most part, fell on doubting ears.

Other suggestions also came to nothing once again disenchanted, he asked for a trar in 1954. Fate sent him to Spurs for £30,00 after Arsenal had surprisingly dropped out o bidding at £28,500. This time the club and player could have been designed with another in mind.

Blanchflower approved of the style cultured ways at Tottenham . . . and Spurs, a t

It was Cup Final day in 1961, with the flags fluttering along the rim of Wembley Stadium. The band trooped off, and down in front of the royal box Leicester and Spurs were being introduced to the Duchess of Kent.

The Duchess, walking down the line of white shirts, paused and turned to Spurs captain Danny Blanchflower. 'The other team have their names on their tracksuits,' she commented, raising a quizical eyebrow. 'Ah,' he mused, 'but *we* know each other.'

The reply was typical of the man. No occasion was too big for him. He had style and he had wit. He was elegant and he was eloquent.

Blanchflower was the player who led Spurs to the first League and Cup double of the 20th century. History would doubtless accommodate him willingly for that distinction alone. But with this man there was so much more.

It wasn't even that he won 56 caps for Northern Ireland and led his countrymen to heights they had not dared contemplate. Nor that he became only the second man to be twice voted Footballer of the Year.

Danny Blanchflower's impact on British football was so much wider, if somewhat intangible. His contribution was in the realms of ideas— in the approach to the game, in tactical switches, in technical appreciation. Some of his proposals may have been a little hare-brained but, self-confident and articulate and a player of abundant skill, he did not find it difficult to defend them.

Moreover, Blanchflower was always a rebel, a thorn in the side of football's establishment. Sometimes his revolt was born of superior knowledge or deeper perception, sometimes it was destructive, misplaced and unnecessarily perverse. But people took notice.

Above all, though, there was his skill. He was the constructive wing-half who had everything— an armoury of exquisitely timed passes, an arrogant ability to read and transform the game, and an indisputable knack of being prominent throughout a match.

For Robert Dennis 'Danny' Blanchflower life began on 10 February 1926 in a terraced house in one of the quiet streets in the Bloomfield district of Belfast. His father worked in the shipbuilding

Blanchflower arrives too late to stop Leeds' ... Charles making his cross in 1956.
...ow The Spurs skipper wraps up the 1962 Cup ...l against Burnley with a penalty.

encouraged thinkers, approved of the ...ghtful ways of their new recruit.

...evertheless the club were conscious of the ... that they were moving towards the close of ...ra. The team who won promotion in 1950 ... the League Championship the following year ... getting on, and manager Arthur Rowe ...ed to Blanchflower as the logical successor to ...amsey as captain.

...ot long after Blanchflower played his first ...e for Spurs—at Maine Road in December ...—Rowe became ill and Jimmy Anderson ... over as manager, with former wing-half Bill ...olson to aid him. With Ramsey ending his ...er Blanchflower was duly appointed skipper ... as events were to show, his captaincy was not ...edals and Wembley steps.

... the quarter-final of the 1955-56 FA Cup ...rs were trailing 2-1 to West Ham and Blanch-...er decided to send centre-half Maurice ...man up into the forward line. Spurs equalized, ... the replay and their captain was acclaimed as ...enius. In the semi-final against Manchester ..., with Spurs 1-0 down, Norman was again ...ed forward. This time it failed to save the ... Certain directors questioned the right of a ...ain to make drastic tactical switches of that ..., and Blanchflower was no longer in charge ...n the season closed.

...oo many captains in the past had done no ...e than carry out the ball and call "heads" or ...s",' commented Blanchflower later. 'Too ...y clubs and countries had wanted nothing ...e from them. I was determined to be more than ... a captain in name only. I wanted to face the ...ands of the position, to challenge its problems ...act on my decisions. Better to learn from ...rience than to do nothing.'

...ith Northern Ireland he had just that sort of ...ority, and the fact that manager Peter ...erty backed him all the way certainly helped ...eir World Cup march of 1958.

Blanchflower was much more than just a great professional footballer

...aly and Portugal were in their qualifying ...up, and few had expected the Irishmen to ...h the finals in Sweden, let alone get into the ...eight. But the story of how a team of injured ..., inspired by their captain, beat the Czechs in ...deciding game of their group is part of foot-...ing legend. With a 3-2 win at Wembley ...rious November—their first defeat of England ...30 years—that season was to be Northern ...nd's brightest hour. But, for Footballer of ...Year Danny Blanchflower, it was only another ...se in a rise to greatness.

...n March 1959 Bill Nicholson, who had ...eeded Jimmy Anderson as Spurs manager a ...months earlier, reappointed Blanchflower as ...n captain. The same month Dave Mackay ...ved from Hearts and, with the signing of the ...curial John White from Falkirk later in the ...—on the virtual insistence of Blanchflower ...r he had played against the Scot in Belfast—...rs quickly became the dominant force in ...ish club football. For most people they were ...most cultured League side they had ever seen.

...1960-61 they opened with 11 wins and ...ted away with the League title on 66 points. ...chflower led his men to victory 37 times that ...on—31 in the League and another six in ...Cup, when the 2-0 win over Leicester at ...mbley made Spurs the first side to do the ...4 years.

...lanchflower, almost inevitably voted Foot-...er of the Year by the press, had already moved ... sports journalism himself. And he was ...ictably controversial in print, wasting little ... in launching a full-scale attack on the ...ball League and the FA. 'There are too many

sacred cows in this game of ours,' was one of his damning comments. He sometimes left the impression, however, that he was disagreeing with a generally held view merely for the sake of being different.

In the years that followed he wrote a spectacular condemnation of Alf Ramsey; he found himself banned from the Arsenal press box; and, perhaps best known, he refused to be the surprised subject of 'This is your Life'. 'I consider the programme an invasion of privacy,' he explained. 'Nobody is going to press-gang me into anything.'

Off the field he remained a loner, preferring to choose his own company and rarely mixing socially with the team. 'I respected them professionally,' he said, 'and they respected me. That was all that mattered.'

In 1962 Spurs dropped to third place in the League and lost in the semi-final of the European Cup, but Blanchflower once again led his side up the Wembley steps—after he had made it 3-1 against Burnley with a penalty. The next season Spurs thrashed Atletico Madrid 5-1 in the Cup Winners Cup final—a match where the captain had to use all his wiles to convince his team they could win. After that, the ambitions of Robert Dennis Blanchflower appeared to be quenched.

The end to his playing days was sadly anti-climatic. In April 1964 Spurs went to Old Trafford for a League game and Manchester United boss Matt Busby, convinced that Blanchflower was no longer the power of old, told his players to take him on at every opportunity. The Irishman had what was probably the worst game of his long career, Spurs crashed and, armed with some cruelly honest and advising press reports, Bill Nicholson informed Blanchflower that, at 38, he was no longer irreplaceable. Understandably Blanchflower refused to drag on in the reserves;

predictably, too, he claimed he was being unfairly treated on the basis of one bad game. Many managers, players, pressmen and spectators would testify differently—that it had been on the cards for some time.

It was unfortunate that a player and man so elegant with a career so constructive and distinguished should have such a decision made for him. It would have been so much more fitting had he ended his days proudly holding aloft a trophy.

Those who saw Danny Blanchflower in action would no doubt prefer to remember him playing at his peak.

Danny BLANCHFLOWER

Honours: European Cup Winners Cup winners medal 1963
League Championship medal 1960-61
FA Cup winners medal 1961, 1962
Footballer of the Year 1958, 1961

Club	Season	League		Int'nls	
		Mtchs	Gls	Mtchs	Gls
Barnsley	1948-49	1			
	1949-50	36	1	2	
	1950-51	31	1	3	
Aston Villa	1950-51	11			
	1951-52	42		1	
	1952-53	41	4	4	
	1953-54	40	4	3	
	1954-55	14	2	2	
Tottenham Hotspur	1954-55	22		1	
	1955-56	40		3	
	1956-57	39	1	6	
	1957-58	40		10	
	1958-59	36	1	4	
	1959-60	40	2	3	1
	1960-61	42	6	5	1
	1961-62	39	2	5	
	1962-63	24	3	4	
	1963-64	15			
Total		553	27	56	2

The star who just had to top the bill

Insert top In 1949, di Stefano Argentina to join Los Millionari
Insert centre Three and a half y later, Real Madrid finally secure transfer. Here Stef poses with Pus another of Real's world stars.
Insert bottom In August 1 amidst great controversy, di Ste left Madrid and moved to Espano
Above April 1970, and di Stefa now a manager—with Valencia.
Right One of di Stefano's many tributions to Real's European d nance—a penalty against Fiorenti

Alfredo di Stefano is a name which can be spoken anywhere in the world and command respect. For it is the name of one of the most famous of all footballers, a name that immediately springs to mind when the discussion is about the best players the game has produced.

Fame, often hero-worship, has long hovered around di Stefano's shoulders. In the fifties and the sixties it was for his greatness as a player . . . as the seventies began, as a successful championship-winning manager.

During his playing days Alfredo was granite-hard and dour, silent and unapproachable. He rarely gave a press interview and always stood aloof from his many friends: his manner was terse, abrupt, almost rude.

But di Stefano's talents were abundant. He was a fine leader, had a sprinter's acceleration coupled with faultless control, and could pass the ball superbly—often to Gento, whom he could find instinctively on the left wing, or to Puskas, usually

splitting the defence. And Stef's accurate, powerful shooting brought him many goals. These abilities were welded together by his exceptional stamina, and permeating his whole game was a mature understanding of football: his strategy was almost beyond analysis.

But after packing away his famous boots—he was past forty then—he quickly realized that the aura of his playing days would not last for ever, nor would it carry him very far in the altogether different and uncertain managerial world.

He realized he had a new job to learn, one that involved diplomacy, handling men and the creation of a good press and public image. So di Stefano matured. He became more friendly and quickly appreciated the value of communication; he even started talking to the press.

Born in Buenos Aires on 4 July 1926, di Stefano received his first football lessons from his bus-conductor father, himself a useful amateur centre-forward. Alfredo says, 'I was right-footed, so he

wouldn't let me play unless I shot only with my left foot. He always said that with one foot I'd never be a footballer.' It was sound advice for a six year old all those years ago.

However, when he was fifteen, Stef was nearly lost to football. His

At fifteen, Stef is very nearly lost to football

family, rallied by his mother, thought that he should become a farmer and carry on an old family tradition. But di Stefano's father was adamant. 'Alfredo was born and bred in the city . . . I'm not banishing him to the lonely prairie. Besides, he can't play football with cattle!' And so Stef entered a business college, where the facilities for sport gave him the opportunity to develop what—even then—were obvious football talents.

At 17, the young di Stefano was the 'veteran' player of his district team, Barracas, ('We never lost a

match'), where one day he was covered by the manager of R Plate, Lubrowski, and signed a amateur. 'In River's amateur te there were so many of us tha were all substitutes for the stitutes,' recalls di Stefano.

Di Stefano moved to Huracar loan, for one year, and returned to River Plate as a fessional. Immediately he gain first-team place and overnigh became the idol of River's cro During his three-year stay at R Plate, di Stefano won a league medal and was once the leag leading scorer. He played in s internationals for Argentina.

Then came the first di Ste 'mystery'. In 1949-50, at the he of his Argentine fame, he sudd left River Plate and signed for Millonarios of Bogota, a ne formed club with ambitions to the best players. The Buenos A public just could not understan logic of his move to Colombia, criticism arose.

But di Stefano maintains, 'I

no mystery. Colombia were ~ous to improve their football and y needed experienced players.

Millionarios offered financial ~s that were 15 times higher ~ in Argentina. Many players ~ed to Colombia. In fact, it was ~ exodus, I'm afraid, that was ~onsible for the eclipse of ~ntina in the 1958 and 1962 ~ld Cups.'

~i Stefano stayed with Los Mil-~arios for three and a half years, ~ing them win two league titles, ~950 and 1952.

~is departure from Los Mil-~arios surprised everyone and ~ted another furore, this time in ~n. In September 1953, Spanish ~spapers went wild with delight ~n Real Madrid announced they ~ signed the Argentine star, ~edo di Stefano, then 27 years of ~, for four years. Real paid Los ~ionarios £10,000 for his transfer ~ di Stefano received £4,000 a year ~n them. His contract with Real ~ twice renewed on improved ~ns, and at the peak of his career, ~ Stefano was the highest-paid ~er in the world. In the late ~es di Stefano commanded a ~,000 signing-on fee, a salary of ~0 a week and bonuses of £150 ~ a win and £90 when the team ~v. Investments, businesses, adver-~ments, signed articles and ~alties added considerably to ~ Stefano's fortune—just reward ~his amazing talents.

~ut within hours of di Stefano's ~ing for Real came a fierce protest ~n Barcelona. They, of course, ~ heard of di Stefano's fame and

ability and, behind the scenes, had made moves to obtain his signature. Their disappointment at losing him to their rivals created one of those 'affaires' which have rocked Spanish football through the years.

It was not until the president of Los Millionarios personally inter-vened in the public controversy over di Stefano, officially declaring that he had promised di Stefano to Real more than a year before, that the dispute in any way abated.

Madrid's president, D Santiago Bernabeu, was first impressed with di Stefano during Real's mid-40s South American tour. Bernabeu wanted to sign him 'before anyone else realizes how good he is'. Fellow directors calmed his enthusiasm and persuaded him to wait. And he did. But in 1952, when Los Millionarios played in Real's Golden Jubilee

The idea of buying Alfredo di Stefano obsesses him . . .

Anniversary tournament, Bernabeu saw a more developed di Stefano and was even more obsessed with the idea of buying him. He spent hours trying to persuade the Colombian club to release their star player, and even enlisted the aid of di Stefano's wife. But he was unsuccessful, though he was told by Millionarios 'When we decide to transfer him you will be first to know.' A year later the Bogota club kept its word.

Di Stefano scored in his first league game for Real, against Santander on 27 September 1953,

and during the 11 subsequent years he was a Real player, he remained continually in the world headlines . . . winning five European Cup medals, one World Club cham-pionship, eight Spanish League medals, becoming the league's lead-ing goalscorer five times and collect-ing countless other honours. Strangely enough, he won only one Spanish Cup medal with Real. In 1957, after he had taken Spanish nationality, di Stefano made the first of 31 international appear-ances for Spain. His 23 goals for Spain were a record for his adopted country.

His popularity was unbelievable, in spite of his strange, tempera-mental character. The public worshipped him, though for his talent alone; di Stefano never gained the affection that crowds would show Bobby Charlton, Puskas or Pele. But such was his obvious con-tribution to Real's supremacy in the fifties and sixties that he earned a tremendously loyal, though never adulatory following.

Indeed, many people attributed the fabulous, glittering 'Golden Era' of Real Madrid between 1956 and 1964 entirely to Don Alfredo. That would be to exaggerate his role, however. Di Stefano undoubtedly played a vital part in Real's success, but Real's world-beating displays were never a one-man show. Stef was the brain and, until Puskas arrived, scored most of the goals, but the ceaseless service and co-operation of his often equally brilliant colleagues paved the way.

In August 1958, Alfredo's 'won-

derful world' was disrupted a little by the signing of Didi (Waldyr Pereira). The talented Brazilian player signed for Madrid amid a fanfare of publicity. Nothing quite like it had ever been seen in the capital. But, a few months later, after completing only part of his contract, Didi returned mysteriously to Buenos Aires. It caused a sensation.

Years later, Didi gave his story. 'I arrived in Madrid hailed as the best player in the 1958 World Cup in Sweden. Everyone was talking about Didi. It was Didi, Didi wherever you went. Di Stefano didn't like this excitement; he naturally felt it might reflect on his own popularity and he became very anti-Didi both on and off the field. In many matches I was completely ignored.

'Naturally this kind of thing reflected upon the team's form. Rather than see a great team dis-integrate, I approached president Bernabeu for a release of my con-tract. He understood the problem and we parted the greatest of friends.'

When di Stefano was asked about the 'affaire' he said, somewhat tersely, 'I had no problem with Didi. He neither reached his normal form nor fitted into the side as Real Madrid thought he would. If a player is incompatible, that is not the fault of another player. Didi was just unable to produce his best form or fit into the side. Nothing more.'

Whatever the reason, Didi cer-tainly did not fit in. And nor did a number of other stars like Canario, Tejada and Kopa—though Kopa did last three years. But why should so many players leave Real so soon after joing the club?

Their departure left di Stefano *the* player of Real Madrid, which, of course, he liked, although with the arrival of Ferenc Puskas a little after Didi, the limelight had to be shared. The Hungarian was a different, more cheerful, carefree character than Stef . . . but the two became famous friends, linking almost magically on the field, and with Rial, Gento and Kopa, there emerged the greatest forward line of any team, anywhere in the world.

The story behind Puskas' somehow hitting it off with di Stefano has passed into football's folklore. It concerns the last match of Puskas' first season with Real, when he and di Stefano were joint leading goalscorers in the Spanish First Division. Puskas, with an easy chance to score, made a gift of the ball to di Stefano, and from then on they were firm allies. In the 1960 European Cup final, when Real gave their memorable exhibition against Eintracht Frankfurt at Hampden Park, these two scored all seven of Real's goals between them.

Di Stefano leaves Real Madrid—and the arguments rage

Time marched on, slowly and successfully for Alfredo. Then in 1964 came the news of his move from Real Madrid to Espanol, the first division Barcelona side. The transfer came as a shock, and gossip spread. 'Di Stefano was a law unto himself. The team had to conform to di Stefano. He was temperamental. The player had become at cross-purposes with his colleagues and Miguel Munoz.'

Real manager Munoz never once entered the controversy. Six years later he did break his silence, and although he still spoke cautiously, the point was taken. 'A manager had to do his job, and when the moment comes to fulfil his obligations on behalf of the club that pays him, he has to do what is necessary.' And so di Stefano left for Barcelona.

'I did not leave Real Madrid with enmity,' he says. 'Why should I? Every manager has his obligations and there always comes a time when he has to rescind the contract of a renowned player. If it's in the best interests of the club, well. . . .'

Di Stefano stayed with modest Espanol for two years, years that must have been frustrating, even an anti-climax. Later, after taking the Federation's managerial course, he took up his first appointment with Elche, which turned out to be one of the few unsuccessful periods of his life. Then di Stefano embarked on his Argentine adventure.

In 1968-69 Alfredo returned to his homeland and became personal adviser on technical matters to Don Alberto Armando, president of Boca Juniors.

Unfortunately, di Stefano's dour, unapproachable character had preceded him and from the beginning the Argentine press was anti-di Stefano. No one questioned his playing and his technical abilities or his experience. His remarkably unwavering dedication to the game

Top *In perhaps the most famous of all European Cup finals, Real's 7-3 win over Eintracht in 1960, di Stefano scores one of his four goals.*
Above *Stef prepares to unleash a shot during a friendly in Cairo.*

Alfredo DI STEFANO

Honours: European Footballer of the Year 1957, 1959
World Club Championship medal 1960
European Cup winners medal 1956, 1957, 1958, 1959, 1960
European Cup runners-up medal 1962, 1964
Spanish League winners medal 1954, 1955, 1957, 1958, 1961, 1962, 1963
Argentine League Championship medal 1947
Argentine League leading scorer, 1947 (27 goals)
7 Argentine caps
31 Spanish caps, 23 goals

510 games for Real Madrid, 428 goals (49 in 58 European Cup games)
81 games for Espanol, 19 goals
Spanish League leading goalscorer 1954 (29 goals), 1956 (24), 1957 (31), 1958 (19), 1959 (23)

was immediately held as an example to all. But his manner and his inability to establish cordial relations with people and the press brought the most bitter criticism from sensation-seeking sports writers. He was 'difficult', they said, and 'totally unsuitable as a presidential adviser and as a club official'.

But with one or two selected aides, he patiently made a thorough search of the country for new and unknown players. 'I want young players . . . players with spirit and fight . . . tough but fair players . . . and most important of all I want footballers, not matadors.' And so the rebuilding of the ailing Boca Juniors began.

The following season, 1969-70, di Stefano was appointed manager-coach of the club, and the real transformation took shape. Defensive thinking and the old 4-3-3 system were discarded. Di Stefano had Boca Juniors play with two authentic wingers and at times with

seven forwards. Ruthlessly he dropped long-serving players and blooded his discoveries—all of them promising youngsters, and all hitherto unheard-of players.

The most difficult task di Stefano had to face was telling the famous Antonio Rattin that there was no place for him in the new attacking set-up. Rattin, captain of the national side and idol of Boca Juniors for 12 years, the greatest stopper centre-half the Argentine had ever produced, was the architect and pillar of the negative, defensive outlook which di Stefano maintained had caused Boca Juniors' decline.

Rattin took the news philosophically for, despite his martyrdom in the 1966 World Cup, he was a true professional. He retired gracefully into the shadows. But the newspapers erupted as never before. Rattin's photograph occupied the full front page of several newspapers. Leading

articles demanded his imme reinstatement, petitions were or ized, demonstrations launched. press demanded . . . and howled di Stefano rightly refused t intimidated, remained unmove continued with his policy of venation. To his credit, An Rattin remained silent.

As the season progressed Stefano's radical policies bro success. Inspired by 'Old Man Boca Juniors won the nat championship in a grandstand f —an away draw—with their et rivals and Stef's old club, River F A record, police-limited crow 75,000 people acclaimed B achievement.

When his year's contract Boca Juniors ended, he u trusively rejoined his large fami six children—in Madrid. He could not settle down in his h land, he had become too Spa Soon after his return, Alf signed his first contract Valencia on 2 April 1970.

Twelve months later, Vale became Spanish League ch pions for the first time in long and very frustrating y Formerly a mediocre team, acquired, through the guidance influence of di Stefano, a fessionalism and dedicatio though not brilliance—w brought them the consistency necessary in Spain's short lea programme.

Di Stefano—the greatest forward of all time?

Di Stefano's comments on success at Valencia show just much he had changed. 'Ever talks about my success. But it's mine. The success belongs to players. I have helped them physical and technical preparat but it was they who fought throw out the season with such unbe able enthusiasm and determinat That—giving credit to other pe —was certainly not the old Ste

When he was with Real Mad Alfredo di Stefano was a phenc non, a player with all the skil player whose remarkable s second precision passes wrecked ablest of defences, a genius harrying defenders, a man who mastered to perfection the abilit draw out the skills of others.

Di Stefano had uncanny intuit He was always in the right plac figure of perpetual motion, lea the attack, automatically mo to dominate the midfield and, w necessary, switching to becom stalwart of the defence. His f balling skills, remarkable foot brain and exemplary dedica meant that Stef did not need a pu relations staff; what he did for I on the field brought him world fa And he has since learned to apply knowledge of play to the trai ground as a manager.

There may have been be players than Alfredo di Stefan some minor details, but none c challenge him as *the* complete pla the greatest forward of his time, with the possible exception of I perhaps of all time.

KEYSTONE

UNITED PRESS INTERNATIONAL

The man with nothing left to win

ove A clash of the 'incomparables'. Bobby Charlton and Pele fight for the ball in Mexico, 1970.

FOTOSPORTS INTERNATIONAL

Armstrong knows Manchester Victoria on only too well. He has lost count of the ber of times early morning trains have ied him to some remote part of the British in search of that elusive goal—the great baller—for his employer, the Manchester ted Football Club. He had no reason to ve that 9 February 1953 would be different most other days as his train pulled out.

rmstrong's destination was Newcastle; his ct to watch East Northumberland Schoolboys Hebburn and Jarrow Schoolboys. Someone given Matt Busby a tip. Occasionally some-g came of these trips, usually they were a

waste of time. Perhaps once in a lifetime, if he was lucky, a football scout would find what Joe Armstrong found that cold winter's day.

Mrs Cissie Charlton, proudly watching her son from the touchline, tells of the United scout's reactions: 'Joe came up and said, "I don't want to butter you up, but your boy Bobby will play for England before he's twenty-one." And he did.'

And he did much more. Not only did Bobby Charlton become the most capped player in England's long footballing history, he also un-disputably took the mantle of the best loved player of his time. It's no surprise to learn that within

twenty-four hours Armstrong was telling Busby that he had made the find of his career.

This is how Joe recalls his first sight of Charlton: 'It was one of those thin February days, with frost on the ground. In fact we had to peer through the mist. Bobby didn't do so much at first, but what I saw was enough for me.

'He was like a vision. This kid could run like a gazelle, drift past opponents with a shrug of the shoulders. And a shot: well, it was unbelievable that a kid of 14 could kick so hard and accurately. I knew we'd just got to have him, so of course I made a few enquiries and eventually we got him.'

There have been few more improbable talent spotters in football than Joe Armstrong, a former GPO official who went on scouting into his seventies but who never played football profession-ally and walks with a slight limp.

Yet it was this man, who had devoted his life to schoolboy football as a hobby, whom Busby entrusted with the massive assignment of finding the raw young talent of football for Manchester United. In that one appointment Busby showed his ability for spotting the right man for the job, for in his time Armstrong had an eye and a hand in the discovery and signing of such stars as Duncan Edwards, Denis Viollet, David Pegg, David Sadler and Brian Kidd—to name but a few.

Thus, when Armstrong presented his glowing report on his latest discovery, Busby realized he would have to move fast. By then he knew that all four of Bobby Charlton's uncles, his mother's brothers Jack, George, Jimmy and Stan Milburn had been League full-backs; and her cousin Jackie Milburn was none other than the Newcastle United and England centre-forward.

18 clubs wanted his signature, but Busby got him for United

In July of that year, 1953, the 15-year-old Charlton arrived at Old Trafford with his father. Bob Charlton senior, a miner, was not at all convinced that his son should move so far from home. After listening to what Matt Busby and his chief aide Jimmy Murphy had to say, he said abruptly: 'Send for our kid!'

Into Busby's office came Bobby Charlton junior, to be asked by his father: 'What do *you* want to do son?'

'I want to come Dad. This is my type of club.' 18 clubs had wanted his signature—one is said to have offered his father £800 for it. It is one of the greatest tributes to Busby and Armstrong's talents that he went to United. Later, Charlton admitted: 'It was probably the wisest decision I have ever made. I never wanted to leave that club.'

And yet those early years with Manchester United were not easy. The schoolboy wonder boy was plunged head first into the realities of the professional game. He was now under the direct control of Bert Whalley, the club coach, and Jimmy Murphy, a tough Welshman who was no respector of schoolboy reputations.

These two men were already busily honing the skills of perhaps the finest group of young foot-ballers ever assembled at one club... the kids who in a few years were to become the 'Busby Babes.' By the time that Charlton joined the club, they had already revealed to a startled football public one of those young stars: a boy, by name Duncan Edwards, who on Easter Monday 1953, before Charlton had joined the club, had played his first game in the First Division against Cardiff City aged 16 years 285 days. With a young star like that on the books, who was Bobby Charlton but a very promising young player? Indeed Murphy, now one of Charlton's closest friends, says of those days: 'A nicer, more genuine kid you couldn't wish to meet. He was loaded with talent, but oh dear! Bobby was one of the hardest pupils Bert and I ever had to coach at Old Trafford. Even as a 15 year old he had that thunderbolt shot in his left foot. And has there ever been a more graceful mover with the ball at his feet?

'He had all of that, as a boy. Maybe he had too many talents, because our job was to get them co-ordinated. He would keep hitting these stunning long balls to right or left wing, then standing still, instead of realizing the game was one of continual movement.

'Many a kid would have had his heart broken by our treatment of Bobby. Bert and I would bring him back in the afternoons when the other lads had a free period. We would get behind him, building up triangular short-passing moves screaming at him: "Play it short Bobby . . . play it short son . . . don't give the long ball until it's on." He learned.'

Charlton himself remembers those apprentice years with a tolerant smile now: 'I think if it hadn't been for Jimmy and Bert I might have given up the game. But I used to think that if they could give up their time to coach me, I had to try and improve my game to prove them right. It wasn't easy, but their love of the game was infectious.'

In the youth team and Central League side young Charlton was scoring plenty of goals, and United fans were anxious for Matt Busby to push a teenage shooting star into the first team along with the other youngsters. Busby hesitated, for Charlton was not as mature as the astonishing Duncan Edwards, only a year older and already a fully fledged international becoming, at the age of 18 years and 6 months, the youngest footballer ever to play for England. That was against Scotland at Wembley, April 1955, while Bobby Charlton was still playing in the reserves and was a virtual unknown outside Manchester.

A two goal first team debut—against Charlton Athletic

Busby was keeping the boy under wraps but a series of injuries to his regular first team inside trio—England centre-forward Tommy Taylor, Eire international Bill Whelan, and quicksilver Denis Viollet—forced the Manchester United manager to experiment. He gave Charlton his first chance against, appropriately enough, Charlton Athletic, and the boy responded with two goals. He didn't win a regular first team place. Busby explained: 'Bobby is going to be a great footballer, but at the moment he thinks the game begins and ends 30 yards from the opposing goal. Once he realizes he has the whole pitch to play in . . . he'll be great. Just great.'

Charlton's chance came when Tommy Taylor fractured a small bone in his leg which resulted in Viollet moving to centre-forward with Charlton at inside-left. In the 1957 FA Cup semi-final at Hillsborough, Charlton showed his goalscoring prowess with an astonishing acrobatic shot on the half-turn from a David Pegg corner, which helped to put United into the Cup Final by beating Birmingham City 2-0.

Now he was in the big time, playing against Real Madrid in the European Cup semi-final that year and at Wembley a month later in the FA Cup Final side against Aston Villa. Charlton remembers that match, because in the first few minutes he could so easily have put United one up, but at 19 he was too inexperienced and shot too hurriedly. United lost the game by the odd goal in three.

In that first season, Charlton experienced the happiness and heartbreak of big-time professional football, winning a League Championship medal, then ending on the losing side at Wembley. But everything that had gone before paled into insignificance compared with an event which lay just a few months away.

Charlton was just the 'boy' of that United team, although many of his team-mates such as Duncan Edwards, Eddie Colman, David Pegg and Bill Whelan, were not so very much older. The side, with an average age of just over 23, had already won the League Championship twice in succession, and had failed only narrowly to achieve a remarkable treble by losing to Aston Villa in the FA Cup Final and Real Madrid in the semi-final of the European Cup.

As season 1957-58 dawned Matt Busby said: 'Our matches with Real Madrid were a contest

between the two best sides in Europe, one experienced, the other still only youngsters. Our turn will come. My ambition is for this team to win the League three times in three years as Herbert Chapman did with Arsenal in the 1930s.'

On a wet soggy pitch from which the snow had been swept on the Wednesday afternoon of 5 February 1958, Charlton played for the last time with the young men he idolized. They were already in the last 16 for the FA Cup, and favourites to win it; if they beat Red Star Belgrade they were in the semi-final of the European Cup for the second year running; and they had shown a welcome return to form in the League on the previous Saturday, beating Arsenal 5-4 after taking a 3-0 lead at one point in a non-stop

thriller at Highbury.

By half-time in Belgrade, United were lea 3-0, Charlton scoring two of them and hav third mysteriously disallowed. True, Red levelled the scores in the last minute, but Ur were through on aggregate and a happy p set off home, with a cheery Tommy Taylor say 'I find it great playing alongside Bobby. I nod 'em back and he whacks 'em in.' A few h later Tommy Taylor, England's centre-forv was dead, and so too were Roger Byrne, M Jones, Eddie Colman, David Pegg, Bill Wh and Geoff Bent. Duncan Edwards died l Two other players, Jackie Blanchflower Johnny Berry, were so severely injured that never played seriously again.

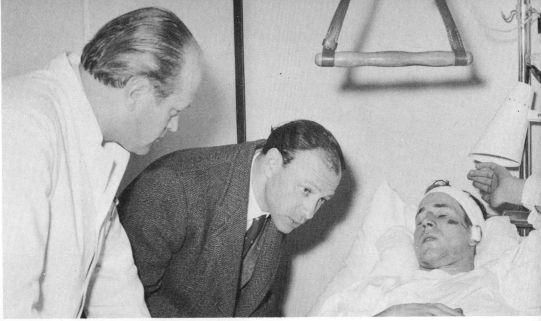

POPPERFOTO

COLORSPORT

Opposite top Charlton lets loose a characteristic thunderbolt from his famous right foot.
Opposite bottom A jubilant Charlton with Sir Matt Busby, Jimmy Murphy and Jack Crompton after the long-awaited European Cup win in 1968.
Above left An anxious moment for Manchester United.
Above Charlton recovers in a Munich hospital after the tragic air crash in February 1958.
Left Charlton moves away from Leicester's Nish to start yet another dangerous United attack.

obvious skills.

The move paid off handsomely for a few weeks later Charlton made a goal for Colin Webster in the last minute of a replayed quarter-final, so knocking out West Bromwich and putting Manchester United into the FA Cup semi-final against Fulham. Inspired by Bobby Charlton and Ernie Taylor (who was signed from Blackpool), United beat Fulham 5-3 after a drawn game and reached the Cup Final.

For the second year running Charlton ended on the losing side and sadly, also for the second year running, he might so easily have changed the course of the game when one of his thunderbolt shots beat Eddie Hopkinson, the Bolton goalkeeper, smashed against a post and rebounded into the grateful arms of the keeper.

His first cap against Scotland was to be followed by another 105

In a matter of weeks after the tragedy it seemed that this new, more serious, Bobby Charlton had matured, and he was honoured by being awarded his first cap for England against Scotland at Hampden Park in April 1958.

It is a game still remembered for an astonishing Bobby Charlton goal when he met a Tom Finney centre with a violent volley. Naturally, the sporting press went into eulogies about the Munich survivor, hailing him as soccer's new 'golden boy'.

That description left Charlton cold. He has always been basically too shy a person to allow himself to be projected in that way. Once when described as the 'greatest ever English footballer', he said, rather embarrassed, of the author: 'Well, he's entitled to his opinion.'

Despite the 106 England appearances, and all the honours showered upon him, Charlton has suffered his setbacks. There was the losing Cup Final in 1957; the Munich air crash which left him with a deep dread of flying; the doubts about his future in the game; a second losing Cup Final; a bright first appearance for England and then the frustration of being picked for the 1958 World Cup party and having to sit and watch it from the sidelines while the press clamoured for his inclusion.

After the 1958 World Cup series he became an

Charlton was picked up some 60 yards away from the Elizabethan airliner which crashed on its third attempted take-off after re-fuelling at Munich. He had broken no bones, but there was a deep cut on his head, and he was still strapped in his seat severely shocked.

So shocked, in fact, that when he returned to Manchester some days later Jimmy Murphy, who had taken over as acting manager until Matt Busby recovered from his terrible injuries, despaired whether young Charlton would ever play again. It seemed that Charlton was still mourning the loss of so many close friends, so Murphy sent him back home to Ashington to be with his own folk for a week or two.

For a time Charlton appeared to have no interest in ever playing the game again. He says it was a talk with the family doctor that finally made the difference; off he went to kick a ball around in a local park and watch some kids doing the same. The experience convinced him that he could never be anything else but a professional footballer.

When he returned to Old Trafford it was, says Murphy, a new and far more serious Charlton, who seemed determined to play his heart out in memory of and to keep faith with the friends who had died. Says Murphy: 'Before Munich Bobby was playing as a striking inside-forward. After Munich I thought we could get more out of him, and protect him, by switching him to the left wing where he would have more room to use his

automatic choice for England as a left-winger, yet very often to the crowd and to the experts he was a frustrating enigma. Despite his reputation, there are those who say that he has never been a great player; at least not in the way that Best, Pele or Puskas are great players. It was probably not until the 1966 World Cup that the Charlton on the field was really recognized as being much more than an emotional reminder of Munich. This feeling was perhaps best summoned up by Joe Mercer when he said in the early 1960s: 'So much talent, but if only Bobby would just go forward and tear 'em apart.'

Perhaps the answer is in Charlton's own self-effacing personality. In 1963 he was back at Wembley again with Manchester United for his third FA Cup Final appearance. That season Manchester United had struggled so badly in the League that for a long time there were fears they would be relegated. But Busby put the picture in perspective when he said to the team on the eve of the match with Leicester City: 'If we can't win with men such as Charlton, Law, Quixall and Herd in the forward line, backed by Crerand at half-back, we have no right to be at Wembley. This pitch was made for you . . . now go out and enjoy your game.'

United replied with a thrilling 3-1 victory in one of the best post-War Finals. At last Charlton had his Cup medal and with it there came a dramatic change in his approach to the game. For some seasons he had appeared, at times, either diffident or dangerous. Now with the sweeping tactical changes altering the face of football Busby made his gambler's throw.

'Where else is there a player with such a wide range of abilities'

With men such as Denis Law, Johnny Giles and Albert Quixall on the books he decided to give the job of midfield general to Charlton because, as he said: 'Where else in the world is there a player with such a range of playing ability. He can find a team-mate with a 40-yard pass; he can still come from behind the other forwards to have a crack at goal. Besides, Bobby is now at the stage where he needs responsibility. He can become one of the world's great players.'

Busby's plan and faith in Charlton brought dividends not only to his club but eventually for his country. For, in Bobby Charlton, Alf Ramsey, England's newly appointed team manager, saw the footballer around whom he could build his World Cup winning team. It is well known in football that at one time Ramsey was not exactly a Charlton fan. Like many other top managers in the game, he felt the Ashington wonder boy had never quite lived up to the exciting promise of his youth.

Charlton answered the call with a thrilling enthusiasm which is now history. There were three factors which probably caused him to burst through the strait-jacket of self-doubt. He had by now married a lovely model, Norma, who says of him: 'Bobby has always been devoted to football. But when he started, the maximum wage was still in force and he felt he would do well to save enough capital from his playing days to set up in a greengrocer's shop or something like that. He has never really lost that simple dedication to the game, although his career, of course, has bridged the vast financial change in the position of footballers.'

At the time of his switch to centre-forward Manchester United's fortunes, with George Best another exciting player in the line-up, began to improve. And, as United became a power in the game again, Charlton faced his greatest challenge . . . the challenge of the 1966 World Cup in England.

Charlton's contribution to that glittering success was perhaps not so dramatic as his skipper Bobby Moore's consistency nor the thrilling finality of Geoff Hurst's hat-trick in the Wembley final over West Germany. Yet few could deny that Charlton's presence on the field struck

Top *Bobby Charlton, then England's most-capped player, with the majority of his 106 caps.*
Top inset *A quiet airport drink with brother Jack prior to leaving for the Mexico World Cup in 1970.*

Above *A pre-season cross-country training run for the Manchester United players. Dedication to physical fitness has played a large part in Charlton's long run of success in top level football.*

a disabling fear into many of England's opponents, and his ice-cool distribution of the ball in midfield played a big part in England's rapid breaks from defence to attack, a crucial factor in England's eventual triumph.

Certainly he scored one of the memorable goals of that series, when he ran from just inside his own half to crash the ball in from some 25 yards against Mexico. Asked afterwards why he didn't score more goals like that one, Charlton gave a clue to his introvert personality by reply-

ing: 'You've got to be joking. I just ran forward looking for someone to pass to. But the Mexicans didn't come to tackle me. They just retreated so I ran on, until I saw a gap and let fly. Those shots either go in or miss by a mile.' Even so perhaps his most relevant contribution was almost negative. His stunning display against Portugal—when he scored two fine goals—so impressed the Germans that their most creative player, Beckenbauer, was detailed to close-mark Charlton for the final and as a result the German attack lost much of its own

RAY GREEN

Gornik Zabrze, in the quarter-finals, Charlton and his men found themselves losing 3-1 to Real in the semi-final in Madrid. Now Charlton, with Crerand, took hold of the game and forced Madrid back and, quite unexpectedly and some would say undeservedly, United drew 3-3. Thus, having won the first leg 1-0 at Old Trafford, they were in the European Cup final at last.

On 29 May 1968, at Wembley, Bobby Charlton became one of the few footballers ever to fulfil all of his major ambitions. It was a night of highly charged emotion; of agony and ecstasy, as Londoners linked arms with Mancunians and became Manchester United supporters for the night; United against Benfica in the final of the European Cup.

Charlton, trying desperately to keep his own nerves and those of his team-mates cool, scored a rare goal with his head to put United ahead early in the second-half. 'It must have skidded off my bald patch,' he modestly explained afterwards. Benfica equalized, almost won the match with a Eusebio thunderbolt and so the match went into extra time.

This was Charlton's finest half-hour, running, chasing, urging his flagging muscles to a final effort. Three times United scored in the next ten minutes; the last a matador's thrust from Charlton as he coolly swept a centre from Brian Kidd into the net.

Too tired and too moved to attend the European Cup celebrations

They threw a big party for United's players, past and present, in the Russell Hotel, London, where they wined and dined and talked of the great days for hour after hour until dawn broke. There was one important absentee: Bobby Charlton. His wife Norma, looking elegant in evening gown, went bravely into the reception on her own to join all the other wives and sweethearts, while her husband who had done so much for the club slept soundly above: 'He was too tired and too full up to come,' explained Norma.

He played on for another five years, the same spirit and dedication remaining even in a struggling United side. Despite widespread advice that managership would not suit the sheer pleasantness of his own personality, he was soon in charge at Preston North End on a quest for a different type of success.

Yet of all the honours that Charlton has won, the biggest and best and perhaps the most lasting is the respect he has earned from his fellow professionals. When the Bobby Moore affair blew up in Bogota and the England captain was falsely accused of the theft of an expensive bracelet, no one believed it. As everyone said: 'It couldn't have happened. Bobby Charlton was with him...'

Left *A snapshot for the family photo album— Bobby in the garden with his three children.*
Above *Back in Ashington, the scene of his own childhood, Bobby visits his mother.*

luency and potency.

As Wembley went wild with delight after England had won 4-2 in extra time, the Charlton brothers embraced in midfield.

'What else is there to win?' asked Jack.

'Just one thing more,' said Bobby.

He was referring to the European Cup; the motivating force of his life, as it was in Matt Busby's. It was something they didn't speak about very often, but deep down Charlton, like Busby, felt that they owed it to the boys who had lost

their lives returning from that European Cup tie.

They had already thrown away one glorious opportunity, losing in Belgrade to Partizan when favourites to win the trophy in 1966. And Charlton knew when Manchester United won the League Championship in 1967 that possibly this would be his very last chance of making that dream come true.

In fact, once again they very nearly made a mess of it. After beating the tough Polish side

Bobby CHARLTON

Honours: World Cup winners medal, 1966; European Cup winners medal, 1968; League Championship medal, 1957, 1965, 1967; FA Cup winners medal, 1963; FA Cup runners-up medal, 1957, 1958; European Footballer of the Year, 1966; Footballer of the Year, 1966

Club	Season	League		Int'nls	
		Mtchs	Gls	Mtchs	Gls
Manchester United	1956-57	14	10		
	1957-58	21	8	3	3
	1958-59	38	29	9	8
	1959-60	37	17	6	2
	1960-61	39	21	9	8
	1961-62	37	8	12	4
	1962-63	28	7	6	5
	1963-64	40	9	10	3
	1964-65	41	10	3	1
	1965-66	38	16	16	6
	1966-67	42	12	4	1
	1967-68	41	15	9	5
	1968-69	32	5	8	1
	1969-70	40	12	11	2
	1970-71	42	5		
	1971-72	40	8		
	1972-73	36	6		
Total		606	198	106	49

Too little time

There are some who say that Duncan Edwards was the best footballer England has ever produced. Others suggest that he would have won more caps than anyone who has ever played international football, others still who contend that Bobby Moore would not have led England through the 1966 World Cup had Edwards still been playing the game, at 29 the perfect choice for captain.

But, sadly, all has to be conjecture. For Edwards was one of the eight Manchester United players to die in the Munich air crash of 1958. In a way his death was even more of a tragedy than those of his team-mates, not because he was the youngest player ever to don an England shirt, nor because of the enormous expectations the game had of him, but because he so nearly survived. For 15 days he held on despite terrible injuries, and then, just as hopes were beginning to rise that there might be a chance, he quietly slipped away.

Among his last words were an enquiry of Jimmy Murphy, Matt Busby's assistant manager: 'What time is the kick-off against Wolves Jimmy? I can't afford to miss that match.' He was undoubtedly serious. Apart from the fact that Wolves were one of his local teams—he came from Dudley where the local church has a stained glass window in his memory—they were also United's main rivals for the supremacy of English football. And it was Edwards who had been one of the keys to United's revival and challenge to the Wolves in the mid-1950s.

He was born on 1 October 1936, and played his first League match for Manchester United against Cardiff City on 4 April 1953. He was just 16 years of age. On 2 April 1955 he became the youngest player ever to appear in a full England side. He was eighteen and a half. And on 5 February 1958, in Belgrade, he played his last competitive football match. He was then only 21, and already a legend. Ever since, the world of football has asked the question: Just how good was Duncan Edwards?

Don Revie, manager of Leeds United, is in no doubt: 'Duncan was one of the three greatest players thrown up in British football since the end of the Second World War. I put Tom Finney top, with Duncan close behind—although we had not seen the best of him before he was killed—and then John Charles.'

The Duncan Edwards story must inevitably be charged with emotion, because of the tragedy which struck him down. Yet the measure of his greatness can be told in capsule form.

In four and a half seasons of actual top class competition, he played 151 League matches, scoring 19 goals. He also played in 18 full internationals scoring five goals—in all a remarkable goal every six matches from the half-back position.

That Duncan Edwards was a bit special was soon quite clear to schoolmaster Eric Booth, secretary of the Dudley Schools FA. At the age of 11 Duncan was playing for his home town team, where the average age was four years older.

Maybe it was the experience of playing so young with much bigger and older boys which gave Duncan his remarkable aplomb and cool confidence when he was later called as a teenager to play in First Division and international football.

Sir Matt Busby, who played such a big role in his development, summed it up when he said: 'Duncan was never really a boy. Certainly he had

a boy's enthusiasm for some things, like collecting long playing records of jazz stars. But when it came to playing football, he seemed a man even when he first came to Old Trafford in 1952. He had this air and confidence about him; a maturity, which some of my other fine young players never had. That's why I had no qualms about giving him his chance when he was only 16. I remember seeing him as a schoolboy and deliberately trying to find some fault in his play. I gave up. I couldn't find any.'

If Busby's praise of his protege seems over effusive, then listen to Bobby Charlton: 'When I think back to Duncan I feel the rest of us were like pygmies. He was terrific. A professional through and through.'

There was no doubt that Duncan's tremendous physique—even at 16 he was just short of 6ft and weighed around 13 stone—stood him in good stead. For it gave him the power in the tackle that few men outside of Dave Mackay have ever equalled. Allied to that was a tremendous right foot shot, just as devastating as Bobby Charlton's

and a left-foot which was strengthened over years by application and practice until it wa equal of the other.

Few players have made such a stagge impact in so short a time. As a schoolbo partnered his cousin Dennis Stevens, who later to play for Bolton Wanderers and Ever but it was always the younger Duncan who wa senior partner. He was capped at schoolboy youth international level. In 1954 he wa England's first Under-23 team, which lost 3 the Italians in Bologna. The following yea earned his first full cap, against Scotlan Wembley. And what a debut this was, as Eng crushed Scotland 7-2. That great Scottish in national Bobby Johnstone insists: 'I still t Duncan is the greatest wing-half I ever pl against; he didn't give me a kick at the ball day.'

Once launched on his international care was honours all the way, and in season 1956 while still in the army, he chalked up staggering number of 94 matches in representa football and for his club, the Army and his unit

It was his sheer versatility which makes hi memorable. A fact taken up by Don Revie, played both with Edwards for England and aga him when he was a Manchester City player: ' professionals talk about greatness,' says Re 'because it is so rare. What made Edwards g was that you could play him anywhere. I've him at left-half, inside-left, centre-forward centre-half for Manchester United, and for var England teams. You could always rely on doing a job. That's what made him so unfor table. Had he lived he would have switched a matically to centre-half, for his club and country. He was the sort of player a man dreams about.'

Certainly few players in the last quar century have attracted so much attention. A schoolboy international practically every F Division club was chasing him. In fact, Whalley, Manchester United's coach, dr through the night and got Duncan out of h still in his pyjamas, to sign for Manche United in the early hours of 1 October 195 Duncan's 16th birthday.

It was a signing which comple revitalized the club, for Manchester Unit classic post-War side which won the Leag the FA Cup and four times finis runners-up in the League were startin get old. There followed a few lean ye until Sir Matt Busby unleashed on astonished game his teenage star known ever-after as the Busby Bal The first, and the greatest, Duncan Edwards, with his non-s driving energy and skill. Uni won the League Champi ship in 1955-56—agai season 1956-57. The sa year they were also los semi-finalists in the Europ Cup and losing finalists in the FA Cu

There is no doubt but for the injury to th goalkeeper Ray Wood against Aston Villa in Cup Final, Manchester United would ha become the first team this century to have d the League and FA Cup double. For it was dur this season that Matt Busby declared: 'I beli I have the finest young side in the world. they lack is experience to become the great and supersede Real Madrid. And in Dune Edwards I believe I have the greatest footba in the world. Alfredo di Stefano is a mat artist; John Charles is bigger and has all skills, but in Duncan Edwards I have a pla who can play anywhere without question, a do a great job either preventing goals, scor goals or "knitting" things together in midfie The great thing about Duncan is that he alwa wants to be involved in the game.'

A few months later Duncan Edwards v dragged out of the wreckage of the Elizabeth airliner at the end of the Munich runway, thigh shattered, his kidneys irreparably damag Sometimes the bulletins were good. Sometir

Above Edwards in the England shirt he wore 18 times. He was his country's youngest-ever player.
Opposite Part of the stained-glass memorial to Edwards that can be seen in Dudley Church.

PRESS ASSOCIATION

God is with us for our Captain.

Thanking God for the Life of Duncan Edwards, died at Munich, February 1958.

they were bad; until, 15 days later, at 1.12 on the morning of 21 February 1958, he died still only 21 years old.

The world of football was shattered that the young colossus had gone. Walter Winterbottom, then England team manager and preparing for the 1958 World Cup, summed up the feelings of many when he said: 'It was in his character and spirit I saw the true revival of English football.'

Winterbottom knew him well. On the field he was a giant, off it Duncan tended to be the strong silent type, rarely speaking unless spoken to. Not that he was unfriendly, but his whole life was so wrapped up in soccer that his conversation—when he could be drawn—was almost certainly either about the last match he had seen or played in, or the next one he was due to take part in.

Once, when accused by an opponent of chucking his weight about, Duncan reproved him with the short comment: 'I don't chuck my weight about . . . I just know how to distribute it in the right place at the right time.'

He was, undeniably, a hard player, but never a dirty one. Nevertheless, Henry Rose, the northern sports columnist of the *Daily Express* once felt constrained to write an open letter in the *Express* criticizing Duncan for what he felt was unnecessarily hard tackling. Later Henry breezed up to the teenager Edwards saying: 'I hope you don't think I was too tough on you with that article I wrote?'

'You wouldn't get me near a plane if it wasn't for a football match'

Duncan smiled: 'I didn't read it Mr Rose,' he said. 'In fact I'm too busy playing to bother reading many reports. I always think if I'm playing badly or doing anything wrong then Mr Busby will soon let me know. And if he says nothing I suppose I must be doing all right.'

When dealing with the press it always pays professionals to have a sense of humour. And when playing for England against Wales at Cardiff, he happened to be taking a throw-in next to his guide and mentor Jimmy Murphy, then the Welsh team manager. Wales were losing handsomely, and as he picked the ball up Duncan whispered to Jimmy: 'I don't know what you're wasting your time for here Jimmy . . . You've just got ten minutes to catch the next train to Manchester.'

And although fearless on a football field, Duncan was perhaps shy and unsure off it. He never really relished flying, for instance. He would sit tense, trying to read, usually at the rear of the plane.

On a six hour flight in an ancient Dakota from Manchester to Bilbao, Duncan arrived looking very green about the gills. 'Thank God that's over,' he said, 'I thought I was going to be air sick.'

'Do you think you'll be fit enough to play tomorrow?' he was asked. 'Fit to play?' thundered Duncan, 'You wouldn't get me anywhere near an aircraft if there wasn't a soccer match at the end of the trip. It's the only reason I've come.' He was devoted to the game, would do anything for it. All the more bitter that he should lose his life in an air disaster before he had shown the world his best.

Duncan EDWARDS

Honours: League Championship medal 1955-56, 1956-57
FA Cup runners-up medal 1957

Club	Season	League		Int'nls	
		Mtchs	Gls	Mtchs	Gls
Manchester United	1952-53	1			
	1953-54	24			
	1954-55	33	6	4	
	1955-56	33	3	5	1
	1956-57	34	5	6	3
	1957-58	26	5	3	1
Total		151	19	18	5

RAY GREEN

Johnny Haynes: no pay-off for perfection

The career of Johnny Haynes was one of the most contradictory in the history of British football. He was the country's first £100 a week player; he was one of the first to use his fame for advertising and to have an agent; and he was captain of England on 22 occasions.

Yet for all that he left the game, after nearly 20 years, without an honour to his name. The reason was a simple one; he spent the whole of his professional career with Fulham.

For years Haynes and Fulham were synonymous: even more so, perhaps, than the contemporary associations of Finney and Preston, Lofthouse and Bolton, or Matthews and Blackpool. Unlike those stars he spent half his career in the Second Division, winning 32 of his 56 caps as a Second Division player; unlike them he never appeared in a Cup Final; and unlike them he never won the accolade of Footballer of the Year.

By birth and upbringing he should not have been a Fulham player at all. Born and raised in Edmonton, North London, he should logically have joined Spurs. But after playing for Edmonton and England Schoolboys—producing a superb display of neat and precise passing in the televised win over Scotland in 1950, one which Dave Mackay (of the losing side) still remembers with awe—he chose to join lowly Fulham.

Haynes considered that Spurs had too many talented youngsters and 'I fancied my chances better at Fulham.' The reason Fulham took preference over any other London alternative was because of one Tosh Chamberlain, a friend of Haynes as a schoolboy player who had gone to Craven Cottage the year before, and a man whom Haynes was to partner on the left-wing in so many matches.

Haynes made his debut on Boxing Day 1952, and over the next 18 seasons was to play over 700 games for Fulham. In 1961, after former Fulham colleague Jimmy Hill had secured the removal of the £20 maximum wage, club chairman Tommy Trinder declared that 'Johnny is worth £100 a week'; and within 24 hours the negotiations for a revision of his contract were complete.

'If the maximum wage hadn't been lifted I'd have gone to Italy'

Thus Haynes continued to play for another nine years for Fulham. But it had been a near thing: 'If the maximum wage hadn't been lifted,' he explained, 'I'd have gone to Italy.' Instead of following John Charles, Joe Baker, Denis Law and Jimmy Greaves and Gerry Hitchens to the glamour of Milan or Turin, he stayed in the less salubrious SW6.

The only other time it looked at all possible for Haynes and Fulham to part came soon after the tragic death of John White, Tottenham's brilliant young Scottish international inside-forward. After White was struck down by lightning on a golf course in July 1964, Spurs manager Bill Nicholson was left with a huge problem. He thought deeply about the person to replace White, who was only 26, and came up with Haynes.

Nicholson offered £90,000—it would have been a record fee between British clubs—for the 30-year-old; but the deal did not go through. 'Bad business,' says Haynes, looking back to a transfer that could have revolutionized his life and given

him a taste of success late on in his career.

Was he sad at the lack of success at Craven Cottage? Haynes is philosophical. 'We never had a good side,' he says. 'We were in the Second Division the best part of the fifties and, although we got plenty of goals and played a lot of good football, we let in plenty too.

'After we reached the First Division in 1959 it was years of struggle. We sold players when, at the time, it looked as if we only needed a couple to make us a really good side.'

Haynes gained his major satisfaction from his career with England, particularly the 1960-61 season when the side, managed by Walter Winterbottom, had a magnificent run. It was especially pleasing for Haynes: his first two games as captain, in May 1960 against Spain and Hungary, had resulted in 3-0 and 2-0 defeats.

A car crash ends Haynes' international career—at 29

The first part of the run comprised the first six games of the 1960-61 season, when England were undefeated and scored 40 goals against eight. Haynes, who had scored three in a 5-0 win over Russia at Wembley in 1958, lists the fifth match of the run, the 9-3 defeat of Scotland, as the best international performance of his time. Dave Mackay was again on the receiving end that day.

In August 1962, soon after poor displays in the disappointing World Cup in Chile, Haynes was involved in a car crash at Blackpool. It was to end his international career and put his whole playing future in jeopardy. Then 29, he did not play for a year and was even told by doctors that he would never play again.

A few months after the crash the Winterbottom era ended and Alf Ramsey took over as England team manager. He never called on Haynes. 'He never had the chance because of the car crash,' says the player. And he refused to speculate whether he might have fitted into the new manager's plans: 'Alf never had the chance to pick me.'

The myth grew up that, even after Haynes had fully recovered, he was an obsolete player. It was thought that the emergence of the back four in defence had blunted his most effective weapon— the through-pass to the winger inside the full-back. By any serious standards it was a false and oversimplified assumption. Haynes, with all his skill and experience, had the equipment to adapt his game and, as he proved with Fulham, he was able to do it with ease. Apart from George Eastham's delicacy, it was not until Bobby Charlton switched to midfield that England found a comparable replacement; and it could well be argued that, without the crash, Haynes would have won considerably more caps.

In September 1964, three months after England's poor showing in the 'Little World Cup' in Brazil, the *News of the World*, the *Sunday Mirror* and *Football Monthly* were among those who campaigned for a return of Haynes. 'If, as Ramsey has admitted,' said *Football Monthly*, 'some of England's failings were due to inaccurate passing, who better than Haynes, the most precise, most telling distributor in the game?

'He is keen to win back his place. The question of whether he returns as captain is not really

important.' But it was not to be: Haynes' national career had finished.

To a generation that has not known an before the removal of the £20-a-week maxin wage it may seem hard to imagine Haynes superstar of the soccer scene. To a top play the seventies £100 a week would be only a sta But Haynes *was* big. He was a 'Brylcreem Boy' smoothly oiled hair being a symbol for the s young man of the day.

Haynes' face was everywhere. And the N predictably, liked it the least. He was regarde the South's golden boy and had a reputa (which he helped create) as a 'big-head'.

He could pinpoint a pass with great accur he had the ability to read the game and to kr without looking, where a player should be; reverse passes were models of accuracy.

But Haynes was a perfectionist. He was a professional. He did not like to lose. And, w things went wrong on the field, he had a pos way of expressing his disgust: he stood hands on hips and delivered a withering look.

'I accept that I gave this image as a fectionist,' he says. 'I still am, even in business I get the needle the same way and, even if I d express myself quite the way I did as a footba the reaction is still the same.'

His contribution at Fulham was always a source of controversy

Possibly the greatest feature of Hay character is his loyalty. He has always been l to his parents; he has stayed loyal to his frie and he stayed loyal to Fulham for 20 ye Players and journalists and fans who were v Haynes at his peak remained his friends. maintained close contact after his playing day England became confined to charity games.

Considering his role as a leader of men v Fulham and England it is strange that Hay did not consider himself cut out for foot management. He did, in fact, take over Ful for 17 days when his former England and Full playing colleague, Bobby Robson, was sac But he told the Fulham directors that he was interested and he soon drafted in another for colleague, Bill Dodgin, as coach, and stood d in favour of him as manager. 'Not my cup of t was his usual explanation.

It was ironic that Bill Dodgin senior sho have been one of the managers of Fulham Haynes' early days of Haynes in the fifties— that the Haynes era at Craven Cottage sho have ended with a free transfer under his man ment.

Over the years Fulham were criticised both keeping Haynes and for not strengthening t side to help him achieve some success with club. The critics said that Fulham were a one-n team, that tactics revolved around Haynes, t Johnny was too strong for any manager at Cra Cottage.

What was the truth? Fulham certainly k Haynes—but compensated him by paying money at the first chance. They might h spent on building the side—the £72,500 tran of Alan Mullery to Spurs was an example o criticised deal—but the clubs answer could be t the side was always full of international play to back Haynes.

On that same basis, with players of the calibre of Bobby Robson, Beddy Jezzard, Jim Langley and George Cohen, Fulham could hardly be labelled a one-man team. Tactics did not revolve around Haynes, although full use was always made of his ability, and it was a fallacy to say that Haynes was too strong for the managers he played under. Personalities such as Jimmy Hill were every bit as strong as Haynes, who played alongside, and was prepared to work under, managers such as Jezzard and Robson.

He received the fan-mail a player of his calibre deserved, but mingled with it were the critical letters saying that Fulham would be better off without him. Haynes merely shrugged his shoulders at these.

Some idea of the impact he had on the London scene was that the testimonial Fulham staged for him raised £11,000. Haynes, who owns his home at Epsom, left the club a comparatively young and wealthy man. 'I'd have been a millionaire by now if the maximum wage had been lifted earlier,' he claims. 'But I've no regrets. I've never been a big saver and should have put by more money than I have.' He later improved his position with shares in a firm with a string of betting shops.

Haynes was tipped to join Jimmy Hill as a television personality when he left Fulham, but instead he moved to South African football and, ironically, won his first honour in 20 years—as a member of the Durban City side that clinched the league title.

'I was sitting a yard from the biggest name in English football'

Some of the awe in which Haynes was held is told by England international Alan Mullery when he talks of his first day as a footballer, in April 1957. Young Mullery and his father caught a bus to Fulham, and sitting across the aisle was Johnny Haynes. 'I had never met him before and he didn't know me,' says Mullery. 'I was too embarrassed to speak to him or introduce myself. Here I was sitting a yard or two from the biggest name in English football.'

Mullery rates Haynes as one of the greatest world-class players in the post-War era and reckons that his former Fulham colleague possessed extra-sensory powers as a footballer, picturing moves ten seconds before they happened.

'Johnny was the greatest passer of a ball I've known,' he says. 'He could lay it to within six inches of a colleague. A yard just wasn't good enough for Johnny. In years to come when my children grow up and they ask me about the greatest footballers, I'll tell them how Johnny Haynes could send a 40-yard pass inside the full-back to the winger streaking in towards goal.'

It was a pity for Haynes that he did not achieve an unspoken ambition: to find another ten Johnny Haynes' to play alongside the perfectionist original. He was happy playing for England, but he also enjoyed his football at Craven Cottage. Because there he was the king.

Johnny HAYNES

Club	Season	League		Int'nls	
		Mtchs	Gls	Mtchs	Gls
Fulham	1952-53	18	2		
	1953-54	41	16		
	1954-55	37	8	1	1
	1955-56	40	18	7	3
	1956-57	33	4	5	2
	1957-58	38	15	11	3
	1958-59	34	26	8	4
	1959-60	31	10	4	1
	1960-61	40	9	9	4
	1961-62	38	5	11	
	1962-63	8			
	1963-64	40	8		
	1964-65	39	6		
	1965-66	32	6		
	1966-67	36	6		
	1967-68	34	5		
	1968-69	28	1		
	1969-70	27	3		
Total		594	148	56	18

The tragic ghost of White Hart Lane

John White, one of the greatest of a great line of Scottish inside-forwards, was killed by lightning on a golf course in July 1964.

It was a bizarre end to the life of a magnificent footballer. Yet the extraordinary way he died should not be allowed to cloud or overshadow what had gone before in his brief reign.

'The most beautiful player I've ever seen,' claims Danny Blanchflower. Not beautiful in the sense of physical appearance—though White was handsome in a boyish way—but beautiful with regard to style.

White was slender, with long legs made to appear still longer by his habit of pulling his stockings up as far as they would go. He moved easily and always looked neat, but it was only when he had the ball that his real style became apparent. No matter what the pitch was like, no matter what the opposition was like, no matter what his own form was like, White had a grandeur all his own.

He seemed to move in his own private vacuum, cushioned against feet and elbows, mud and rain. He coaxed and cajoled the ball to his liking, used his feet almost to caress it, then placed it perfectly, short or long, forwards or sideways. Nobody, not even Blanchflower, could pass a ball with White's combination of economy and accuracy.

A flash of lightning robs football of one of its finest players

In his brief prime with Spurs and Scotland, John White was perhaps as close to perfection as an inside-forward could be. Anyone who saw him, weaving in and out of tackles, switching one of those effortless passes to a colleague, should prize the memory. Thoroughbreds come on the football scene so rarely that they merit treasuring. And he proved that physique is not all that important, for at a fraction under 5ft 8in and around 10 stones he was physically unexceptional. Like an even smaller genius, Tommy Harmer—the man he eventually replaced in the Tottenham side—he relied on skill, not strength.

White was the victim of a freak accident, struck down by a flash of lightning so fierce that it melted the wedding ring on his finger. He had been playing golf at the Crews Hill course in Enfield, near his home, when a storm broke. He was later found dead at the foot of a tree, presumably having tried to take shelter there from the rain.

White was then only 26 years of age, with the prospect of many more fine seasons in front of him. On a personal level, his death was a tragedy: he was married (to the daughter of Tottenham's assistant manager, Harry Evans) and had a two-year-old daughter and a son of six months. To football in general, fate had struck a malignant blow. To Spurs in particular, White's absence left a gap that could not be filled. The same applied to Scotland: White had gained 22 caps and was obviously a key figure in his country's preparations for the 1966 World Cup.

An international, in fact, had played a large part in White's arrival at Tottenham. In October 1959, while with Falkirk, he played in a Scottish forward line with Leggat, St John, Law and Mulhall, who carved up the Irish

defence in a 4-0 victory at Belfast. Goalkeeper Bill Brown and wing-half Dave Mackay returned to London full of praise for the slim inside-right and manager Bill Nicholson, who had already watched White for himself, was now further impressed. Blanchflower, who had captained the Irish side that day, was even more voluble than usual in support. White, he said, was going to be a great player. 'Falkirk want £20,000,' said Nicholson, knowing that such a sum, although nowhere near a record, was still high for a largely unknown player. 'You're kidding,' replied Blanchflower. 'That's not a transfer. It's a robbery.'

So Nicholson travelled to Scotland. He was still worried about the frailty of White, but when he was informed that he was a cross-country star—he was to run for the Army that week—his doubts about the little lance-corporal's stamina were dispelled. As it was White did not turn out for the Army that Saturday: he went to London and, five days after the game in Belfast, on 8 October 1959, he signed for Spurs.

White had never been to London before, but he liked what he saw. Being as canny as most Scots, he also liked the thought of a £20-a-week wage once his national service was over: before joining the Army he had been getting £3 a week as a joiner, plus £4 as a part-time footballer. And he had never had much money. His father died when John was six and his mother brought him up, with his two brothers and a sister, in a three-room house in his native Musselburgh, near Edinburgh. Even when he left Alloa Athletic for Falkirk he received only £10 from the £4,000 fee.

Moving to London was an enormous step for a basically shy young man to take. Although he began well, with a goal in his first match (away to Sheffield Wednesday) the rest of that 1959-60 season was undistinguished. His style was similar to that of Harmer, and although the pair sometimes worked well together (as in the 13-2 FA Cup rout of Crewe) the presence of two such delicate ball-players was rather a luxury when the going was tough.

In addition White was still stationed at Berwick, and even for home matches he had to make a round trip of some 700 miles. This and a spate of Army games in midweek meant that he ended the season a very tired young man.

By the following August, however, he had been demobilized, had moved into digs in London, and had met Sandra Evans. The marriage that followed enabled him to settle in a 'foreign' city, and the confidence his manager and playing colleagues showed in him brought about a surge in his ability that soon became evident when the new season began.

'John had taken a bit of time to settle, just as I did when I left Hearts,' says Dave Mackay. 'But once he was in full-time training we all knew he had talent.'

With Blanchflower, Mackay, Smith, Jones and the rest around him, White visibly grew in stature. No longer did he tend to fade from a game; instead he became a major directional figure, imposing his will on the patterns of play. He and Blanchflower were the twin conductors of a Tottenham orchestra who, after they had narrowly missed the Championship in 1959-60, swept to the double the following season, shattering record after record. They won 31 of their 42 League games, including the first 11 in succes-

PRESS ASSOCIATION

Above John White, Spurs player who wa tragically killed by li ning in July 1964, a age of 26.

Top right *Though renowned for his style skill as a constructive inside-forward, White sc many fine goals. This one (White is second from ri was against Aston Villa in Spurs' double season.*
Centre *Blanchflower and White, who formed midfield inspiration of Spurs' double side, par the FA Cup after the success of 1962.*
Far right *White meets club colleague Jin Greaves at Wembley in 1963. White was automatic Scottish choice for seven years.*

John WHITE

Honours: European Cup Winners Cup winners medal 1963
League Championship medal 1960-61
FA Cup winners medal 1961, 1962

Club	Season	League		Int'nls	
		Mtchs	Gls	Mtchs	G
Falkirk	1957-58	12	6		
	1958-59	25	6	3	1
	1959-60	*	*	1	1
Tottenham Hotspur	1959-60	28	6	4	
	1960-61	42	13	4	
	1961-62	36	8	5	
	1962-63	37	8	3	
	1963-64	40	6	5	1
Total		220*	53*	22	3

*No record of appearances with Falkirk available for 1959-60.

n, collected 66 points, and failed to score only one match. With Cup ties they scored goals. White claimed only 13 of them, but de many more, and those he scored were ally vital. One, against West Ham, was a ically brave diving header.

Although Spurs failed to retain the title in 1-62 they kept a grip on the Cup—thanks gely to White. He had been somewhat nymous against a handicapped Leicester at mbley the year before: but now he did much ter. And he turned the game back to Spurs mediately after Burnley had cancelled out an ly goal by Jimmy Greaves. Jimmy Robson ced the ball in, early in the second half, and rnley rejoiced. Amid the celebrations, the right k of their defence was badly positioned when y restarted . . . and White spotted it.

He ran wide to the left, calling for the ball. es supplied it, and White had time to asure a centre for Smith to turn and slam it st Blacklaw. Spurs were ahead again, and they nt on to win 3-1.

This was typical of White, always so cool in es of crisis. Had others shared his calm achment in the second leg of the European Cup ni-final with Benfica that season, Spurs might ve survived instead of losing 4-3 on aggregate. t, on a night of wild passion, too many of ite's colleagues acted in haste instead of ying on precision.

In this and in earlier rounds, White had been cellent. Like Blanchflower he responded to challenge of European football, relishing the opportunity to match his wits with opponents of the highest class. The same applied in 1962-63, when the second Wembley victory enabled the club to take part in the Cup Winners Cup—and to become the first British side to win it.

Methodical, relaxed, unflagging in his determination, White steadied them in various times of stress. Rangers arrived in London with hordes of fans for a tie labelled 'the British championship'. White—often watched by Ibrox scouts in his Alloa days, but turned down for his apparent frailty—reiterated their missed chance with two early goals, both headers from corners by Greaves. Spurs won 5-2, and in Glasgow White turned on a magical show in front of his countrymen to inspire a 3-2 victory.

'He was ready for it,' says Blanchflower. 'He was going to be a king'

So Spurs proceeded to the final, in Amsterdam against Atletico Madrid—and a 5-1 victory. Here again White scored an unexpected goal, moving to a cross from Terry Dyson and striking a thunderous shot high into the net while the defenders looked for him to lay the ball off.

The 1963-64 season, which sadly turned out to be White's last, was a difficult one for him. Blanchflower and Mackay were out through injuries, and much more depended on the slim Scot. Spurs won nothing, and were decried as failures—though they still finished fourth and scored 97 League goals.

The strain of being something of a one-man organizer told on White, who was left out of the team for a vital match with Liverpool at Easter, when defeat ruined their last hopes of the title. He had, however, been a dominant figure throughout the season. For all his love of a joke—he and Cliff Jones did a marvellous cancan act—he took his job seriously. 'He was never any trouble,' says Nicholson. 'He loved to play, but unlike some he loved to train as well. He was a fine boy.'

Blanchflower knew that White was taking over his role as number one on the Tottenham pitch. 'He was ready for it,' says Danny. 'He had the skill and the confidence. He was going to be a king.' White made more than 200 appearances for Spurs between the first match with Sheffield Wednesday and the last, at Leicester. Of the 17 competitive matches he missed in that time, the club lost nine, drew seven and won one. That is some indication of his part in Tottenham's greatness.

White scored the only goal in what was to be his last match at Leicester. Then came that lightning flash, followed by the deeply moving scenes at the funeral, when players, officials and public joined the family in mourning, and heard Maurice Bayliss, Vicar of Enfield, say: 'White Hart Lane will be a stricken place . . . much of its glory will pass away with John White.' The wreaths included one in the club colours, with the simple message 'Thanks for the memory,' in pencil from a boy of 12.

Martin Peters– ten years after

THE
MIDDLE-MEN

Below *Martin Peters and Geoff Hurst play against Rumania during England's defence of the World Cup in Mexico. Three months ea[rlier] Peters had become a Spurs player for £200,0[00] but he continued for his country in the famous [link] with Hurst and Moore that had begun at West H[am].*
Bottom *Peters' second-half goal made it [1-1] against West Germany in the World Cup quar[ter-] final at Leon—but it did not prove enough.*
Right *Britain's first £200,000 footballer h[eads] out Phil Beal at Molineux. Peters took some [time] to settle with Tottenham, but by 1972 he [had] overcome the problems and assumed the captaincy when Alan Mullery had left.*

Martin Peters struggled to sleep the night England manager Sir Alf Ramsey described him as '. . . a player ten years ahead of his time.'

It was the winter of 1968 and Ramsey was talking on television about the richness of England's playing strength. Peters was one of the players Ramsey singled out as being 'truly world class.'

Initially this praise pitched Peters into a morose mood. 'I lay awake half the night trying to figure out just exactly what Alf meant by me being ten years ahead of my time. My first reaction was that there was no place for me in the present set-up and that this was Alf's way of gently dropping me from the England scene. I thought it was a sort of public pat on the back before being quietly shown the door.'

Peters need not have lost any sleep. Ramsey was to make him as permanent a part of the England establishment as his West Ham club-mates Bobby Moore and Geoff Hurst.

The England boss was later to go deeper into the reasons why he prized Peters so highly—an assessment that was disputed by several prominent people in the game. 'Martin is not just a good player, but a great one. He has a wonderful sense of timing that would enable him to be an outstanding success at any ball game. One of his chief attributes is an ability to see situations and positions that escape the notice of lesser players.

'Not only can he steal quietly into these positions but he has the finesse and the finishing power to take full advantage of opportunities that other people have not realized existed. He is a great asset to the England team.'

'I have grown used to not being the most popular of players'

Peters is one of the most misunderstood and maligned England players of all time. There is a huge section of the paying public that neither appreciate the finer points of his play nor understand the role he performs for club and country.

His public image was hardly improved by the sniping comments of home-based critics during England's World Cup defence in Mexico. Manchester City team manager Malcolm Allison was the chief castigator on television. 'Martin Peters? He's the one that's ten years ahead of his time, so we've got to wait for him to come good.'

Peters' Spurs colleague Alan Mullery also came under the Allison hammer, but gained some revenge by clearly beating him in a verbal wrestling match during a confrontation in front of the cameras. Peters, for his part, preferred to bury his feelings. 'I was more annoyed than hurt by the criticism. The people giving me stick were doing it from 7,000 miles away and judging me from what they saw on the small screen. It was unfair. Everybody is entitled to express an opinion, but from what I could gather little of the comment about me was constructive. I admire Malcolm tremendously as a coach and feel that a lot of what he said was purely for effect. It hurt quite a bit but I have grown used to not being the most popular of players.'

Peters hit a new low in the popularity poll soon after joining Tottenham from West Ham in March 1970—for a record £200,000 deal that included Jimmy Greaves as a £54,000 makeweight.

It reached the point where skipper Mullery had

into the role he preferred. 'I like to go forward from midfield and have the freedom to place myself wherever I feel I can achieve the most for the team. There are obviously specific jobs for me to do in defence when the need arises, but ideally I like to search for goals. This may sound vague but I've a clear picture in my mind of just what I'm trying to achieve.'

It was no real surprise to people close to football in London when Peters moved to White Hart Lane. 'It was as if Martin had been with us for 18 months before the deal,' one Spurs player commented. 'Bill Nicholson was forever bringing his name up at our team meetings. He seemed to have orgasms over his play and kept using him as an example of what he wanted from Tottenham players.'

There was also a wide forecast that Jimmy Greaves would figure in the deal as exchange bait. He and Peters, in fact, had both been discovered playing schools football in Dagenham. 'Jimmy Greaves had been like a god to me when I was a kid,' says Peters. 'I idolized him from the time when I went along with the senior team at my school as a supporter. Jimmy's team won 13–0 and he got 11 of the goals.

'Even as a youngster he was a graceful and elegant footballer'

'I felt desperately sorry for Jimmy when he failed to get into the team for the World Cup final in 1966. I can't recall for sure what went through my mind that day but for a split second the thought might have hit me, "What the hell am I doing here when someone like Greaves is a spectator?"'

The Peters for Greaves-plus-£146,000 deal went through in a hurry on transfer deadline day, 1970. Peters had in fact withdrawn his request by then, after coming to an agreement with Greenwood that he would be allowed to move later in the season. 'There was never any chance of me changing my mind. I'd quietly made four transfer requests during the previous year and purposely made my fifth demand public in the October because I wanted it out in the open.'

So the Moore-Hurst-Peters club partnership was finally broken—though it continued to flourish for England. All three of them had been discovered playing in Essex schools football by West Ham scout Wally St Pier. 'We had a lot of competition for Martin,' he recalls. 'Even as a youngster he was very much like he is today—a graceful, elegant player who could read the game like a book.'

Peters gives three men the credit for having had the most influence on him. 'Alf Ramsey and Ron Greenwood were both of tremendous help in my development, but my father did a lot for me in my early years.'

Martin's father is a lighterman, guiding barges around the Thames dockside—which can be as demanding and difficult as finding a way through a packed defence. 'I thought of following him at one time, but I'm obviously delighted that I settled for football. It's given me the sort of security that people dream about.'

In 1971 he lived in a detached house in Essex with his wife, Kathy, and their two children. Kathy Peters is totally dedicated to supporting her husband in his career and the rumour-pushers blamed her for his break with West Ham. 'That's the silliest of all the stories circulating about me,' claims Martin. 'Kathy did not try to influence me against West Ham in any way. The decision to press for a move was mine and she gave me her full support.'

Peters came out of his shell a lot after joining Spurs. He was always quiet and cautious at West Ham, and conversation seemed to come hard to him. But his personality emerged at Tottenham, where you had to be quick with your tongue to get a word in edgeways.

Indeed he found it easier settling to the social side at Spurs than the playing side. Though he headed a delicate goal on his debut, against

plead with the demanding Spurs fans to give [Pet]ers a break. 'Martin is a players' player and [doe]s not deserve to have the fans on his back. [Th]ose people criticizing him should watch what [he] does *without* the ball. Then they will appreciate [wh]y he is a £200,000 player.

He appears from out of nowhere to take up [g]oat positions, just like the late John White [use]d to for Tottenham in the early sixties. Martin [has] enormous skill and the winning ability to [sen]se where the ball will be a second or two [bef]ore anyone else.'

After a tricky start Peters was soon asserting [him]self as an authority in Tottenham's midfield [and] played a prominent part in the 1971 League [Cu]p success. And he became even more of an [infl]uence on the team in the 1971-72 season, [wh]en he took over the captaincy from the injured [Mul]lery. 'I enjoy the responsibility of being [cap]tain,' he says. 'It means greater involvement in [the] game. I'm pretty quiet on the pitch compared [to] some captains, but I'm not frightened of [giv]ing somebody a volley of words if I feel it will [hel]p the team effort.'

The true reasons for Peters leaving West Ham [are] a mystery and unlikely to be divulged. 'I'm not [pre]pared to tell anybody why I decided I had to [leav]e Upton Park. It was very much a personal [mat]ter between West Ham manager Ron Green[woo]d and myself.'

Greenwood refuses to yield any more facts. 'We [jus]t call it a clash of personalities,' he says. 'We [hav]e no ill-feeling toward each other. Martin is a [gre]at player and gave wonderful service to West [Ha]m. He was well worth the money we got for him.'

He openly asked for a transfer in October 1969, from a West Ham club where he had seemed inseparable as the 'third man' in the Moore-Hurst-Peters trio. They had grown up together at Upton Park, following the treasure trail with both club and country.

It was Peters who scored England's second goal in the 1966 World Cup final against West Germany at Wembley. But whereas skipper Moore and the three-goal Hurst became world-recognized personalities after that triumph, Peters remained something of an obscure figure.

A story gathered strength following his transfer demand in 1969 that he was sick of having to shelter in the shadow of his two colleagues. He dismisses the theory. 'There was a load of nonsense talked about me being jealous of the money and publicity that was going the way of Bobby and Geoff. It's totally untrue. They are good friends of mine. In fact Geoff is godfather to one of my two children. I don't envy them in any way and wish them every success both on and off the pitch. I've never tried to get involved in outside business ventures simply because I feel I have enough to contend with trying to maintain my status in football.'

A more believable story that circulated was that his transfer request was spawned by his frustration at not being able to find an obvious identity inside the West Ham side. He wore every first-team shirt during his nine senior years with the Hammers, and was a victim of his own all-round ability, often playing in positions where he felt shackled. A move to another club, he believed, would give him the chance to cement himself

75

Coventry, it was all of six months before
properly adjusted to Tottenham's tact
manoeuvres. 'I quickly got an understanding v
Steve Perryman and Alan Mullery in midfi
but I took a lot longer to fit in with Alan Gilz
and Martin Chivers up front. Gradually, thou
things started to work out as I knew they wo
Some of the fans were not too patient with m
the early days but it didn't worry me. The
perfectly justified in shouting what they
After all, it's their entrance money that pays
wages.'

There was positive proof of the way Pe
settled in as a commander at Spurs when t
travelled to Rumania, just before Christmas
1971, for the second leg of their EUFA C
quarter-final against Rapid Bucharest. He was
inspiring captain in a match that left a lot of sca

It was a situation that demanded cool
composed leadership, and that is exactly w
Peters gave Tottenham. 'Martin is a captain v
inspires by example,' says Nicholson. 'He h
good temperament and he proved it in Buchar
when he refused to be intimidated by so
unbelievably wicked fouls.'

Peters' accomplished debut made a lasting impression on Ramsey

Captaincy was not new to Peters. He led
England schoolboys team against West Germ
at Wembley in 1959—in his last match bef
joining the West Ham groundstaff. He then m
his First Division debut against Cardiff at Up
Park in April 1962, and collected the first of f
Under-23 caps, against Belgium, that same ye
scoring twice in an impressive 6-0 victory.

In the World Cup year of 1966 he was rat
surprisingly given his first full cap, aga
Yugoslavia at Wembley. Ramsey was plotting
switch to his 4-3-3 formation and Peters'
satility, quick pace and stamina made him an id
man for one of the three midfield positions. 'I
excited and astonished. I did not expect to
given a chance so near to the World Cup finals.'

England beat Yugoslavia 2-0 and Pet
accomplished performance made a lasting imp
sion on Ramsey. It was his springboard into
World Cup squad, and he played in all the Wc
Cup matches apart from the goalless ope
against Uruguay.

Not unexpectedly Peters is unswerving in
loyalty to Ramsey. 'Alf's the last bloke to bla
for our exit,' he said after the defeat by W
Germany in the quarter-finals of the 1970 Wc
Cup, a match in which he had given England
apparently safe 2-0 lead. 'He can't go out on
pitch and play for us. It was sickening to see
criticism he had to take. He does a magnificent
for England and will always have the players
his side because he's a players' manager.'

Peters, at just over six feet and a little un
12 stones, is a gazelle of an athlete. He is go
looking in a clean-cut, boyish way and lo
fresh out of college rather than a harde
professional footballer. 'People who call Ma
soft make me laugh,' said an England team-m
not noted for his physical deficiencies. 'He car
hard when it's necessary but he does it in a qu
almost apologetic way.'

But in 1973 he appeared to add a new dim
sion to his character. At Spurs his leaders
became more demonstrative, and when Sir
Ramsey decided to omit Bobby Moore from
internationals against Austria and Poland,
turned to Martin Peters to lead England.

But again the fates proved unkind. In 1
only the Germans' last-minute equaliser
stopped his goal from winning the World C
Now Poland's obstinacy at Wembley en
Peters' strong chance of leading his country
the final stages in Munich. It was a shatter
blow for a man desperate to get to Germany
try to make up for what happened in Mexico.

He had only five years left before he fin
reached his Ramsey appointed time—perh
not time enough.

Above *Bobby Moore (6) and Alan Stephenson
look on anxiously as Peters clears against
Southampton in February 1970. A fortnight
later, after nine seasons at West Ham, he moved
to Spurs. He had made five transfer requests, but
denies that it was because he had to live in the
shadow of Moore and Hurst, who won more recognition after the 1966 World Cup success than he did.
'It was a personal matter between manager Ron
Greenwood and myself,' says Martin. A more
plausible explanation, perhaps, was that Peters was a
victim of his own all-round ability at Upton Park, and
felt that Spurs could provide him with the role he
preferred.*
Left *Peters with his wife Kathy and two children
at his Essex home in 1971.*

Martin PETERS

Honours: World Cup winners medal 1966
European Cup Winners Cup winners medal 1965
League Cup winners medal 1971, 1973
League Cup runners-up medal 1966
UEFA Cup winners medal 1972

Club	Season	League		Int'nls	
		Mtchs	Gls	Mtchs	Gls
West Ham United	1961-62	5			
	1962-63	36	8		
	1963-64	31	3		
	1964-65	35	5		
	1965-66	40	11	8	2
	1966-67	41	14	4	1
	1967-68	40	14	9	5
	1968-69	42	19	8	3
	1969-70	31	6	4	
Tottenham Hotspur	1969-70	7	2	9	4
	1970-71	42	9	7	3
	1971-72	35	10	8	
	1972-73	41	15	8	2
Total		426	116	62	20

No regrets...

a May evening in 1972, in a pub on a corner aisley Road West, Glasgow, a young man in nowy white shirt was standing at the bar, ing an eye on the proceedings, chatting to uccession of customers. In a way, he was ling court.

he pub was full of football fans, and the was of the Scotland-England international ch that had been played that afternoon at npden—a miserable match full of brutal fouls, assless match that had damaged the image of ball itself. The young man in the corner mostly ned. In a Geordie accent somebody said, e, you should have been there, Jim. You d have shown them something.'

Turn it up,' said Jim Baxter. 'Nice of you ay so, all the same.'

ne of the customers came from Nottingham. had a tattered old poster, folded many times, still unmistakable as an advertisement for ther Scotland-England match, the one played Wembley in 1967. Baxter signed the poster him. 'Now,' said the fan, 'I'll get it framed.' he was an Englishman.

ut there were men of many accents who ted a word with Baxter in his pub that ning. Would it be pretentious to call it a pilgrim- Perhaps, but it happens regularly enough.

m Baxter played senior football for Raith ers, Rangers, Sunderland and Nottingham est. To each of these clubs he brought a nt which was unique and yet not always reciated. There were people, who, after that ettable match at Hampden, went to Jim ter's pub for a drink—and to be reminded of eone who was able to play football the way it ht to be played. And that, of course, is where difference of opinions comes in.

Ramsey and the England players have never forgiven Jim Baxter

t all depends on what you want from the ie. If you incline towards the bustling, exciting men, you would have had strong reserva- s about Baxter. If you think speed and power integral factors of football, you might der how Baxter earned his reputation. An lish manager of stature was once quoted as ng: 'I want men who will run through a door me.' Baxter would never have run through any rs: more likely, he would have balanced ball on the tip of his toe while somebody ked for a key. At his best, he was so slim to be fragile, and he was not interested in ving quickly. But he remained one of the tiny d of world footballers who could do things a ball that nobody else could do. And, lly, if you think footballers should be disciplined agons of virtue, Baxter was hardly your man.

lenty of players, of course, have fine trol of a football. This should be one of the cs in a professional. But, to absolute control, Baxter added grace. Watching him, it was ays clear that this was what he had been n to do; and he knew it. With one pass he d break the hearts of half-a-dozen defenders alter the course of a match. In timing and accuracy, his passing was not equalled in career. He could gather around him a ter of frustrated opponents, show them the , tease them, sway to one side and release

a pass of infinite sweetness to a point exactly the right distance ahead of a forward in full flight. Or, depending on how he felt, he would take them all on. Whatever he decided to do the common factor was—grace.

Yet these were physical talents. He would not have reached the heights he did reach without something else, something in the mind. And that could best be described as a monumental arrogance. Without that, he would still have been a very good player, but he would not be remembered in quite the same way for quite the same reasons.

That fan with the 1967 poster was remembering how Baxter, aided and abetted by Denis Law, inflicted a terrible humiliation on England in the year after Ramsey's men had won the World Cup. The score was only 3-2 for Scotland, but the gap between the two sides was vast. In short, Baxter took the mickey—and at Wembley of all places.

Once, inside the English half, he placed his foot on top of the ball, glanced around him with a massive disdain, and strolled away from it: knowing, of course, that Law would get there before any Englishman. Soon after, on the edge of the home penalty area, he played what is known in Scotland as 'keepie-uppie'—juggling the ball in the air with his knees and feet for several seconds. The proud England players, a magnificent side unbeaten since their World Cup triumph,

were reduced to the level of a clumsy bull before a matador. The crowd, or at least the Scots in the crowd, laughed, and laughed hysterically. And while any team can get over a defeat, neither the England players—notably Alan Ball—nor Ramsey, have ever forgiven Jim Baxter for making them the subject of mirth.

Most professional managers, including Bill Shankly, have since said that Scotland would have done better to score more goals that day. Why did Jim Baxter choose instead to taunt the English? The answer to that question could be the answer to his whole personality, and he answers it himself, cautiously.

'I know I've been called arrogant,' he says. 'Well, maybe that's how it looked, and I can't help what people say. But I'll tell you a story about that. When I was about 18, I was picked for the Scotland Under-23s, my first cap. It was against Wales, at Tynecastle. A big day for me.

'I was with Raith then. I go over to Edinburgh, full of myself, all dressed up in my best gear. Really sharp, you know. And I see these lads from Glasgow and England, now they really look something, and suddenly I'm a country yokel. I'm a nobody. All the kids are queuing for their autographs. Me, I'm asked a couple of times, and they look at my signature to see who I am. Well, that was the day I made up my mind I was going to be noticed. I knew I could play, but I had to make sure everybody else knew. But remember this, I never attempted anything on the field that I wasn't confident of bringing off.'

James Curran Baxter was born on 29 September 1939, in a little Fife mining village called Hill O'Beath. His father was a miner, he was an only child and, in due course, he followed his father down the pit. 'Funny thing,' he says, 'at school, all we did, every chance we got, was play football, yet I never got a game for the

Not the 'Slim Jim' of the early sixties, but still unmistakably Baxter; in action for Rangers against Dundee United after his return in 1969.

COLORSPORT

school first team until about six months before I left. I was too skinny I suppose.'

The scouts who watched his school team—Cowdenbeath High—must have been of that opinion. They may well have realized that here was a rare talent, but, even then, the game was beginning to rely overmuch on physical strength. No senior club took a chance on Baxter the schoolboy. But a Fife junior club, Crossgates Primrose, in the person of its coach, Willie Butchart, saw him play for Halbeath Boys' Club. It is recorded that Crossgates Primrose signed Jim Baxter for the usual £2.50 fee—plus £30 extra, which he gave to his mother for a washing machine.

The next stop was Raith Rovers. Remarkably, no other senior club offered Baxter a trial, even though he was holding his own in that hard, tough world of Scottish junior football with its ferocious local rivalries fought out by part-time professionals of all ages.

It may be considered appropriate, all the same, that Raith Rovers also used to employ one Alex James, whose place in Scottish football legend probably exceeds that of Baxter. Bert Herdman was manager of Raith in 1957, when Baxter went to Stark's Park, Kirkcaldy, as a part-time senior professional, while his other labours were in the mine. The signing-on fee was £200, and Herdman never doubted that, for this comparatively tiny sum, he had secured the services of Scotland's finest footballer for many years. 'His fantastic confidence attracted me almost as much as his ability,' he said at the time.

Towards the end of the decade Baxter really began to be noticed, first by the aficionados of the game, then by fans everywhere. But if he was the king of Fife, so to speak, his subjects knew perfectly well that, before long, he would be moving on. No club from a county so sparsely populated as Fife could hope to keep a young player of high class, then or now. He had learned that lesson in the Under-23 international, the game in which he was figuratively cut down to size, and he proceeded to make up for it—in his own mind, at any rate. One match, in 1958 against Rangers at Kirkcaldy, was indeed a significant one. Against the club then recognized as the best in the land, and still thin as he was, he handed out some memorable lessons in the art of playing football; and, in Fife, they still remember that 3-1 Raith victory with fondness.

'If you're good at something, why not give value for money?'

Rangers could not beat Baxter, so they persuaded him to join them. Not that much persuasion was needed. To Baxter, Ibrox promised the ideal vehicle for his talents. For Raith Rovers, the £17,500 fee was a lot of money, and the club needed it. So, in the summer of 1960, Jim Baxter signed for Glasgow Rangers.

Perhaps he was lucky, at least in one respect. His arrival at Ibrox coincided with the emergence of a superb Rangers side, one of the best in the club's entire history, and that's saying something. Of course, it could be put another way: that Baxter's arrival inspired the emergence of that team. Anyway, Rangers fans—so soon to be dominated by Jock Stein and Celtic—were then happy to chorus the praises of their side, with Baxter usually at left-half, partnering Davis and Paterson.

Over the next few years, Rangers won everything there was to win domestically—and Baxter was the centre-piece. In Glasgow he was idolized, and he started to amass his total of Scotland caps. In his first appearance at Wembley, in 1963, he scored the two goals (including a penalty) that gave Scotland victory, and the following year he was chosen to play for the Rest of the World against England at that same stadium. As it happened it was not until the second-half that he was asked to display his talents in the company of such as di Stefano and Puskas, but when he did come on (replacing Josef

Masopust) almost his first touch of the ball was a gloriously casual pass to Puskas which came within inches of resulting in a goal. In such a setting, playing with some of the finest footballers on Earth, Baxter belonged.

With Rangers, he liked nothing more than teasing Celtic—'unless it was England,' he says. After one cup final between the two, won convincingly by Rangers, he tucked the ball up the front of his jersey and walked off with it. He knew the fans would love this, and that he would be 'noticed'. He made no apologies for his showmanship then, and makes none now. 'If you're good at something,' he says, 'and you're paid to do it, why not give value for money?'

During a game he did not hesitate to show off, to clown around a bit. But, all the while, he was seldom less than the most effective part of the team. The manager, Scot Symon, did not have to give any elaborate tactical talks. With Baxter and that other very fine ball-player, Ian McMillan, in the side, briefing could be kept to a minimum. In building up a move, all that was required was to give the ball to either Baxter or McMillan, and they could be relied on to do the rest. Up front, of course, there was Ralph Brand—recalled by Baxter as the sharpest forward he ever played with—Jimmy Millar, and those two most dangerous of wingers, Willie Henderson and Davie Wilson. No wonder the Rangers of that period were virtually unbeatable in Scotland.

'If I had my time over again, I'd probably be exactly the same'

Baxter's best years with Rangers ended with one of his best yet most tragic games. In a European Cup second round tie against Rapid Vienna in the Austrian capital in December 1964 he broke his leg in the last minute of the match. Before that, his superb skills had not only enchanted the 70,000 Viennese but had turned a potentially brutal match into one of composure.

He found it difficult to recapture his real form when the injury healed but, in May 1965, he was still worth the highest fee ever paid to a Scottish club—£72,000—to Sunderland. He could have persevered and kept his exalted status in Glasgow, but money was unquestionably a factor in that transfer. He has never been a man to deprecate the value of hard cash. He explains cuttingly: 'Go into Wylie and Lochhead in Glasgow and order a three-piece suite, a bedroom suite, a new fitted carpet, and then tell the salesman when he talks about payment: "Well, I've got so many Scottish Cup medals, lots of international caps, and some championship medals." What'll he say? He'll reckon you're round the bend, right?'

Baxter continued to play a great deal of elegant football at Roker Park, also winning ten more caps, but it was the beginning of the end of his playing career, though he was only 26 when he joined them. They know what football is all about on Wearside, and they admired his skills, but he simply could not produce them often enough in the demanding Football League, where the competition—if not necessarily the quality—is so much higher than in Scotland. Even so, Nottingham Forest paid £100,000 for him in December 1967. Few people could understand, since it was obvious that, even at 28, he did not have much longer left in big-time football. He stayed less than two years at the City Ground, eventually being given a free transfer after there had been no customers at £40,000 and then at £20,000. He played just 50 times for a sadly unsuccessful Forest. Add on his wages and he had cost over £2,000 a game.

He was then snapped up by Rangers in a blaze of publicity, played a few games for them, and was given another 'free'. Then, at the age of 30, Jim Baxter packed it in. He now has his pub, an exceedingly attractive wife, Jean, and two boys. Many would envy him. And many criticize him. A fool to himself, they say. If only he had

Jim BAXTER

Honours: Scottish League Championship medal 1960-61, 1962-63, 1963-64
Scottish Cup winners medal 1962, 1963
Scottish League Cup winners medal 1960-61, 1961-62, 1963-64, 1964-65

Club	Season	League		Int'nls	
		Mtchs	Gls	Mtchs	Gls
Raith Rovers	1957-58	3	1		
	1958-59	26			
	1959-60	32	2		
Rangers	1960-61	27	1	4	
	1961-62	29	2	6	1
	1962-63	32	5	7	2
	1963-64	26	4	4	
	1964-65	22	6	3	
Sunderland	1965-66	35	7	6	
	1966-67	37	3	3	
	1967-68	16		1	
Nottingham Forest	1967-68	22	2		
	1968-69	26	1		
Rangers	1969-70	14			
Total		347	34	34	3

2

5

3

6

4

SYNDICATION INTERNATIONAL/POPPERFOTO/ASSOCIATED PRESS/PRESS ASSOCIATION

Jim Baxter takes advantage of a throw-in to shelter from the rain at Airdrie in August 1969. Rangers, with whom he had enjoyed his greatest years, had taken him back on a free transfer from Nottingham Forest. The week before 2 Baxter had played against Raith, his first club. But he could not hold a regular place at Ibrox, and retired at the end of the season—at 30.

3 Jim scores from the spot against England in 1963—his first Wembley appearance. The Scots won 2-1—and Baxter scored both goals.

4 In December 1964, after a superb display against Rapid in Vienna, Baxter broke his leg in the last minute. When he recovered he moved to England, but in a sense it proved to be the start of the slide, despite the fact that he was only 26.

5 Baxter gets in a header for his first English club, Sunderland, against Fulham in 1966.

6 Sunderland had paid £72,000 for him the previous year. He was never at his peak at Roker Park, but in 1967 Forest reckoned he was worth £100,000. He was to cost them over £2,000 a match.

looked after himself, if only he hadn't been so fond of the *dolce vita* . . . if only . . .

Jim Baxter listens to all this impatiently. 'Listen,' he says, 'don't talk to me of regrets. You've heard the song. No regrets. That's me. Anybody who goes around moaning about what they should have done in the past should see a head-shrinker. You know this . . . if I had my time over again, I'd probably be exactly the same.'

In truth, Baxter might have played for two or three more years, had he looked after himself. But he did like a drink, he did like a night out as often as possible and, towards the end, he was a far cry from being the 'Slim Jim' of the early sixties. 'What I did? I enjoyed myself, that's what,' he says.

So what is the criterion? Jim Baxter not only enjoyed himself, he gave enjoyment to others. How could it be said that he abused his talent when he played such a wealth of memorable football at the highest level? Even in his decline with Sunderland and Nottingham Forest, he

sometimes gave glimpses of his best, and, despite a certain chubbiness around the waistline, his best could be better than anything else seen in the immediate vicinity.

Again, it's all a matter of opinion. There are those who pay their admission money and who are not satisfied unless they see 90 minutes of running. Then there are those who will happily pay to see just a few minutes of class. Each school of thought has its own validity.

It is also doubtless arguable that during his five years with Rangers, Baxter was the best half-back in the world. But it surely cannot be a contentious statement that, in the rich history of Scottish football, James Curran Baxter ranks among the top ten. For many, his status is considerably higher than that. He had his crowded hour, all right, and that Geordie who, on the night of the 1972 Hampden international, told him in his pub that he should have been out there on the park in the blue shirt of Scotland . . . well, the tragedy is he was still young enough.

Above *In the 1970 FA Cup Final against Che[lsea],
Billy Bremner moves towards Johnny Giles [who]
breasts down the ball. Working together, these [two]
are the lynch-pin of Leeds.*

Inset *Giles blasts in a penalty past Gordon [West?].
At moments like this, Bremner prefers to look awa[y]*

**THE
MIDDLE-MEN**

Giles and Bremner - a two-man army

Johnny Giles places the ball almost lovingly on the penalty spot, retreats a few paces, accelerates into that fluttering stride of his and places the ball wide of the goalkeeper.

Yet, however often it may happen, it is a sight that Billy Bremner has not seen very often. Superstition demands that he must not look at such critical moments, so he turns his back and squats on his heels. This is one of the rare moments when Leeds United are in action that Bremner cannot bear to watch, one of the moments when the highly productive midfield partnership, which brought Leeds so near so many of football's greatest triumphs, breaks down.

Hair so red, face so pale, his colleagues called him 'Chalky'

At first glance the Bremner-Giles link seems to have been an unlikely partnership—Bremner small and frail in appearance, hair so red and face so pale that his colleagues call him 'Chalky'; Giles slightly more muscular and yet almost delicate as he hovers over the ball.

Appearances could scarcely be more deceptive. Both are men who know how to look after themselves. Bremner plays with a belligerence that is a product of his humble Scottish upbringing, which demanded that he should be first or nowhere. He hurls himself into a game, making extravagant demands of himself and of his team.

He is as expressive on the field as he is outspoken off it. Studiously thoughtful about football, he still has an inborn sense of fun which emerges in lighter moments, even in moments of stress.

When Billy Bremner fell and banged his head on the ground during Leeds United's European Cup semi-final against Celtic in 1970 he suffered concussion and blurred vision. But, as on so many other occasions, the pitch probably suffered more damage than he did. His bones might be constructed of steel and his muscles of reinforced concrete. His energy might be the by-product of an atomic power station. He just does not know how to stop.

It is only when you look into his steel blue eyes beneath the conspicuous flame hair that you appreciate the character of the man.

He has the outstanding qualities demanded of a leader, of the captain of Leeds United in an era when the club achieved more than ever before in their history.

Giles is a leader, too, though in a different way. Persuasive, thoughtful, with a quietly spoken voice which has its roots in Dublin, he is a considerate man, a businessman type.

He is rated by players and managers alik[e] one of the most accomplished midfield pla[yers] in the world and yet, because he plays for I[reland] he has rarely had the chance to establish him[self] in the international arena.

Unlike Bremner, who pays little heed injuries, Giles is often prone to injuries, som[e] which have had a lasting effect.

He was not always a midfield player. Be[fore] he was transferred from Manchester United £37,500 in August 1963—the signing [must] surely rank among the bargains of all time—[he] played on the right wing, collecting an FA [Cup] Final winners medal against Leicester City a [few] months earlier.

For years he waited on the wing for his chance to move inside

But it had always been his ambition to di[rect] and general a team from midfield. For s[ome] years, both with Manchester United and Le[eds] he waited on the wing for the chance to m[ove] inside.

He had to be patient, but when Bobby Co[llins] broke a leg in Leeds's first away Europea[n tie] in the Fairs Cup in Turin in 1965, man[ager] Don Revie knew without question or hesita[tion] the player on whom the midfield responsib[ility] would fall.

Giles was ready and equipped for it characteristically he dismissed the burden saying: 'There's a lot of responsibility physical effort involved, but it's the job

...ove Johnny Giles goes in to a tackle with ...ncis Lee, another player who doesn't dodge trouble. ...et Flat on his back in a Scottish international ...inst Wales, Bremner was to get up and play on as ...ugh nothing had happened. His tough, wiry body ...ns immune to the inevitable knocks.

...nted ever since I joined Manchester United ... boy.'

...The success he made of it has been reflected ...the results which have made Leeds one of the ...st consistent teams in English football.

...When Bremner and Giles are in action there ...ms to be some sort of mental telepathy between ...m—a mysterious quality more often described ...football as understanding. But it goes deeper ...n that.

...They have a great respect for each other, ...reciating each other's skills. Bremner has a ...n eye for an opening. He can thread the ball ...ough a defence. He knows when to go forward ...en Giles is in possession and expects rather ...n demands the ball to be placed at his feet.

...Giles's strength is not so much in his ability ...produce through passes as to change the ...ection of an attack unexpectedly, to fling ...g passes over a defence into an unprotected ...a. He searches for the vulnerable points and ...ds them with a chilling certainty.

One headline read: 'Bremner can go, say his club, Leeds'

Yet the partnership might have foundered ...ore it flourished. It might never have existed.

...the months when Giles was assisting ...nchester United to reach Wembley in 1963 ...emner became restive. He was a young man ...th a young man's ambitions and Leeds United ...that time did not seem to offer him the scope ...achieve them.

...One headline of February 1963 read: 'Bremner

can go, say Leeds.' The asking price was £30,000, a figure which sounded ridiculous some eight years later. Possibly it may have been a move merely to satisfy him without any intention of letting him go because Don Revie, then settling in as manager, knew his exceptional value. In the early seventies, it seemed unlikely that Leeds would sell him at any price.

He stayed and helped Leeds to become a power in football. But his fiery nature, evident from the moment he made his League debut a month after joining the Elland Road club in 1959, frequently landed him in disciplinary trouble.

He collected suspensions and fines like other players score goals. He learned his lesson the hard way, but having learned it he still contrived to retain the aggression which was such an essential part of his game.

He once called himself: 'The biggest little fool in football.' His record of misconduct branded him throughout the game and it is a tribute to his character that he has overcome it so successfully that, when he became Footballer of the Year in 1970, he was paid this tribute by Vernon Stokes, the chairman of the FA disciplinary committee. 'I could not be happier that the trophy has gone to Billy. He is a changed man completely. He has always been a first-rate player but his temper has let him down in the past. In the last couple of seasons he has learned to control himself. He is now an example to the game.'

Bremner's fury often stemmed from his refusal to believe that the opposition had any right to control the play. 'I hate to see the opposition having that ball,' he says. 'After all it's my job in midfield to see they don't have it too often.'

Men who appreciate the physical and mental demands on the modern footballer are at a loss to explain how a player with such a slight frame can produce such prodigious effort. It is beyond even Don Revie. 'It is a constant mystery to all of us,' he says. 'I think more than anything it stems from dedication and character. I don't

think there is a comparable player in the modern game, not when you bear in mind the weight and frame of him. There can have been few others in the past who poured so much into a game. Hughie Gallagher perhaps. Where he gets it from is beyond me. I think he must have been well fed when he was a youngster.'

Billy knows the source of his energy stretches back to the days when he played as a skinny little lad with bigger boys and even men in his formative years in Scotland. He was not big enough, but he had to be good enough to compete and the only way he knew was to throw himself into a game and if necessary straight at an opponent.

Why did Bremner find himself in so much trouble to start with?

Maybe that is why he landed in so much trouble in his early seasons in League football. He continued to throw himself at bigger men. Even when he learned the error of his ways he continued to flog himself unmercifully, but insisted: 'You don't feel the physical part of it while you're playing. Immediately afterwards there might still be no reaction. Then about midnight you flop.' And he has been known to sleep for 12 or 13 hours after a game.

The reaction of opponents during a match is much more immediate and startling. After Bremner learned to calm his fiery temperament, the opposition still frequently tried to take advantage of him, goading him, provoking him, but he met them all with a controlled aggression that was a delight to his manager and team-mates.

Bremner, one of the few personalities who have had race horses named after them, illustrated his resilience in 1970 when he played for seven weeks with a knee ligament injury that would have put most players out for a month. 'That is Billy Bremner and the character of the man,' said

Above *Challenged by Bobby Charlton, Giles de*
turns the ball past him.
Inset *In the Fairs Cup final 1971, which Leeds*
on the away-goals rule, Bremner and Jack Char
leap up to cause panic in the Juventus goalmo
It was the second time Leeds had won the trophy.

Don Revie almost in awe.

There are two men in football who have sometimes been likened to James Cagney. One is
Bill Shankly, the other Billy Bremner. But
Cagney, even if he could play the game, could
never achieve what Billy has achieved without a
machine gun in his hands.

'He's a marvellous skipper, leading by the
example of his skill and tenacity, temperament
and fight,' says Don Revie. 'He's like Dave
Mackay and Frank McLintock. Both of them
rolled into one if you like. A born captain. Billy
on one leg is better than a lot on two. I get a
warm feeling just thinking about what he's done
for this club—and what he's going to do.'

One of the most influential games Bremner
ever played was in the FA Cup semi-final replay
against Manchester United at Nottingham
Forest's ground in 1965 after a brawl of a draw at
Hillsborough, Sheffield.

As players began to flag in extra time, drained
by the exacting demands and tension of such a
critical match, Bremner summoned reserves of
energy. It was unbelievable that he should have a
reserve at all after the effort he had poured into
the game already. And though never unobtrusive
in a match, he has the ability to steal silently
into the penalty area, as he did at Nottingham
to score the winning goal and send Leeds to
Wembley.

When the footballer
makes earls, managers
and directors sing

The tension did not end there for him because,
once again, Bremner was in disciplinary trouble,
and lived on a knife-edge of uncertainty
about whether he would be suspended at the time
of the Cup Final against Liverpool. His luck
held. The FA was compassionate, fined him £100
and suspended him for seven days.

His dominance and leadership extends beyond

the pitch and the dressing-room. Even in moments
of celebration when the Leeds players forget
their dedication and let their hair down Billy is
the leader.

He takes over the stage, underlines his
authority with a walking stick which he always
seems to unearth from somewhere and demands
that everybody must sing individually. Directors,
Don Revie, even the Earl of Harewood, who is the
club's president . . . nobody is safe. They all
have to do a turn.

Giles is quiet and restrained in comparison.
There is nothing of the showman, no hint of the
Cagney about him. While Bremner is acting as
master of ceremonies at the occasional party,
Giles can usually be found quietly sipping a drink.

He has one prized possession of which the
other Leeds players were envious for so long, the
FA Cup winners medal that was his prize for
playing in Manchester United's Wembley team
of 1963.

Since then he has helped Leeds to reach more
Cup Finals. The first in 1965 they lost in extra-
time to Liverpool and they lost the second to
Chelsea in 1970 after a draw at Wembley and a
replay at Old Trafford.

'One losers medal is more than enough,' he
said then. 'Two are unbearable. It must have been
heartbreaking for the other lads to lose a second
time. At least I have had the consolation and the
exhilaration of winning at Wembley.'

It was a satisfaction he at last shared with his
Leeds team-mates in 1972 when they beat Arsenal
by the only goal at Wembley. But there was
further heart-break the following year when they
lost dramatically to Sunderland.

He had joined United at 15 from the Dublin
junior club Stella Maris and was already an
Eire international at schoolboy level. He learnt
much of his football from his father Dicky
who played for Shelbourne.

Somehow though, Giles felt that he did not quite
fit in, that his talent was not completely
appreciated, and he became convinced of it at

the start of the 1963–64 season when, al
with other Manchester United players, he
dropped in one of the rare purges that Sir M
Busby carried out after indifferent performanc

'It was the worst day's
work Manchester
United have ever done'

Giles asked for a transfer and the club gran
it. His brother-in-law Nobby Stiles, who marr
Johnny's sister Kay, maintains: 'I still think
day Manchester United let Johnny go to Le
was the worst day's work the club have ever do
Don Revie is inclined to agree with that opini
'He was just the kind of player we needed
what we decided was to be an all-out push
promotion.'

But he could hardly have realized at the ti
just how valuable Giles would be, the v
part he was destined to play in what beca
Leeds United's annual pursuit of the gan
major prizes in the sixties and early seventies.

Leeds won promotion in 1964 with Giles on
right wing, and finished runners-up in the Lea
Championship and the FA Cup the following ye

'When I left Old Trafford I closed one d
and opened another at Elland Road,' says Gi
'Somehow I felt I wasn't improving quic
enough at Old Trafford.'

He served a second apprenticeship with Le
on the wing until Bobby Collins broke his l
He was the perfect successor for a man who l
been in at the start of the Leeds revolution.

His game did not have the raw edge of
belligerent Collins, but he compensated for

The winning combination of Bremner and Giles ...res another victory against Crystal Palace.

...ve Once Bremner was continually in trouble ... referees, but Revie wisely made him captain, ...uraging his sense of responsibility.

...ht Bremner stands waiting alert at the goalpost.

...a more subtle approach. His acute sense of ...nce enabled him to conceal passes which often ... the opposition by surprise. Opposing teams ...uently detail a man to shadow him, to ...ent him from creating space for himself, ...lam the door in his face. 'But Johnny has ... fantastic ability to shake them off,' says ... Revie. 'He always seems to have time, if ... to spare, but time to get in the most damage.'

...ve all Giles rarely becomes ruffled, refuses ... provoked—and once suffered for it.

...uring a Fairs Cup tie against Real Zaragoza ...pain he was punched in the back and grabbed ...he throat. The offender was sent off—and ...as Johnny for the first time in his career.

...ven then he remained calm and collected, ... dignified. Later that same evening he was ...rly hurt by the referee's decision, but refused ...ear a verbal strip off the referee. He merely ...ad his hands in a gesture of amazement ... said simply: 'I don't know why I was sent ...oo. I didn't do anything wrong.'

'A player of my size has got to be able to look after himself'

...ater he was exonerated by the FA disciplinary ...mmittee, a decision which did not surprise him ...he least. Justice, he felt, had been done.

...ut Johnny Giles is far from soft. He can be ...tly tough when the situation demands it. ...onents have used the word sly to describe ... in his tougher moments. Any player who has ...e into contact with him at such moments will ...lily testify to his ability to look after himself

—sometimes with bruises to show for the confrontation.

Giles does not find his size a handicap. 'It's easier for a small player to avoid physical contact than a taller one because being so nimble he can usually get out of trouble before it arrives,' he says. 'A player of my size has got to be able to look after himself, otherwise opponents might take advantage of it. You have to give them the message that they aren't the only ones who can dish it out. It makes them think before doing it again.'

If Giles does have a criticism of his game, a weakness, it is in his inability to score more goals. 'I did have a spell at Leeds when I was used as a pure striker and it made me appreciate the difficulties of playing in the thick of it. It is my job in midfield to create goals rather than score them. But I feel I ought to be able to go through and score more often.'

He is the player who always takes the penalties. He has so perfected the art that his failure rate is remarkably low. 'I never remember the ones that scored,' he says, 'but I can tell you right away the ones that didn't. Penalties don't worry me until I miss one. People say a professional should never miss from the spot which is why it's a greater strain than trying to score an ordinary goal.'

If there is a strain on him it certainly does not show. 'The calm way he approaches the job, often at a vital stage, is quite remarkable,' says Revie.

Over the years Leeds have benefited from both Bremner's and Giles' change of loyalties. As a boy Bremner was Celtic-daft, but turned his back on the Glasgow club because he felt they had too many good players and went to Elland Road because of the greater opportunity offered there. Manchester United was Giles's first love. The love affair ended in 1963 and so began one of the greatest partnerships in modern football, a partnership that seemed certain to continue for as long as their football lives.

Billy BREMNER

Honours: FA Cup winners medal, 1972; FA Cup runners-up medal, 1965, 1970, 1973; Fairs Cup runners-up medal, 1967; Fairs Cup winners medal, 1968, 1971; League Cup winners medal, 1968; League Championship medal, 1969

Club	Season	League		Int'nls	
		Mtchs	Gls	Mtchs	Gls
Leeds United	1959-60	11	2		
	1960-61	31	9		
	1961-62	39	12		
	1962-63	24	10		
	1963-64	39	2		
	1964-65	40	6	1	
	1965-66	41	8	6	
	1966-67	37	2	3	
	1967-68	36	3	2	
	1968-69	42	6	8	2
	1969-70	35	4	3	
	1970-71	25	3	2	
	1971-72	41	5	9	
	1972-73	38	4	5	
Total		479	76	39	2

Johnny GILES

Honours: FA Cup winners medal, 1963, 1972; FA Cup runners-up medal, 1965, 1970, 1973; Fairs Cup runners-up medal, 1967; Fairs Cup winners medal, 1968, 1971; League Cup winners medal, 1968; League Championship medal, 1969

Club	Season	League		Int'nls	
		Mtchs	Gls	Mtchs	Gls
Manchester United	1959-60	10	2	2	1
	1960-61	23	2	4	
	1961-62	30	2	3	1
	1962-63	35	4	2	
Leeds United	1963-64	40	6	7	1
	1964-65	39	6	1	
	1965-66	40	6	4	
	1966-67	29	12	2	
	1967-68	20	6		
	1968-69	32	8	2	1
	1969-70	32	13	3	
	1970-71	33	13	1	
	1971-72	38	6		
	1972-73	33	6		
Total		434	92	31	4

THE
MIDDLE-MEN

Return of the rebel

On the face of it, Gunter Netzer seemed to be the perfect fit for the role of playboy. His car? A Ferrari DT Gino Sports. His girl? A delightful blond called Hannelore. His business? A discotheque named Lovers Lane. His wage? A cool £30,000 a year. The title of his biography? The Rebel of Football.

Up to a point the image is accurate, but inevitably it ignores a lot. In the first place it is the game itself and not the life-style that goes with it that is Netzer's first consideration. He knows that Netzer the footballer will be remembered long after Netzer the playboy. So he takes his job seriously, training hard and keeping regular hours. The applause for his performances in the early seventies was a reward for a lot of hard work in leaner years before.

Netzer's earlier career had been fitful. The same age as Franz Beckenbauer, by 1973 he had won half the number of caps as the West German captain. That can be put down to a number of factors, not least the coolness of his relationship with Helmut Schoen, manager of the West German side. A player who could say, as Netzer did, that he 'acts according to the will, in football just as in outside life' was not the easiest to fit into the methodical kind of team that Schoen wanted.

The tension between the two frequently flared up in public. Netzer put it on record in no uncertain terms: 'It's no secret that Schoen and I were at loggerheads in Mexico. I wanted to play in the team in such and such a way, and he wanted to do things that I disliked.'

It was, perhaps, the very arrogance of statements like that which cost Netzer his place in the team. Certainly with Beckenbauer, Wolfgang Overath and Helmut Haller in West Germany's midfield positions, it was hardly an attitude he could have afforded to take.

The clouds, which had then seemed to have set in for his career, cleared suddenly in late 1970. Overath was injured, Haller lost form, Beckenbauer moved to the back four, and Netzer won his place in midfield. A string of brilliant games allayed all previous doubts about his temperament and consistency. He dominated the European Championship game against England at Wembley in 1972, several times taking the ball from one penalty area to the other on single runs.

His long passing would have been a credit to Haynes at his best. For West Germany's vital second goal against Belgium in the semi-final of the European Championship he swerved a pass from the centre-spot to the edge of the opponents' penalty area, setting up Muller with the chance. Gyula Lorant, centre-half in the Hungarian side that beat England 6-3 at Wembley compared him to Josef Bozsik, right-half that day: 'The same confidence, technique, accuracy in passing; only Netzer is more dynamic.'

It was a remarkable change from the situation around the time of the 1970 World Cup, from which he was barred by injury. Reflecting on those days, Netzer said, 'I didn't kick a ball for nine weeks, and I felt like giving the game up altogether. It's like a roller coaster, football. One minute you're on top of everything, the next you're at the bottom again.' That may or may not be true for football, but it certainly is for Netzer.

He was born on 14 September 1944. He first played for IFC Monchengladbach in the summer of 1963. He gained two international caps as a schoolboy and was also selected once for the B-team, as well as for Germany's Youth side. He received his first cap in a friendly against Austria on 9 October 1965.

Leave Netzer to me—Storey

Left A Russian defender's boot finds its mark on Netzer's knee. Although he did well in West Germany's 3-0 win against the Russians in the 1972 European Championship final, Netzer has often been intimidated by determined marking.
Above Peter Storey lived up to this dubious boast, driving Netzer deep into his own half in the second leg of the quarter-final of the 1972 European Championship. At Wembley in the first leg Netzer had been given a free run of midfield, and played brilliantly in West Germany's 3-1 win.
Below left Netzer, taking the captain's part for Borussia Monchengladbach. In 1972-73 he captained his club side from a central defensive position.
Below Netzer awaits the attentions of another Russian defender.

After a 4-1 win, manager Helmut Schoen picked Netzer for the next game, a World Cup qualifying tie against Cyprus, which Germany won 6-0. But after an appearance against England at Wembley in February 1966, which the Germans lost 0-1, he was dropped and eventually omitted from the World Cup squad.

Throughout the late sixties, Netzer was in and out of the national side—with more outs than ins. He was sent off in Chile on a South American tour in 1968 when he fouled an opponent, incensing another enough to punch him before they were both dismissed. That incident cost him his place for nine games, and his return was no happier. Selected to play against Spain in Seville in February 1970, he was alleged to have said, after a bad 2-0 defeat for which he was severely criticized, that he would never again play for West Germany.

The end of this rather wayward period coincided with the tremendous improvement of his club side, Borussia Monchengladbach. Built by Hennes Weismeiler around Netzer, the captain, they twice won the Bundesliga (1970, 1971). Netzer acquired enormous confidence.

This connection between Netzer's form and that of Borussia Monchengladbach is more than just coincidence. In an average team, which Borussia Monchengladbach were for several years in the late sixties, Netzer would only spasmodically appear very much more than an average player; only in a team as good as his club's or country's in the early seventies could he look a really great one. Netzer feeds off the quality of those around him, in particular his partners in midfield for Borussia Monchengladbach and West Germany, Jupp Heynckes and Herbert Wimmer. 'I owe a lot to Wimmer,' Netzer has pointed out. 'Without him I would never have the time to put on my tricks and set my sights for long passes.'

If there is any weakness in Netzer's play, it is his dislike for being closely marked. Jurgen Friedrich, a Kaiserslautern player who several times marked Netzer out of the game, once remarked, 'The answer to Netzer is simple. All you have to do is detail a strong, forceful man to mark him, to follow his every move and prevent him developing those devastating forward rushes.'

In the second leg of the European Championship tie against England, Peter Storey did just that. Netzer reacted—as he usually does—by retreating as far back as his own penalty box. It is in that area of the pitch that he prefers to play, and it was there, performing a similar role to Beckenbauer, that Netzer was playing for Borussia Monchengladbach in 1972-73.

It is perhaps to escape from close-marking that Netzer exaggerates the effects of any harsh tackle made against him. It is something he is quite open about. Asked why he did it, he replied blandly, 'To intimidate my opponents. The crowd always howl when a player is pole-axed, while most referees are more likely to send the fouler off.'

It was all a bit unconventional, but then that is Netzer, admired in Hollywood (Elke Sommer was rumoured to be his most ardent admirer) and even mentioned in government circles—he once had a two hour discussion with the leader of the West German opposition party, Dr Reiner Barzel.

There was doubtless more to the conversation than the German equivalent of 'It was never a foul', but one can only speculate what Dr Barzel would have made of Netzer. In 1972, at 27 and at the peak of his career, Netzer still had all the radicalism of youth in character.

In the summer of 1973 he turned his back on Borussia Monchengladbach and moved to Real Madrid. Inevitably the transfer added further controversy to his career. Helmut Schoen was reported to say that Netzer would never play again for the national side. With the World Cup finals so imminent one doubted whether he could afford such a decision. It was yet another twist to the story of the Rebel of Football.

Gunter NETZER

Honours: European Championship winners medal 1972
West German League Championship medal 1970, 1971
West German Footballer of the Year 1972
UEFA Cup runners-up medal, 1973

**THE
MIDDLE-MEN**

Alan Ball— made, not born

Alan Ball was not born to be a football great. He was made into a footballer by an ambitious father, and he made himself into a great one with his own dedication and determination.

Everton manager Harry Catterick, who bought him from Blackpool in 1966 and set what was then a transfer record between British clubs of £110,000, had a bargain. 'Of course every player has his price,' he said some years later. 'Alan's is one million pounds.'

When asked if he would sell at that price, Catterick replied: 'No, but I would consider it first.'

Yet in December 1971 Ball *was* sold, to Arsenal. The fee was somewhat short of Catterick's earlier valuation, but at £200,000 it was then a British record. Everton fans were aghast at the sudden deal. So were some players.

In the eyes of Howard Kendall, team-mate and one of his midfield partners, Ball was: 'A player beyond price. To my mind he's worth more to his club than any player in Britain. It's impossible to put a price on his value to Everton. Others may be more talented, but no one can give to a team over a long, hard season more than Ballie gives to Everton.'

Kendall had said this of Ball in the days before the player and Everton lost faith in each other. But what made Ball, only 5ft 6in and 10st, worth such tributes, worth such a fee?

For one thing he can, better than almost any

other player, make others play. He is always going for space, making it easy for others to find him. His running without the ball, taking weight off his colleagues, is tremendous. He has a sharp brain that helps him to 'steal' the ball in midfield. He can go on and on through a game winning it without making a tackle. Most sides in modern football have equipped themselves with a hard man to win possession for others. Ball has done this job by thinking quicker than his opponents—and then he has used the ball better than most.

He can score goals, too, although his annual tally has become progressively smaller. This could have been due to a persistent groin injury— one that forced him to take a complete rest from the game in the autumn of 1971, much to the disappointment of his fans. Certainly, from the summer of the previous year, after doing so much to make Everton Champions and helping England in the World Cup in Mexico, he had a long, depressing spell when he was only a shadow of his former self.

But at his best he did score goals. Most often they were important ones. For a man who worked so hard in midfield, his scoring record in the First Division was impressive.

With struggling Blackpool—they were relegated the season after he left—he registered 41 in three successful seasons. In his first four years with Everton his League total was 60. In

four of those seven campaigns, though he ne[ver] played as an out-and-out striker, he was [top] scorer at his club.

Most of those goals came because Ball had [fast] reactions, superb control and courage that t[ook] him into situations where the studs were fly[ing] and the bigger men were in command.

Above all, he can, by example, lift a team [to] new efforts. He is the man, as the 1966 Wo[rld] Cup final against West Germany showed, w[ho] never stops running.

In those memorable but exhausting two ho[urs] at Wembley Ball not only sold himself to [the] football public as a player of world stature, [he] also sold himself to Everton.

He was 21. All the other Everton regulars [at] the time were older. But he transformed the[m.] The week before the opening of the next seas[on] Everton, the FA Cup holders, were beaten [by] Liverpool in the Charity Shield match at Goodis[on] Park. Liverpool were so much the better te[am] that the 1-0 scoreline was an injustice.

A unanimous opinion: 'Only Alan Ball could have scored that goal'

Two days after that game Catterick went quietly to snap up Ball, who was then unsett[led] with Blackpool and apparently set for Leeds. [In] his first appearance for his new club he sco[red] the only goal to give them victory at Fulham. [A] week later he went in among fearsome defend[ers] like big Ron Yeats and Tommy Smith, sco[red] twice in 17 minutes, and led Everton to a [4-1] triumph over their old rivals from Anfield.

Later that season he broke the deadlock in [an] FA Cup meeting between the Mersey giants w[ith] a goal that summed up his main qualities [—] quick reactions, courage, control and accuracy [—] chasing a ball that everyone else had given up [as] dead and scoring from an almost impossi[ble] angle. The other players were unanimous: 'O[nly] Alan Ball could have scored it.'

Over the years he went on lifting Everton—

GERRY CRANHAM

RAY GREEN

SYNDICATION INTERNATIONAL

ft Alan Ball in a goalmouth incident in the 1966 World Cup final. After ng sent off in an Under-23 match against Austria he was terrified that msey would leave him out of the World Cup squad. Ramsey didn't—and s never given cause to regret his decision.

ove But Ball has never been one to keep his feelings bottled up. In a match inst QPR in 1969 he makes them very clear. Though he now controls his per when playing for England, he has had more trouble doing so with his club.

Top Alan Ball and Johnny Giles, another tough little fighter, race to the ball, neither prepared to give an inch to the other.
Above Young Alan plays chess with Big Alan. If ever a father influenced his son, it was Alan Ball senior. A professional footballer himself, though never in the big-time, he was determined that his son should be the best footballer in the world. And his father's determination was matched by that of Alan himself. Ballie wanted only one thing—to win!

the League title in 1970, to high First Division cings in every other year except 1971, to mbley in 1968, and to two semi-finals.

His consistently high level of performance s remarkable. Ray Wilson, Everton and English orld Cup colleague, said: 'You rarely see a yer in the modern game string together more n three outstanding performances. I've seen lie play 12 blinders on the trot.'

By the time he was 26 his claims to greatness d been underlined at international level by Ramsey, who had played him 50 times for gland.

Alan James Ball was born 12 May 1945 at rnworth, near Bolton. This is an area in ncashire where many of the great names in tball like Tommy Lawton, Nat Lofthouse and ancis Lee first saw the light of day. But Ball s not blessed with the physique or talent at marked him out as a natural.

Tony Waiters, Blackpool and England goal-eper, remembers seeing him for the first time en he was a kid sweeping out the dressing-oms at Bloomfield Road. 'He was small, almost ny, and he had this Bolton twang. My first pression was that he would not make the grade football. But I was to find out that he had s total dedication to the game. He talked about thing else. Everything was geared to it.

'He became a great player because he was termined to become a great player. Everything s come as a result of this determination—even skill. He's not a natural. He's a manufactured yer. But that doesn't detract from his greatness.'

Those few who would detract from it point to deficiencies. He cannot stand and deliver like bby Charlton, hitting long, raking passes with th feet; he cannot crack spectacular 20-yard

goals like Francis Lee; he cannot dribble like George Best, outstrip a defence like Steve Heighway, soar to produce headers like Denis Law; he cannot always be relied on in the heat of battle to keep his temper.

It is his temperament that points up the major inconsistencies in the Alan Ball career. His fiery temper has made him a fierce competitor on behalf of every team he has played for and a wonderful team-mate. It has also made him his own, and his side's, worst enemy.

'I've seen him burst into tears when we've lost a game'

But Kendall, who has been his room-mate on away trips and probably knows him better than anyone in the game except Alan Ball senior, who manages Preston North End, looks on the credit side:

'He takes defeat worse than any player I've ever known. I've seen him burst into tears when we've lost a game. It's not my way and most of the other lads are the same as me. But we don't mind Ballie being different. We know this hatred of defeat helps him to be the great player he is. And he doesn't just hate losing a match—he hates losing the ball.'

Ball hates to lose at anything. To lighten the mood in training the Everton players awarded a booby prize to the man voted the worst per-former in five-a-side games. Once, for a joke, Ball was presented with the special jersey. He was never given it a second time.

On the debit side are the dismissals and cautions, the suspensions and fines. Ball has

always been acutely aware of the problem, right from his first few matches at Blackpool. Manager Ron Suart and Ball's father worried about the problem, and both had long talks with the impetuous young player about it.

Ball recounted later: 'My father felt it would be a good thing to try to get on with referees. He said it wouldn't do me any harm to show them respect and chat them up a bit. I tried it at Bolton. As we all lined up for the kick-off I chatted pleasantly with the ref, addressing him very respectfully, talking about the weather and wishing him a good game. He booked me later on.

'Another time my father advised me to show what a good sport I was by collecting the ball when it went out of play, even if the throw or the kick wasn't ours. I tried that when Blackpool played at Everton. I ran behind for the ball after it had gone behind for a goal-kick, picked it up and ran back with it. The ref told me to stop taking the Mick. It really seemed I couldn't win.'

In 1965 Ball feared he was finished with England almost before his international career had properly started. He was sent off in an Under-23 match in Austria for throwing the ball at the referee—most of his trouble has been through showing dissent.

A year later, after helping England to win the World Cup, he talked about that fear: 'I thought I had thrown away my big chance. I had a reputation as a bad boy and this was bound to make things worse. I had been foolish and I was going to pay for it.

'But Alf got hold of me and told me he was looking to me to help England in the World Cup —but he couldn't risk playing with ten men. I could see his point. I was a risk. But he seemed to have a lot of confidence in me and picked me

COLORSPORT

Single-minded concentration shows on Ball's face as he sits on the sidelines in his unaccustomed position of substitute for Everton. At that moment nothing else exists. He is more than in love with the game—he is totally obsessed by it.

again. From that day I have never been in trouble while playing for England.'

And he stayed out of trouble until his temper let him down in Katowice in 1973.

Indeed, Ball even began his career with his new club, Arsenal, under the shadow of a suspension, having collected three cautions in his last year with Everton. Arsenal had paid a large part of that enormous fee for Ball's spirit, now they had to wait to discover whether they could get the spirit without the temper.

Ball admits to a different attitude towards his club and his country: 'I would play for England for nothing, but not for a club. I am employed by them, I should get paid for doing the job.' Arsenal wages, reputed to be not less than £12,000 a year, seemed to suggest that the job they expected from Ball would be demanding.

The eternal optimist, the leader who will never admit defeat

They hoped for the effect he had on Everton both as player and captain. Allthrough his career he has had this ability to lift a side through his example. He has always been the eternal optimist, the man who will never admit defeat, whether in a five-a-side, a League game or a World Cup final. He always looked a natural leader.

But after he took over the captaincy from the quieter Brian Labone in 1970, Everton slumped. There were letters in the local paper in the early struggling days of the 1971-72 season demanding that Catterick should relieve him of the captaincy. The break-up had begun.

It is not difficult to see where Ball derives his fighting heart and temper. His father, another fiery redhead, has been in trouble with authority as a coach at Stoke and manager at Halifax and Preston. Both father and son hate to lose. Alan junior showed just how badly he took it when he threw his losers medal down on the Wembley turf after West Bromwich beat Everton in the 1968 FA Cup Final.

Big Alan—he is not all that big, but the family use the term to differentiate between father and son—was a professional who never made it to the top, doing the rounds with Oldham, Birmingham, Rochdale and Southport. He was determined that his son would be a great footballer. When

Young Alan had achieved that status Big Alan looked back on the years when he did all he could to get him accepted as a professional:

'At four I just didn't know. At six we knew how many times he could bounce the ball on his foot. At seven people would stand and watch him on the beach. At eight I thought he had a chance. At 12 I was convinced he would be a player. At 14 he had a trial for Lancashire Boys, played brilliantly for 20 minutes and was called off because they said he was too small. At 15 he was turned down by Bolton. He then joined Blackpool and at 17 signed pro.'

The rejection by Bolton really hurt the Ball family—Wanderers were their team. Years later, as Young Alan celebrated the 1970 League title triumph, his grandfather recalled: 'I'm still bitter about it. I'd have given anything to see him run out at Burnden Park in the white shirt of Bolton.'

The Balls were a close-knit family. Alan gave his winners medal from the 1966 World Cup to his mother. But there was a great deal of friction in the early days about the way Big Alan was pushing him. His mother worried about him having a weak chest. So he took up cross-country running to improve his breathing—reassuring his mother and proving the stamina that has always been there by winning the races he went in for with ease.

Big Alan reflected, 'When I was manager of Ashton United in the Lancashire Combination I put him in the first team. He was 14 and only a little chap. His mother wouldn't speak to me for ages!'

He added: 'I didn't feel guilty about what I was doing then, although I sometimes do now. Maybe I should have let him play Cowboys and Indians. Then I look at him today . . .'

The father kept pushing his son like a Tin Pan Alley song-plugger. 'I'm telling you,' he sang to talent scouts up and down the country, 'this boy's going to be great.' Eventually Ron Suart, who was then manager of Blackpool and later became assistant to Dave Sexton at Stamford Bridge, listened to the song and believed.

At 17 the little lad from Farnworth made his

first appearance in the First Division—on August 1962, against Liverpool at Anfield. At age of 18 he established himself as a Black regular.

He set himself a target: to play for Engl before he was 20. This he felt, was the best of repaying his father. He made it, in Belgr with three days to spare. His reaction to selection was typical. Alf Ramsey called to during a training session for the tour ma against Yugoslavia: 'Well son, I'm show you into the cauldron and it's bubbling. I h every confidence in you to play well. Have got confidence yourself?' Back came the re 'You're bloody right I have!'

Alan Ball gives his V-sign to those who had rejected him

He played against Yugoslavia, West Germa and Sweden in the space of eight days. Wh others went off on holiday after that Engl tour Ball went off with the England Under party. It was not such a happy tour—he was off in Austria—but he still played three m games in eight days.

This was Alan Ball giving his V-sign to th who had rejected him, those who had said he not big enough, not strong enough for demands of modern professional football.

He is the little man who took on the wo and won—the boy who moved from a terra house in a cobbled backstreet to a rich ma residence, his beautiful white house in suburb Worsley just outside Manchester, and later to equally high-class home near London.

His life-style is evidence of that success— house, the smart wife and daughter, the cloth the friends like George Best, pop stars a successful young businessmen, the cars. Parti larly the cars. He changes them like many m change ties. 'E'-type, Lotus, Barracuda. Y name it, there's a good chance Alan Ball has it—at least for a few weeks.

He did not even allow an early business fail —he owned a garage at one time—to put h off the good life. He is a gambler who owned racehorses in partnership with Best a Alex Young.

He is the joker who can also laugh at hi self. Some forecast disaster when he was ask to lend his high-pitched voice to after-din speaking on Merseyside. Harold Wilson, Dan Blanchflower and Cliff Morgan have all h their say at this monthly gathering. Ba brought the house down.

He concluded: 'I've three wishes—for Evert to win the European Cup, England to win t World Cup again, and my voice to break bef I speak to you again.'

Sadly Ball's involvement with World Cup ball ended in a flash of that inevitable temp In Katowice in June 1973, he intervened duri a scuffle between Martin Peters and a Pol player and was shown the red card.

But for Arsenal his enthusiasm, his obsess with winning, remained. They may not have h to pay a million for him, but every game he out to prove that was what he was worth.

Alan BALL

Honours: World Cup winners medal, 1966; FA Cup losers medal, 1968, 1972; League Championship medal, 1969-70.

| Club | Season | League | | Int'nls | |
		Mtchs	Gls	Mtchs	Gl
Blackpool	1962–63	5			
	1963–64	31	13		
	1964–65	39	11	3	1
	1965–66	41	17	11	
Everton	1966–67	41	15	6	1
	1967–68	34	20	7	2
	1968–69	40	16	8	
	1969–70	37	10	10	3
	1970–71	39	4	6	
	1971–72	17	3	2	
Arsenal	1971–72	18	3	3	1
	1972–73	40	10	9	
		382	122	65	8

PART 4
THE WINGERS

Billy MEREDITH

Honours: League Championship medal, 1907-08, 1910-11; FA Cup winners medal, 1904, 1909

Club	Season	League		Int'nls
		Mtchs	Gls	Mtchs
Manchester City	1894-95	18	12	2
	1895-96	29	11	2
	1896-97	28	11	3
	1897-98	30	14	2
	1898-99	33	29	1
	1899-1900	33	11	2
	1900-01	34	6	2
	1901-02	33	7	2
	1902-03	34	25	2
	1903-04	34	9	1
	1904-05	33	11	2
	1905-06*			
Manchester United	1906-07	16	5	3
	1907-08	37	10	3
	1908-09	34		3
	1909-10	31	5	3
	1910-11	35	5	3
	1911-12	35	3	3
	1912-13	22	2	3
	1913-14	34	2	3
	1914-15	26		
	1919-20	19	2	3
	1920-21	14	1	
Manchester City	1921-22	25		
	1922-23	1		
	1923-24	2		
Total		670	181	48

*Suspended during season 1905-06

Billy Meredith playing for Manchester Un⟨ited⟩ against QPR in the 1908 FA Charity Shield ga⟨me⟩

THE WINGERS

30 seasons of 'Old Skinny'

Billy Meredith was to the early twenties what Stanley Matthews was to the fifties—a phenomenon, a footballing freak, an ageing genius who refused to grow old and who, well into his forties, was still able to make full-backs wish they had never been born.

The parallels between the two men are extraordinary: each was the outstanding right-winger of his day; each played top-class football well past the age when most men would be content with pipe and slippers on a winter Saturday afternoon; each had a very similar club record, making their name with one team, moving on to another for their years of maturity and—an uncanny coincidence—returning grey-haired to play out their final years of first-class football with the side of their youth.

Meredith's figures are staggering. He played top-class football for no less than 30 years; from 1894, when at 19 he joined Manchester City from Chirk, his home town just across the Shropshire-Wales border, to 1924, when he was accepted for every Cup-tie in City's run up to the semi-final. He played 367 League games for City, and another 303, almost a career in itself, for Manchester United between 1906 and 1921. He scored 181 League and 56 Cup goals.

His international record is equally impressive. In the days when Wales's opponents were limited to England, Scotland and Ireland he was selected for 71 consecutive matches between 1895 and 1920; but because of the demands of his clubs (particularly City) he was released for only 48 of them, plus the three victory internationals in 1919. Nevertheless the total was not surpassed by a Welshman (Ivor Allchurch) until 1962.

A side with Meredith on the right wing was virtually assured of dominance on that flank.

Tall, gaunt and shambling, almost casual in appearance, he became transformed with a ball at his feet. His runs to the corner flag and the devastating cross might be varied by his sudden cut inside—he was as fast as he was skilful—for a shot at goal. This disconcerting habit became such a menace that opponents were forced to reorganize their defences: the full-back dropped back as a second line of defence, and the left-back was given the unenviable task of shadowing 'Old Skinny'. Not, as a rule, with a great deal of success: in 33 games in 1898-99, for example, he scored 29 goals.

Three internationals, a League game, and three days at work—in a week

When faced with a blanket of close-marking defenders, as he so often was, Meredith's answer was as unexpected as it was brilliant. With a jink of his tall frame he would lean right in to the would-be tackler, then accelerate past him; 99 times out of a 100 the tackler would give chase, only to find that Meredith had, with his jink, flicked a back-pass to his own right-half, drawn off a whole battalion of defenders, and left the field open for attack.

As celebrated as the shot and the back-pass were the toothpick and the penalty. The first, rolling ceaselessly from one side of his mouth to the other throughout his career, was a unique trademark—all the more so, perhaps, for the fact that he never once swallowed one. The penalty was a piece of inspired and effective clowning. At the turn of the century a goalkeeper could advance to the six-yard box, and Meredith

was a master of looping the ball over his head.

Meredith's relationships with his two cl⟨ubs⟩ were not as serene as his long service wo⟨uld⟩ suggest. He appears to have been an outspo⟨ken⟩ and headstrong young man, furious at his cl⟨ub's⟩ frequent refusals to release him to play for W⟨ales⟩ and disgusted with the miserable wages.

He always spoke with amused irony at ⟨the⟩ nightmare week of his first international ca⟨p in⟩ 1895. On the Saturday, after an agonizing ⟨sea⟩ crossing, he played against Ireland in Belf⟨ast;⟩ then another night of sea-sickness on the ⟨way⟩ back; on the Monday, the game with Englan⟨d in⟩ London; on Tuesday, home to North Wales f⟨or a⟩ day's work down the pit (his Manchester C⟨ity⟩ wages were insufficient to feed him and prov⟨ide⟩ the allowance he paid his parents; on Wednes⟨day⟩ a League game for City; on Thursday and Frid⟨ay⟩ shifts down the pit; on Saturday, up the roa⟨d to⟩ Wrexham to play for Wales against Scotl⟨and.⟩ For those internationals he was paid just £⟨a⟩ game, and throughout his 30-year career ⟨he⟩ averaged £4 15s a week from football.

It was money that led to his move to Un⟨ited⟩ in 1906, two years after he had scored the g⟨oal⟩ that gave City the FA Cup. Eighteen City play⟨ers,⟩ Meredith among them, were suspended ⟨for⟩ receiving 'illegal payments'—that is, 5s a⟨nd⟩ bonuses. Immediately after the suspension ⟨he⟩ moved to United and, within three seasons, ⟨had⟩ won League and Cup medals with his new cl⟨ub.⟩ In 1921 a free transfer saw him back with Cit⟨y.⟩

If one memory of a lifetime's football wa⟨s to⟩ recur during his last years—he kept a hote⟨l in⟩ Manchester for some time, and died, aged ⟨83,⟩ in 1958—it was not the two League Champi⟨on⟩ships, the two Second Division championsh⟨ips⟩ or the two Cup winners medals. It was a da⟨y in⟩ 1920, with England meeting Wales at Highb⟨ury.⟩ The occasion was a special one even before ⟨the⟩ match started, for T E Thomas, Meredith⟨'s⟩ headmaster at Chirk School, was retiring. T⟨his⟩ remarkable man had introduced no fewer t⟨han⟩ 49 future Welsh internationals to footbal⟨l as⟩ pupils at his school, and on this day the ⟨many⟩ Chirk Old Boys in the Welsh team made hi⟨m a⟩ presentation before the game.

Then, with their 44-year-old right-winge⟨r to⟩ the fore, Wales beat England for the first t⟨ime⟩ in their history. As he left the field the laco⟨nic,⟩ unemotional Meredith gave way to tears; it ⟨was⟩ the proudest moment of his life. Sadly he ne⟨ver⟩ played for his country again.

The following year he returned to Manchester [City], an incredible 27 years after he had first [worn] their colours. His return match was against [Aston] Villa, played at City's ground in Hyde [Road]. Meredith performed with much of his [old] audacity, delighting a crowd of 35,000. [Villa] were beaten 2-1, and the veteran Welshman [played] a large part in the scoring of the first [City] goal.

[A] further two years later, as his 50th birthday [approached], there was further proof of his [remarkable] stamina. Manchester City were at [Brian] Park for an FA Cup tie, Meredith, as [ever], was on the right-wing and marking him [was] a young full-back.

[After] ninety minutes, neither side had managed a goal in a match that had been fought at the traditional hectic pace of Cup encounters. The game went into extra time. And it was here that Meredith struck. His immediate opponent, less than half his age, flagged the longer play continued. Meredith did not. And inevitably he broke free along the right touchline.

He crossed with all his perception and accuracy, and a City team-mate put the ball into the goal to win the match. City went on to reach the semi-final, where they were beaten by Newcastle United, the great side of the era.

By this time he had finally come to terms with retirement. His final appearance came at the end of April 1925, by which time City were playing at Maine Road. That day, for his testimonial, a team of his own choosing played [a] combined Rangers and Celtic eleven. The game, a 2-2 draw, was played with such panache that it was totally worthy of Meredith's achievements.

At an age when many coaches are considering retirement, he joined their ranks. In 1931, he returned to Old Trafford in a coaching capacity at a time when the club was going through [a] period of turmoil.

He retained more affection for United than for the Maine Road club, sometimes quietly visiting the ground to watch the team in action. As late as 1950, funds were made available from Old Trafford to help him overcome a small financial problem. His stamina remained in life as it had on the field and he was 81 when he died in 1958.

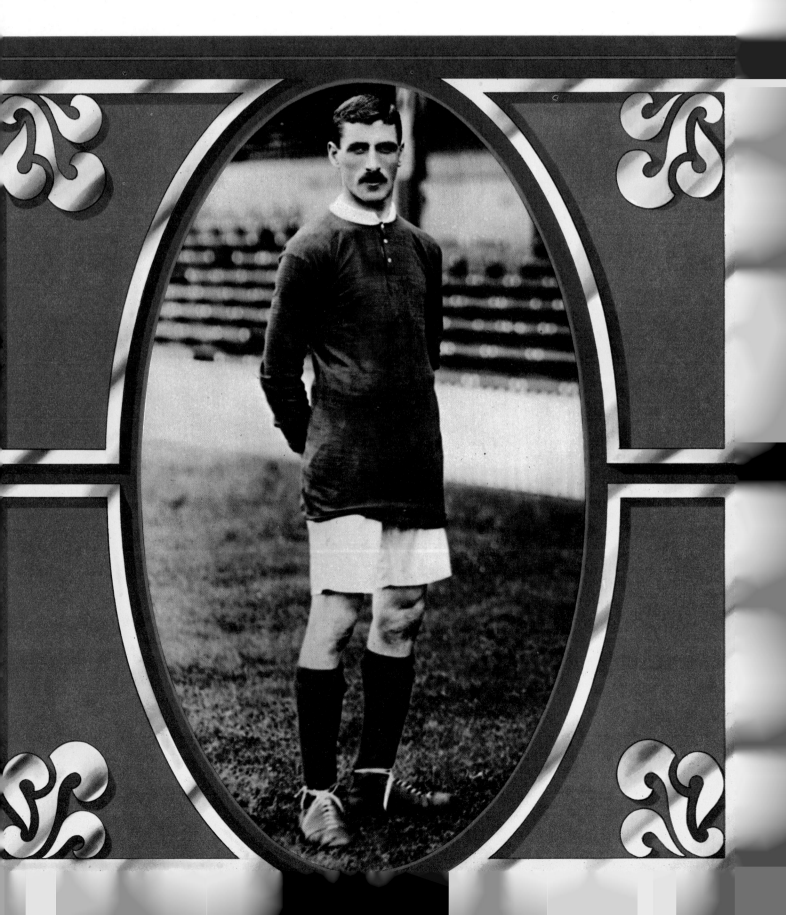

THE WINGERS

Alan Morton – the devil on the wing

He would stand just behind the halfway line, waiting for the kick-off. He would stretch the elastic round his waist, hitch up his pants, stamp his left foot on the ground and then wash his hands with imaginary soap and water. The pre-match rigmarole was almost as individualistic and as entertaining as his play. But not quite.

Even when Stanley Matthews was at his Wembley best in 1953 there were still some to argue that he was not as good as Alan Morton. That is a true measure of Rangers' little left-winger, the man the English called the 'wee blue devil'. His two inside-forward partners at Ibrox, Tommy Cairns and Bob McPhail, were no doubt biased, but the fact that they backed Morton against Matthews had some validity.

At the time when the Matthews cult was hypnotizing football, Morton's two old partners were defending his memory. 'He was always going in a straight line . . . for the goal,' said McPhail, scorer of 307 League goals. 'He could take the ball into the opponents' penalty area quicker than anybody else I ever saw. He never pulled his tricks until a game was won and then he would give the crowd the entertainment they wanted.'

Tommy Cairns emphasized the same theme of directness. 'In the other arts—accuracy of the pass and the cross, dribbling, and team sense—he was Matthews' equal. And in directness and goalscoring Morton was the master.' They both insisted that they would rather play with Morton than with Matthews; he never stopped the game the way Matthews did.

Apart from the excellence that these two great wingers showed in ball control and in trickery they also shared a scorn for anything that was ungentlemanly on the field. Indeed Alan Morton was so highly regarded both for his play and for his sporting attitude that when the Scottish FA held their annual diamond jubilee dinner in 1933 he was the only player to be invited as a guest.

England tried every type of full-back against him —but never subdued him

In his day Morton was feared as no other winger, at international as well as club level. He played some of his best games against England and it was an English journalist, Ivan Sharpe, who called him 'yon wee blue devil', after hearing a spectator with a Lancashire accent so describe him during a game at Hampden. The nickname became 'the wee blue devil', and stuck.

Morton played for Scotland against England 12 times between 1920 and 1932. England tried every type of full-back against him—big and small, tough and clever, slow and fast—but never succeeded in subduing him. Such was his ball control, his speed, his jinking and the perfection of his balance that to use the word of the day he was 'ungettable'. Once, in a League international at Goodison Park, Hill of Burnley chased Morton to the corner flag and seemed to have him trapped there. Morton doubled back to the halfway line, cut along it with Hill still chasing, and then turned to go through the middle. The redoubtable Hill then stopped with hands on hips and gave up.

Though only 5ft 4in Morton had an exceptionally long stride—and even had an insert sewn into his shorts to allow for it. When he played with Queen's Park the other winger was J B Bell, Scottish 220 yards champion; Morton could match

him over the first 20 yards and give him a good race over the full furlong.

Morton was born in the Jordanhill district of Glasgow in 1896 but his father, a coal master, moved to Airdrie while Alan was still young and steered his five sons to mining as a career. Alan became a mining engineer and he practised his profession throughout his football life. In fact he used to work on the morning of an international.

From the house to the local shops in Airdrie there was a long stretch of wall. Alan, who was never without a ball in his pocket, used to kick one against this wall as he went on errands for his mother, keeping it going with one foot on the outward journey and with the other on the way back. Thus, though he was naturally right-footed, he had exceptional control with both feet by the age of 11. Controlling the ball as it broke awkwardly from the uneven wall also developed his burst of speed over the first ten yards—an asset later so useful in taking him clear of defenders.

On his debut Morton dribbled the ball round an international keeper

The Morton boys (Jimmy, William, Bob, Jackie and Alan) formed a good basis for a team. They played on a rough piece of ground and Alan, being the youngest, had to be fast and elusive to stay out of trouble. But balance and poise came almost naturally.

Morton had what he called his own football teacher. At his Airdrie home there was a grass plot and a coal cellar. The boys cut a hole in the cellar door, just big enough for the ball to pass through. The object was to chip the ball from the grass through the hole and take it first time off the door if it missed—as it usually did. This called for various contortions but it was all good for developing a body pivot.

It was this pivot, from the hips up, which used to put Morton behind the ball and which gave him his balance. And it explained the different studs he wore: the normal was four studs in a rough square on the centre of the sole; but Morton used three in a triangle, with the apex just below the toes. Thus, when Morton rose on his toes to put his body behind a cross, there was no drag on the standing foot. He always insisted that, even at the height of his career, he used only the tricks and the skills he had developed as a boy in Airdrie.

When he left school he followed his brothers round various teams, including Cairnhill Hearts and Menstrie Thistle. Bob was a powerful player, either at centre-forward or centre-half, and he eventually signed for Queen's Park. Shortly afterwards Alan was given a trial and, although he was tempted to turn professional by several clubs, he signed the amateur Queen's Park form which Bob placed in front of him. The goal he scored for Queen's Park on his first team debut in 1913 was an omen: he calmly dribbled the ball round the Third Lanark and Scotland goalkeeper Jimmie Brownlie, then rashly reckoned the best of all time.

Morton always pulled out something special on the big occasion. In his first international against England, at Hampden Park in 1920, he scored with his famous lob from the touchline.

Though Morton is automatically associated with Rangers he was a full international before he

went to Ibrox. He had played in the ann[...] Glasgow-Sheffield match in 1914 (at outs[...] right) and then, when still on Queen's Pa[...] books, he played against Wales at Cardiff[...] February 1920. His first international coinci[...] with the 50th birthday of Billy Meredith, the gr[...] Welsh winger. Meredith played that day for [...] 47th cap, and Morton was always to remember [...] fervour of the Meredith jubilee.

There were many attempts to entice Mor[...] away from Queen's Park. One offer was £5,0[...] a house and a job as a mining engineer—[...] considerable inducement in those days. [...] obstacle for all, including English clubs, was [...] team he admired most of all and the one for wh[...] he wanted to play—Rangers. During Mort[...] six years with Queen's Park the amateurs ha[...] one time or another defeated every other Scot[...] team but the 'Blues'.

In 1920 A L Morton of Queen's Park became Alan Morton of Rangers

Rangers manager Willie Wilton had b[...] drowned in an accident and trainer Willie Str[...] had taken over. Struth made a tempting offe[...] Morton and, though his father did not want [...] to play professional football, he finally agreed[...] the condition that Alan would continue with [...] career in mining.

Rangers were all full-timers but Str[...] reluctantly agreed to this condition and, in J[...] 1920, A L Morton of Queen's Park became A[...] Morton of Rangers. He was Struth's first sign[...] and although he never divulged the signing-on [...] it is known that a substantial sum of money [...]

DAILY RECORD, GLASGOW

GLASGOW HERALD/EVENING TIMES

ead over a number of years and that he
ame the highest paid player of his day.

Only a Scottish Cup winners medal eluded him for some years

Morton played for Rangers for over 12 years.
ring that time he made 495 appearances for
m (not once did he play in the reserves), scored
goals, and helped them to nine League
mpionships. Then, after six matches of the
2-33 season, he retired from the field and was
mediately invited onto the board. There he
ained, an active director, until ill-health
fined him to his home in 1968. He died three
rs later.

The combination of Struth and Morton began
ntage era in Rangers' history. They had much
common, especially in the meticulousness of
ir dress. Struth was noted for the smartness of
clothes, while Morton used to go to Ibrox to
n straight from his office, usually dressed in a
l-fitting black coat with bowler hat and rolled
brella. He usually carried an attache case.

Although he trained only on two evenings a
k and was a fairly heavy smoker (the first
ng he reached for in the dressing-room after
atch was a cigarette), Morton was remarkably
His training schedule was simple, running and
ctising with the ball.

Ie had only one serious injury throughout his
er, a fact that says much for his elusiveness.
e injury, a knock on the calf, cost him an
rnational cap.

Morton collected every honour with Rangers,
the Scottish Cup winners medal eluded him

for some years. In 1922 Rangers seemed to have
the Cup won with only Morton (the club), who
they had beaten twice that season, as opponents
in the final. But they lost 1-0. The winners medal
eventually came in 1928 during a season when,
with Morton playing at his peak and partnered by
Bob McPhail, Rangers played 38 League matches
without defeat and then beat Celtic 4-0 in the
Scottish Cup final.

One of Alan Morton's claims to fame was as
a member of the 'Wembley Wizards', the team
who beat England 5-1 in 1928. In the second
minute of the match Morton raced past the
England right-back, Roy Goodall, and with a
cunningly placed cross found Alec Jackson at the
far post to head the first goal. That day Jackson
scored three goals, and all of them from Morton
crosses. Goodall could do nothing to stop him
and his famous hanging cross, the 'Morton Lob',
often had goalkeeper Ted Hufton in trouble.

He would be the obvious number 11 in any all-time Scotland selection

Some argue that Morton was only good in his
day. But it is difficult, if not futile, to compare
different generations. There is no point in taking
Alan Morton out of context: he was one of the
finest examples of a specialist player. Suffice it to
say that so good was his ball control, so perfect
his balance, so impressive his speed, so daunting
his directness, so keen his appreciation of what
was happening around him, that he has to rank
with the great players of football. He would have
few if any rivals for the number 11 position in
any all-time Scottish side.

Far left *The full-size portrait of Alan Morton that
hangs in his sister's house at Airdrie.*
Centre *Morton leads out Queen's Park. He followed his brother Bob to Hampden as an amateur
and stayed there until 1920 when, despite the competition from England, he joined Rangers.*
Above *A fast, ball-playing winger who could also
score goals, Morton was Rangers' outstanding star
during their most illustrious period.*

Alan MORTON

Honours: Scottish League Championship medal
1920-21, 1922-23, 1923-24, 1924-25, 1926-27,
1927-28, 1928-29, 1929-30, 1930-31
Scottish Cup winners medal 1928, 1930, 1932
Scottish Cup runners-up medal 1921, 1922, 1929

Club	Season	League		Int'nls	
		Mtchs	Gls	Mtchs	Gls
Queen's Park	1913-14	22	3		
	1914-15*				
	1915-16*				
	1916-17	38	4		
	1917-18*				
	1918-19	26	3		
	1919-20	25	7	2	1
Rangers	1920-21	39	6	1	1
	1921-22	30	4	2	
	1922-23	35	3	3	
	1923-24	34	6	3	
	1924-25	36	8	3	
	1925-26	29	5		
	1926-27	31	10	2	3
	1927-28	34	11	3	
	1928-29	37	13	3	
	1929-30	23	5	3	
	1930-31	32	7	3	
	1931-32	13		3	
	1932-33	6	3		
Total		490*	98*	31	5

*Incomplete totals, no figures available for some
wartime seasons

93

Bastin and Hulme –raiders on the wing

Joe Hulme and Cliff Bastin could scarcely have been more contrasting; one an extrovert, expansive and jolly, the other an introvert, cool and remote. As a pair of wingers for the conquering Arsenal teams of the thirties, they were perfect. The development of the third-back game and the 'W' formation called for raiding wingmen and Arsenal, the pioneers of these tactics, had the best examples of all.

Hulme, on the right, was fast, particularly off the mark. Bastin, on the left, was not as quick (though fast enough) but a skilled ball player with a magnificent left-foot shot that brought him the record total of 33 goals from the wing in 1932-33.

'Flying' Joe Hulme was born in Stafford on 26 August 1904. Bastin was born eight years later in Exeter. Both retired at almost exactly the same age, Hulme after playing his fifth Cup Final (for Huddersfield Town) in April 1938, and Bastin, less dramatically, in November 1946, at a time when his pace had long since gone.

Whereas Hulme was a natural winger, Bastin was made into one. After playing on the left-wing once for Ladysmith Road School in Exeter, he did not figure there again for nearly nine years until Herbert Chapman, the Arsenal manager whom he revered, put him there partly to save him from the buffets and bruises of League football.

Bastin was more worried about his tennis match than joining Arsenal

Bastin made his debut for Arsenal in August 1929—at inside-right to Hulme—at Everton. The result was a 1-1 draw, with Hulme scoring the Arsenal goal. After a home match against Derby, however, Bastin went back into the reserves, re-emerging some months later as Arsenal's first-team left-winger.

He cost Arsenal £2,500 from Exeter City, but when Chapman had come down to sign him he was characteristically phlegmatic. Chapman talked to him at his home for hours but Bastin, by his own admission, was more concerned about a tennis match he was due to play. He had been a schoolboy international inside-left in 1926, and was now a Third Division star at 17. Finally it was his mother, rather than Chapman, who decided him on signing for Arsenal.

It was this extraordinary coolness that allowed Bastin to become the youngest player ever to win a Cup medal the following April. Wembley and its dramas held no terrors for him.

Hulme, by contrast, came to Arsenal as a seasoned player. His first club was Third Division York City and in February 1924 Blackburn Rovers, then a major force, paid a mere £250 for him. In 1926, the year Bastin became a schoolboy cap, Blackburn made a handy profit by selling Hulme to Arsenal for £3,500.

It might be justifiably said that Alex James was the making of both players. The brilliant little Scottish inside-left joined Arsenal from Preston at the same time as Bastin, and after a period of adaptation became the team's midfield orchestrator. Bastin would stand 10 to 15 yards in from the touchline to exploit James' beautiful diagonal passes, cutting in to shoot with his killing left-foot. Hulme, out on the right, would benefit from James' marvellous

crossfield balls, which he would pick up at full gallop. He was a splendid sight under full sail—to all except those left-backs unlucky enough to oppose him.

Jack Crayston, who played right-half behind him on so many occasions, used to tell the story of sitting on the substitutes bench at a Racing Club de Paris-Arsenal game, when the French defender marking Hulme came off and sat beside him. The only words Crayston could make out, he said, were 'Hulme,' 'greyhound' and 'fatigue'.

As a fine cricketer, Hulme used his speed to great advantage in the deep field. He was a more than useful batsman, and in 1934 set up a record sixth wicket stand for Middlesex of 212 with the illustrious 'Gubby' Allen.

The story is told of him that once, out in the deep, he ran as hard as he could after a ball which always seemed to keep just ahead of him, until at last he realized he was chasing a low flying bird. There is also the tale of Hulme facing the demon bowling of West Indies' Learie Constantine, quite failing to connect with the first deliveries, until the umpire at last shouted 'no ball!' 'So *that's* what it is,' said Hulme.

When Herbert Chapman called Bastin into his office at Christmas in 1929 to tell him he would be playing outside-left against Portsmouth, Bastin was shocked. He still regarded himself as an inside-forward, and indeed would have some of his finest games there for England in the early thirties. But Chapman convinced him, as he had convinced so many others; even though Bastin felt that Chapman himself was probably surprised by just how well things went.

When Hulme arrived at Highbury, he was partnered at inside-right by the legendary Charlie Buchan, then at the tail end of his career but still a marvellous strategist and frequent scorer. 'Joe,' said Buchan, before his first game, 'if I call for the ball, give it me straight at my feet.' Hulme agreed, but when Buchan first called for it, Hulme went racing upfield with the ball. When Buchan asked him why, he replied, 'There was a player right on top of you.'

Hulme and Bastin: 53 goals from the wing in the 1932-33 season

But that was just Buchan's point—he wanted to take out a player in this way. After a few months, however, they were working smoothly together and their partnership helped Arsenal, and Hulme, to reach the first of their many Cup Finals in 1927, when they lost 1-0 to Cardiff. The goal was tragically given away by the goalkeeper Danny Lewis who, curiously enough, was an even faster man than Hulme.

Bastin, nicknamed 'Boy' Bastin for his precocity, had won every honour in the game at the age of 19. He played a key part in the 2-0 Cup Final win over Huddersfield Town in 1930, when James gave him the ball from a quickly taken free-kick and then slipped into position to convert the return pass.

His first England cap came at outside-left against Wales in November 1931—when his Arsenal colleague Charlie Jones marked him out of the game. He had to wait nearly two years before he returned to the national side, playing brilliantly on the European tour and scoring England's goal in a 1-1 draw against Italy in Rome.

That was the day the Roman crowd shouted 'Basta Bastin!' 'Enough of Bastin!' The previous season he had scored his 33 League goals—record for a winger.

Bastin had great admiration for Hulme as player and as an all-round athlete, pointing out that to make a century at billiards, let alone cricket, was nothing to Hulme, and that when he took up golf he rapidly became one of the finest golfers in the club.

'Joey was one of the best outside-rights have ever known,' he wrote. 'Yet he could also be one of the worst. His nervousness sometimes made him play far, far below his normal form.' He paid tribute to Hulme's speed and 'astonishing ball control', his ability to put over centres at top speed, and singled out a superb performance Hulme gave in an international trial at Portsmouth, when he pulverized the famous Ernie Blenkinsop. Bastin called it the best display of wing play he had ever seen.

'The other side objected because I was playing on my home ground'

The first of Hulme's nine caps came against Scotland, France and Belgium in 1926-27, with the last, after that international trial, against Scotland in 1933. Bastin won 21 caps, the last of them on England's European tour in 1938, when he gave a fine performance in the famous 6-3 win in Berlin against Germany and also scored (from penalties) in the matches against Switzerland and France.

Between them Hulme and Bastin amassed plethora of medals. Both shared in Arsenal League Championships of 1931, 1933, 1934, and 1935, plus the Cup victories of 1930 and 1936, while Bastin won another Championship medal in 1938—the year Hulme played in his fifth and last

PRESS ASSOCIATION

up Final for Huddersfield when, he had joked, 'he other side objected because I was playing a my home ground.' Hulme had joined Town the January, having played 333 League games d scored 108 goals for Arsenal.

Bastin was certainly the more complete player. s an inside-left, he was perfectly capable marshalling a forward-line, whether it was at of Arsenal or England. During the War, hen his speed had largely deserted him but his aft had not, he played most of his football r Arsenal in that position and also played number of successful games at right-half.

He was particularly admired on the continent. n the eve of the 1934 World Cup, Hugo Meisl, e father of Austrian football, told his brother illy that if he could have one player his red team would win the tournament. The player as Bastin.

Perhaps Bastin's insulation, his unvarying lm, had something to do with the deafness hich afflicted him more and more as his career vanced. Though he was a sensitive and vulner- le man, serious and withdrawn, nothing seemed touch him on the field. He was cool in the avest crises of play, and was thus able to score me decisive goals.

One came in the last minute of the 1932 Cup mi-final against Manchester City. A weary rsenal side was getting much the worst of it hen Bastin sent Jack Lambert away down the ght and glided into position to score from his ntre.

In the Final an injury to James meant that astin had to play at inside-left, and he began e move with a crossfield pass to Hulme, from hich Arsenal scored an unavailing first goal. ulme went down the wing, his cross confused e Newcastle defenders, two of whom collided, d Bob John (the emergency outside-left) put e Gunners ahead. But the famous 'over the ne' goal equalized for Newcastle, and Arsenal lost 2-1. Even the abilities of Bastin and Hulme were not the same without James.

Bastin played regularly for Arsenal through the War—when he was rejected for military service and served as an air-raid warden. Perhaps his extraordinarily early beginning had something to do with the fact that his career ended a little early. His last game in Arsenal colours was against Cardiff City on Boxing Day 1946, and he scored a goal in their 4-0 win. He then retired to run a cafe and report matches for the *Sunday Pictorial*. Later he became the landlord of the Horse and Groom pub in his native Exeter.

Hulme, in the immediate post-War years, became manager of Tottenham Hotspur, but the cares of the job took the edge off his famous good humour, and he seemed glad when he left Spurs to go into journalism with *The People*. He continued with them into the sixties before he eventually retired.

Far left Cliff Bastin, consistent and outstanding member of the great Arsenal sides of the thirties. Signed from Exeter by Herbert Chapman for £2,500 in 1928, Bastin won five League Championship medals and two Cup winners medals in nine years and in 1932-33, the first of Arsenal's hat-trick years, he scored 33 League goals—a record for a winger. The same season Joe Hulme, on the other wing, scored 20.
Below Bastin (right) and Hunt in action against Wolves during the fourth round FA Cup tie at Molineux in 1938.
Below bottom Bastin (far right) poses with four more Arsenal players—Copping, Hapgood, Male and Drake—who were chosen for the England side to play against Ireland at Goodison Park in 1935. England won 2-1, with Bastin scoring both goals.
Right Joe Hulme, who in 1938 became the first man to appear in five Wembley Cup Finals when he played for Huddersfield in the 1-0 defeat by Preston. It was his last competitive game.

Cliff BASTIN

Honours: League Championship medal, 1930-31, 1932-33, 1933-34, 1934-35, 1937-38
FA Cup winners medal, 1930, 1936
FA Cup runners-up medal, 1932

Club	Season	League Mtchs	League Gls	Int'nls Mtchs	Int'nls Gls
Exeter City	1927-28	3	3		
	1928-29	14	4		
Arsenal	1929-30	21	7		
	1930-31	42	28		
	1931-32	40	15	1	
	1932-33	42	33	2	3
	1933-34	38	13	5	1
	1934-35	36	20	3	2
	1935-36	31	11	4	1
	1936-37	33	5	2	2
	1937-38	38	15	4	3
	1938-39	23	3		
	1946-47	6			
Total		367	157	21	12

Joe HULME

Honours: League Championship medal, 1930-31, 1932-33, 1934-35
FA Cup winners medal, 1930, 1936
FA Cup runners-up medal, 1927, 1932, 1938

Club	Season	League Mtchs	League Gls	Int'nls Mtchs	Int'nls Gls
Blackburn Rovers	1923-24	11			
	1924-25	42	4		
	1925-26	21	2		
Arsenal	1925-26	15	2		
	1926-27	37	8	3	1
	1927-28	36	9	3	
	1928-29	41	6	2	3
	1929-30	37	14		
	1930-31	32	14		
	1931-32	40	14		
	1932-33	40	20	1	
	1933-34	8	5		
	1934-35	16	8		
	1935-36	21	6		
	1936-37	3			
	1937-38	7	2		
Huddersfield Town	1937-38	8			
Total		415	114	9	4

THE WINGERS

Tom Finney—a king without honours

Tom Finney had just turned 38 when he played his last League match. It was not of particular importance as Preston were comfortably placed in the First Division and the visitors, Luton Town, were already certain to be relegated. Yet Finney's admirers proved their regard for him by turning up to the number of 30,000 and making his farewell a touching and memorable occasion. Their idol had been playing for some time at centre-forward—thereby creating a club record by playing (and scoring) in all five forward positions—but to please them he reverted to his original role of outside-right.

For over a decade Finney *was* Preston, and Preston *was* Finney. There were other notable players—Eddie Quigley, Charlie Wayman, Alex Forbes, Tommy Docherty—but none were local, none stayed very long, and none were ever in the same class. Finney, by contrast, never considered playing for any other club. When he retired in 1960 he held all the long-term appearance and scoring records for Preston, and had played 76 times for his country—a number then exceeded only by Billy Wright, with whom he figured in all but two of his internationals.

Finney was not forgotten in Preston, where he was thought of as the greatest player who had ever lived—a feeling reinforced by the fact that the club dropped from ninth place to relegation the season after he retired. As head of an expanding firm of plumbers and electricians, and a Justice of the Peace with an OBE, 'Sir Tom' (as he was affectionately known) became a prominent local figure.

Tom Finney's interest in football started early with his father taking him regularly to Deepdale. His idol was Alex James, the inside-forward wizard who spent his first four years in English football with Preston. He left in 1929, when Finney was only seven, but the youngster had seen enough to shape his ideas and, a natural left-footer, he chose inside-left as his position. He even persuaded his mother to make him long baggy pants in the style favoured by James, though as he was small and frail they nearly smothered him. It broke his heart when James was transferred to Arsenal.

'Move that little chap to the right-wing. He'll get more room there'

Finney furnished himself with two deft feet by dribbling a tennis ball along pavements and 'selling the dummy' to lamp-posts on his newspaper delivery rounds. As he says, he was a nippier inside-left than scholar. After homework he hurried to a nearby recreation field to feed his passion for football. Though he was never to be a reserve while a Preston player he had that role many times as a boy because he was small and, perhaps, too fond of the ball.

In 1937 Preston North End decided to father local teams and foster schoolboy talent by providing equipment and improving the training facilities. Finney went to the ground (which was near his home) at every opportunity, and was among the lads who received regular coaching and free pints of milk. Now at 15, 4ft 9in and only five stone, he still clung to his favourite inside-left spot and his baggy shorts.

It was by chance that he found his true position—a left-footer at outside-right. In his first trial for the club the chairman, Mr Taylor, exclaimed to the trainer, 'Move that little chap to the right-wing, he'll get more room there.' Though a success he turned down a ground staff job at £2 10s a week on his father's advice to continue playing as an amateur until he had learned his trade as a plumber.

Like so many of his generation Finney lost several of his most promising football years through War service. He was only 19 when he played brilliantly against Eddie Hapgood, Arsenal's long-established England full-back, in the 1941 War Cup Final at Wembley, and contributed to Preston's victory in the replay at Blackburn. But he then disappeared from the scene to serve abroad with the Eighth Army.

Finney or Matthews— a controversy ended by chance and inspiration

Towards the end of the War his exploits with other accomplished players at international level in Italy and Austria made it clear that England had found a winger of exceptional ability, possessing all the attributes. Good judges were satisfied he was a naturally gifted genius in the Stanley Matthews' mould, and the England selectors did not lose any time giving him an international trial, taking the earliest opportunity of putting him in the team. Thus, in September 1946 at Belfast—a month after a belated League debut (at 24) for Preston in the First Division—he made the first of 76 appearances for his country. He was an immediate success as understudy for the injured Matthews.

Two days later, in Dublin, England won again, with Finney scoring the only goal in a hard struggle against the Republic of Ireland. Matthews was available for the next match, against Wales at Maine Road in the November, but to the consternation of all who regarded the maestro as an automatic selection when fit, Finney was retained. So began a controversy which raged and persisted to the personal embarrassment of the figures involved, who were firm friends, for some time.

The controversy grew after Finney, through seeing little of the ball, had been inconspicuous in a 3-0 defeat of Wales. Nevertheless he was not discarded and was on the winning side for the fourth time when the Netherlands were beaten 8-2 at Huddersfield.

He so often called the tune, yet his fondness for holding and working the ball made it inevitable that he should be dubbed 'Finney the Fiddler' by those who did not care for his often elaborate, though never ostentatious, style of play. There was a tendency to magnify his faults if he did not perform wonders, as if he were expected to produce a glossy display in every match. He could score a goal and make one or two and still not escape the discouraging jab. It annoyed him because he was instinctively a purposeful player (an artist with either foot) with his own positive views on how and when he should part with the ball.

Some selectors would have played him anywhere in the England team rather than leave him out, but not everyone revelled in his artifice and deception. There were sneers about 'his footling foolery diddling away chances', such questions as 'when will he cut in and show his shooting

powers?' and 'when will he stop trying to beat [his] man too many?' and 'when will we see the Pre[ston] edition of him in an England shirt?' They [cer]tainly did at Hampden Park a number of ti[mes] and he scored four goals at Lisbon in 1950 in w[hat] he considers his best international.

It seems inconceivable that in 20 report[s of] Finney's play in one England match there c[ould] be ten applauding all he did and as many fin[ding] fault. Yet it happened. Some critics hamme[red] him; others, commenting on the same disp[lay,] wrote that 'Finney was always the danger m[an]' 'The best England forward was Finney,' [and] 'England's goal came through a wonderful dri[ve] by Finney!'

There was a local controversy early in [his] Preston career when a critic bluntly asked [how] many more goals would other forwards [have] scored if Finney had done his job the ortho[dox] way, stopped beating a second or third man, [and] put his centres across slickly in the Matth[ews] style. Seeing Eddie Quigley as the ideal sco[ring] foil for Finney, Preston broke the national tr[ans]fer fee record to sign him from Shef[field] Wednesday in 1949. But the two never fo[und] accord as partners, and the unhappy Qui[gley] expressed relief on being moved to inside-[left.] Preston nevertheless scored plenty of goals [as] did Finney) with the team thriving when [it] adopted a slightly more direct approach.

The England problem, however, remaine[d a] sore spot. Matthews regained his place aga[inst] Scotland, lost it again to Finney after a [dis]appointing match, and then returned to be on [the] losing side at Zurich after Finney had shone [in a] 3-0 defeat of France at Highbury in May 1[9—.] The dilemma was eventually overcome b[y a] combination of chance and inspiration. Bo[bby] Langton was injured in the Swiss match [and] Finney, who was in the party, was told by Wa[lter] Winterbottom that he would be at outside-[left] against Portugal. Finney, although a nat[ural] left-footer, was never to care for the position. [Yet] he occupied it 33 times for England and score[d —] goals, five more than his total in 40 appeara[nces] at outside-right. His other three caps cam[e in] 1956-57 at centre-forward, with Matthews o[n the] right-wing and Colin Grainger on the left. [He] scored on his England debut in each new positi[on,] and the one at outside-left came in that matc[h at] Lisbon, where a stunned crowd saw Port[ugal] routed 10-0 by what Finney has always descr[ibed] as one of the finest exhibitions given by [an] England side.

'I might have been a spectator for all the damage I did'

The experiment, which was as successful [as it] was logical, quietened the arguments about [the] gifted wingers, but it did not kill the controve[rsy:] it was to rear its head again a few years la[ter.] Finney has often said he would rather have [been] in the background and enjoyed his football t[han] endure it again. The majority have been conte[nt to] accept his England colleagues' ready endorse[ment] of Matt Busby's expressed view of Finney as [the] best footballer of his generation, irrespectiv[e of] position, and agree that he did as much [as] anyone to uphold his country's prestige.

In Scotland, going back to his vivid debu[t at] Hampden Park in 1948, he was immen[sely] admired. He and his close friend Willie Thor[nton] of Rangers were warmly greeted before the ma[tch] as former 'Desert Rats' by Field Marshal L[ord] Montgomery, the Eighth Army commande[r. A] wonderful goal by Finney just before half-ti[me,] when he cut in and shot superbly to give Engl[and] a winning lead, gave the renowned soldie[r so] much pleasure that he took the trouble to sa[y so] in a personal letter to the Preston player, [en]enclosing an autographed programme of [the] match and a photo of himself.

Never happier in his international career t[han] when playing at Hampden, Finney was suprem[ely] at ease in the glowing atmosphere of the cro[wd's] appreciation of the type of talent Scot[s]

tionally tried to cultivate. But with reason was a player the Scots loved to hate, for and never lost at Hampden on the six sions Finney was in the team. He also liked iff, where he played the best of his many games against Wales, especially when Wilf nion (his favourite England partner) was side him.

ke every great player Tom Finney had pointing games when he was described as 'strangely ineffective', notably when and beat Wales 4-2 at Sunderland in 1950. fully recovered from appendicitis, he could do ing right and was dropped for the next match. t his biggest flop, on his own frank admission,

remained the 1954 Cup Final—his saddest day with Preston since his inspiring efforts in a last-match-of-the-season win at Liverpool failed to save the team from relegation in 1949. Having just missed a League Championship medal the previous season, when Arsenal edged Preston into second place on goal average by winning their last match, Finney yearned to lead his side to a Wembley triumph in the Cup. So much was expected of him after a great season; but his contribution to a mediocre Final that West Bromwich Albion won 3-2 was a small one, and he never produced anything resembling his normal form.

'My performance was awful, and I can only assume that my game suffered because of the tense Wembley atmosphere. I was excited, perhaps, but not nervous. Most of the team were on edge, but this wasn't responsible for our disappointment. I might have been a spectator for all the damage I did. I had no fire or zest and Len Millard, who was marking me, played a blinder.'

But, after inspiring his team in the previous rounds, there were other reasons for the Wembley failure. Too much had been taken out of him by the stress of that week. Scores of friends and acquaintances badgered him for tickets; there were interviews, photographic sessions, television appearances, and, as a last straw, the presentation to him of the trophy he had earned when sports writers elected him Footballer of the Year.

This climax of a demanding week took place at a dinner in London on the night before the Final, an unrealistic procedure that was later dropped. Finney looked drawn and tired long before the junketting was over and must have longed to be back in the peace and quiet of Preston's Cup headquarters at a Weybridge hotel. He is abstemious, but it was wearying, and he still had to face the return journey to Surrey. It was little wonder that, at breakfast time, with the great occasion only a few hours away, he felt devoid of the energy needed to play in a Cup Final.

Finney took a lot of punishment—and injury robbed him of 100 games

One thing on which all who played with or against Finney are unanimous is that, with all his skill, he never lacked courage. In his time he took a large amount of punishment—reflected in the fact that he missed 115 matches, most of them in singles, two and threes, through injuries of one kind and another. Injury also cost him 11 international appearances. 'Tom Finney was one of the hardest and pluckiest players I have seen,' said Jim Milne, respected as a player, trainer and manager at Deepdale. 'He went into the tackle like a defender, and often came away with the ball. Though apparently fragile he was deceptively strong. I don't think I ever saw a harder forward playing and he had some tough nuts to tackle. Nothing frightened him. Bill Shankly used to say he would go through a mountain. Today he would be just as good as he was then. Make no mistake about that. He was the greatest.'

There are many who would agree.

1 Tom Finney playing for England in 1950. 2 'Sir Tom' on the job. He was a plumber both during and after his long football career. 3 Players and officials sing Auld Lang Syne at Deepdale before 38-year-old Finney (centre) plays his last match for Preston in May 1960. 4 Admiring eyes as the veteran takes a corner in that game. For a long time Finney and Preston had been synonymous to the football public. His contribution to the side was only really apparent after he left: the season after he retired they slumped from 9th place in the First Division to 22nd—and relegation.

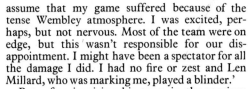

Tom FINNEY

Honours: FA Cup runners-up medal 1954
Footballer of the Year 1954

Club	Season	League		Int'nls	
		Mtchs	Gls	Mtchs	Gls
Preston North End	1946-47	32	7	6	5
	1947-48	33	13	6	6
	1948-49	24	7	6	3
	1949-50	37	10	10	4
	1950-51	34	13	4	2
	1951-52	33	13	7	
	1952-53	34		8	3
	1953-54	23	11	7	1
	1954-55	30	7	1	
	1955-56	30	17	5	2
	1956-57	34	23	7	1
	1957-58	34	26	7	2
	1958-59	16	6	2	1
	1959-60	37	17		
Total		431	187	76	30

THE WINGERS

The one-trick magician who fooled them all

Created OBE in the birthday honours in 1957 and knighted in 1965 'for services to football', Stanley Matthews was a player for 35 years; and for most of that time he was known all over the world as the greatest in English football. He played more than 50 games for England and appeared in three Cup Finals, gaining a winners medal at the third attempt, when he was 38. He was still playing in 1965 and, living in the sunshine of Malta, he was still not an old man in the early seventies; yet his fame, especially to the younger addicts of the game, was already that of a historical figure, a portrait in the select gallery that holds the frozen likenesses of such heroes as Steve Bloomer and Billy Meredith.

What was it like then, to see him in action at the height of his talents? The first feeling, as he runs out on to the field, seemingly unaware of his reputation, is one of surprise. His figure, neither noticeably tall nor short, is unimpressive; his face spare; his skin not ruddy nor brown, as might be expected of an athlete, but pale, tight over his cheekbones and forehead, with the thin hair drawn well back. His raised eyebrows and hooded eyes give him an almost Chinese air of impassivity. He holds himself nervously, with a kind of brittle stiffness, his hands closed and his arms slightly bent. He tries his legs, shifting his weight from one to the other—carefully, as if he were taking an inventory of his muscles, confirming that he has overlooked nothing in his meticulous preparations. There is a tension in him, a restrained anxiety, suggesting that of a schoolboy who hopes he will do well. He pays no attention to the crowd.

As the whistle goes and the ball moves upfield, he jogs forward with that same careful movement, wasting no energy, but with his cool eye shifting, watching intently. He is a little behind the rest of the forward line, with a clear space ahead of him, when the ball comes to him for the first time—as he likes it, straight to his feet. The ball comes fast, but he stops it dead as it reaches him. It is already perfectly controlled

as he turns and, at little more than a fast wal takes it towards the back.

The back, like every other in the game, h heard all about Matthews. He knows th Matthews likes to beat his man by going outsi him; he knows that if he rushes his tackl Matthews will be round him; so he stays near t touchline, watches, and retreats. Matthews co tinues, in his leisurely way, to bring the ball him; retreat becomes dangerous. The back hol his ground. Another man comes across in suppo Matthews is now very close; the back is with a stride of the ball. Matthews shrugs h shoulders and sways to the left. In that secon with a kind of desperate clarity, we can re the back's mind; this time Matthews is goi inside. The ball is held in the curve of Matthew right foot and that lean, wonderfully balanc figure has swayed so far to the left that it is alm too late to catch him. But not quite—he is quick strong back, and he goes across in a sw lunge. There is no one there: Matthews is gone on the outside—flying past him, already yar beyond him, imperturbable as ever; slowing dow now to his trot as he obligingly shows the ba to the next crouching defender.

The speed of that sudden sprint, over tho few yards, was Matthews' essential secret. Wi all his other gifts he could still outwit ar wrong-foot his opponents, but he would not ha left them grotesquely and completely beate staggering off-balance, or sitting helpless facing in the wrong direction—all of which did, over and over again, to the best defende in the world.

It would be difficult to convey, to anyo who had never seen Matthews, the extraordina *moral* effect of his presence in a team. A si facing Matthews—particularly a foreign si whose players had not seen him bundled about League matches on muddy Saturdays—expecte the impossible. They thought so hard abo stopping Matthews that they often forgot to gi proper attention to the rest of the forward lin It is true—and this is the main point h critics always had against him—that he ofte gave the defence time enough to assemble i forces; but then the assembly tended to take plac around Matthews himself. Wide spaces were le in the middle, and Matthews always knew exactl where those spaces were.

He was never a purely ornamental dribble He would stop the game sometimes, standin still over the ball, or tap-tap-tapping it with thre men round him, but it was more than ba control: it was command. With all his certaint of touch, he could look away from the bal watch the other man's feet, take in the di position of the field with one cool flickerin

Stanley MATTHEWS

Honours: FA Cup winners medal 1953
FA Cup runners-up medal 1948, 1951
European Footballer of the Year 1956
Footballer of the Year 1948, 1963

Club	Season	League		Int'nls	
		Mtchs	Gls	Mtchs	Gls
Stoke City	1931-32	2			
	1932-33	15	1		
	1933-34	29	11		
	1934-35	36	10	2	1
	1935-36	40	10	1	
	1936-37	40	7	1	
	1937-38	38	6	6	5
	1938-39	36	2	7	2
	1946-47	23	4	3	1
Blackpool	1947-48	33	1	5	
	1948-49	25	3	5	1
	1949-50	31		1	
	1950-51	36		2	
	1951-52	18	1		
	1952-53	20	4		
	1953-54	30	2	5	
	1954-55	34	1	7	
	1955-56	36	3	2	
	1956-57	25	2	7	1
	1957-58	28			
	1958-59	19			
	1959-60	15			
	1960-61	27			
	1961-62	2			
Stoke City	1961-62	18	2		
	1962-63	32	1		
	1963-64	19			
	1964-65	1			
Total		698*	71	54	11

* Matthews also made 3 League appearances in the abandoned 1939-40 season

Below left *Stanley Matthews as a young Stoke player. He made his first team debut in March 1932, and in his first full season the club won promotion. Matthews stayed for 16 years at the Victoria Ground before going to Blackpool for a bargain £11,500.*
Below *By the outbreak of war Matthews (here in action for the RAF) was a big star.*

e, and place his passes to an inch. No other
r in English football ever carried such
tmosphere with him, and his opponents'
ledge of his reputation and fear of his
ery was a weapon for him: and he used it
ilessly. For all his diffidence, skill and
acy, he was a ruthless player. He would never
a man, or retaliate when fouled, he was never
us; but he would beat a man, expose his
iority, beat him again, and coldly destroy
onfidence.

atthews was a maker of goals. He often scored
ng his early years with Stoke City, he
d in his first international and (playing
nside-right) he had a hat-trick against
hoslovakia in 1937, when England won 5-4.
after a few years he changed his tactics. Out
he touchline, he would take the ball right
n to the corner-flag, and work in towards
. His characteristic high centre curved
ss to drop just beyond the far post, out of
h of the goalkeeper; his ground pass was
ed back to the edge of the penalty area.

Matthews' durability was the result of rigid physical habits

n both cases the forwards were running on to
ball and the defenders had to turn. Matthews
so far forward with the ball that it was
ost impossible for the man receiving it to be
ide, his control was so extraordinary that
could hold the ball until a clear opening
made. He was not rushed into bad passes and
never passed at random. The principle is
le. The execution of it, as he did it, required
eculiar temperament and a skill that was
ost genius—in fact it required a Matthews.
vas a school of football in himself.

lis father was a boxer: Jack Matthews, 'The
ting Barber of Hanley', with a record of 350
ts, and good enough to appear at the National
rting Club. He, too, was a lean smallish
, a featherweight, quick and skilful, and
all accounts exceptionally fast and neat
his feet. He drank no alcohol, he never
ked, and he wore waxed moustaches.
thews remembers that when he was only a
ll child the clothes were pulled off his bed at
o'clock every morning, and he had to join his
er and two brothers at their dawn exercises;
deep breathing at the open window, then a
l with the chest expander.

Matthews says that, looking back, he is grateful
his father's severity. As a footballer he had
on to be: his wonderful durability was the
ct result of that foundation of rigid physical

Below Matthews finds Spurs left-half Ron Burgess
difficult to pass in the 1948 FA Cup
semi-final at Villa Park. Blackpool won 3-1 to
reach the first of their three finals
in six years. But they lost to Manchester United
that time and to Newcastle in 1951.
Below right Chaired along with his captain
after the 'Matthews Final' in 1953.
At 38 he had mesmerized the Bolton defence in
leading Blackpool's great come-back.
Below left Scottish full-back Stephens resorts
to the use of both arms in a desperate attempt
to stop Matthews at Wembley in March 1944.

habit—one which he continued—but it must have
been hard going at the time.

His unusual quality as a footballer was discovered early. He was a centre-half when he
played for his school at 11—certainly not a
defensive one, because he scored eight goals one
afternoon—but they soon made him into an
outside-right, and within a year of the change he
was an office-boy at Stoke City Football Club;
at 15 he played two games with the reserves;
at 16, 22 games; and on his 17th birthday he
signed as a professional, making his first-team
debut in March 1932.

Through these years he was still under the
severe eye of his father. The physical training
continued, and when he was an office-boy his
father took charge of his money. With no bus fares,
the boy walked the two miles between Hanley and
Stoke every day, because the exercise was good
for him; when he became a player, half his wages
went into a Post Office savings account.

At 18 he was in the first team, Stoke City
were promoted, and young Matthews won a
Second Division Championship medal; at 19 he
played for England. That first international,
against Wales at Cardiff, was in September 1934;
his last was to be against Scotland in April 1957,
when he was over 40.

If Matthews had retained his place throughout
that period he would have gained 119 caps in
official matches. As it was he won 54 (plus 26
in wartime and victory games) in a rather
sporadic international career. Indeed the start
was not a good one: the first two displays, against
Wales and Italy, even induced one of the leading
football writers of the time to accuse him of
'slowness and hesitation' and to conclude that
'perhaps he has not got the big match
temperament'.

Thousands demonstrate their feelings over his request for a transfer

But Matthews undeniably became a great star,
and there was an intensely dramatic quality
in the way his great performances were matched
to great occasions. Yet none of this was reflected
in his personality off the field. There was
no flamboyance, no distinction in his manner or
his dress, little variety in the flat intonations of
his voice, with its accent of the Potteries. His
manner was understated and self-contained, his
only interest the playing of football, his obsession
that of physical fitness. He was rarely in the news
except for his performances on the field.

But he had a precise notion of his own value.
He stayed 16 years with Stoke, and twice asked

for a transfer. The first time produced an extra-ordinary local demonstration. Thousands of handbills and posters appeared all over the city, bearing the words 'Stanley Matthews Must Not Go!'; 3,000 people attended a public protest meeting, and a thousand more paraded outside with placards. Matthews stayed—for nine more years, and then, after being out for a few weeks through injury, he was asked to play in the reserves, rather than force a change in a winning team. He refused, and in 1947 he was transferred to Blackpool. He owned an hotel there (he was thrifty, as one might expect from his background), he trained on the Blackpool ground, and had made it clear he would go nowhere else. So Blackpool got him for what was even then a bargain price—£11,500.

For all his great games, the 1953 Final is the one that is remembered

He stayed with them until 1961, and with them found the opportunity to capture a major honour: an FA Cup winners medal. These were Blackpool's good Cup years. They reached the Final in 1948, against Manchester United, and on the eve of the game the Football Writers' Association named Matthews as their first Footballer of the Year. But United won the Cup. 'I would have liked the medal,' Matthews said. 'It's always been my great ambition. I wanted to give it to my son Stanley'—the talented son who did not follow his father into football but, with his approval, made a name for himself some years later in tennis.

Against all probability, Blackpool were back again at Wembley three years later, up against Newcastle United. Matthews was 36 and must have been sure it was his last chance; but Jackie Milburn scored twice and Blackpool lost again.

By this time Matthews' medal, like Gordon Richards' Derby win, had become an object of popular mythology. Thus when Blackpool reached the Final again in 1953 the most unexpected people seemed to be emotionally involved in the result, and the stage was set for what was possibly Matthews' greatest game—though this is an almost impossible selection to make. There had been, for instance, the game against Czechoslovakia in 1937 and the 6-3 win over Germany in Berlin the following year; there were yet to come the 1955 match with world champions Germany at Wembley—when towards the end it was the young men who looked tired and clumsy—and England's 7-2 trouncing of Scotland the same year, with Matthews making five of the goals. That was Duncan Edwards' first international, and

Below Matthews centres in a League game against Chelsea in 1963. He had returned to Stoke for a nominal £2,500 in 1961, aged 46, and in his first full season played 32 matches in their promotion campaign—thus helping Stoke back up for the second time.
Below right Di Stefano is beaten and Masopust turned in Matthews' testimonial match at Stoke in April 1965. Aged 50, this was the last professional game for 'the maestro'.
Below left A scene from one of Matthews' many tours, this time Ghana in 1957. To many countries Stanley Matthews was football.

Matthews had been playing for England before was born. These were only a few of the thousa of games he played; yet for most people the Final of 1953 has to be the most memorable.

With only 20 minutes to go, Blackpool w 3-1 down. Then Matthews, at 38 the oldest n on the field, lifted his play into a new dimension faster, lighter, younger than all the n covering the field in his search for the b doing miraculous things with it when he captu it, slipping through the narrowest openin dancing over lunging tackles. His oppone seemed pinned to the ground by their own wei as he flitted through them. His high c found Mortensen by the far post, and it 3-2; with two minutes to go, Mortensen slamm in a free kick from outside the penalty a and Blackpool were level. With less than seconds left Matthews had the ball again, w inside the back this time, feinted and went side the next man, took the ball right dowr the line, and cut back a hard ground pas behind them all, behind the defence, Mortensen racing in—but right into the path Bill Perry, who met it first time. Blackpool won the Cup in the most theatrical fashion Matthews had achieved his last ambition.

Perhaps not quite the last. In 1961 he w back again to Stoke City, then 19th in the Second Division and drawing an average gat 10,000, for a nominal £2,500. There were 33, in the ground on 18 May for the last match the 1962-63 season, against Luton To Matthews was 48. Again the situation see dramatically contrived: Luton had to win to av relegation, while Stoke needed a point for Second Division championship and promotion half-time they were one up—not enough. T just after the interval came the goal that settle —and Matthews scored it. It was his only goa the season and his last in professional footb

48-year-old Matthews' last goal in football wins Stoke promotion

It was a fine finale to an astonishing play career. There followed a brief period on administrative end of the game, which en unhappily. Matthews went from Stoke to take o as general manager of Port Vale, in the Fou Division, and in 1968 the club were fined £4, and expelled from the Football League making illegal payments to players. They w immediately re-elected but he, much distres by the affair, resigned. He later managed Hibe ian of Malta—just one of the corners of the wo where, for years, Matthews *was* football.

PART 5
THE GOALSCORERS

The man who set the goal standard

There is one story, above all, which illustrates the prowess of Steve Bloomer as a marksman. It was best told by Harry Storer.

'Bloomer was in his late fifties and employed on the Derby County groundstaff,' said Storer, himself a Derby player at the time, in the thirties. 'We were chatting together and standing with our backs to a group of players having shooting practice in the goalmouth. Suddenly a ball was mis-hit in our direction and was hurtling towards our backs. One of the players shouted "Duck!".

'I did. But Bloomer turned quickly, sighted the dropping ball and, perfectly balanced, volleyed it into the net. We were all left speechless. He was about 40 yards from goal.'

Storer, who over 20 years later became manager of Derby, completed the story: 'In that flash of sheer genius, Bloomer showed why he was the greatest scorer of his generation and why he broke so many records.'

Those records—in a career that started with his League debut for Derby County at Stoke in September 1892, and ended shortly before the First World War, after he had also played for England, Middlesbrough and once more for Derby—made impressive reading: 352 League goals, plus 28 goals for England in only 23 matches. He also scored in the unofficial international against Germany in 1901.

A playing career that ended at an internment camp in wartime Germany

It was in Germany, where he was enjoying a full-time coaching appointment following retirement, that Bloomer was living when War was declared with Britain 13 years later.

The last survivor of his four daughters, Mrs Doris Richards, recalls the result: 'He was awakened in the middle of the night at his digs by the Kaiser's guards and taken away to be interned as a civilian prisoner-of-war.

In the camp at Ruhleben he met up with other Britons who had been helping the growth of German football, including England internationals Fred Pentland and Sam Wolstenholme, and together they persuaded the commandant to allow the formation of a league with daily matches. So ended, in these bizarre circumstances, the playing career of Steve Bloomer.

Shortly before his death in 1938 at the age of 64—he had been troubled by bronchial diseases since the War—Bloomer went on a health cruise sponsored by the Derby County directors and his testimonial committee. Although it was 24 years since he had last pulled on a Derby shirt in competitive football, he was still held in such esteem and regarded as the finest player ever produced by the club. The Bloomer testimonial was supported by the Football Association and many big clubs in England.

When he had left Middlesbrough, after four seasons on Teesside, to return to his first love in 1910, he was greeted by an emotional public reception at Derby station, with cloth-capped and overalled supporters welcoming back the hero they had never wanted to lose. Bloomer responded by scoring more goals until his

ammunition finally ran out at 40.

At 38, the 'second Bloomer', as Derby fans called him, led their team back into the First Division after relegation. After the First World War he became coach before finishing his days on the groundstaff.

His retirement age of 40 was almost another record. Even in those apparently less exerting days few players lasted so long. Later, Stanley Matthews playing for Stoke in the First Division beyond 50 was phenomenal, but a precedent had already been set by the great Welshman Billy Meredith.

The famous winger of Manchester City and Manchester United played well past 50. Years later Meredith reacted to the mention of his contemporary: 'Bloomer? There'll never be another Steve. He hit the ball so hard and so low that there wasn't a goalkeeper who could stop 'em. Not even "Fatty" Foulke.'

Fatty Foulke, the Sheffield United, Chelsea and England goalkeeper, weighed around 20 stones for most of his career. With Foulke and his bulk seemingly covering most of the goal, he and Bloomer were inevitable rivals in the public eye. It was certainly a challenge to Bloomer's precision of shot.

Despite the elephantine obstruction that appeared before him, Bloomer was more often than not the winner—although in their first vital clash—in the 1899 Cup Final at Crystal Palace—Foulke was beaten only once, not by Bloomer, and Derby lost 4-1.

The previous season Derby had lost their first Final, by 3-1 to Nottingham Forest, with Bloomer getting their goal.

When, in 1903, they reached Crystal Palace for the third time in six seasons, they were again losers, this time by a record 6-0. It is often forgotten that Bloomer was unfit to play and that Fryer, the Derby goalkeeper, was injured early in the game and had to leave the field.

It was another member of Preston's double side, the great Johnny Goodall, who had more influence on the young Bloomer than any other player. Derby had bought Goodall from Preston before Bloomer, who was born at Cradley Heath in Staffordshire in 1874, had arrived at the County Ground.

'Goodall was a wonderful footballer, brilliant captain and one of nature's gentlemen,' reflected Bloomer. 'In my first match for Derby I was very nervous and I shall never forget what it meant to me when, in the course of that game at Stoke, he encouraged me with the advice: "Go on yourself, lad, and shoot."

'The fact that someone of his reputation and ability told me to do what I myself might have thought a little too cheeky for a greenhorn gave me the confidence I badly needed. So I went on and shot and scored the first of my goals for Derby County. Another one followed the same afternoon.' Goodall later advised the England selectors to overlook him in order to give Bloomer his first cap.

Bloomer eventually became captain of Derby. 'I was skipper for four seasons, but I never rated myself a 'Nudger' Needham in that capacity. In fact, I contended that our centre-half in three of those four campaigns, Frank Buckley

(later Major Frank Buckley, the Wo manager) should have had the job, not me.'

Despite his supposed popularity at all le in the game, Bloomer was not invited to the jubilee banquet in 1913. This caused a mi sensation. Professional players had alre formed their own union, ran a magazine a under the heading 'The Incomparable Ste these comments appeared:

'No one knows Stephen better than the gen secretary of the union, Harry Newbould, v was the Derby outside-right before Bloomer ever heard of and was the Derby secretary at time the great discovery was made.

'Bloomer is the greatest inside-forward v has ever played for England. His name has years been a household word wherever foot has been played and, after 21 years, he is s getting goals in League football.

'He has done as much for the game as any pla who has ever kicked a ball—and he is not go to the FA banquet.'

'There never was a player more deceptive in his appearance'

The author of the article went angrily 'And some of the guests there never kicke football in a match of importance in their lives.'

The article recalled Bloomer's rise. 'He v just 17 when he first turned out for Derby. P: thin, fragile, ghost-like, almost ill-looking, caused the Derby crowd to laugh when tl first saw him. But they didn't laugh for long.

'There never was a player more deceptive in appearance. As a boy he had followed the occu tion of a striker (not the modern term for g scorer, but a foundry worker) and, for all slender build, he had muscles of steel in arms a legs.'

The union author was clearly over-sensitive the omission of Bloomer on the banquet invitat list. The FA appreciated Bloomer, and in f presented him with a portrait of himself gaining the most England international caps up that period.

'He was not a subtle or really scient

Steve Bloomer was not only one of the grea goalscorers of his time but also one of the m enduring. Billy Meredith (top left) was one of few whose careers lasted longer. His playing cai over, Bloomer went back to Derby (centre) first coach (bottom) later just to talk.

Steve BLOOMER

Honours: FA Cup runners-up medal, 1898, 1899

Club	Season	League		Int'nls	
		Mtchs	Gls	Mtchs	Gl
Derby County	1892-93	28	*		
	1893-94	25	*		
	1894-95	29	*	2	3
	1895-96	25	*	2	6
	1896-97	29	*	3	4
	1897-98	24	*	1	2
	1898-99	28	*	3	4
	1899-				
	1900	28	*	1	1
	1900-01	27	24	2	5
	1901-02	29	15	3	
	1902-03	24	12		
	1903-04	29	20	1	1
	1904-05	29	13	3	1
	1905-06	23	12		
	1906-07	9	6		
Middlesbrough	1906-07	34	18	2	1
	1907-08	34	13		
	1908-09	28	16		
	1909-10	20	8		
Derby County	1910-11	28	19		
	1911-12	36	18		
	1912-13	29	13		
	1913-14	5	2		
Total		600	352	23	28

*Figures are unavailable or unreliable for the seasons before 1900-01. It is known that Bloomer scored 352 League goals—297 with Derby County and 55 with Middlesbrough.

player,' wrote football author Ivan Sharpe, who played at outside-left in the Derby side captained to the Second Division championship by Bloomer in 1912, 'but he had the golden gift of splitting the defence with one arrow-like, pin-pointed pass . . . and he scored most of his goals by sudden shooting.'

Bloomer himself remarked that 'any shot that scores is a good shot.' But, according to Sharpe, 'it came from nearer the toe than the instep,' enabling him to kick the ball fractionally faster than most forwards, and lending some point to Bloomer's own cryptic explanation of his success: 'I try to get there first.'

Bloomer's international career was as distinguished as his League scoring feats, and he often played between the much-capped G O Smith, the Old Carthusians centre-forward, and Billy Bassett, the West Bromwich winger.

Of the Bassett-Bloomer wing pair, a newspaper correspondent wrote: 'When England beat Ireland 9-0 in 1895 (the match was at Derby) the understanding of the pair was amazing. First, Bassett would make a brilliant run; then Bloomer. Then would come a series of most baffling passes from one to the other.

Bassett himself said of Bloomer: 'You never know what he is going to do. He will give you the most beautiful passes, five or six in succession, and the opposing half-back would instinctively turn towards my direction every time Bloomer got the ball.

'Unexpectedly, he would then cut in at great pace, run straight for goal and score with a powerful shot—absolutely unstoppable.'

Billy McCracken, the Newcastle United and Ireland full-back whose tactics helped produce the change in the offside law, was a contemporary of Bloomer. 'We were great pals,' he recalled at the age of 88. 'He wasn't an artist like Jimmy Hagan or Raich Carter, the best inside-forwards I've ever seen. He was a simple ball-player and a deadly finisher. I saw him play for England against Scotland at Newcastle one day. He picked up the ball about ten yards inside the Scotland half and hit it from there. It shot into the net about three feet from the ground.'

'I sent Steve home with a bottle of Scotch underneath his arm'

Bloomer's highest haul in a match was six goals for Derby County against Sheffield Wednesday at Derby on 21 January 1899. But the match he liked to recall the most was a strange, long-winded affair with Sunderland at Roker Park five years before.

'It was the most remarkable League match of my lifetime. It lasted two and a quarter hours. Why? Simply because the appointed referee did not put in an appearance at the right time. Play started with a substitute referee and we got to half-time, with Sunderland leading 3-0, before the official man arrived.

'Then we started all over again and Sunderland won the "second" match by 8-0, making 11 against us during the afternoon!'

Bloomer, who was signed by Derby at wages of 7s 6d (37p) a week and ended up with two benefit payments totalling £400, made a special journey to Merseyside in the thirties to see a match at Goodison Park, when Everton centre-forward Dixie Dean was expected to overtake his total of 352 League goals.

Dean tells the story. 'I didn't get the goal I needed to break Steve's record that day. I apologized to him in our dressing-room after the match.

'Then we left the ground and had a few beers together. I sent him home to Derby with a bottle of Scotch under his arm because he'd taken the trouble of coming all that way.'

From one immortal goalscorer to another.

THE GOALSCORERS

Gentility, grace... and goals

If Steve Bloomer was the greatest professional footballer of the period before the First World War, there is little doubt that G O Smith was the greatest amateur—'the only footballer ever to have matched the immortal W G Grace in being known to the public by his initials alone,' according to Geoffrey Green. Between them, in a way, an amateur in a hard professional league, a goalscorer like Bloomer but with the delicate skills of Smith, stands Vivian J Woodward, to many the equal of Smith, to some even his better as a centre-forward.

Looking back at these players, it is difficult to estimate their place in the historical spectrum of the game. It is easier to take the word of their contemporaries.

'One can count the great centre-forwards of the last decade on the fingers of one hand,' stated *Caxton's Association Football and the men who made it* (published in 1905), 'J Campbell of Sunderland, J Goodall of Derby County, R S McColl of Glasgow Rangers and G O Smith. And the greatest of these is Smith. One day we may probably have to add the name of Vivian Woodward to the illustrious list....

'There will always be differences of opinion about favourite players, but universal testimony agrees that never in the history of the game has there been a centre, for consistency over a number of years, who has equalled G O Smith. For at least ten years the old Charterhouse boy stood without rival in England.'

Despite the fact that he was to become one of England's finest amateur players, Gilbert Oswald Smith was not obvious material for football stardom. As a junior at Charterhouse, playing at outside-right, his report was strikingly indifferent: 'Improved towards the end of the season. Dribbles and passes well, but is rather slow.'

He continued to improve, playing for four years in the Charterhouse team (three as captain) before going up to Oxford University. There he pursued his studies and other sports—his century won the day in a sensational varsity match against Cambridge at Lord's—while his football developed.

His ball control and finishing became second to none, while a slight build and a reluctance to head the ball were more than compensated for by his emergence as a shrewd tactician. 'What made him,' wrote another great amateur all-rounder, C B Fry, 'was his skill in elusive movement, his quickness in seeing how best to bestow his passes, his accuracy and his remarkably penetrative dribbling.'

Above In the England team that met Scotland in 1902. The captain was Gilbert Oswald Smith, better known by his initials. One of England's finest ever centre-forwards, Smith was an amateur, and won the first of his 20 caps, in 1893, while still at Oxford. His passing was renowned, and what he lacked in physique—G O was slightly built—he made up for in his 'quickness in seeing how best to bestow his passes.'

These qualities were not lost on the Engla selectors and in February 1893, when still Oxford, Smith won the first of his 20 caps, scor his side's fourth goal in the 6-1 win over Irela at Perry Bar in Birmingham.

On that occasion he played inside-right in all-Corinthian forward line. He had alrea started to play for the famous club while university, and afterwards when he becam teacher (later a headmaster in London) he sha his affections between the Corinthians and Old Carthusians. It was with the latter, his school side, that he won his Amateur Cup winn medal in 1897 and his runners-up medal in 18 He scored in both finals.

Among all Smith's qualities one stood ou his passing. 'It was in making and receiving pas that he excelled all others,' says *Caxton*. 'And was in making the pass that he was most dead No defender could anticipate what he was go to do. He was such a deadly shot that he co not be allowed to dribble too close to goal. A if one back went for him he would pass to undefended wing with unfailing accuracy a promptitude.

'In the wettest, muddiest days, when the b was heavy with clay, or greasy as a Christm pudding, his passes never went astray. His cont of the ball was no less remarkable than his abi to part with it to the best advantage.'

Smith was far from the crashing type tha often associated with the old style centre-forwa 'G O had not the physique to play a hard, dash game had he desired to do so,' explains Caxt 'His gentler methods bore better fruit. opposed subtlety to force; intellect to m strength. Slightly over middle height, with winsome face that bore traces of the pale cast thought, Smith fought his way to the front sheer diplomacy. If he could not win by f means he would not win by foul. Nor did he m a charge provided it was fairly delivered. He not belong to the drawing-room order of play

'He knew that football is a manly game, calli for qualities of pluck, grit and endurance, a when he got hurt—as all men do—he nev whined or grumbled ... To see him walk quie on to the field, with his hands in his pockets, a watch the fine lines of an intellectual face, c wondered why the student ventured into the are of football. But watch him on the ball wi opposing professionals—maybe the best in t land—in full cry after him, and you saw veritable king amongst athletes.'

Anyone could knock Smith off the ball—if they could catch up with him

It was these same attributes that so impress another contemporary, James Catton. In *Wick and Goals*, he describes Smith as 'rather frail physique, gentle in manner, and kind in dispo tion. On the field he was courageous and m unselfish. In his case, mind triumphed over musc by quickness of decision, the quickness of h movements, the perfect simplicity of his style, t swerve and balance of his body, and his neatne of footwork. Anyone could knock him off the b if he could get in contact with him. But he w difficult to find, so elusive was he. His val consisted chiefly of wonderfully accurate pass to either wing; either to the inside or the outsi man. And his body balance and swerve were su that when he left the arena not a hair of his he was out of place—John Goodall said it was trouble to play with him, and called 'Jo' the fine centre he ever saw, because he was such a mast of doing the right act at the right moment.'

Though for historical convenience Smith a Woodward are often lumped together as 'pr First World War', they almost belonged different football generations. They never play in the same England side, though that might ha been possible had not Smith given up the fir class game at the early age of 29. Woodward,

Gilbert O SMITH

Honours: FA Amateur Cup winners medal 1897
FA Amateur Cup runners-up medal 1895

Club	Season	Int'nls	
		Mtchs	Gls
(Old Carthusians	1892-93	1	1
& Corinthians)	1893-94	2	
	1894-95	1	1
	1895-96	3	3
	1896-97	3	
	1897-98	3	2
	1898-99	3	5
	1899-1900	3	
	1900-01	1	
Total		20	12

COLORSPORT

adopted G O as his schoolboy hero, and on
...y occasions admitted consciously modelling
...tyle on that of the great Corinthian.
...Woodward nevertheless remained 'sufficiently
...vidual in style to make the final single-handed
... on goal with a big chance of success.' This,
... his excellent ability in the air, meant that he
... a much more prolific scorer than his idol.

Woodward won 16 of his England caps while he was a non-League player

...ike Smith, however, he was slightly built and
...d much of his success to science and skill
...er than brawn and speed. 'The ease and
...ncy with which he escapes the attentions of
...osing players is hardly less marked than his
...ng run which frequently carries the ball half
...length of the field,' asserts Caxton. 'Woodward
...ssentially a brainy player . . . The fact is that
...dward has the rare power of thinking on his
... . . . His mind is full of ideas which he is
...stantly putting into shape . . . He can develop
...an as he runs, and while the defence is anti-
...ting the conventional pass out to the wing he
...swing towards the centre, feint to pass to a
...rade, and go sailing on with the ball at his toe.
...then heaven help the goalkeeper!'
...Woodward began with Chelmsford in the
...thern League and 16 of his 23 full England
...s came while he was a non-League player. In
...8, after helping Great Britain to win the
...mpic soccer tournament in London—he
...tributed several goals, including one in the
...l—he signed for Spurs. He remained, as he
...ld do all his career, a dedicated amateur: his
...enses for one North v South international trial
...e to 1s 6d (7½p). His 19 goals in 27 matches
...ed Tottenham win promotion to the First
...ision that season, their first in the Football
...gue. Chelsea then persuaded him to serve
...n, and he stayed until the outbreak of War,
...ving twice more for the full England team and
...ing Britain to retain the Olympic title at
...kholm in 1912.
...Unlike Smith, Woodward faced the rigours of
...lar League football. 'In looking at Wood-
...d,' states Caxton, 'he does not impress one as
...ntre-forward who could stand the rough wear
...tear of weekly League matches. A modern
...re-forward of any class is at once a marked
... . . . He is certainly not built to be used as a
...ledore or shuttlecock, but he is quite man
...ugh to look after himself and take his share
...he hard knocks that invariably fall more upon
...expert than upon the moderate players.'

'One could not mistake him for anything other than an amateur'

...What did he look like, this anomalous gentle-
...n? 'Woodward is easily recognized in a crowd.
...is built rather after the greyhound pattern,
...l moves with great speed and freedom on the
...d. His is a pleasant face to look upon. To a
...r complexion are added a firm mouth,
...ngly-marked eyebrows, and a keen clear eye
...t takes in a situation at a glance. One could
...mistake him for other than an amateur, and
...ugh he has played many times for England,
...is not averse to assisting his original club,
...elmsford, nor does he object to turn out for
...beloved county of Essex.'
...Woodward's international career was indeed
...emarkable one. He won two Olympic gold
...dals; he played 38 games for the England
...ateur side, including the very first, a 2-1 win
...r Ireland in Dublin in 1906; his 29 goals for
...full England side remained a record until both
...ney and Lofthouse bettered it by one in 1958;
...ve all, perhaps, was his reputation abroad.
...h Bob Crompton he played in all seven of
...gland's games in Hungary, Austria and

Bohemia in 1908 and 1909, scoring 15 goals.
There, in Central Europe, where he had toured
with the Pilgrims club in 1905, his position
bordered on the saintly, and his style was constantly emulated. He also visited South Africa,
captaining the Corinthians as a guest there and
playing for a representative England side in
several test matches.

'No ambassador of sport had a greater influence on the European continent than V J W—
the man with over 60 caps,' wrote Ivan Sharpe,
the journalist, who also won an Olympic gold
medal, at outside-left, in 1912. 'No forward has
ever seemed to jog through the game in such an

Above *Vivian Woodward's schoolboy hero was
G O Smith, but there were those who thought
Woodward eventually excelled Smith as a centre-
forward. He certainly scored more goals. Like Smith,
Woodward was a 'thinker'. But then he had to be,
because he was no more strongly built than G O.
After winning a gold medal in the 1908 Olympics—
he was to win another four years later— Woodward
signed for Spurs, though still as an amateur.*

effortless way, to create openings with so little
subtlety, and score goals with smaller fuss. He
was a quiet, simple, transparently honest sportsman, and that is how he played the game. The only
spectacular phase of his football was the way he
rose to the ball amid the press of players and
headed goals. I played with Woodward a dozen
times and relished the way he rolled the ball into
an open space. It looked so easy, and Woodward
certainly made life easy for his partner. He was a
leader by example and simple inspiration.'

Sharpe was not the only one to be impressed
by Woodward's effortlessness. 'Rarely have I
seen another forward do so much with such little
effort,' maintained Charlie Buchan, whose
illustrious career began when Woodward was at
his peak. 'He made the ball do all the work,
opening up the play with beautifully timed
passes. He seemed to stroll through the game . . . I
could not tell, really, if he were fast or not. He
seemed to have no concern with speed.'

With the increasing emphasis on success at all
costs, and therefore on goals, the great centre-
forwards have come to be judged largely from the
number of goals they scored. While in this respect
Woodward stood the test of time, it has hit
Smith harder. Though for most of his career he
played centre-forward and was expected to score
his quota of goals, he was in many ways, as was
Woodward, an early version of Hidegkuti or
Revie.

'There never was, and never will be, another like him'

Smith died in December 1953, Woodward the
following year. Where they rank in the history of
football can be measured from all the tributes
accorded them. Peter McWilliam, the fine
Newcastle and Scotland half-back and successful
Tottenham manager, put Smith as the centre-
forward in his all-time team; J T Howcroft, the
famous referee, plumped for Woodward. These
were tremendous tributes to players who were
never paid a penny for entertaining the public
and played for the love of the game.

Certainly Smith has no shortage of support,
either from the amateur or professional ranks.
Pa Jackson, founder of the Corinthians, in
Sporting Days and Sporting Ways, called him: 'An
athlete of extraordinary talents . . . he became
the greatest centre-forward England has ever
produced.' Confirmation comes from Steve
Bloomer, the most prolific of pre-First World War
scorers, who reckoned he 'was fortunate in internationals to be playing between Billy Bassett at
outside-right and G O Smith at centre-forward—
the best men in those positions I have ever seen.'

Geoffrey Green probably put it best. 'Those
who saw him for the Corinthians and for
England . . . say that there never was, and never
will be, another like him. Let that be his
testimonial.'

Vivian J WOODWARD

Honours: Olympic gold medal 1908, 1912

Club	Season	League		Int'nls	
		Mtchs	Gls	Mtchs	Gls
(Non-League clubs)	1902-03			3	4
	1903-04			2	
	1904-05			3	2
	1905-06			1	
	1906-07				
	1907-08			7	10
Tottenham Hotspur	1908-09	27	19	5	11
Chelsea	1909-10	13	5	1	
	1910-11	19	6	1	2
	1911-12	14	2		
	1912-13	27	11		
	1913-14	27	4		
	1914-15	6	3		
Total		133	50	23	29

Woodward also played in 38 amateur internationals for
England, scoring 53 goals, and represented the United
Kingdom in six Olympic matches, scoring five goals.

COLORSPORT

Gallacher's last word was: 'Sorry'

When Hughie Gallacher was scoring goals as only he could and arguing his way through football and glowing from the adulation of the crowds then life was tolerable. He made the final break with this world on the night of 11 June 1957 when, distraught with trouble and worry, he stepped into the path of the Edinburgh to York express as it sped over Dead Man's Crossing at Low Fell near his home in Gateshead. He was 54 years old.

The last word he spoke was, 'Sorry,' as he brushed against a passer-by. It was an appropriate word for although he had little to be sorry for as a football player he had much to be sorry for in his life. There was a broken marriage and a divorce and a story that he had accepted illegal payments. The day after his death he was due to face a charge of ill-treating his daughter.

Hugh Kilpatrick Gallacher was born in Bellshill, a Lanarkshire village in mining country. He was born in the early hours of 2 February 1903, the second son of Matthew Gallacher, an Ulsterman who made a modest living from farming. He was to become the greatest centre-forward of his time.

He scored 387 goals in 543 League matches—only Jimmy McGrory and Jack Rowley have scored more. He played 19 times for Scotland between 1923 and 1935 and scored 22 goals. Few internationals have averaged better than a goal a match.

His first competitive game of football was for the school team. He played in goal and played well and before he had left school he had played centre-half, inside-left and centre-forward and he was captain of the team. One of his team-mates· at school was Alex James and the two of them were later to go into football history as forwards in the Wembley Wizards, the Scotland team which beat England 5-1 in 1928.

Hughie Gallacher continued to play football after he left school although he worked long hours. World War I was raging and he went to work in a munitions factory at Mossend near his home. When the War ended and the factory closed he went to the pits.

Long hours at the coal face toughened him, and it was as well that they did for during all his football life he took hard knocks, for to tackle roughly was often the only way to stop him. He was fast and elusive and jinky and difficult to dispossess as he worked towards goal.

His second sport was boxing and this, too, went some way towards strengthening him. He trained at a famous gymnasium in Hamilton used by British champions Johnny Brown and Tommy Milligan and was a fair fighter. He often carried his fighting over to the football field and it was aggressiveness that had him so often suspended.

While he was still 16 he played junior football, which was then a hard grade. He played as an amateur with Tannochside Athletic and then for a miners' team, Hattonrigg Thistle, and by chance for Bellshill Athletic. He went to watch them on a day when they were a man short and they asked him to play. Afterwards, they persuaded him to sign for them for a ten-pound fee. He never got the money and that was the start of the ill luck which plagued him.

When he was 17 he was selected to play for Junior Scotland against Junior Ireland. On 29 December 1920, he headed the winning goal from ten yards out when there were but two minutes left to play. That spurred the senior club Queen of the South to act.

They had had him down to Dumfries for a trial but before he left the pavilion after that international they had persuaded him to accept terms of six pounds a week. It was a lot of money then and he was just 17 and it gave him notions outside football.

He had met a girl at the pit where he worked, and, when he signed for Queen of the South, he told his parents that he was going to marry her, in spite of their objections.

It was soon clear that his parents had been right and that he should not have married. He and his wife stayed together for only a year. They had no home of their own and stayed in rooms and then with both parents. A son was born to them and he was called after his father. That might have strengthened the union but he died before he was a year old.

Then a daughter was born and for the sake of the child they decided to try and live together again. They did, but only briefly and parted permanently in 1923 when Hughie was 20. He waited almost seven years for a divorce and when it did come it took almost £4,000 to pay the costs and he was left broke. He almost died himself when he contracted double pneumonia and for days he was on the danger list at a Dumfries hospital. During his convalescence he was visited by Airdrie directors who offered him nine pounds a week to play for them. He accepted for he wanted to play in the First Division.

Public demonstrations as Gallacher looks set to go to England

He was all Airdrie needed to make a fine team. Quickly he settled in to score goals, and he did it in batches of threes and fours. Twice he scored 30 goals in a single Scottish season. In season 1923-24 Airdrie won the Scottish Cup and by that time were attracting the notice of English clubs with money to spend.

There were demonstrations in Lanarkshire when it was learned that approaches had been made for the transfer of the county's favourite goalscorer but, nonetheless, on a November night in 1925, he was transferred to Newcastle United. Airdrie were paid £6,500. He played his first game for his new club on 8 December 1925.

The Newcastle supporters were not encouraged by their first sight of him for he was only 5ft 5in tall. But they were quickly won over. He scored, then made a goal for Stan Seymour, and then scored again.

Hughie Gallacher was immediately king of Tyneside and was soon the centre of controversy when he was made captain. Some argued that he was too young and it was revolutionary to have a centre-forward captain of a team. Gallacher answered them in the best possible way. In his first season as captain, 1926-27, Newcastle United won the League Championship.

He lorded it over Newcastle and lived life to the full. He was known round the Newcastle pubs and among the Newcastle ladies but despite his enjoyment of the situation he was always fit. He lived hard but he trained hard.

Then he met the second lady in his life. She was the 17-year-old daughter of the landlord of a hotel whose bar was a favourite of his. He was

Hughie GALLACHER

Honours: Scottish Cup winners medal 1924
Football League Championship medal 1926-27

| Club | Season | League | | Int'nls | |
		Mtchs	Gls	Mtchs	G
Airdrieonians	1921-22	11	7		
	1922-23	18	10		
	1923-24	34	33	1	
	1924-25	32	32	3	
	1925-26	16	9	1	
Newcastle United	1925-26	19	23	2	
	1926-27	38	36	3	
	1927-28	32	21	2	
	1928-29	33	24	3	
	1929-30	38	29	2	
Chelsea	1930-31	30	14		
	1931-32	36	24		
	1932-33	36	19		
	1933-34	23	13	1	
	1934-35	7	2		
Derby County	1934-35	27	23	1	
	1935-36	24	15		
Notts County	1936-37	32	25		
	1937-38	13	7		
Grimsby Town	1937-38	11	3		
Gateshead	1938-39	31	18		
Total		541	387	19	2

constantly in her company but he had omitted mention that he was still married and there v trouble when her brother found out. T appeared in court and were bound over to k the peace.

The family naturally were opposed to couple meeting but that did not stop them a when Hughie was transferred to Chelsea, followed him to London. They were married ye later when he obtained his divorce.

In Newcastle Hughie Gallacher set out to the best dressed footballer in Britain. He l well-cut suits supplied by a Newcastle tailor, usually wore white spats and on occasion white hat. Usually he carried a tightly rol umbrella. He was equally fastidious about football dress and took special care of his f and legs. They were the tools of his trade and matter how frivolous he might be in his outside football he was always deadly seri about the game.

He had returned to Bellshill after the Scotlan France match of 1930-31 and after having a hec time in Paris and needing a rest. Such notions w shattered when the Chelsea chairman came to him after agreeing on a £10,000 fee with Ne castle United. He had considerable difficulty agr ing terms with Gallacher who had the advant in the dealing.

The day he was transferred from Newcas United to Chelsea, the manager Andy Cunni ham gave him the usual civil send-off and wish

Far left Playing for Chelsea, Hughie Gallacher wins a mid-air duel in front of the Arsenal goal—no mean feat if you are only 5ft 5in tall!

Left In the famous 'Wembley Wizards' match of 1928 Scotland's Gallacher lets fly at the English goal. Scotland won 5-1 and Gallacher was acclaimed the finest centre-forward of all-time.

Below After an FA disciplinary hearing in 1934, Chelsea captain Andy Wilson (left) discusses the 'heavy punishment' with Gallacher. It was a symbolic headline, for Gallacher was in trouble, personal and professional, all his life.

Bottom Fourth from the left, Hughie Gallacher stands out in a group of Chelsea players as the snappiest dresser in the side. While he was with Newcastle, he was easy to recognize by his white spats, white hat, well-cut suits and rolled umbrella.

him well. Said the cocky Gallacher, 'I did well at Airdrie, I have done well at Newcastle, I'll do well anywhere.' He was right—as long as he meant at football. When Hughie Gallacher returned to Newcastle for the first time as a Chelsea player there were 68,386 spectators in St James' Park. That crowd set the record for the ground and it was reckoned that there were another ten thousand outside who could not get in.

The year 1928 was a notable one for Gallacher. He played for Scotland in the wonderful Scotland forward line of Jackson, Dunn, Gallacher, James and Morton in the Wembley Wizards match and was acclaimed the greatest centre-forward of all time. But there was another side to him shown during a tour of Hungary at the end of the season. In Budapest, he was accused of being drunk and disorderly on the field but an FA inquiry accepted his explanation and exonerated him. He explained that it had been a very hot day and that he had washed out his mouth with whisky and water.

Eventually he deteriorated and began the downward trek that comes to even the greatest of stars. Nevertheless he left a tremendous store of tales and anecdotes behind him. And none were stranger than those involving the referee Mr Fogg. They first met during a match on an ice-bound pitch when Mr Fogg let it be known that he was not going to tolerate hard tackling because of the dangerous state of the ground. Hughie Gallacher was aggrieved when he took some painful tackles. The referee did not like his reactions and asked him his name. Gallacher told him, 'If you don't know my name you've no right refereeing, what's your name?' The referee taken by surprise answered 'Fogg,' and was told, 'I could have guessed. You've been in a fog all afternoon.' That bit of repartee cost him a 2 months suspension but 14 days after the suspension was up, he was chosen for the Scotland v Ireland match of 1929. Strangely, Mr Fogg was referee and in an 'I'll show you' mood Hughie Gallacher scored five goals. Again when Mr Fogg was referee he scored five for Derby County against Blackburn Rovers.

He reckoned that his greatest goal was the one against Wales at Tynecastle Park in Edinburgh when he took the ball from his own half of the field past three defenders and lobbed it over the goalkeeper as he came out. He once scored by slipping the ball between the legs of Harry Hibbs, Birmingham's international goalkeeper and once he took the ball from his own half beating defenders all the way and then pretended to shoot. As the goalkeeper dived he walked the ball into the other side of the goal.

But he was on the downward slope with Derby and on it went through Notts County, Grimsby Town and Gateshead and, as the football in his life faded, his personal problems grew. Finally there was the humiliation of having been charged with ill-treating his daughter.

One can understand the torment in his mind the day before he had to face the court. He was a faded football idol, a memory, and all the glories of the past could bring him was drink from those who wanted to talk of the old days. He brooded and then walked out in his cloth cap, and then the express thundered past and the little man stepped in front of it and was no more.

TOPIX

PRESS ASSOCIATION

THE GOALSCORERS

Dean and Lawton –the immortals

The team that made England feared in football again—the World Cup side of 1966—was a team of all-purpose players. But it wasn't always so; the style that made English football dominant until after the Second World War was based on men who knew their place—the specialists. And the greatest specialists of them all were the centre-forwards.

'Dixie' Dean and Tommy Lawton were two such men; great centre-forwards and men of star quality—a very different matter—and men who, at a time when the absence of television meant that there were few such figures, became folk heroes.

They had much in common. Both were tall, powerful and fast; both were dark—Dean with curly hair and a full-cheeked, round-featured face, Lawton with his hair a slick patent-leather black, a broad forehead and a jutting nose; both were supreme artists at heading the ball; both showed their talent young; both went to Everton, Arsenal's rival as the glamour team of the period, where every boy from the north wanted to go, as they might now want to go to Manchester United.

Dean arrived first. Born in Birkenhead in 1907, he was christened William Ralph Dean,

accepting 'Bill' from his friends. The poin[t] worth underlining because the nickname 'D[ixie]' that followed him all through his career is [one] that he detested, and still does. He began [in] football with Tranmere Rovers, making his de[but] at the age of 15 in 1923, but it was only a b[rief] appearance in a shop-window. When he was [only] 17 Everton offered £3,000 for him—a size[able] sum then—and Tranmere were forced to let [him] go. They were in the same unhappy position a [few] years later, when they had to part with ano[ther] centre-forward who played for England, 'Po[rky]' Waring. Dean stayed with Everton from 1[925] to 1937, and with them won two First Divi[sion] Championship medals, one Second Divi[sion] medal (when the team bounced back into [the] First after only one season of relegation), [one] FA Cup winners medal, and 16 internati[onal] caps.

The new offside law and why it became a centre-forward's charter

It was an interesting period in the developm[ent] both of football in general and centre-forw[ard] play in particular. In 1925 the offside [law] had been changed to its present form, so th[at a] man was 'onside' if only one opponent, beside[s the] goalkeeper, was between him and the goa[l,] instead of two. It was a couple of seasons be[fore] defences adjusted themselves to the new situat[ion,] and during that time centre-forwards, tea[ring] through the newly-opened space in the middl[e of] the field, cut them to pieces.

Two in particular profited. George Cam[sell] of Middlesbrough, later to play for Engla[nd,] scored 59 goals in the 1926-27 season— [but] that was in the Second Division. In 1927-28 ca[me] Dean's most remarkable achievement, when [he] set a record that looked unlikely ever to [be] broken over 40 years later. That season he sc[ored] 82 goals in first-class matches—League, C[up,] internationals and in international trials. I[n] First Division matches he scored 60 goals. W[ith] only three games to go, he was still ten short of [the] record. When the last game arrived—aga[inst] Arsenal—he still needed three.

There were fifty thousand people at Goodi[son] Park, and an almost unbearable atmosphere [of] excitement. Arsenal scored, Dean equali[sed.] Dean scored from a penalty, Arsenal equali[sed.] Then, with only twelve minutes to go, anot[her] centre came over, Dean leapt to it, met it, [and] the record was broken.

That was the great day of his career—grea[ter] even than the one in 1927, when England b[eat] Scotland at Hampden Park for the first t[ime] for more than 20 years. The score was 2-1, [and] Dean got both the England goals. He was [not] yet 21.

Clearly, after this astonishing season, [the] point was made that the new offside law ca[lled] for new defensive techniques. The game ha[d to] adjust itself, and it did—by the introduct[ion] of the 'stopper' centre-half, whose business it [was] to block up the clear path to goal down [the] middle. Herbie Roberts, of Arsenal, was the firs[t to] perfect the 'policeman' third-back game and [he] and his kind bottled up many centre-forwa[rds] who had been anticipating a period of ease a[nd] plenty.

Dean, though, could not be subdued, even [by] this smothering close-marking method. In the [first] place, he was admirably gifted to deal with [a] defender man-to-man. He had muscular l[egs] full of spring, fine judgment for the flight [of] a high ball, and could head it with a force a[nd] accuracy comparable to most men's shoot[ing.] The stoppers had little luck with him beca[use] he beat them in the air, and was too str[ong] and courageous to be forced aside. More imp[ortant]

Left above One of football's first immort[als,] Madame Tussaud's entertains an Everton team o[f the] 1930s to a viewing of the waxwork of Dixie De[an.]
Left Sir Frederick Wall, secretary of the FA, D[ixie] Dean and the FA Cup won by Everton in 1933.

KEYSTONE/RADIO TIMES HULTON PICTURE LIBRARY

he developed new techniques himself. He
ame a goal-maker as well as a goal-scorer. He
uld rise to a high centre, and then, instead
eading for goal, would nod the ball neatly
n to one side, into the path of an advancing
de-forward. In 1936, towards the end of
n's career, the 17-year-old Tommy Lawton
e to Everton, already a brilliant player and
markable header of the ball. He learned this
k from Dean, and more than ten years later
making goals for Jackie Sewell of Notts
nty, just as Dean had made them for Dunn in
thirties.

Dean was the most famous goalscorer since
legendary Stephen Bloomer of Derby County,
se total passed 350. Dean scored 379 during
career, 349 of them for Everton, and a high
portion of them headed. Yet when he had
there only two years, the whole of Liver-
l was shocked to hear that he had fractured his
ll and his jaw in a motor-cycle accident in
es, and would never play football again. The
ries were, as reported, grave, but he recovered,
so did the spirits of his followers. His popu-
ty was amazing, and on Merseyside it was near
ration. He was caricatured, imitated, and
subject of music-hall jokes. Sandy Powell,
comedian, had a song about him with the
ain 'Nodding 'em in, nodding 'em in'. It
said that when Dean met the great Liverpool
lkeeper Elisha Scott in the street, and wished
good morning, nodding sharply as he did
Scott dived into the gutter with his arms
stretched.

He left Everton in 1937, had a short spell with
ts County and then with Sligo in the Irish
gue (where he played his last game in Decem-
1940), and then took over a pub, 'The Dublin
ket' in Chester. This was not a success, his
lth broke down, and he went to hospital. John
ores, the millionaire chairman of Everton,
nd him a job as a porter with the Littlewoods
anization, where he has been happily employed
some years. In 1964 there was a benefit for him
Liverpool—a match between English and Scots
yers drawn from the Liverpool and Everton
bs. It was well attended, and he had a great
tion as he walked out to kick off. He is still
uch respected local figure, and an expert and
using after-dinner speaker.

Tommy Lawton, the pupil who outshone the master, Dixie Dean

Tommy Lawton, his disciple and successor,
ne to be an even greater player, partly because
npetition was fiercer in his time, and the
ne itself faster and harder, but also because
added to equal skill in the air a truly formid-
e shooting power. He was tall, powerfully built,
ecially in the shoulders, neck and legs,
manner was cool and observant, his move-
nt deceptively leisurely. He would range about
field with his long easy stride, his head
ing forward, pounce smoothly on a loose
l, and glide swiftly through the defence,
utifully balanced, moving like a skater, con-
ling the ball in quarter-circles with the
side of either foot. The shot, when it came, was
cuted with what seemed a lazy swing of the leg,
it travelled like a shell. 'He was the
ntest mover', said Alex James, 'of any big
n that ever played football.'

The famous Russian ballet dancer Nijinsky
s once asked how he managed to perform so
ectively into the air. He answered, 'First I jump
gh—and then I wait a little.' This ability to
ver in the air, almost to wait above his
ponents' shoulders, is the mark of a world-
ss header of the ball, a quality which Tommy
wton showed to the delight of the football

ght above Dean (right) at Highbury on the day
passed Steve Bloomer's League goalscoring record.
ght Like Tommy Lawton, Dean spent some time
h Notts County. It was in their striped shirt that
scored the last three of his 379 League goals.

crowds for over 20 years.

Lawton played 45 times for England—including wartime and victory internationals—and scored 46 goals. In first-class football altogether his total was around the 500 mark. The feeling he commanded was not so much affection as respectful admiration, and his fame was international. Because of his skill and strength he was a threatening and dangerous opponent, yet, as Billy Wright said, 'Although he took tremendous hammerings, I never saw him lose his temper or his pose. Never can I recall Tommy Lawton deliberately fouling an opponent.' In 20 years of football, with various clubs, at various levels of the game, he was never booked and never sent off.

Lawton would rise, head and shoulders above all the rest

In the fine England sides between the end of the War and 1948, the lessons he had learnt from Dean, and then perfected, were seen at their best. On the right wing was Stanley Matthews, who could place a high centre into a crowded penalty area as precisely as any man that ever tried it. In stadiums all over the world, a sigh of admiration breathed from the crowd as Lawton rose effortlessly, head and shoulders above the rest, and with the speed of a striking snake, met the ball just where his centre parting met the forehead, and drove it into goal. Beside him, at inside-forward, was the brave and tireless Stanley Mortensen, tearing through to fasten on to the passes that Lawton glided down to him.

Lawton was born in Bolton in 1919, a natural genius of football if there ever was one. In three seasons of schoolboy football he scored 570 goals, and there were times, it was said, when the talent-spotters outnumbered the other spectators. Burnley was the club that got him, when he was 16, and he was in their League side before he was old enough to sign as a professional.

Four days after his seventeenth birthday, the day he became a professional, he played for Burnley against Tottenham Hotspur, where the man marking him was Arthur Rowe, already an international centre-half, and later to be the startlingly successful Spurs manager of the fifties. Lawton scored a hat-trick, one of the most prophetic debuts ever. Two minutes from the start, he hit the ball with all his force into the back of the net. A few minutes later, he scored his second goal, a header from a fast out-swinging corner, met exactly at the top of a perfectly judged jump. He then missed another couple of chances in the first half, the 17-year-old understandably showing his nerves, before completing an unforgettable hat-trick in the second. Within the year, in December 1936, Everton bought him for £6,500.

He spent nine of his best years there, won his first England cap when he was only 19, and, in 1939, a League Championship medal. Then, in November 1945, with the War over, the clubs started rebuilding, and Chelsea needed a centre-forward. For a record fee—£11,500—they bought the best in the country, Lawton. There were cries of anguish in the papers about this scandalous sum of money—as there have been ever since Middlesbrough bought Alf Common for £1,000 in 1905.

Lawton was not merely a footballer, and he was certainly something more than a faithful club

1 and 2 The last three years of Lawton's playing career were spent in the red shirt of Arsenal. 3 After his demob from the army in 1945 he and his wife moved to London, where he joined Chelsea. 4 The deal which took Lawton to Third Division Notts County for a record £20,000 in 1947 caused a sensation; he was still England's centre-forward. 5 Lawton in a Nottingham snooker hall with a long-retired County star, Albert Iremonger. A goalkeeper, Iremonger is best known for the time when he took a penalty, hit the crossbar and in the ensuing scramble managed to boot the ball into his own net.

RADIO TIMES HULTON PICTURE LIBRARY

RADIO TIMES HULTON PICTURE LIBRARY

1

2

3

4

5

servant. He was a star, and he was always news. At every stage of his career there were headlines. He was difficult, and some said mercenary. He was certainly not in the game for fun, much as he liked it, yet when one considers the thousands who were drawn to any ground where he played, simply to see him, he can hardly be said to have given any club less than their money's worth. At £12 a week in the season, with £2 for a win and £1 for a draw, and £10 a week in the off-season, he was unlikely to make a fortune. Dean played for most of his time for £8 a week. No wonder both of them reflect, looking at the modern game, how different it would have been if they had been born 20 years later.

Lawton had only one full season with Chelsea, but it was a good one. He scored 26 goals in 34 games, an individual record for Chelsea in the First Division, and, playing between two fine inside-forwards, Goulden and Walker, made many more. Then the headlines started appearing. He had asked to go. The club refused to release him, put a big fee on his head, and said they had received no 'acceptable' offers. There was talk of arbitration, and of appeal to the players' union, but then there was a decision, and with it the biggest football story for years.

Lawton, the England centre-forward, was going to the Third Division, to Notts County, for the first ever £20,000 fee. He played four more internationals while he was there, helped them to promotion in 1950, and in the same season was top scorer in the Third Division. It was ten years since, with Everton, he had been top scorer in the First.

Then, in 1952, after rumours of internal disagreements, he left 'at his own request' and returned to London, to Second Division Brentford. He was 33.

He had lost some speed, but he was still much faster than he looked; he still led the line, though he lay a little further back; his experience and authority were impressive—yet, with all this, the time was obviously coming when his career must take a new turn. It was not clear what it would be, especially since he had not enjoyed being player-manager with Brentford, and had returned to being simply a player.

The next development was astonishing and unexpected, and 'The Lawton Story' was all over the sports pages again. Lawton, at 34, was back in the First Division—and with Arsenal. Arsenal had played their first eight games of the 1953-54 season without a win, though they had begun it as champions. They had young players coming up, but they needed the maturity and confidence of a player like Lawton. For three years he served his purpose admirably.

With Arsenal Lawton was the goalmaker rather than the goalscorer

He was even more the goalmaker now, and Lishman and Tapscott were the inside men who ran through on to his nodded passes. He balanced the line, and swept majestic low passes to the wings. Under his leadership, a disorganized, though enthusiastic, attack became steady and coherent. Lawton, on tour with Arsenal, spent his thirty-fifth birthday in Moscow, and the Russian footballers threw a surprise party for him, with a cake two feet square.

This period was the end of Lawton's big-time football. He and Arsenal parted with dignity, and with manager Tom Whittaker's assurance that he would be advised when a good opportunity as a player-manager came along. An opening appeared with Kettering Town, in the Southern League. Lawton filled it well, and from it might have built a new career. Unfortunately, after a year, Notts County offered him a good salary as manager there and, overlooking his earlier unhappy experience with them, he took it.

It could never have worked. The directors were not unanimous on the appointment, and said so publicly. Some of the players felt a greater

loyalty to the acting manager, Frank Broome, and once again there was money trouble—money to buy players, money to pay Lawton's salary. After a year he was dismissed.

In 1958, Lawton announced he was finished with football, and took over the Magna Charta Inn, at Lowdham in Nottinghamshire, and for a long time nothing was heard of him. Then, on a television programme, it was mentioned that he was looking for work, and as a result of it he was offered a job as a salesman with a firm that makes seats for football grandstands.

Lawton has a son, who, at 15, had a trial with Leeds United—difficult for him, because he must have known it would take a truly remarkable player to be only half as good as his father. The trial was not a success and both father and son were disappointed. But it is some measure of Tommy's reputation that he had to stop his son playing local Sunday football—so persistent were the scouts who wanted to give the lad a try.

With great players of the past it is always easy to be tempted by the question of whether they would succeed in modern times. The answer must be that they would. What makes a great player in any period is his great gifts as an individual, and, more important, his ability to adjust to changing circumstances. Both Dean and Lawton lived through transitional periods. Dean survived the change in the offside law, which put an end to the promise of many of his contemporaries. Lawton played through the period when foreign influences were beginning to affect the English game, and through the unrest that eventually led to footballers being adequately paid. With their talents, their physical equipment, the intuitive speed of their reflexes, they would have been ornaments and assets to any team playing today. The pity is, especially in Dean's case, that their gifts were not displayed in the setting they deserved.

Dixie DEAN

Honours: League Championship medal 1928, 1932; FA Cup winners medal 1933

Club	Season	League		Int'nls	
		Mtchs	Gls	Mtchs	Gls
Tranmere Rovers	1923–24	2			
	1924–25	27	27		
Everton	1924–25	7	2		
	1925–26	38	32		
	1926–27	27	21	5	12
	1927–28	39	60	5	4
	1928–29	29	26	3	1
	1929–30	25	23		
	1930–31	37	39	1	
	1931–32	38	45	1	1
	1932–33	39	24	1	
	1933–34	12	9		
	1934–35	38	26		
	1935–36	29	17		
	1936–37	36	24		
	1937–38	5	1		
Notts County	1937–38	3			
	1938–39	6	3		
Total		437	379	16	18

Tommy LAWTON

Honours: League Championship medal 1939

Club	Season	League		Int'nls	
		Mtchs	Gls	Mtchs	Gls
Burnley	1935–36	7	5		
	1936–37	18	11		
Everton	1936–37	10	3		
	1937–38	39	28		
	1938–39	38	34	8	6
Chelsea	1946–47	34	26	8	10
	1947–48	8	4	3	4
Notts County	1947–48	19	18	3	2
	1948–49	36	20	1	
	1949–50	37	31		
	1950–51	30	9		
	1951–52	29	12		
Brentford	1951–52	10	2		
	1952–53	34	13		
	1953–54	6	2		
Arsenal	1953–54	9	1		
	1954–55	18	6		
	1955–56	8	6		
Total		390	231	23	22

'Wor Jackie'

One Christmas morning the young Jackie Milburn saw lying on his bed, among other presents, the gift he wanted most of all—a pair of football boots. Hurriedly he put them on and ran outside to play football. There were so many boys in their new boots in the street that he had to wait some minutes to find out which side he could play on. Not a particularly remarkable thing to happen on a Christmas Day perhaps—except that all this was taking place at four o'clock in the morning. It was still dark, and the play was by the light of streetlamps and torches.

That was Ashington, Northumberland.

Ashington was a township obsessed with football—and the pit. From the bedroom in Sixth Row where he was born in May 1924, he looked into the pityard and the shaft used by his father, and the fathers of his friends, every working day and night.

When the young Milburn was first chosen to play for his school he was twelve—he lay in bed on the Friday night wondering if he should tell his father about it when he came in off his shift at two in the morning. He decided not to but, sleep being out of the question, when he heard his father come in and go to bed, he got up, put on his football strip including his boots, and spent the rest of the night downstairs sitting dressed for the match before the kitchen fire. He was on the field two hours before kick-off and he scored two goals—in front of his father, mother and two sisters.

Ask Milburn what made him and he will answer, 'Ashington. There were games going the full length of every street. We were kicking a ball before school, during breaks, at lunch-time and after school. Sponge balls, tennis balls—you learn control better with them than with these full-size balls youngsters have now.

'Ashington and the family. We were steeped in football. Ever since my great-grandfather played in goal for Northumberland in 1888. And the women played too, you know, in Ashington. All the women who married the Milburns seemed to play football.'

Milburn can't remember not having the want and ambition to be a professional footballer. Three of his older cousins played for Leeds: Jack, George and Jimmy Milburn, all defenders. They were proof that the Milburns could make it. A younger cousin, Stan, played full-back with Chesterfield and Leicester, and another cousin, Cissie Milburn, married in Ashington and became the mother of Jackie and Bobby Charlton born in Laburnum Terrace, three doors away from where Jimmy Adamson was born.

What lifted Milburn's football above that of his friends? More than anything else it was his desire to win; his clear, undoubted aim; his willingness to practise and to train on and on.

'I would kick into an empty goal, on my own, pretending there were three or four defenders to beat: then I would go for the ball, bring it back and start again. Then I used to kick a ball against a wall for hours.'

Watching Ashington play early in the War he was tremendously impressed by Stan Mortensen, then guesting for Ashington. He had never seen such dynamic effort in a goalmouth. Mortensen revealed to Milburn what a determined man could do. For Milburn, 'Morty' is still the best centre-forward he has seen. As it happened, when Milburn played his first game for England he was at centre-forward, with Mortensen on his

right. That match took place in 1949.

Milburn's shooting is part of football history. Those goals lashed in; those long-range shots disappearing into the net, hardly visible, scarcely believable, with the goalkeeper just beginning to move and the players transfixed and gaping.

Milburn played for Ashington when he was an apprentice fitter at the colliery and continued to train hard. He was then selected for Northumberland, and wrote to Newcastle United asking for a trial. He had two good trial games, signed as a professional at thirty shillings a match plus expenses to and from the ground and was put straight into the first team.

The trainer at St James's was Norman Smith, a man Milburn, if anything, respects even more today than he did then. 'He didn't tell you, but advised you.'

Milburn once spoke to Stanley Matthews in admiration, hoping to get some little tip. 'You ask me?' said Matthews. 'I'd give anything to be able to hit a ball like you.'

'Hughie Gallacher, you will never be good enough to lace his boots'

Milburn remembers with some amusement: 'Hughie Gallacher used to come down and have a word with me, after the matches at St James's, when he was doing some reporting. He gave me some tips. "Hughie Gallacher," my father would say, "you'll never be good enough to lace his boots".'

Milburn played in an inside position, mainly inside-left at first and then, because of his speed, he was usually played on the wing, especially on the right. He was not keen on being tried at centre-forward because his only game there as a schoolboy had been a dismal failure.

At the end of the War, Stan Seymour, resolved to get Newcastle out of the Second Division, assembled a formidable side, and in 1946-47 attendances at St James's actually averaged 56,351.

Milburn's dreams were being realized now. He was playing dramatically before huge, enthusiastic crowds in a talented and spirited side destined soon to gain promotion and to win three FA Cup Finals at Wembley. And the crowd took to him. They called him, 'Wor Jackie'.

In October 1947, Charlie Wayman, Newcastle's centre-forward, was transferred to Southampton. Before this, centre-forward Albert Stubbins had gone to Liverpool. Newcastle's new manager George Martin talked Milburn into the centre-forward position. Before his first game in his new role Milburn had two sleepless nights.

Len Shackleton, who was in the Newcastle side that day, says: 'Jackie Milburn is the fastest player I've seen: once he was moving, once he got going. His speed is needed today when defences have a tendency to be a bit square. An ideal player would have Tony Green's quickness off the mark and Jackie Milburn's speed from there. The important thing for Jackie was that switch to centre-forward, although he'd have come to the fore in any case—his talent would have brought him through. Whenever I think of Jackie Milburn I think of a greyhound going out of a trap.'

That is how it was at Wembley in the 1951 Final against Blackpool. In the second half, just

over the half-way line, Milburn quickly looked round to see that he was on-side to a pass from Robledo, then he streaked the long, lonely run to the goal and drove the ball past Farm.

Five minutes later he settled the issue with one of the most spectacular goals ever seen at Wembley. Spotting a chance from thirty yards he called to little Ernie Taylor to backheel the ball. It came slightly late for his run and he was very nearly too far over it, but this kep

Far left *Jackie Milburn hammers a left-foot shot as a despairing defender abandons his challenge.*
Left *Another left-foot rocket from Milburn which Arsenal keeper Jack Kelsey can do nothing about.*
Below left *The Argentinian goalkeeper puts up his hands in a gesture of dismay as Milburn (in a number 9 shirt of unfamiliar colour) scores England's second goal at Wembley on 9 May 1951.*
Bottom left *On the way to his third Cup winners medal in five years, Milburn heads Newcastle's first goal against Manchester City in the 1955 Final.*

there were some seconds of silence before the unbelieving crowd accepted the evidence of the ball in the net.

Milburn had one of the happiest of football careers. He thought his team-mates were the best he could be playing with; he played before his own people, knowing that they liked him; and he was happy at home. 'Happy in work, happy in life,' he says. He met his wife, Laura, at Letchworth, when the team was training there. He has two daughters, both married and, in the tradition of the Milburns, living not too far away from his home in Newcastle. He has a son, still at home.

In the close season of 1957 the scarcely credible happened: Milburn left Newcastle United. He reversed the customary direction for footballers and went to Northern Ireland as player-coach with Linfield. He averaged 50 goals a season for over three seasons and also gained some experience of managing.

He then went to Yiewsley in the Southern League as player-coach. He did some coaching with Reading at this time, and when Alf Ramsey left Ipswich Milburn took over as manager there —not, however, with much success. Since 1964 he has earned his living as a sports journalist.

A modest man, he says: 'I had a lack of devil in front of goal. I would give the ball to George Robledo. Perhaps I should have held it more: I would have scored more goals—like Greaves, like Charlie Wayman, like Malcolm Macdonald.

'Then there was my heading—although I averaged eight goals a season with my head. I used to hold back, hoping to get in a ground shot. But heading a lot, the jumping, used to bring on fibrositis. I'd be off three or four days. I'd come off holding my neck. That all started with not wearing enough when I was a boy. It was through living in my football strip. I just wouldn't take it off, and I used to get cold up the back.'

He says: 'The crowd and players now seem to be poles apart. At one time they were a unit. And there's a lot of unnecessary running about by young players. I like to see the older heads: knowing what to do.' What saddens him is to meet some of the great footballers of his day who were not able to make anything for the future out of the game.

'I enjoyed every second,' he says. 'Everything was there—the crowds, the excitement. It was all laid on. When it was all gone, I really missed it. For two years it was hard to take. I used to agree then with what Wilf Mannion said: "They should take old footballers to the knacker's yard and shoot them".'

His great contemporary Len Shackleton says: 'Jackie Milburn's cost now? It would be like the reference number on my gas bill.'

he shot low and, before anybody knew it, it was in the net.

Mortenson, at centre-forward for Blackpool, shook hands with Milburn after that goal. 'Jack,' he said, 'that deserves to win any match.' Milburn says having Mortenson say that to him in a Cup Final was one of his proudest moments.

His other two Cup Finals, in the next year, 1952, and in 1955, were marred by bad injuries to Barnes and Meadows which meant both New-

castle's opponents, Arsenal and Manchester City had to fight a man short.

The best game Milburn can remember playing was the classic Portsmouth-Newcastle sixth-round tie at Fratton Park in 1952. Portsmouth were at their peak with the renowned half back line of Scoular, Froggart and Dickinson. Milburn got the first three goals in Newcastle's 4-2 win. His third, which put Newcastle ahead, was such a sudden long-range bullet of a shot that

Jackie MILBURN

Honours: FA Cup winners medal 1951, 1952, 1955

Club	Season	League		Int'nls	
		Mtchs	Gls	Mtchs	Gls
Newcastle United	1946-47	24	7		
	1947-48	39	21		
	1948-49	34	19	4	3
	1949-50	30	18	4	3
	1950-51	31	17	3	4
	1951-52	32	25	1	
	1952-53	16	5		
	1953-54	39	16		
	1954-55	38	19		
	1955-56	39	19	1	
	1956-57	32	13		
		354	179	13	10

THE
GOALSCORERS

The other Stanley

Stanley Mortensen is lucky to be alive. He admits the fact with a cheerful nod in fate's direction, something he has been doing on and off for 30 years. His life is lived to the full: he is grateful for what he has, grateful that he was spared instead of becoming a statistic on the roll of honour in World War Two.

In the period since he was taken from a crashed Wellington bomber with severe head and back injuries, Mortensen has lived as if determined to enjoy himself. That, as much as his individual style, was a characteristic of his play for Blackpool and England—even during the darker period towards the end of his active days, in the lower divisions and in non-League soccer Mortensen looked as if the game and its quality was the prime objective, irrespective of the result.

When he dropped out of football he ran a post-card shop on Blackpool's Golden Mile, then a sports shop, then betting shops. He became a member of the local council and was elected chairman of the entertainments committee—a fitting choice.

In due course Blackpool made him their manager, though too late to avoid relegation in his first season, 1966-67. In his second season the club missed promotion on goal average after winning their last seven matches, and they gained 58 points—the highest any team has obtained without going into the First Division. Mortensen shrugged off the blows and remained the same as ever, infectiously good-humoured.

Even when Blackpool summarily dismissed him a year later—by his own admission a terrible blow—he took it in his stride. He left through a corridor thronged with reporters, smiling that Mortensen smile.

Then, after he became head of sports pro-motion for a holiday-camp firm, he was still as large as life. That has always been his way.

His ability to turn disaster aside, bedded into his character by nature, was ingrained still more deeply during his playing career. He had more good moments than bad, but he certainly had some bitter disappointments. He never won a

Below *Stan Mortensen in action against FIFA at Wembley in October 1953, his penultimate game for England. He won 25 caps, scoring 23 goals.*
Bottom *Earlier in the year 'Morty' (here hooking in his second goal) became the first man to score three in a Wembley Cup Final. But despite the hat-trick that enabled Blackpool to beat Bolton 4-3, the glamour went to Stan Matthews.*

UNITED PRESS INTERNATIONAL

Championship medal; he was on the los side in two FA Cup Finals, the first of th after scoring in every round of the comp tion that season, including the last; he wa member of the England team humiliated the USA in the 1950 World Cup; and th years later his international career was en by the Hungarians in the celebrated 6-3 match Wembley.

Even his triumphs did not gain the accla they deserved, in those pre-television days. first full international, against Portugal in Lisb in 1947, brought him four goals, but hardly Englishman saw them. Against Italy in Tu a year later he inspired an outplayed Engla team with a magnificent goal from an acute ang and a possible rout became a 4-0 win. Again, supporters in the crowd were minimal. months earlier he had scored a hat-trick agai a very good Swedish team—on a midweek aft noon at Highbury. And even when he became first player to score three times in a Wemb Cup Final, his feat was overshadowed beca of his friend and colleague, Stanley Matthe The shuffling magician on the right flank is man the people remember from 1953: Mortense hat-trick comes to mind virtually as an aft thought.

Mortensen certainly had his share of m fortune. But he is the first to point out that, w or lose, he was lucky to be playing at all. Doct said his football career was over, almost in infancy, after he had survived that bombe crash early in the War. He still carries a fo inch scar on his skull, plus another legacy: t of insomnia. Ever since then he has had di culty in sleeping for any length of time.

Even in his prime, 'Morty' never looke particularly good advertisement for a seas resort like Blackpool. In Rio for the 1950 Wo Cup, the players all collected a healthy tan . . . except Mortensen. 'He would come down in morning looking as if he'd spent the night wit ghost,' said centre-half Laurie Hughes. 'He j couldn't nod off. But he took some matching energy.'

Energy was another of Mortensen's rec nizable virtues. There was not a lot of h (much less than there is now) but he could l the fiercest pace, streaking into action with t high-stepping run, shoulders hunched over ball. His speed might not be exceptional in toda era of sprinters, but in his day there were few match him, certainly not over those first v yards.

Morty also had a strong shot; and though headwork was never particularly brilliant, was always dangerous near goal. Like many f forwards he had an instinctive 'nose' fo chance, nature taking him to unlike places to cash in on rebounds

ections. He was also immensely brave, scoring
[va]riety of injuries to carry on plying his trade
[as a]goalscorer.

[D]uring ten post-War seasons with Blackpool
[he a]veraged roughly two goals every three games,
[incl]uding a record 30 in the FA Cup. Many came
[from] crosses by Matthews, but he also collected
[a lo]t on his own, beating a defence by speed
[or a]through ball and then shooting past the
[adva]ncing goalkeeper.

[I]ronically it was a similar goal by Newcastle's
[Jack]ie Milburn that turned the 1951 Cup Final
[awa]y from Blackpool. Three years earlier,
[desp]ite Mortensen's earning a penalty (tripped
[from] behind when clear) and after scoring himself,
[Man]chester United had twice come from behind to
[win]4-2.

[T]here is more irony here. Mortensen blames
[him]self, in part, for Blackpool's defeat. The teams
[wer]e level 2-2 when he slipped past Chilton and
[faced] himself with a clear if angled chance. 'I put
[it to]o close to the goalkeeper, Jack Crompton,' he
[expl]ains. 'He dived and held it, cleared upfield,
[and] inside a few seconds Stan Pearson had scored
[thei]r third—while I was still in United's penalty
[area.]'

[B]ut third time paid for all, in the amazing
['53]match with Bolton. Nat Lofthouse (with
[Milb]urn a main rival for Mortensen's England
[plac]e) emulated the Blackpool man by scoring
[in e]very round: the goal that gave him the set
[pac]e in the first minute. Morty equalized, in
[off]Hassall's foot—'I think it would have
[gon]e in anyway'—but Bolton went into a
[3-1]lead. With 20 minutes left, Hanson failed
[to]hold a Matthews cross and 'I poked it in
[as]well as banging into the post.' With time
[alm]ost up, Mortensen thumped a 20-yard
[free]-kick high into the net for the equalizer
['the]y lined up the wall carelessly, so I just
[whac]ked it and hoped'), and then Matthews made

the winner for Perry in the last few seconds.

Further irony: on the same ground a few
months later the Hungarians vanquished the
myth of English soccer supremacy. 'A wonderful
team,' says Mortensen. 'They had superb ball
control, and always had a man spare.'

But England's performance was perhaps better
than the critics, and history, allowed. Certainly
Mortensen did as much as any man could. He
made the equalizer for Sewell, after Hidegkuti's
first-minute shock, with a glorious diagonal pass.
At 4-1 down he ran at a packed defence, lost
the ball, won it back, and swept it wide of Grosics.
At 2-6, he hurtled into the heart of the defence

Below *Mortensen scored 197 League goals for
Blackpool and 30 in the FA Cup—a record for the
competition—before moving to lesser clubs.*
Bottom *The England star (white shirt) sees his
diving header go in against Charlton at the Valley.
He could count himself lucky to be playing: after a
crash in a Wellington bomber early in the War he
had been told he would never play again.*

yet again, only to be bumped and bored and felled
for Alf Ramsey's consolation penalty. Humiliation
for England, yes: but Mortensen had little
personal reason for reproach. He had scored 23
goals in 25 full internationals.

His first international appearance, however,
had been against his own country, as a substitute
for Wales, in one of the many high-scoring
unofficial wartime matches. Mortensen travelled
to Wembley as an England reserve in September
1943: the Welsh, harder hit by service duty, had
no such luxury. When Ivor Powell went off
injured, Welsh FA secretary Ted Robbins suggested that Mortensen might make up the
numbers. Officialdom agreed—with a refreshing
lack of protocol—and Morty was on before anyone
had a chance to change the decision. The fact that
Wales lost 8-3 hardly lessened his enjoyment of
the occasion: 'Wembley was always a special
ground for me, win or lose,' he says.

A stunning display against Scotland in 1945
brought him two goals and a place in the top
rank of striking inside-forwards (the match
was also memorable for a remarkable display of
goalkeeping by the amateur Bobby Brown, who
later became Scotland's team manager). And so to
peacetime, and the decade with Blackpool, its
triumphs and its tragedies.

When the batteries that gave Mortensen his
pace began to run down, his days in the top
class ran down too. But he carried on playing,
with Hull, with Southport, then with Bath City
(where he had appeared during the War) and
finally with Lancaster City. He kept turning out
when he was past 40, yet a decline that could
have seemed pathetic with a less jovial personality
hardly seemed a decline at all. 'I had a job to do,'
he says. 'I knew a bit, and I tried to pass it on.'

He tried the same philosophy as a manager,
and to a large extent it worked. He bought wisely
with a limited budget, young recruits like Tony
Green and Tommy Hutchison indicating his
shrewdness. The blow of his dismissal after
little more than two years in the job was
worse for its unexpectedness (Blackpool
finished eighth in the Second Division in his
third season) and worse still for its deliverance of a
man who had given so much to the club. Football,
often short of sentiment, was particularly short of
that quality on the day Morty was shown the door.

Yet Mortensen did not bear a grudge, and
nobody was more pleased than he was when his old
club gained promotion in the following season—
with a team largely composed of men he had
chosen.

He went back into business, with the accent
on entertainment. That was in character, for
throughout his life he had been an entertainer,
with his skill and determination on the field, his
humour off it. The game could do with a few
more like him.

[S]tan MORTENSEN

[Ho]nours: FA Cup winners medal 1953
[FA] Cup runners-up medal 1948, 1951

[Cl]ub	Season	League		Int'nls	
		Mtchs	Gls	Mtchs	Gls
[Bl]ackpool	1946-47	38	28	1	4
	1947-48	34	21	6	7
	1948-49	32	18	5	3
	1949-50	37	22	9	6
	1950-51	35	30	2	1
	1951-52	37	26		
	1952-53	34	15		
	1953-54	31	21	2	2
	1954-55	28	11		
	1955-56	11	5		
[Hu]ll City	1955-56	21	8		
	1956-57	21	10		
[So]uthport	1956-57	11	5		
	1957-58	25	5		
[To]tal		395	225	25	23

THE GOALSCORERS

The happy Wanderer

Whenever football conversation turns to 'real' centre-forwards then there is one name that is certain to be mentioned—Nat Lofthouse. In a past age, when individual roles in a team were more distinct, Lofthouse was paramount among his contemporaries, one in a succession of great number nines that included Dixie Dean and Tommy Lawton.

Lawton, in fact, was Lofthouse's idol and model: 'I had become a terrific Tommy Lawton fan. Whenever I could get away on a Saturday afternoon, I went to see him play for Everton, and when eventually I got a trial for Lancashire Schools—in his footsteps—I felt proud as Punch. As I got off the coach at the bus station after playing in the trial, I received the shock of my life. Waiting for a bus was Tommy Lawton. We were introduced. I stood there tongue-tied and could only nod like a dim-wit when Lawton said "Always try to bang in one or two, Nat, and remember, it's goals that count".'

Nat Lofthouse followed his hero's advice: goals became his trade. Before nagging injury ended his playing career in the early sixties he scored over 300. They flowed from both feet and the famous forehead with exciting regularity: 256 in 452 League appearances between 1946 and 1961; 30 in 33 internationals between 1950 and 1959. He even achieved the schoolboy dream of a hat-trick in each half—for the Football League against the League of Ireland at Molineux.

But Nat Lofthouse was more symbolic of his era than the itinerant Lawton. He was big and strong, just as most centre-forwards were supposed to be, but in that age of the maximum wage he was also loyal to his only club, Bol Wanderers. He was proud of his ability status but always remained a member of local community. There was none of the ele tion to the social stratosphere that isolates many modern stars from the local foot public.

Nathaniel Lofthouse was Bolton born, 27 August 1925, and bred. His father was h horsekeeper for Bolton Corporation and Nat the youngest of four sons. His first proper ga of football was not a happy one; pressed i service as an emergency goalkeeper, the 11-ye old debutant suffered the indignity of picking ball out of the net seven times. But that ma gave him an insight into what organized fo ball was all about and on his own request he included in the school team—at centre-forwa Size was the determinant factor then but made steady progress, and when he made debut for the Bolton Schools XI against B the neighbouring team were hammered 7-1— Lofthouse scored all seven.

It was the Mayor of Bolton himself, Alderm Entwhistle, a Bolton director, who asked hi join the Wanderers. They signed him as a 14-ye old amateur in 1939. Although the War int rupted British football it gave Lofthouse unique opportunity to play in improvized f teams that included players like Finney Shankly. He made his first-team debut in 19 and Bury again provided the victims, though time Lofthouse was content with only a pai goals. Aided by the sympathetic George Hu the former Spurs, Arsenal and Sheffield Wedr day international, the young number n improved rapidly, acquiring a powerful left-f shot to add to the natural right and consolidat his heading ability. Professional terms were reward—£1 10s (£1·50) per match, plus 2s (12½p) expenses—and Nat's childhood ambit to make the grade with Bolton Wanderers fulfilled.

He still had to prove himself. Wartime fo ball wasn't easy. Bevin Boy Lofthouse's Saturd went like this: up at 3.30 am, catching the 4 tram to work; eight hours down the pit push

KEYSTONE

bs; collected by the team coach; playing for ▪lton. But work down the mine toughened him ▪ysically, and the caustic humour of his ▪low-miners made sure he never became ▪rogant about his success on the field.

When the War ended, the chance to play along-▪le established professionals returning from ▪e forces gave Lofthouse the final confidence ▪ needed, and he was a regular in the League ▪le from the resumption in 1946. Wanderers ▪ned him full-time on the maximum wage of ▪0, and the Bolton lad who so admired Tommy ▪wton was on the road that would lead to his ▪lowing Lawton as England's centre-forward.

Goals flowed regularly, attracting favourable ▪ess comment as it became obvious that ▪fthouse had international potential. In 1949 ▪ scored four goals for the FA XI against the ▪my—three from pin-point Stanley Matthews ▪sses—and the following year he was selected ▪r the FA's summer tour of Canada. The success-▪ tour culminated in a match against the ▪ World Cup team in New York, when Johnny ▪ncocks scored the solitary goal with a ▪mendous shot direct from a free-kick. Home-▪rd bound, the FA party suffered unmerciful ▪es from American fellow-travellers on the boat ▪en the news came through that the Senior ▪ngland side had suffered inglorious World Cup ▪feat at the hands of the same US team in Belo ▪rizonte.

The call to full international honours came ▪e following November, against Yugoslavia. ▪nong the first to congratulate Lofthouse was ▪mmy Lawton, who sent a telegram to Burnden ▪rk. The game was played at Highbury, and ▪spite the presence of ex-ballet dancer Beara ▪ goal and 6ft 4in Horvath at centre-half, both ▪agland's goals in the 2-2 draw were scored ▪ Lofthouse. Within a year he was established ▪ England's centre-forward and from October ▪51 to November 1953 he did not miss a ▪agle game for England. One of those eighteen ▪atches, against Austria in May 1952, was to ▪ve Lofthouse the famous nickname, 'The Lion ▪ Vienna'.

Though unbeaten over eight games when ▪riving in the Austrian capital, the England side ▪ere not in peak form. Their tour had begun ▪th an unsatisfactory 1-1 draw against Italy ▪d there was much press criticism. National ▪ide was running high in Austria, with local ▪pporters fervently hoping that their team ▪uld trounce that belonging to one of the ▪cupying powers.

They had grounds for optimism. In November ▪51 the Austrians had gone to Wembley and ▪ngland had been lucky to draw 2-2. Austria had ▪so beaten Scotland in Glasgow—the first ▪ntinental side to do so—and rubbed the point ▪ by trouncing them 4-0 in Vienna. Of Austria's ▪ previous games, only two had been lost, with ▪n won convincingly.

Before a capacity crowd of 65,000 in the ▪ater Stadium the stage was set for a match that ▪th sides desperately wanted to win. Austria ▪gan with a series of furious attacks. Lofthouse ▪ored. Huber equalized and the stadium ▪upted. Sewell restored England's lead. Hysteri-▪l scenes greeted Austria's second equalizer, ▪ored by Dienst. Austria attacked with renewed ▪enzy, but to no avail. One raid ended when ▪ngland keeper Merrick plucked the ball off ▪ienst's head, and swiftly threw it upfield ▪ Tom Finney. Finney's shrewd through-▪ll put Lofthouse clear. With the desperate ▪fence in pounding pursuit, Lofthouse slid ▪e ball under the advancing Musil before being ▪lled by a crunching tackle. It was a great ▪iumph, but as he regretted: 'I never saw

▪pposite top Nat Lofthouse beats Kuznetsov to ▪ore the last of his 30 international goals, against ▪ussia at Wembley in October 1958.

▪pposite below Just five months earlier Lofthouse ▪d placed this shot in the very same net to help ▪feat Manchester United in the Cup Final.

▪ight During the last of his many years at Burnden, ▪fthouse acts as coach and manager.

the ball enter the Austrian net for the best goal of my life.'

But that magnificent moment was followed by a set-back to Lofthouse's international career. A wrist injury put him out of the game, and it took him some time to recover his form. Perhaps he was fortunate, missing England's eclipse by Hungary in 1953, but won recall for the 1954 World Cup, scoring three goals, including one in England's 4-2 quarter-final defeat by Uruguay.

Strangely, his international career seemed to be over after the 1955-56 season, one of his best—32 League goals in 36 games, four inter-national goals in five games. The 1958 World Cup came and went, then Lofthouse was surpris-ingly recalled to the England team for two games, and he scored his 30th international goal (equal-ling Tom Finney's just-established record) with a powerful shot against Russia.

During this fine international career Loft-house remained content to play for Bolton. He was a classic example of the loyal club man under the maximum wage system; proud to play for the same club for 15 seasons.

The Lion of Vienna, King of Burnden Park, but susceptible to time

They were good seasons too, despite the 1946 tragedy (when 33 spectators died when crush barriers collapsed at Burnden Park) and the fact that Wanderers did not recapture the success of the twenties. They were still a successful First Division club. The slump later to affect Bolton, Blackburn, Preston and the other provincial Lancashire teams was not yet even a shadow on the horizon. For Lofthouse, and stars like him, life was simple and fulfilling. True, they would travel to the ground by bus and go home to the wife and family after the game. But they were pleased to enjoy the recognition and acceptance reserved for a local hero—and international honours were an added bonus for the more successful. When the alternative to football was working down a pit for less money, Lofthouse felt himself entitled to be happy with life.

'For me football is pleasure with pay,' he wrote in 1954. 'Just think for a moment what a top-class man receives every week. During the season his wages are £15 a week. In the summer they come down to £12 a week. For a win he receives a bonus of £2. A draw means a bonus of £1 . . . Speaking as a Bolton Wanderers' player, I must say we get the best of everything, and from all parts of the country I have heard other players pay a similar tribute to their clubs . . . From the moment I signed a pro form I've been treated everywhere with kindness and under-standing . . . Drop into any League ground and you'll find footballers who will tell you they've been given a fair deal by their clubs . . . I have no real grouses as a professional footballer.' How many pros would agree with Lofthouse today?

Lofthouse earned his £15 a week. His bread-and-butter League scoring consistency, coupled with his international success, brought him the accolade of Footballer of the Year in 1953— the trophy being presented the night before the Cup Final, in which Bolton faced a Blackpool side containing Stanley Matthews, twice on the losing side. Every uncommitted fan was for Blackpool and the maestro. Dedicated Boltonians, on the other hand, were prepared to go to any lengths to secure their side's victory. One fan even forwarded a treasured lucky charm to the team—a bent nail picked up at the centre of the new Wembley pitch in 1923, to which Bolton's win was, in the fan's opinion, attributable.

Lofthouse took to the pitch needing a goal to complete a remarkable record of scoring in every round. He didn't have to wait long. Within two minutes, a long crossfield pass found Holden on the right wing. His quick inside pass found Lofthouse, who hit the ball home from 25 yards.

But the winner's medal, of course, eluded him.

Nat LOFTHOUSE

Honours: FA Cup winners medal 1958
FA Cup runners-up medal 1953
Footballer of the Year 1953

Club	Season	League		Int'nls	
		Mtchs	Gls	Mtchs	Gls
Bolton Wanderers	1946-47	40	18		
	1947-48	34	18		
	1948-49	22	7		
	1949-50	35	10		
	1950-51	38	21	1	2
	1951-52	38	18	7	7
	1952-53	36	22	8	8
	1953-54	32	17	5	6
	1954-55	31	15	5	2
	1955-56	36	32	5	4
	1956-57	36	29		
	1957-58	31	17		
	1958-59	37	29	2	1
	1959-60				
	1960-61	6	3		
Total		452	256	33	30

In that memorable 'Matthews' Final' Bolton went down 4-3. It was 1958 before Lofthouse gained the coveted prize in the 2-0 defeat of Manchester United. He scored both goals that day—though not without sparking controversy. The second saw United keeper Harry Gregg hit the back of the net as hard as the ball after Lofthouse's charge caught him off the ground. But that was in its way appropriate. Though scrupulously fair, Lofthouse understood that football was a hard game, and always gave 100 per cent.

In return, he took his share of knocks. After Bolton's Cup Final triumph, he only enjoyed one more good season as his career tailed away.

After a spell out of the game, when he kept a pub, he returned to Wanderers in 1968 as manager. The experiment was not a success, and Bolton languished in the Third Division. He was replaced briefly, then re-appointed. In 1971, Jimmy Armfield was appointed manager and Nat Lofthouse left the club, a redundant figure after over 30 years at Burnden.

It was a sad ending to a connection that had once been so rewarding. The Lion of Vienna had finally been overtaken by the march of time.

RAY GREEN

Back from the dead

In the great Hungarian team of the fifties, the team that sensationally destroyed England's unbeaten home record against foreign opposition, Hidegkuti was regarded as the perfect ball artist, Kocsis the master header of the ball. Yet it is Ferenc Puskas who is best remembered, because Puskas always had an air of the 'con-man' about him, full of swagger and impudence, which made everything he did look just that bit better.

The Ferenc Puskas story is the classic rags-to-riches story—but with a difference. For few players in the history of football have ever carved out two such separate, equally dazzling careers—both of them studded with remarkable achievement.

Puskas, the son of a mediocre footballer, was born on 2 April 1926. His parents' second son, he was immediately nicknamed 'Ocsi', which means 'kid-brother', and Puskas has always signed his letters with this affectionate childhood tag. The dusty streets of Kispest were not as picturesque as the sandy beaches of Copacabana in Brazil, but nevertheless barefoot boys still kicked a ball about—a ball made of rags and old socks—just as enthusiastically. 'Ocsi' often says that his father could only afford one pair of shoes between him and his brother. He always wore the right one and did not dare kick a ball with it—and that was how, he said, he had developed the greatest left foot in the game.

Even at thirteen, Puskas shows he has exceptional talent

At the age of 13 Puskas joined the local First Division club, Kispest, as a 'cub' player, and under the watchful eyes of his father, then a coach, began a career which made the name Puskas famous throughout the world. It was obvious from the outset that this stocky little lad had exceptional talent, and after playing for Hungary at youth level he made his League debut for Kispest when he was just 16. Immaculate ball-control, a deadly shot, intelligence, and speed of thought and action were the hallmarks of Puskas' play. Surrounded by average players, the young star was able to turn a match by creating and taking chances with both coolness and precision.

Puskas' sense of humour and flamboyance, the marks of an exceptionally gifted player, were demonstrated perfectly in a match against Hungary's most popular club, Ferencvaros. With the score at 1-1, Ocsi clashed with one of the opposing defenders and was stretchered off the field. The hushed crowd looked on in sympathy as the young man lay motionless, apparently badly injured. But as the ambulance men reached the tunnel leading to the dressing-rooms, Puskas jumped off the stretcher, ran to the touchline and, as the ball was out of play, rejoined his team-mates. Seconds later he picked up a loose ball in midfield, moved effortlessly past the Ferencvaros defence, and from 25 yards hit a stunning goal. The Ferencvaros fans, incensed by this mixture of clowning and artistry, bayed for his blood, but the youngster returned to the centre circle with an unashamed grin on his face.

At 17 years old, Puskas made his full international debut, against Austria, wearing a number ten shirt. Officially an inside-left, he was the general of the team which included such seasoned forwards as the Ujpest pair, Szusza and Szengeller. Szengeller made Puskas an early goal which no doubt gave him added confidence, and Hungary won 5-2: Puskas was to keep his place in the team for the next 11 years.

That match against Austria took place in 1945. Football in Hungary had been virtually unaffected by the War, and the players had suffered no restrictions; indeed, rather than call them up, the government had found them work in hospital depots and the like, and had been uncharacteristically liberal with leave to play football. Not until March 1944, and the siege of German-occupied Budapest by the Russians, did football have to make even a temporary halt—because of fierce fighting in the capital.

With the speedy resumption, a new era began in the history of Hungarian football—an era to which young Puskas was to contribute much.

The Magyars, World Cup finalists in 1938, were past masters of the typical Central European game, one which suited Puskas. They shunned physical contact, relying instead on sheer ball control and clever, short passing moves. The emphasis was solidly on attack. By then, the 'W' formation was the universally accepted tactic for clubs and national teams alike. Within the rigidity of this system forwards like Puskas flourished, because they only had to beat one man, either with the ball or by intelligent positioning, and the way was clear towards goal.

Besides a style of play that admirably suited Puskas, as the much-battered capital came back to life, the Hungarian FA, following political directives, re-organized club football—to Puskas' advantage. Kispest became the official Army

club and was renamed Honved. In order to create exceptionally strong teams, several leading players were ordered to join either Honved or MTK, who had suffered a great deal during the previous ten years; indeed they had disbanded in 1943. So, suddenly, the hitherto struggling suburban teams, including the newly-christened Honved, became the stronghold of Hungarian football. Honved could field such notable players as goalkeeper Grosics, wing-half Boszik and forwards Kocsis, Puskas and Czibor—all members of the legendary Hungarian side. Now, at last, Ocsi found himself playing regularly with top-class footballers, and the responsibility of 'carrying' a team was taken off his shoulders. As a result his game improved dramatically, because he could safely leave more of the donkey-work to others and concentrate on scoring goals.

Despite his international status, Puskas was still not content with his prowess and worked endlessly to perfect his skills. He would spend hours after training kicking a ball against a brick wall, controlling the rebound with his body, or balancing it up and down his thighs. This master-and-slave game was patiently played out night after night until he had achieved complete mastery over the ball.

Puskas and his Honved team mates were ostensibly members of the People's Army, but they did very little military training. They fought on football pitches, not battlefields, for promotion and higher earnings, and Puskas rose to the rank of major without ever carrying a rifle. However, these crack footballers were a

EPOQUE LTD., U.P.I., PRESS ASSOCIATION, ASSOCIATED PRESS, ASSOCIATED NEWSPAPERS, LONDON EXPRESS

Puskas dies in battle says report

HUNGARY'S king of the Soccer field, Ferenc Puskas has been killed

1 *Ferenc Puskas was still playing for Real Madrid at 41. But by this time his weight was slowing him down.*

2 *and* 3 *Two of Puskas' four goals against Eintracht in the 1960 European Cup final. This game was Puskas' finest moment with Real Madrid.*

4 *His playing days over, Puskas returned to the European Cup final as manager of the little Greek side, Panathinaikos. In London for the final, Puskas displays his own ball skills.*

5 *Puskas with Billy Wright before the 1953 England-Hungary game at Wembley. Puskas captained the Magyars to a magnificent 6-3 win.*

6 *In 1956, Puskas was rumoured killed during fighting in Budapest. But the rumours were just that.*

7 *Football made Puskas wealthy, though it also limited the time he could devote to his investments. One, a sausage factory, lost money as a result.*

times supposed to sleep in the barracks—not the most convivial accommodation—and so, after curfew, Puskas and company would put on their best suits, wave a cheerful goodbye to the understanding guards, and walk out into the night life of Budapest. They were caught only once, drinking in a bar around midnight by an officious captain who disliked football and was jealous of the freedom and affluence the players enjoyed.

Next morning, the commander sent for Puskas and ordered a 50 mile march as a punishment for the escapade. 'Thank you, sir', said Ocsi. 'But you realize that we won't be able to play against MTK next Sunday. It's up to you, sir. Either we march, or we play!' Luckily for Puskas the commander was a Honved supporter and readily suc-

cumbed to this obvious piece of blackmail. That skirmish won, the squad were left alone to concentrate on their football.

In the meantime, Gustav Sebes had taken over control of the national team and was working hard on a new tactical plan, a kind of 4-2-4. Nandor Hidegkuti became the first-ever withdrawn centre-forward, and Sebes gave Puskas, as well as Kocsis, a free-wheeling, buccaneering role. The combination of this tactical ploy and the presence of Puskas and several other brilliant footballers produced a near invincible team. Their magnificent football expressed the philosophy, 'No matter how many goals we concede, we can always score at least one more.'

Ocsi, by then known as the 'Galloping Major', was the kingpin

of this excellent Hungarian team, and was largely responsible for the effectiveness of their attacking style of play. Puskas scored 85 goals in 84 internationals for Hungary, an impressive average over such a large number of games. He got most of his goals with shots hit with his famed left foot, usually from well outside the penalty box. This ability to regularly fire goals from a distance of 20 yards and upwards was perhaps his finest attribute, one he used to good effect throughout his international as well as his club careers.

Of Puskas' 84 internationals for Hungary—he also played four for Spain later on—three games stand out, all of them part of the golden era of Hungarian football; the unforgettable 6-3 win over England in 1953 at Wembley, the subsequent 7-1 thrashing of England in Budapest, and Hungary's tragic 3-2 defeat in the 1954 World Cup final against West Germany. Ocsi played a major part in that sadly important set-back, as well as those previous triumphs, when he did much of the damage to England. For earlier in the 1954 World Cup finals he was injured and could not play in the quarter- and semi-finals. He passed a late fitness test on the morning of the final, but his inclusion was still a brave gamble on the part of Sebes—a gamble that failed. The struggling Puskas had a relatively poor game for Hungary, even missing a sitter at a vital stage of the game, and the winners' medals went to West Germany.

Two years later he was on tour with Honved when the 1956 uprising erupted in Hungary. Puskas, like Kocsis and Czibor, decided not to return home because of the possible personal consequences of the Russian intervention. It was a hard decision for Puskas to make. Hungary was his home, and in his own words, Hungary had 'treated him like a king'. He had probably enjoyed a better standard of living there than the head of state. He was paid well, if somewhat furtively, in goods. When he went abroad he and the other Hungarian players were allowed to bring back virtually what they liked—25 bolts of cloth or a few thousand razor blades for example—to be sold in Hungary. In this way they were able, provided they won their games often enough, to live quite well.

Now, however, Puskas left all that behind to set up home in Vienna. There he was joined by his wife and daughter.

Puskas forms part of a package deal offered Real Madrid

After a year in the football wilderness—Puskas could not get a player's permit—he was approached by Emil Oestereicher, the ex-manager of his former club. Oestereicher, a likeable man and an excellent coach, was eager to work in Spain, and saw Puskas as the trump card he needed to clinch a job there. So, with Puskas' agreement, Oestereicher offered a package deal to the greatest club side of the time, Real Madrid. The package included a 30-year-old overweight footballer and a coach who could not speak the language. But, despite these handicaps, the offer was accepted by Real Madrid's chairman, Santiago Bernabeu, and a partnership began which turned out to be as beneficial for Puskas as it was for Oestereicher and Real Madrid.

Puskas became part of the best club side ever to run the European gauntlet, and besides the satisfaction this brought to such a talented craftsman, it was also financially rewarding. Puskas amassed over £250,000 during his stay in Spain, though he lost a considerable part of that money with the collapse of a business in which he was involved. He invested in a sausage factory, but others took advantage of the little time Puskas could afford to devote to the business, and the value of his investment dwindled.

Ferenc PUSKAS

Honours: World Cup runners-up medal 1954
Olympic gold medal 1952
World Club Championship medal 1960
European Cup winners medal 1960
European Cup runners-up medal 1962, 1964
Hungarian League Championship medal 1949-50, 1950, 1952, 1954, 1955
Spanish League Championship medal 1960-61, 1961-62, 1962-63, 1963-64, 1964-65
Spanish Cup winners medal 1961-62

Leading Hungarian scorer 1947-48 (50), 1949-50 (31), 1950 (25), 1953 (27)
Leading Spanish scorer 1959-60 (26), 1960-61 (27), 1962-63 (26), 1963-64 (20)

International appearances: Hungary 84 (85 goals)
Spain 4

Puskas in the green and white of Panathinaikos. As manager, he took them into the 1971 European Cup final.

SYNDICATION INTERNATIONAL

The initial problem that Puskas had to overcome when he moved to Madrid was to regain his match fitness. Once he had lost weight he then had to establish himself in the Real Madrid team—no easy task for even the most accomplished footballer. For this was the era of Alfredo di Stefano. Di Stefano was the acknowledged boss of the Real Madrid dressing-room, and a newcomer, no matter how much he cost or however good his credentials, had to earn the maestro's approval before he was fully accepted as one of the team. Before Puskas' arrival, such outstanding foreign internationals as Brazil's Didi and Sweden's Simonsson had failed to impress di Stefano, and their stay in Madrid had been both short and far from sweet.

But Puskas still had a swagger and a personality which endeared him to the afficionados of Madrid. He did not go to Spain cap in hand but as a rival to di Stefano's hitherto unchallenged leadership, and during the first few months there was an uneasy atmosphere in the Real camp. Di Stefano and Puskas hardly spoke to each other, and both players had their small and separate group of friends. But the issue was to resolve itself in quite a dramatic fashion.

In Spain it is a greater honour to finish top scorer in the first division than in most European countries; the player is publicly crowned and receives cash prizes and gifts from various sources. At the end of one particular season Puskas and di Stefano were way ahead of their rivals with 26 goals each. Real had just one more game to play, against Elche.

The championship was already won—as usual—and the crowd had turned up merely to celebrate and crown the king of goals. In the first half the two stars scored a goal apiece and everything depended on the last 45 minutes. Neither of them

had increased their total when, just before the final whistle, Puskas waltzed past the defence and drew the goalkeeper. But instead of shooting past him, Puskas merely pushed the ball sideways for di Stefano to bang it into the net. At the end of the game, Alfredo ran over to Puskas and warmly embraced him. Di Stefano was the top scorer, but Puskas, once again using his wits, had won an important victory in cleverly settling the difference between them.

From then on they blended perfectly. And they never played better together than in the marvellous European Cup final in Glasgow, when di Stefano scored three goals and Puskas four to give Real a 7-3 victory over Eintracht Frankfurt.

In 1962 Pancho (Spain's affectionate nickname for him) scored another hat-trick in a European Cup final. But nonetheless Real lost, 5-3 to Benfica. Puskas also ended four seasons as top scorer in the Spanish First Division, the honour he had selflessly allowed di Stefano to steal in that game with Elche.

Puskas was vastly amused when Pele was feted as the only man to score a thousand goals. 'I got at least 1,500, but who's counting?' he said. This kind of remark is typical of Puskas. He is a difficult man to interview, because he has a habit of puncturing pompous questions with wry remarks. 'Was the Wembley game your best match?' 'No, I played better against Turku in Finland, when we won 17-0.' 'Which team would you most like to manage?' 'One which wins every game.'

Puskas however, is more open when talking about his old Hungarian team-mates. 'Hidegkuti was the finest centre-forward I ever played with, and Grosics certainly the best goalkeeper.' Puskas was always fiercely loyal to his Hungarian colleagues. 'They would have been an asset to any side. They always gave their best and that was

usually more than good enough.'

Puskas himself overstayed [his] welcome as a player. He loved [his] football so much that he was relu[c]tant to step down.

When he finally retired fro[m] playing, he was just a shadow [of] his old self, slow and ponderou[s.] After his retirement he took [up] coaching with a small-town Spani[sh] outfit, and afterwards tried his lu[ck] in Canada.

Then came an offer to take ov[er] the management of the Greek cha[m]pions, Panathinaikos. The offer w[as] worth £20,000 a year to Puskas, [as] well as a rent-free villa in Athen[s.] He happily accepted this offer, a[nd] began commuting between Athen[s] and his own villa in Madrid. He us[ed] his immense personal prestige to [line] up lucrative friendlies for th[e] little-known semi-professional tea[m,] and this experience against stron[g] foreign opposition, plus Puska[s'] persuasive, multi-lingual tongu[e,] transformed these part-timers an[d] took them into the final of th[e] 1970-71 European Cup—a com[petition where previously no Gre[ek] team had ever reached the sem[i] finals. Panathinaikos achieved th[is] distinction because they were com[pletely dominated by Puskas' co[n]fident personality.

Puskas marched with his tea[m] into an hotel in London, where t[he] final was to be played, like t[he] manager of a travelling circus. [A] great showman, he always had [an] entourage of admirers around hi[m.] Now Hungarians from all over t[he] world, Spaniards who remember[ed] him with affection from his days [in] Madrid, and Greek shipping ma[g]nates who just wanted to grab so[me] of the reflected glory were there. T[he] match was lost, as Puskas had quie[tly] predicted all along, but Panat[hi]naikos gave Ajax a hard fight.

'... perhaps it is a little bit special to be Ferenc Puska[s]'

Ajax took an early lead throu[gh] Dick Van Dijk, but were still clin[g]ing to their slight advantage when [a] late goal from their substitute fina[lly] ended Panathinaikos' challenge.

Puskas regards Spain as his hom[e,] and indeed has a magnificent hou[se] just outside Madrid. His daughte[r,] Aranka, is engaged to a Spani[sh] architect and the Puskas family [is] hoping that Ocsi will be asked [to] manage a Spanish first divisi[on] club. By 1972, that seemed a distin[ct] possibility, for Puskas' reputation [as] a manager was fast approaching th[at] which he had earned as a player.

Towards the end of 1971 Pusk[as] was guest of honour at a dinn[er] where he presented prizes to som[e] outstanding players. After the me[al] Billy Wright and Bobby Moo[re] praised in their speeches the co[n]tribution Puskas had made to foo[t]ball, and other notable gues[ts] applauded him. Puskas said afte[r]wards, 'Until today, I thought [of] myself as a professional doing a jo[b] just like a dentist, a plumber or an[y]one else. But hearing people li[ke] Billy and Bobby Moore speak [so] highly of me makes me feel that pe[r]haps it is a little bit special to b[e] Ferenc Puskas.'

Il buon gigante

ts Special, predecessor to *Match of the Day*,
l to have an opening sequence in which a
commanding player broke from his own
lty area, ran the length of the field and
e an easy goal for a colleague. The teams
e Wales and England, the venue Cardiff, and
player John Charles.

he Italian equivalent programme was also,
years, prefaced by a shot of a player in a
ntus shirt rising above the defence to head
equally spectacular goal. The player, of
se, was John Charles, and the moral of the
introductions is unmistakable.

or a man to command the instant recogni-
and admiration of two soccer publics is
anation enough of why he takes his place
gside the handful of players who have won
iine world acclaim.

le dominated his games with Leeds United,
ntus and Wales. When he returned to Leeds
i Italy, the club began to draw crowds in
Manchester United class for away matches.
joined Juventus when they were an Italian
gue flop, and led them immediately to the
with his ability to score against packed
nces. When he played for Wales they were
ble of matching anyone, as they showed in
World Cup. Welsh team manager Dave
en said of his selection sessions: 'I used to
the names of John Charles and Ivor Allchurch
n and start from there.'

lis versatility was endless . . . centre-forward,
re-half (his favourite), midfield or even
back. And he succeeded in two countries,
very different soccer environments. One
iager used to say, when asked what position
would play Charles if he were lucky enough

to have him, 'Where I was weakest.'

Charles was admired by his co-professionals,
respected by his opponents, and held in awe by
the fans. In Turin he received the film star
treatment, unable to walk down a street without
signing an autograph or being publicly
applauded. 'Il Buon Gigante', the Gentle Giant,
showed no temperament in the land of temperament and was idolized for it. When a friend's
briefcase was stolen from Charles' car in the
street, it was front page news. How could anyone stoop so low as to rob John Charles?

Charles was never seen to commit a petty
foul. He wrote in his autobiography: 'Players
will have to realize that the public does not pay
good money to see pettiness and childishness.'
Even when a young player at Leeds, he said:
'If I have to knock them down to play well,
I don't want to play the game.' This, from a man
built like a heavyweight at over six feet and
thirteen stone.

Some years later his attitude had hardly
changed. 'Some people despise me for not using
my size and weight. Sometimes I think I would
have been a better player with more devil. When
I look back on the players who gave me a
bashing I kind of regret not bashing them back.
But it's nice to know I've gone through a long
career without hurting anyone.'

That was as true of his international as his
club career. Italian League secretary Luigi
Scarambone said in 1961: 'Wales should give him
a medal. He's put it on the map. Nobody in
Italy knew where or what it was before.'

Born in Swansea in 1931, Charles joined the
groundstaff of Swansea Town as soon as he was
old enough. But he did not stay long. His talent

was quickly spotted by Leeds manager Major
Frank Buckley and, still an amateur, was
persuaded to go to Elland Road. The cost to
Leeds was £10.

In January 1949 he signed professional forms
and three months later made his League debut
against Blackburn—at centre-half. The following season he did not miss a League game and,
on 8 March 1950, he made his debut for Wales,
against Northern Ireland at Wrexham, to become
the youngest Welshman ever to represent his
country. He was eighteen years and three months
old. But not until 1953 did he win a regular
place. This came after the great transformation
in his career, when Buckley decided to play him
at centre-forward: the experiment quickly paid
rich dividends, with 26 goals in the first season
and then 42 (to break the Leeds club record and
lead the League) in the second.

On 19 April 1957 he was chosen as captain of
Wales for the first time and led them in a goalless
draw against Northern Ireland in Belfast. But this
was a milestone in Charles' career for in the
crowd was Umberto Agnelli, wealthy president of
Juventus of Turin. And so began one of the most
talked about of all transfers.

Juventus were, at the time, struggling near the
bottom of the Italian First Division. In English
terms it was as if Arsenal were in danger of
relegation. They needed players and, with
Agnelli of Fiat in charge, the money was there.
For footballers in England, the money most
certainly was NOT there. It was four years
before the lifting of the maximum wage restric-
tion and Charles was to start a minor emigration
of star footballers from Britain to Italy.

Within a week of the Belfast international
Leeds and Agnelli had agreed terms. It took
Charles a little longer, months of negotiation in
fact. But he signed in August in time for the
Italian season and for the sort of money English
footballers had only dreamed about up to that
moment. It was all cloak-and-dagger stuff with
Kenneth Wolstenholme and Terry Sommerfield
representing Charles and negotiating between
Sam Bolton, Percy Wood and Raich Carter of
Leeds and Agnelli and his agent, Gigi Peronace,
for Juventus.

He received a guarantee from Agnelli which
read: 'I make myself personally responsible to you
for the due performance in both the letter and the
spirit of all the obligations undertaken by FC

*ow John Charles drives the ball past Sunderland
er Fraser for the first of the two goals he
ed on his final appearance for Leeds United
re his transfer to Juventus.*

*ht Despite the vigorous attentions of the
oa defenders, Charles still manages to win the
in the air. Although he was regularly fouled
provoked, he rarely retaliated, earning himself
nickname 'the Gentle Giant'. His bravery in the
lty area brought him a large number of goals
he Italian League—by tradition the hardest
e to score regularly.*

entus and whether or not such obligations
ll conform to present or future federal rules
the same extent as would have been the case
such contracts been made with me personally
so that this document shall be legally
orceable against me to the fullest extent.' With
Charles was naturally satisfied, and he began
most successful and rewarding part of his
eer. The cost to Juventus was £65,000, a
ord fee for a British player.
Within a year a poll by the Italian football
er 'Il Calcio Illustrata' elected Charles the
player in the country, and put his value at
ut £280,000, more highly rated then than
tefano.
Charles enjoyed it all. He bought a share in
restaurant, acquired a villa on the Italian
iera as well as one in Turin, and he had two
s. He struck up a devastating playing partner-
p with Omar Sivori, the Argentinian who had
ed for Juventus at the same time. Helped by
arles' 28 goals, Juventus won the championship
t year, and two years later won both the
mpionship and the cup, reaching a record
points and scoring 92 goals, with Charles,
ugh not always acting as a goalscorer, getting
of them. In the 1961-62 European Cup he was
right-half in the side that became the first
beat Real Madrid on their own ground in
ropean competition.
n the 1958 World Cup in Sweden, Charles was
centre-forward in the Wales team that
w with Hungary, Mexico and Sweden before
ting Hungary in a play-off and reaching the
arter-finals. But he was absent from the side
t lost 1-0 to Brazil, the eventual winners.
all he collected 38 caps for his country, and
ld have had far more had he been available.
Charles sang on records and made a film with
ori. But there were black spots. Juventus
nped down on his personal appearances, saying
y were affecting his game. He was fined by
club for returning a day late from holiday
h his family and his home life suffered at
hands of the club's rigorous training
edules. He was so often away from home that
marriage began to collapse. And he was tired
manufactured press reports of a non-existent
ht life.
The trouble came to a head at the time of his
f return to Leeds and his equally brief
eer with Roma afterwards. Twice divorce
eatened although he and wife Peggy patched
ngs up when he finally returned to Britain to
. As early as 1960 he was beginning to worry
ut his sons' education. One offer to return
his native land was from Southern League

Barry Town, who would have paid £50 a week
as they were not bound by the Football League's
maximum wage.

Press reports were to reveal conflicting statements from Charles about his stay at Juventus.
At one and the same time Charles was quoted
as saying in 1961, 'I like it here. I miss
my bacon but that's about all.' And, less
enthusiastically, 'I stick it out for my wife and
the family.'

More recently Charles has revealed his true
feelings about the Italian episode. 'If I do have
regrets,' he said in 1965, 'it is that I ever left
Juventus. That was my one big mistake.'

His 'mistake' arose from a temporary homesickness and a growing dislike for training
schedules, coupled with concern over his
children's education. His discontent mounting,
he even wrote a book called 'Goodbye Juventus'.
But the negotiations were even more protracted
than his original signature had been and it took
from April 1962 until August for it to be settled
that Leeds would pay the Italians £53,000 for his
return. In the meantime there had been rumours
that his brother Mel, of Arsenal and Wales,
or even Cliff Jones of Spurs (and previously
Swansea) would come out to take his place. The
departure was not a happy one—there were
squabbles with the Agnellis over his contract—
and he left a lot behind, both physically and
in less tangible forms.

Charles returns to Leeds—but for just three months

With Leeds he was an immediate attraction,
although his own regrets were not long coming.
By September he was saying it was all a big mistake
and by November he had been sold back to Italy
again, this time to Roma at a fat profit for Leeds,
not to mention a good one for Charles.

At Rome he began well, scoring within 15
minutes of his first home match against Bologna,
the League leaders. But injuries and loss of
form limited his appearances for the club to a
costly ten, he was dropped by Wales and finally
signed for Cardiff for only £20,000 at the end
of that season. For a time the Football League
refused to accept his resignation because of
money still owed to Leeds by Roma and Juventus.

It was obvious, too, that his greatest playing
days were past and, after a short spell with
Cardiff, he was transferred to then non-League
Hereford United. Life there was pleasant enough.
He soon adjusted to a more muted admiration

than he had been used to in Italy. Said Charles,
'Last week I signed four autograph books and
the back of a Woodbine packet. And that was one
of the better weeks. The *dolce vita* is certainly
over.' But he enjoyed the rest from constant
publicity. 'Life at Hereford is a far cry from
Turin. Cafes don't empty as we stroll along a
street. And there aren't any photographers lurking
under the tables.'

As a player he had weight troubles but
found little difficulty in scoring a large number
of goals. And the crowds he helped draw to Hereford's small ground were a major factor in the
club ultimately being elected to the Football
League.

He left Hereford in September 1971, less than
a year before the club attained their ambition
of Football League status and before the stunning
run in the FA Cup. He had been star player,
player-manager, and plain manager but he was not
prepared to uproot his family from Cardiff, not
to mention his business, and live in Hereford.

In the interim there had been moments recalling the old fame. He went back to Juventus for
benefit games and in 1969, when the Italian club
were trying to persuade Manchester City's
Malcolm Allison to become their team manager,
Allison was saying that he would only go to Italy
if Charles was given a job at the club too.

His name was linked at various times with
playing and managerial jobs at Plymouth,
Birmingham, Wrexham, Barnsley and Doncaster,
but nothing came of them. By 1972 Charles was on
the periphery of soccer, still running his sports
shop in Cardiff and being called on to take charge
of the Welsh Under-23 side, but puzzled and
saddened by the lack of demand for his services.

He said in January of that year, 'I have applied
for a few jobs since leaving Hereford, but I am
mystified to find that nobody wants to use my
experience. I am not bitter. After all, 20,000
Welsh fans turned up at Ninian Park last month
for my testimonial. But I would feel a lot
happier if someone would explain what I have
done to be branded a managerial flop.'

The saddest thing about John Charles is that
with all his talents he will not be remembered
as well as lesser men in decades to come. He left
his country as he was approaching his peak and
its fans never saw the best, just the promise and
the aftermath. When children yet unborn ask their
fathers about the 1950s they will hear the names
Billy Wright, Ronnie Allen, Stanley Matthews
and Nat Lofthouse—but probably not John
Charles. And there is good cause to suggest not
only that he ranks with them but, in many
respects, above them.

*Charles, Mike Bailey and Bill McGarry. McGarry
asked Charles to accompany the Wolves party to
Turin as liaison officer for the away leg of their
1972 EUFA Cup tie against Juventus.*

John CHARLES

Honours: Italian League Championship medal 1958,
1960, 1961
Italian Cup winners medal 1959, 1960

Club	Season	League		Int'nls	
		Mtchs	Gls	Mtchs	Gls
Leeds United	1948-49	3			
	1949-50	42	1	1	
	1950-51	34	3	1	
	1951-52	18			
	1952-53	40	26	3	2
	1953-54	39	42	4	3
	1954-55	40	11	4	5
	1955-56	41	30	4	
	1956-57	40	38	3	1
Juventus*	1956-57			3	
	1957-58	34*	28*	6	1
	1958-59	34*	19*		
	1959-60	34*	23*	1	1
	1960-61	32*	15*		
	1961-62	21*	8*	4	1
Leeds United	1962-63	11	3	1	1
Roma*	1962-63	10*	4*		
Cardiff City	1963-64	33	11	1	
	1964-65	28	3	2	
	1965-66	8	4		
Total		377†	172†	38	15

†Football League total only.
*Italian League (total 165 games, 97 goals)

PRESS ASSOCIATION

**THE
GOALSCORERS**

The European Pele

He was stalking the midfield when the ball was pushed through to him. Gathering it and accelerating in one movement, he was streaking for goal before England's defence had time to form. Racing into the penalty area, he glanced menacingly at the far corner of the goal the second before his right foot pummelled the ball out of Springett's reach.

But for the second time in the match, the dark-skinned youngster was beaten by the cross-bar. His expressive face showed all the frustration and disappointment of a small boy who has found the sweet cupboard but cannot open it.

Luck was not with Eusebio that October day in 1961. And when Wembley emptied, England had an unsettled defence and an alarmed goalkeeper, but two goals. Portugal had just Eusebio's near misses.

Eusebio had taken everybody unawares. Before the game, his name had meant nothing to players, press or public. But so devastating was his performance that he was soon the focus of everybody's attention. With each electrifying run past defenders, with each of his massive shots, there was a general shaking of heads and reference to the programme from the press box to the stands.

In the sports pages of the newspapers and in pubs all over the country, there was one topic of conversation the next day, and it was not England's victory. It was unbelieving discussion of Eusebio.

The black, athletic forward—still a teenager—had won his first cap only days earlier against Luxembourg. Then, with only Eusebio's 25 appearances for Benfica to draw on for experience of top-class football, it had seemed that Fernando Peyroteo, the Portuguese manager, was either desperate for players or astonishingly confident in the youngster's abilities. He was not desperate.

And on his international debut, just 19 years old, Eusebio had justified his manager's confidence in him with the kind of goal that would become the hallmark of his game: pouncing on the ball, twisting and sprinting past two or three defenders, then smashing it into the net.

It is that shot, one of the most powerful in the history of association football, plus his speed of thought and action that make Eusebio one of the world's most explosive strikers. But he is far more than that. Not for him simply the parasite-like feeding off his fellow forwards in the goalmouth.

Far from it. Eusebio will hector and chase for the ball, far into his own half if need be, and it is these all-round individual skills which soon earned him the considerable nickname, 'the European Pele'. For like Pele, Eusebio can win matches on his own.

This was never more in evidence than in England in 1966, in Portugal's World Cup quarter-final

against North Korea. As the lightweight Koreans scampered to a 3-0 lead over the powerful Portuguese, the 1,500 or so Iberians scattered around Goodison Park clung to Eusebio's reputation like a drowning man to a lifebelt.

And it was entirely due to the pride of Benfica that Portugal were not, after Italy and Brazil, the third fancied team to leave the World Cup prematurely.

Eusebio first struck terror into the Koreans with a murderous shot on the half-hour. His direct penalty minutes before half-time sounded the death knell. Fifteen minutes after the change round, Eusebio sent Simoes racing clear down the left touchline, then tore forward to meet his cross with a right-foot volley that ripped into the net and was just a blur on the action replay.

Once more Eusebio was to run on into the Korean goal, retrieve the ball he had put there and carry it urgently back to the centre circle. North Korea 3, Portugal—in the person of Eusebio—4. Augusto added a welcome fifth, but the

Koreans' resistance had long si been destroyed.

But the Black Panther, as Euse is often known, could on occasi be tamed. One such occasion presented itself, for waiting Euesbio in the semi-finals v England and Nobby Stiles. And a 90 minutes with Stiles and compa Eusebio left the field crying. V can say whether his obvious cha at the final whistle was nat disappointment at the result—shame at his faint-heartedness?

For despite Eusebio's succes penalty—the first shot to de Gordon Banks in the tournamen the recurrent accusation that Mozambique lacked heart gathered momentum.

To be as dangerous a ma winner as Eusebio means havin live with ferocious tackling. M cenaries know more compass than some of the defenders allo to cancel him out of matches. Nobby Stiles, with a reputation sticking to his man like a leech drawing almost as much blood occasions, had snuffed Eusebio

EUROPA AMERICA

ASSOCIATED PRESS

the game more by his presence ~~than~~ his tackling.

So much so that Coluna shook ~~his~~ fist angrily at Eusebio, while ~~Au~~gusto too gave vent to his feelings, Eusebio hovered hesitantly on the ~~ed~~ge of the penalty area, a safe ~~dis~~tance away from Stiles.

But 1966 was still a very good year ~~for~~ Eusebio. The £1,000 cheque for ~~the~~ top scorer in the World Cup ~~fou~~nd its way—via his nine goals— ~~in~~to Eusebio's luggage. And though ~~he~~ finished third behind Bobby ~~Mo~~ore and Jack Charlton in the ~~vo~~ting for the best of the World Cup ~~foo~~tballers, Eusebio was acclaimed ~~by~~ the world press as 'the most ~~spe~~ctacular player in the World Cup, ~~wh~~o is now greater than Pele.' 'Here ~~is~~ pure and instinctive genius,' ~~co~~mmented one newspaper.

When Eusebio left England with ~~his~~ Portuguese team-mates, it was ~~a t~~ribute to his skills that he should ~~at~~ the same time stay behind—in ~~M~~adame Tussauds! The Madame ~~ha~~d been fortunate than the ~~lat~~ter, Real Madrid and Juventus ~~age~~nts, all of whom had tried unsuc-

cessfully to buy him. Juventus offered Benfica £200,000, but Eusebio's name stayed on Benfica's books.

That Eusebio should be universally known by his christian name is appropriate enough for one of the world's most popular players. One of eight children, the full name given him was Eusebio da Silva Ferreira. It was 25 January 1942, and Pearl Harbour had just changed the course of the War. But in the tiny house in the colourful native quarter of Lourenco Marques, Eusebio's birthplace and the capital of Portuguese East Africa, it was a happy time.

Eusebio was born to poverty. His father died when he was only five years old, and his mother had to bring up Eusebio and the rest of the family single-handed. It was while running errands for his mother that Eusebio played his first game of football, when the local youngsters were one short for a kickabout. From that day on, in Eusebio's own words, 'I had football under my skin.'

Soon, Eusebio was going to

school. And like most football-mad youngsters, he could not wait for school to end every evening, the signal for two hours' football. Eusebio was already a good basketball player, as well as a junior champion at 400, 200 and 100 metres, sprinting the shortest distance in the excellent time of 11 seconds. Most sportsmen in Mozambique knew of Eusebio, few foresaw his destiny.

It was Hilario, at that time just a friend and neighbour and not yet an international, who eventually persuaded Eusebio to join his football club, the Lourenco Marques Sporting Club. Not that Eusebio did not want to play football seriously. It was just that he had always been a supporter of Sporting's rival, Desportivo!

However, he at last agreed—a decision that was to have far-reaching consequences—and by 17, football was Eusebio's livelihood.

He scored a hat-trick on his debut for Sporting Club, against Juventude, and with his help Sporting reached second place in the Mozam-

Top left Eusebio waits patiently to take a free-kick as the Manchester United players prepare a wall to stop one of his famous shots in the 1968 European Cup final.
Far left Eusebio the family man on his 30th birthday.
Centre left The house in Mozambique where he lived before football brought him fame and wealth in Europe.
Above Another European Cup final at Wembley, this time against AC Milan in 1963. Eusebio was on target here but Milan beat Benfica 2-1.

bique championships that season. There was soon talk in the Lisbon press of Eusebio heading towards Europe.

The first formal invitation came from Benfica, whose offer was worth 250,000 escudos (over £3,000) to Eusebio alone. Promptly, Sporting talked in terms of 100,000 escudos for him if he stayed. But it was too late. With the idea of going to Lisbon, to the great Benfica, Eusebio's mind was already made up. 'For me, Benfica was like a tale out of the Arabian Nights. I slept little that

PRESS ASSOCIATION

ASSOCIATED PRESS

night as it happened.

But as soon as Eusebio got to Lisbon, the trouble started. Sporting Club of Lisbon insisted that he belonged to them, because the Lourenço Marques Sporting Club had originally been formed by Sporting Lisbon fans, and the two clubs had for years had an agreement about promising players.

So Eusebio spent the next seven months training furiously on the beaches of the Algarve, while Sporting and Benfica and the lawyers wrangled over his signature. Eventually, in May 1961, everything was settled, and on the 23rd, Eusebio donned the Benfica red shirt. He got three goals for them in what was a private match against Atletico.

His official debut was less exhilarating. The second leg of a Portuguese Cup tie, Benfica kicked off 3-1 up against Setubal. Soon after half-time and 3-0 down, the aggregate score favoured Setubal. Eusebio introduced himself to the crowd with a fine goal that squared the tie, and a penalty award to Benfica soon afterwards invited them into the quarter-finals.

But Eusebio missed it, Setubal scored again, and Benfica were out. A crestfallen Eusebio found small comfort in the agreeable comments of the press about his own performance.

A few months later, Benfica, as European champions, met Santos in the Paris final of the annual international tournament organized by Racing Club de Paris. With half-an-hour to go, Santos led 5-0, and it seemed a good opportunity to try out Eusebio in top-level football.

'I can't imagine any goal giving me a greater thrill than those I got against Santos,' recalls Eusebio. For those 30 minutes were enough for him to force a destructively in-form Pele to share the stage with him. Eusebio scored a hat-trick of superb goals, and all with ten minutes to spare. His reputation was growing—fast.

In September that same year, he was flown out to Montevideo for the third and decisive match in the World Club Championship series with Penarol. As a newcomer to the side, he was strictly ineligible, but he played—Penarol, confident of victory, raised no objections—and scored. But his impressive 20-yard shot only brought him a runners-up medal.

He collected another the following season. Earlier he had been at peak form in 'a game I will always remember for its emotion and suspense.' Amsterdam was the venue for the 1962 European Cup final between Benfica and Real Madrid. Puskas' first-half hat-trick gave Real a half-time lead, but two spectacular goals from Eusebio, both formidable right-foot shots, and his part in Benfica's other three, clinched the man-of-the-match award for him, and the Cup for Benfica.

Eusebio's next three European Cup finals were less fruitful. At Wembley in 1963, he gave his side the lead against AC Milan with a glorious shot, but could not prevent the Italians winning. Two years later, while on the domestic front he collected his third consecutive League championship medal, AC Milan's neighbours, Inter, saw that Eusebio was again on the losing side in the European Cup final.

In 1968, back at Wembley, Nobby Stiles was there again to trouble him—as was Alex Stepney who saved magnificently from Eusebio when he was clear with just minutes to go—and Manchester United beat Benfica in extra time. No doubt Eusebio would gladly have saved one of his 42 League goals that season for the final, for they had taken him way ahead of his rivals in the League scoring lists, for the fifth successive season.

But while those European setbacks were undoubtedly a tremendous disappointment for Eusebio, he has had his share of football's honours. In 1963 he was chosen for FIFA's Rest of the World side to play England, and two years later, he was voted European Footballer of the Year.

Top left *Eusebio's first goal against North Korea in the 1966 World Cup quarter-final at Goodison Park. His four goals won a semi-final place.*
Top right *The disappointment of failure. He could not prevent Portugal's 1-2 defeat by England in the semi-final, though his penalty goal was the first England had conceded.*
Bottom left *One penalty he did not score. Academia's goalkeeper Me... saved this one—the first goalkeeper ever to save a Eusebio penalty.*
Bottom right *The 1966 semi-final and an aerial challenge on Banks.*

With his wife of two months, Flora, and Coluna and his wife, Eusebio was on his way out to lunch when the news came through on the car radio that he was the 1965 European Footballer of the Year. For Eusebio it was the final recognition of his natural footballing abilities; his marvellous control, his amazing acceleration, and the shot . . .

Besides honours, his brilliant play has brought him money too. In 196... there was a long hiatus during which he refused to re-sign for Benfica; ultimately, the club made him an offer which persuaded Eusebio to change his mind. Though he has never approached the fortune that other number 10, Pele, Eusebio lives well. 'I have earned a lot of money. I don't know exactly how much, but it is enough to live without worries and even to save some.'

And though as the seventies got under way, both Eusebio's club and country suffered from ageing sides, he continued to impress. Eusebio has come a long way since that bitter-sweet game against England in 196...

EUSEBIO da Silva Ferreira

Honours: European Footballer of the Year 1965
World Club Championship runners-up medal 1961, 1962
European Cup winners medal 1962
European Cup runners-up medal 1963, 1965, 1968
Portuguese League Championship medal 1963, 1964, 1965, 1967, 1968, 1969, 1971, 1972, 1973
Portuguese Cup winners medal 1962, 1964, 1969, 1970, 1972
Leading Portuguese scorer 1964(28), 1965(28), 1966(25), 1967(31), 1968(42)
Leading scorer in 1966 World Cup with 9 goals

THE
GOALSCORERS

A goal a game for 15 years

the start of season 1971-72 Celtic and their
t mass of supporters paid tribute to Jimmy
Grory on the 50th anniversary of his joining
club. From apprentice footballer in the
ments of Glasgow to idolized goalscorer, club
ager and public relations officer, his had
1 a distinguished career. But he accepted the
itable praise with typical modesty.
What is the latest figure on that goal at
ley?' he asked as he puffed on his pipe. That
a private joke. He, the greatest of all
ttish marksmen, did score a memorable goal
aisley but, over the years, the ten yards he
out from goal as he dived to head the ball had
e than doubled.

McGrory could laugh off much of the legend
had grown up around him—but there was no
of getting past the figures. They show him
e the most consistently prolific scorer ever in
ain. Arthur Rowley did score 24 more in
gue football—but he played over 200 more
es. It is McGrory's remarkable consistency, a
ue average of over a goal per match, that
es him unique.

etween 20 January 1923 and 16 October 1937,
dates of his first and last matches for Celtic,
cored 410 goals in First Division games. His
y in cup-ties and internationals took the total
50.

McGrory was a broad-shouldered, barrel-
sted, courageous player who had a mind for
hing but the goal. It is reckoned that he scored
ut a third of his goals with his head, but when
talk is of heading he likes to recall a Celtic-
fermline League match on 14 January 1928.
that game he scored three goals in nine
utes, then another before half-time, and in the
nd half added another four to bring his total to
t. Yet none was achieved with his head.

ames Edward McGrory was reared in the
ngad district of Glasgow and played for the
l junior team, St Roch, as an inside-forward.
en he first joined Celtic there was for a while no

place for him and he was loaned to Clydebank,
as a winger. He returned to Celtic after scoring
13 goals in a season and, after a short spell at
outside-left, established himself at centre-
forward.

The total of goals mounted rapidly. Duncan
Walker of St Mirren held the Scottish League
record until McGrory passed it in February 1927
—on his way to 49 for the season—and in
October 1935 he scored his 353rd goal to push
Steve Bloomer out of first place in the record
books. It was then discovered that Motherwell's
Hugh Ferguson had scored 362; but McGrory was
soon passing that total.

He recalls the game in December 1935,
against Aberdeen, with ease. 'I remember the
three goals that day which took me past Ferguson's
total, but especially the third. There was a
half-cross, half-shot from Jimmy Delaney on the
right. I threw myself at it, although I thought I
might be yards short, and got my head to it.' That
season he went on to total 50, including four in
five minutes against Motherwell.

'I got my goals through being in the right
place at the right time,' he explained. 'Much of
goalscoring is in the mind. I used to go looking
for goals.

'There was no secret about my success as a
centre-forward,' he continued with unnecessary
modesty. 'I played my heart out for my club and
was always scared of being dropped, right to the
end.'

His total of seven international caps is out of
all proportion to his club feats—he was a
contemporary of Hughie Gallacher—but even
then he scored six goals for his country.

McGrory left Celtic to become manager of
Kilmarnock in 1937, and in his first season they
eliminated Celtic from the Scottish Cup before
losing to East Fife in the final. He returned to
Celtic as manager in 1945 and remained in the
job until Jock Stein took over in 1965. He then
became public relations officer for the club.

Top *Motherwell resort to hand-ball to stop Jimmy
McGrory scoring. With 410 goals in 408 matches he
is the only one of the great British scorers to average
a goal a game in League football.*

Jimmy McGRORY

Honours: Scottish League Championship medal
1925-26, 1935-36
Scottish Cup winners medal 1923, 1925, 1927,
1931, 1933, 1937
Scottish Cup runners-up medal 1926, 1928

Club	Season	League		Int'nls	
		Mtchs	Gls	Mtchs	Gls
Celtic	1922-23	3	1		
Clydebank	1923-24	30	13		
Celtic	1924-25	25	17		
	1925-26	37	35		
	1926-27	33	49		
	1927-28	36	47	1	
	1928-29	21	20		
	1929-30	26	32		
	1930-31	29	37	1	1
	1931-32	22	28	2	2
	1932-33	25	22	2	3
	1933-34	27	17	1	
	1934-35	27	18		
	1935-36	32	50		
	1936-37	25	19		
	1937-38	10	5		
Total		408	410	7	6

1

2

3

THE GOALSCORERS

Jimmy Greaves – last of the goalscorers?

It was with disillusionment that Jimmy Greaves quit his throne as the king of goals at the premature age of 31.

'The game has gone sick,' he said. 'If I was starting again now I wouldn't be allowed to play as naturally as I did when I first went to Chelsea.' Then as a teenage prodigy Greaves had proved that football matches can be won by individual skills and flair.

He came into the game when the most a player could earn for his labour was £20 a week. By the time of his premature retirement, footballers were commanding bigger salaries than Prime Ministers and Greaves was established as a legendary figure.

He was 17 when he played his first Football League match for Chelsea at Tottenham on 24 August 1957. His last game was for West Ham against Huddersfield on 1 May 1971. Sandwiched in between the first kick and the last were 357 First Division goals, 44 goals in 57 England international appearances, spectacular service for Spurs and a brief and bitter affair with AC Milan in Italy.

Greaves astonished everybody with his decision to finish at such an early age. 'I knew I was past my best and wanted to get out with my pride intact,' he said. 'The pressures and tensions in football are now so great that I believe more and more players will be retiring soon after they are 30.'

'I wouldn't like to be someone like Trevor Francis just breaking into the game. The demands on players are increasing every season. They don't get the chance to enjoy the game like when I first came into football . . .'

One aspect of the game that Greaves would have been happy about if he had been starting in the seventies would have been the money. When he took his first uncertain steps into football as a 15-year old tea-boy with Chelsea, fame must have seemed the only reward.

By the time he retired, he and his wife, Irene, and their four children lived in a magnificent, seven-bedroomed house in the stockbroker belt of Essex. As a working partner in businesses with an annual turnover of £500,000, he could afford to smile when he recalled how he ignored his father's advice to 'put football second and study a trade'.

Greaves father was a London tube train driver. His brother and sister are both school teachers. 'I often wonder what I might have achieved had I really concentrated at school,' he said. 'But I was football daft—and in those poorly-paid

days you *had* to be daft to want to do it full-time.'

Born in wartime East Ham on 20 February 1940, he was trailed by a troop of top First Division scouts during his schoolboy days in Dagenham. Tottenham were favourites to sign him, but were outmanoeuvred by Chelsea scout Jimmy Thompson, who whisked him away to Stamford Bridge to become the most productive of 'Ted Drake's Ducklings.'

Drake recalled: 'I always remember how hurt he looked when I rested him from the first team in his first season. He had been going like a bomb for us, but I did not want to burn him out. I recalled him on the Christmas Day against Portsmouth. He scored four goals. Needless to say, I never rested him again.'

In Greaves early days at Chelsea, he wore baggy, knee-length shorts. His wiry, 5ft 8in frame seemed submerged by shirt, shorts and socks. He looked the little boy lost—until he got the ball at his feet.

'What England needed against Poland was a magician—a Greaves'

From seeming disinterest in what was going on around him, Greaves would suddenly look as alert as a hunting dog on the prowl. A dip of the shoulder would send a defender one way while he went the other, sudden acceleration would end the challenge of a second defender, and a third would be deceived by a pretence at a pass.

In a second, the defence would have opened up like a knife wound. Then Greaves, shifting the ball on to his favourite left foot, would finish off a blur of action with a shot that had both venom and accuracy.

With the ball in the back of the net, Greaves used to turn and sprint back towards the halfway line as if eager to try an action replay of the goal. His right arm would be half-raised, the forefinger pointing towards the sky as if he was counting the men he had beaten. He would duck his head almost shyly as team-mates bounced congratulatory pats on his spiky hair.

This was a scene well known at Stamford Bridge. Greaves scored four goals against Portsmouth, five against Wolves, five against Preston, five against West Bromwich, four against Newcastle and, in his final match for Chelsea, he slammed in four goals against Nottingham Forest. He also helped himself to nine hat-tricks,

apart from these four and five goal barrages the way to his haul of 132 goals in 169 Che first-team matches.

'I knew Jimmy was something special whe scored 114 goals in his last season as a y team player,' recalled Drake. 'I remember gratulating him for scoring seven goals in youth match. The next game he went out got eight!'

In November 1960, Jimmy Greaves bec the youngest-ever player to score 100 Le goals, at the age of 20 years 9 months. A v before, he had asked Chelsea for a tran 'Chelsea had a lot of potential that seemed t coming to nothing,' Greaves said later. 'I enjoying my football with them but knew th was little chance of winning anything. It was bition which stirred me into asking for a mo

Greaves got his move from Chelsea—but direction that was to bring only heartache regrets. He was sold to AC Milan in one of most bizarre transfer deals there has ever bee

Soon after he had signed an option tying to Milan, the English players' union wor fight to have the maximum wage abolis Greaves was going all the way to Italy to what was suddenly within reach at home.

'It was like a sick joke—only I couldn't see funny side,' said Greaves. 'I got tied up Milan only for mercenary reasons. I would n have put pen to paper had I realized the m mum wage was going to be kicked out.'

Greaves hired a top solicitor in a bid to an escape route. But he was finally trappe the bait the Italians use so well: money. signed a three-year contract that was sched to bring him a £15,000 signing-on fee earings of around £15,000 a year.

Greaves felt a prisoner in Milan—both on off the pitch. He detested their system of loc players away in secluded training camps be every match and in no time at all he suffocated by homesickness.

He scored 9 goals in 10 league matches Milan, but got no enjoyment out of playing football that was being slowly strangled by defensive systems. The Italian press adde the pressures by presenting him to the publi a layabout playboy and sex maniac—all beca he had been spotted drinking in a nightc accompanied by his wife!

After a series of bitter rows and disputes Milan trainer Nereo Rocco, Greaves was pu for sale. Tottenham outbid Chelsea and sig the player they could once have had for noth for £99,999, manager Bill Nicholson wanting Greaves to be the first player with £100,000 price-tag.

The Italian episode had lasted just over months. Greaves' attempts to earn big me had gone sour. He made just £4,000 from ill-fated stay and this had been whittled d to pennies by the time he returned to Lon to join 'Super Spurs,' the club he had suppo as a boy, who the season before had become first club this century to win the League and Cup 'double'.

'I was tortured by doubts when I first joi Spurs,' Greaves recalled. 'They had achieve much before I was brought in and I wonde

POPPERFOTO

Above *Danny Blanchflower said after this match against the 17-year-old Greaves in 1957, 'His greatest asset is his uncanny deceptiveness. You think he's going one way . . . and then find he's going the other.'* 1 *Jimmy Greaves gets the ball and* 2 *makes his first feint leaving one defender* 3 *bewildered and stretched out on the ground.* 4 *Then, suddenly, the whole line of his body twists round, and another defender has been beaten by the Greaves magic. The whole move comes to its inevitable climax* 5 *with the goalkeeper leaping in a vain attempt to stop a great Chelsea goal against Tottenham.*
Left *The reign is almost over. Jimmy Greaves in pensive mood during one of his last West Ham games.*

Jimmy GREAVES

Honours: European Cup Winners Cup winners medal 1963;
FA Cup winners medal 1962, 1967

Club	Season	League		Int'nls	
		Mtchs	Gls	Mtchs	Gls
Chelsea	1957-58	35	22		
	1958-59	42	32	3	1
	1959-60	40	29	4	2
	1960-61	40	41	8	13
AC Milan*	1961-62*	10*	9*		
Tottenham	1961-62	22	21	7	4
	1962-63	41	37	8	4
	1963-64	41	35	9	8
	1964-65	41	29	6	6
	1965-66	29	15	9	5
	1966-67	38	25	3	1
	1967-68	39	23		
	1968-69	42	27		
	1969-70	29	8		
West Ham	1969-70	6	4		
	1970-71	32	9		
Total		517†	357†	57	44

Football League total only†   Italian League*

ether I would fit in.'

He made his Tottenham debut against ckpool on 16 December 1961. He scored ee goals, the first from a stunning scissors k. The doubts disappeared.

Greaves had eight wonderful seasons with ttenham and emerged as their top scorer ry time. He set a League record by leading First Division scorers in three successive sons and collected a total of 220 League goals the club he still calls 'the greatest'.

Greaves admitted on reflection that the ding-down point in his career started with attack of hepatitis in November 1965. It's a ndice that sucks you dry of energy,' he said knocked half a yard off my speed and from n on I was never quite the same player, ough I refused to admit it to myself for eral years.'

He fought off the after-effects of the illness time to win a place in England's 1966 World p squad. He played in the three qualifying tches against Uruguay, Mexico and France hout scoring and then missed the quarter-l against Argentina and the semi-final against tugal because of a shin injury.

There was no doubt about his fitness for the final against West Germany, but team manager Sir Alf Ramsey—then plain Alf—did what few people would have dared. He left Greaves on the sidelines and England went on to win the World Cup, with Geoff Hurst scoring a historic hat-trick. 'That was the saddest day of my career,' admitted Greaves. 'I *knew* England were going to win the World Cup and desperately wanted to play a part in the final.'

Stories circulated that Ramsey and Greaves had quarrelled, and they gained strength when Sir Alf continued to ignore Greaves even when he showed a brief return to top form in the 1968-69 season. Angry petitions were sent to Ramsey demanding his recall and Greaves fans prepared for a placard-and-chant march on Downing Street. After some weeks of continual harrassment, Ramsey finally burst out, 'They are crucifying me! Greaves has *asked* not to be selected for England.'

Greaves, equally keen to put the record straight, said later: 'There was no question of any argument. I simply told Alf that I did not want to be considered for his training get-togethers if he was *not* going to play me in the

team. I was never one for tactical talks and felt my time could be put to better use in my business. Alf did not want to select me on these terms and I quite appreciate his point of view.'

Greaves entered the last lap of his career when he joined West Ham on transfer deadline day, 16 March 1970. He was valued as a £54,000 makeweight in a £200,000 swap deal that took Martin Peters to Tottenham. He maintained his remarkable record of scoring in each of his major debut matches with two goals against Manchester City at Maine Road.

Greaves marked his retirement in 1971 by cutting himself off completely from football. 'The world's worst spectator'—the words were his—was unlikely to be seen at any League matches in the future.

Greaves had always been a popular player with his fellow professionals. He had a humour that everybody liked and was always scrupulously fair. The only time he was ever sent off was for throwing a punch in retaliation during a roughhouse Cup Winners Cup tie in Belgrade. 'I missed by a mile,' he said later, 'I never was any good at counter punching!'

The God Pele and his God-given gifts

'The name Pele,' said Pat Crerand, the wing-half and philosopher, 'should be spelt G-O-D.' Even allowing for West of Scotland exaggeration, the remark reflects the unique position Pele occupies in the esteem of footballers throughout the world. He is the ultimate symbol of excellence in football, the greatest flowering of Brazil's genius for the game, a player with scarcely a weakness.

Joao Saldanha, former manager of the Brazil national team, said of Pele, 'If you ask me who is the best full-back in Brazil, I will say Pele. If you ask who is the best wing-half I would say Pele. Who is the best winger? Pele. If you ask me who is the best goalkeeper, probably I would have to say Pele. He is like no other player. He is to Brazilian football what Shakespeare is to English literature.' Saldanha is an immensely strong and aggressive personality and his relationship with Pele, who is more deity than mortal in Brazil, was never a blissful one. But Saldanha did not attempt to qualify his tribute to *Negrao* (big negro), as the player is called by those who know him well.

Pele himself accepts that he reached and passed his peak with the 1970 World Cup in Mexico. He has since retired from international football, though he continues to be thrillingly active with his club, Santos. He has climbed every mountain available to the great footballer, won two World Cup winners medals, scored more than a thousand goals in his senior career and been recognized for more than a decade as the most lavishly equipped exponent of his sport, perhaps the most exceptional it has ever known.

Only one player has been regularly compared with Pele

Of all the great players of the last 30 years or so, only one, Alfredo di Stefano, the magnificent Argentinian who was the central influence in the Real Madrid side who were irresistible in Europe in the 1950s, has been regularly compared with Pele in terms of personal capacity to control a match. But even di Stefano, with his iron will, his marvellous perception and superb skills, should take a place just slightly beneath Pele in the pantheon of the game. Di Stefano did not have the Brazilian's gymnastic grace or liquid fluency. There was a hard, functional angularity about his game, and while that quality, by emphasizing his strength and authority, carried its own excitement, it did not produce the shiver in the blood that comes with the sight of Pele in full flow.

Of contemporary players, the man who comes closest to creating that effect is George Best. It is one of the sadnesses of sport that Best will never have the opportunity to exercise his huge gifts in the context of a great side in the greatest of competitions, the World Cup. He deserves the finest company and the biggest stage. In that sense Pele was born lucky. Only the Hungarians of the early fifties could be seen as rivalling the vast store of talent that was available to Brazil in the 1960s.

When Pele burst upon us in the 1958 World Cup in Sweden he was the prodigy of a team brimming with the highest skills; Djalma and Nilton Santos, Didi, Garrincha, Vava, Zagalo; these were giants. When the young Pele proved himself at least as exciting, scoring two goals in an unforgettable victory over Sweden in the final, no one could doubt that football had gained a star of the first magnitude.

Pele is viciously kicked out of the 1966 World Cup

The success in Sweden was followed by another in Chile in 1962, but injury prevented Pele from playing in more than two matches and it was left to Garrincha to dazzle the assembled aficionados. Despite their win, there was disturbing evidence that, as one writer said, the Brazilian team had begun to suffer from hardening of the arteries. But the warnings were ignored and so the World Cup of 1966 became as much a disaster for Brazil as it was a triumph for England. The selectors in Rio, afraid to desert venerated players who were palpably in decline, travelled to Europe with a party that looked more like a pensioners' club than a World Cup squad.

Even the outstanding young Brazilian players had been ill-prepared, and when Pele was systematically kicked out of the competition by Morais of Portugal, a miserable exclusion from the quarter-finals became inevitable. This was an experience to scar the Brazilian psyche and it did so much personal damage to Pele that he talked for a while of turning his back on the Jules Rimet trophy forever. In his career to that point, his country had taken the prize twice and yet Pele himself had never played a full series of matches in the finals. He muttered grimly that he saw no virtue in offering himself as a sacrifice to the hard men. What was the point of his taking the field in the World Cup if violence was to be allowed to invalidate virtuosity?

Fortunately for everyone, Pele's pessimism was short-lived and his

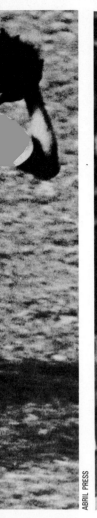

spirit was fully restored by the fresh impetus imparted to Brazil's drive towards the World Cup of 1970. The Brazilian players, under Saldanha, were withdrawn from club football four months before the Mexico finals. It was the first time that Pele had known the luxury of a period of sustained training. Previously he had always been too preoccupied playing matches (as many as 140 a season by the time he had earned the large fees Santos charged for his appearance in exhibition games) and the novelty of preparation had a wonderful effect on him.

Pele announced that he felt really fit for the first time in years. Tension between himself and Saldanha, the one factor that might have undermined his performance in Mexico, helped to persuade the ruling body of Brazilian football that Saldanha should be replaced. Mario Zagalo, Pele's ally of ten years before, took over the managership and Pele's last and greatest assault on the Jules Rimet trophy was launched.

What happened in Guadalajara and Mexico City in that burning midsummer of 1970 can be seen as a dramatic summation of Pele's contribution to football. Encouraged by his sense of physical well-being, his confidence in the vast, mature range of his abilities, and his knowledge that Brazil had been properly prepared, he went to Mexico with a calculated resolve that he and his team would dominate the ninth World Cup competition to a historic degree.

'Pele has created his mood. We are ready to explode'

One of the Brazilian officials said: 'Pele has created his mood. We have timed everything to come to a peak at precisely the right moment. We are ready to explode.' We knew the kind of explosion to expect from Pele. He is probably the most exhilarating runner with the ball the game has known, exercising such astonishing control that he hardly seems to play the ball deliberately at all. It seems to be juggled adhesively between his feet and shins while he moves at maximum speed, free to concentrate on his next decisive stroke. Other players, even great ones, have to caress the ball constantly as they run, but Pele seems to make it a natural appendage of his stride.

Top left Pele, regarded by many as football's 'God', retaliates all too humanly with a punch in the face as his shirt is pulled by a desperate defender.
Left above Pele keeps his eye on the ball despite the kind of over-zealous attention he has come to expect.
Left centre Against England in Mexico, 1970, Pele is floored, though Bell and his England team-mates seem unconcerned.
Left bottom By contrast, Pele is quick to assist Tommy Wright when cramp gets the better of him.
Left Pele disconsolately leaves the field after Brazil's 1966 World Cup game with Portugal. It looked then as if he had been kicked out of the game for ever. But Pele returned to enjoy a superb 1970 World Cup.

'Sometimes you tackle him and you are convinced you have the ball,' says Bobby Moore. 'You have felt solid contact with it and you know it's yours. Then you look round and he's ten yards past you and it's at his feet. He'll play it against your legs and then catch it on the rebound and carry on.'

The first time Pele used that insolent skill, Bobby Moore said he thought it had been an accident. 'But after the sixth or seventh time, I had to realize that, incredibly, he was doing it on purpose. Nothing is too outrageous for him.'

There is the same total lack of inhibition about Pele's passing and finishing. He passes the ball over, round, past and sometimes apparently through opponents, curving and flighting and driving the ball with bewildering variety and relentless precision. And when Pele strikes at goal, his athletic elasticity, inspired timing and spontaneous force give him a deadliness no one has ever exceeded.

His vision on the field, his awareness of what is going on all around him, is so amazing that he gives the impression of having his eyes on the sides of his head, like a bird's. But his sense of what is happening during a match goes far beyond any question of sight. His is a deep, instinctive perception. It is easy to believe that if someone is having his pocket picked at the back of the stands Pele will know about it.

In the 1970 Mexico World Cup, in Brazil's opening match of the competition, against Czechoslovakia, Pele brought the first half to an amazing climax with one of the great moments of the World Cup. Moving into possession well inside his own half of the field, he gave a barely perceptible glance in the direction of Viktor, saw that the goalkeeper had stepped out some yards from the posts, and struck. Pele was still in the Brazilian segment of the centre circle when, raising his right leg in a prodigious backlift and swinging it through with a flow-

The whole stadium throbbed with a special excitement

ing, effortless precision worthy of an iron shot by Ben Hogan, he sent the ball in a fast arc towards goal. Viktor's contorted features revealed the extent of his painful astonishment as he scrambled back under the ball, then spun helplessly to see it swoop less than a yard outside a post. Through the interval the stadium throbbed with the special excitement crowds feel when they have seen something remarkable and know there is more of the same to come.

In the semi-final against Uruguay, a match fraught with the severest pressures for Brazil because of the history of their confrontations with their South American neighbours, there came this crucial moment.

Having adopted a stance about as fluidly aggressive as Edinburgh Castle's, Uruguay were presumably content to hope that an opponent's error would give them a chance of a goal. Such a shamelessly barren philosophy hardly deserved the extraordinary vindication it was granted as early as the eighteenth minute when Brazil contributed not one but two unbelievable mistakes. First Brito, without any excuse, pushed the ball straight to Morales, who curled his pass behind Everaldo to Cubilla. Cubilla controlled the ball on his chest but had to take it too close to the bye-line, so that the shot was struck slackly across the face of the goal. Felix then supplied the second blunder. Moving like a man trying to walk on golf balls, he stumbled and groped across his line as the ball bounced languidly into the net.

Felix looked disgusted. Several of the other Brazilians were on the verge of despair, none more obviously than Gerson, who held his head as if to staunch a wound. Pele ran through the shattered ranks of the team and collected the ball to bring it back for the kick-off. All the way to the centre circle he was talking soothingly to those around him. He knew how debilitating mutual recriminations could be and he did not intend to let anything stand between him and the

'Who'll be first to score against these bastards?'

World Cup. One of his colleagues later recounted what Pele said as he placed the ball for the kick-off. 'Right. Now let's see who's going to be the first to score against those bastards.'

During that game, Pele was not only at his most vigorous, exploding into unforeseen runs as if in response to a gun that only he could hear, checking and swerving and doubling back, the religious medal around his neck glinting in the afternoon sunshine. He was also at his most outrageously ambitious, attempting plays that the fantastic heroes of our boyhood comics would have found taxing.

For at the heart of Pele's game is a joyful pursuit of the impossible. He has dominated the mythology of world football as no man before him ever did, scoring over a thousand goals and creating ten thousand moments of exhilarating beauty. But he is happily dissatisfied. He does not hide the insistent desire to score one goal that will stand apart from all the others, a goal that will be impossible until he makes it possible, one that nobody else can emulate: Pele's goal.

That was the goal he had sought with his incredible arced shot from the middle of the field against the Czechs and he reached for it twice more against Uruguay, first with an instantaneous volley from 35

Top left One of the crucial games in the 1970 World Cup was Brazil—the favourites—against England—the World champions. Here Pele embarks on one of his dazzling runs that always spelt danger, and that prompted Bobby Moore to help Mullery mark Pele.
Top right Afterwards, with Brazil 1-0 victors, Pele delightedly embraces a sporting Bobby Moore.
Right An enthralled crowd watches Pele streak past England's defence.
Far right Pele takes a leaf from the golfer's book as he sets himself for a crucially accurate chip shot.

yards after the goalkeeper, Mazurkiewicz, mis-hit a goal kick, and then with a dummy on Mazurkiewicz that neither he nor anyone else who witnessed it will ever forget. The miraculous goal did not come, though, but a superb victory did, when Italy were outclassed in the final match, and Pele went home happy in spite of the knowledge that his legend would now be even more difficult to live with.

Pele (or Edson Arantes do Nascimento as he should properly be called) long ago gave up any hope of living a normal life. Indeed, all the members of the poor black family into which he was born on 21 October 1940, in common with his white wife Rosel and two children, have found their daily existence overwhelmed by the most pervasive adulation ever accorded to a sportsman.

Autograph-hunting is the mildest form of pestering that Pele is subjected to. More often he is asked for money. There are television programmes which promise cash rewards for anybody who succeeds in bringing Pele in front of the cameras. The day Pele played his last match for the Brazilian team (18 July 1971) a television programme announced that whoever succeeded in bringing Pele to the studio would receive £1,000.

When Pele came back to his hotel he found, shoved under the door, a number of messages written by the hotel staff, each one explaining in painful detail precisely why it was so important for him and his family to get that £1,000. Pele did not go to the programme (he has never been to one), but he helped the staff out of his own pocket.

'If I were to go to a programme they would have to pay me £10,000,' Pele said. 'Not because I want the money or because I need it. But because that is how I can make certain that they are not going to ask me. If I went on one programme, I would have to accept all the other invitations.

Pele's hometown unveiled his statue in 1971

'The television comperes who behave like that are dishonest,' says Pele. 'They know that I am not going to their programmes: they are just giving people false hopes. They put me in an awkward position and force me to spend money to evade their blackmail.'

Tres Coracoes (Three Hearts), the city where Pele was born, unveiled his statue in 1971. Politicians, army officers, everybody striving for publicity was there, standing by Pele to have their photograph in the newspapers. There were speeches, fireworks, the usual scenes.

Pele's brother Zoca, who is four years younger, wanted to be a footballer and he was promising enough to be given a contract by Santos at the age of fifteen, but he never had a chance to make his way in the game. Whenever Santos included him in any team sent into the interior of Brazil the stands would be packed with people prepared to see miracles and prepared to condemn anything else. Zoca was a reasonable player but the pressure on him was intolerable.

Pele's own life has been irrevocably shaped by his talent. He has earned vast amounts of money from football. Yet his best friends say that he is not a good businessman. He tries to compensate for this flaw by a perennial bargaining attitude. If he is made an offer, he does not know whether it is sound or not, because he does not know his real market value, and so he automatically asks for more money. And in most cases he gets it.

He earns almost £4,000 a month playing for Santos, plus victory bonuses. The actual amount varies from month to month, because on top of a fixed wage, he earns £400 for each match Santos play in Brazil and £2,000 for matches played abroad. Advertising brings him at least another £4,000 each month. Apart from that, Pele has a partnership in a plastics company with his ex-clubmate Zito and is a director of Banco Industrial de Campina Grande, in Santos (Sao Paulo).

In 1966, Pele almost went bankrupt with the company he had at the time ('Sanitaria Santista', which dealt in bathroom fittings) and had to be dug out of his difficulties by Santos. It was also at that time that he broke with his then financial advisor Pepe o Gordo (Pepe the Fat) because Pepe had almost ruined him. Pele found that Pepe (a Spanish immigrant), though not dishonest, was absolutely not the economic wizard he had led people to believe. Pepe o Gordo still lives in Santos, but Pele is no longer on speaking terms with him.

That Pele is, after all, not the great businessman he is reputed to be is more than underlined by the fact that the bank where he is a director has forbidden him to grant any loans. The bank administration think that Pele does not know how to say 'no' and that he could lead them to heavy losses. For this reason, Pele is used almost totally for promotional purposes alone, quite an expensive piece of public relations.

But despite his colossal earnings, despite his celebrity, many who know him best envy him least. Says Joao Saldanha, 'He is a king, but he has never been a boy.'

The king has a handsome face, especially when he smiles, and the impossibly white teeth offset the overlong nose. The eyes are large and slightly protruding and the wary steadiness of their gaze emphasizes the overall impression of earnestness. His torso is thick (in the Brazil training camp of 1970 he sat at 'the fat man's table' set aside for those who had to watch their weight) and the back of his neck is heavy with muscle. His legs inevitably are remarkable. The thighs are vast slabs of muscle, the calves slim and tapering as a schoolgirl's. They were once thinner, Pele explains, before the endless succession of kicks left an accumulation of permanent swellings. His feet are surprisingly splayed out.

When he talks of the special capabilities of those feet, he disclaims any personal credit. For Pele is a devout Catholic and is sincerely convinced that his talent for football is a divine gift.

'I feel the greatest skill I have on the football field is the ability to make something out of nothing. Of course, you need balance, and speed of mind and body, and strength. But there is something else, something God has given me, maybe some extra instinct for the game. Sometimes I can take the ball and no one can foresee any danger, and then in two or three seconds there is a goal.

'Eusebio is a great player, but he needs others to work with him to make things happen to suit him. Sometimes, perhaps not very often, but sometimes I can make goals happen out of nothing. This does not make me proud. It makes me humble, because this is a talent that God gave me. All I can do is work to use it well, to make a good life for my family and to give pleasure to the people. Aside from anything I do, there is always the Finger of God. He made me a footballer and he keeps me a footballer.'

God did more. He made Pele *the* footballer.

Top *Pele the businessman. Though he is a director of a Brazilian bank, he is forbidden by his fellow directors to grant loans because, they claim, he is unable to refuse anybody.*
Right *Pele, who plays as many as 140 games each season, enjoys one of those rare moments when he can quietly relax.*
Below *Pele celebrates his 1000th goal, a penalty against Vasco da Gama.*

PELE (Edson Arantes do Nascimento)

Honours: World Cup winners medal 1958, 1970
World Club Championship medal 1962, 1963
South American Club Cup winners medal 1962, 1963
Brazilian Cup winners medal 1962, 1963, 1964, 1968
Sao Paulo League Championship medal 1958, 1960, 1961, 1962, 1964, 1965, 1967, 1968, 1969
Internationals: 110 appearances, 96 goals
Club (Santos): 1036 appearances

HOW PELE SCORED 1000 GOALS

Team	Competition	1956	'57	'58	'59	'60	'61	'62	'63	'64	'65	'66	'67	'68	'69	Total
Brazil			2	9	11	4		8	7	2	9	5		4	7	68
Santos	Sao Paulo Championship		36	53	46	32	47	37	22	34	49	12	15	17	26	426
Santos	Friendlies against non-Brazilian sides		1	13	46	31	35	33	19	16	16	19	24	1	15	269
Santos	Gomes Pedrosa & Taca de Prata Tournaments		4	8	6		9		14	3	5		9	12	12	82
Santos	Friendlies against Brazilian sides	2	22				9	6	7		17	2	5	5	4	79
Santos	Brazilian Cup				2		7	4	6	7	2	2				30
Santos	South American Club Cup							4	5		9					18
Santos	World Club Championship							5	2							7
Santos	Brazilian Championship				7											7
Army					14											14
	Total	2	65	83	125	74	107	97	82	62	107	40	53	39	64	**1000**

In the red shirt of Wales, Ron Davies shoots past the England defence. If he had been born an Englishman, he would almost certainly be known all over the world.

Ron Davies – the saviour of the Saints

THE
GOALSCORERS

The Leicester goalkeeper Peter Shilton swung back his foot and volleyed a massive clearance down the field towards the Southampton end. To the amazement of the crowd at the Dell, the ball bounced past a stationary Southampton defence and rolled—untouched—into the net. Could a team which gave away goals like that possibly survive in the First Division? The answer is they could, so long as they had the extraordinary goalscoring power of their Welsh international centre-forward, Ron Davies.

In a career that began in 1960, he scored goals wherever he played. He scored goals whatever the position and, far more important, he scored goals however weak the side he was representing.

The first eight years of his professional life were one long struggle to score enough goals to cover the vast numbers a succession of leaky defences were letting in. For at Chester, Luton Town, Norwich and in his early days at Southampton, almost every time he hit the back of the net his team-mates celebrated by letting in a goal. Only at Norwich where his side briefly flirted with promotion to the First Division did he taste any flavour of success. 'Even so,' he reflected later, 'when I was there, it was about the only time they didn't have a Cup run.'

Even when his consistent goal-scoring took him into the Welsh international side in 1963, he was often frustrated by playing in a side always ravaged by injuries and the unavailability of players. Yet typically he knocked in a goal on his debut, against Northern Ireland at Wrexham.

He was born at Holywell in Flintshire in May 1942, and a colleague of his in the local school team was Mike England, later to represent Spurs and Wales. England took all the limelight, and overshadowed Davies: 'Mike won all the schoolboy honours. I didn't get a thing.'

It could have been because Davies was so shy. He was once sent home from school because he had not spoken to anybody for two weeks.

But, more likely, it was because he did not develop physically as fast as his future colleague in the Wales side. But, in a school match, he was eventually spotted by John Harris, then the manager of nearby Chester. For two years he made the journey by bus twice a week from Holywell to Chester to train with other schoolboys. For a bashful lad it was an ordeal, but Davies persevered. Still a skinny, anaemic-looking boy, he remembered making no outstanding impact at these sessions, but Harris continued to invite him to come.

At 15 he left school. 'My parents brought me up very strictly, and desperately wanted me to be a success. I passed a few exams in my last year at school, and they got me into the local steelworks as an apprentice moulder. It was quite a triumph, but I only lasted five weeks.'

He lasted five weeks because John Harris encouraged the Chester FC board of directors to take what for them was a radical decision—to employ Davies as a groundstaff boy. He was the first Chester had ever had.

'It wasn't going to break them,' said Harris. 'We only paid the lad £3 a week. I could see then that he would be worth the risk. In the summer after his 15th birthday he had filled out, and it seemed that he had shot up six inches.'

Davies was delighted to sign, and after two years of interminable chores around the ground in between learning the basics of his trade, he signed full professional forms.

At the time Chester were a sagging mixture of ageing 'old pro's' and young hopefuls. Davies was the youngest and, perhaps, the most hopeful—at least for the long-suffering Chester fans.

Still only a 17-year-old he won a place in the side towards the end of the 1959-60 season, but he had yet to show more than the merest glimpse of his future power in the air.

'If anything, in those days I was better on the ground. I could play reasonably well with both feet, and I think they gave you a little more time to play then.'

In that first season he played eight games, and scored one goal. Chester finished fifth from bottom—the highest they were to achieve whilst Davies was with them.

The following season he gained a regular place—in what proved to be the least effective side in the Football League. Chester finished bottom of the Fourth Division. They conceded 104 goals and scored only 61—but out of those 61 Davies netted 23 in 39 appearances.

Playing centre-forward for Chester must have been one of the least rewarding jobs in football at that time, but the young Davies finished the sixth highest scorer in the Division. An example of the frustration he must have felt occurred in Chester's last match of the season, at Hartlepools. Chester needed to win to avoid the humiliation of being bottom of the League. Davies helped his side score four times, grabbing two fine goals himself, but his defence let in four—so Chester were last.

The 1961-62 season followed the same pattern. They were bottom again—conceding fewer goals but scoring even less. The strain began to tell on Davies, whose total for the season fell to 13, but he still scored more than twice as many as the second highest scorer.

'At last I had begun to show myself as a header of the ball'

Chester began the next campaign, predictably, with four successive defeats. Davies was dropped. Aggrieved, he placed a transfer request before the manager, and surprisingly he was put on offer at around £3,000. Before any suitable bid was made, he had got back in the side, and on 3 October 1962 Chester thrashed Southport at the Sealand Road Stadium 6-1. Davies' aerial power devastated the Southport defence and he scored four times. His transfer value rose sharply, and a few weeks later Bill Harvey bought him for Luton Town for £10,000.

'At last I had begun to show myself as a header of the ball,' Davies remembered. 'Bill Lambton, one of Mr Harris's successors, made me jump hurdles wearing Army boots. It was murder, but it may have done the trick. Since then I have discovered that if you get little room on the ground, there is always space in the air. If you can get there.'

Luton were in the Second Division, but if Davies expected to be given more support, he could not have been more disappointed. Luton were relegated. But he more than repaid his transfer fee. In 29 games for his new club, he scored 21 goals—giving him a League total of 28 for the season. But, once again, he was a loser.

One of his matches for Luton was against Norwich City at Kenilworth Road. His opponent that day happened to be Ron Ashman, the 'Canaries' player-manager. Ashman never forgot that afternoon.

'The big lad I was marking did nothing but score four goals. I couldn't believe it.' Davies' recollections struck a different key. 'How can he say I did nothing? As I got the first, Ashie came up to me and said "That's not a bad start lad," and I replied "Wait on, you've not seen anything yet".'

The impression stuck, and Ashman's next visit to Luton early in September 1963 had a more singular purpose. Like John Harris he had reported to his board. Like John Harris he had asked for money—this time a Norwich record transfer fee of £35,000. Ashman obtained the cash and his player, and never had one moment to doubt his judgement.

'At Norwich we had to work on him a bit. He wasn't the best of targets for our defenders' clearances, and we had to improve his ability to lay off passes to supporting players. But for a big fellow, he was extremely well-equipped on the ground—good with both feet—and in the air he came into a class of his own.'

Norwich City played with two wingers whose task was to find Davies' blond head. Alongside him Ashman played another big man, Gordon Bolland, who at that time found goalscoring almost as easy as his new Welsh colleague. Davies revelled in the support he was given, and 27 more goals were added to what was already becoming an impressive League total.

Most of the goals came with strong flicks of the head, but for Ashman the finest came in a different style.

'We were playing Leeds at Carrow Road. I was

still sitting on the trainers' bench. They were challenging for promotion. They went two up with about 20 minutes left, and Don Revie ran on to the pitch to embrace his team. I thought—"Hell, it'll take a bloody lot to make me run on to a football pitch!"

'Davies pulled one back a few minutes later, but there were only minutes left when our right-back hit a long ball up to Ron on the edge of the Leeds box. He was facing his own goal, but he took the ball on his chest, and half-turned to his right. As it dropped, he hit it on the volley with his left foot. It flew past Gary Sprake into the top of the net. And there was I, invading the pitch just like Revie. It was the best I shall ever see.'

While at Norwich Davies managed to fit in wedding. 'I met Sylvia while I was at Cheste I knocked her over in the street, and it all start from there. But with all the football it was diffic to plan a wedding. We even got engaged outsi Crewe Alexandra football ground, and s brought the ring with her.'

Maybe the responsibilities of marriage fir his ambition. 'He always wanted to do we Ashman remembered. 'In fact, in his seco season with us he became a wee bit jealous Gordon Bolland. Bolly had a good patch a notched a lot of goals, but Ron had a spell whe they were hard to come by. For Ron it was enough that Norwich were getting goals—he ha

RAY GREEN

RON DAVIES

In the 1966-67 season he scored 38 First Division goals to become the Football League's top marksman—five further efforts in Cup-ties made him the leading goal-scorer in Europe. Although Southampton's defence had the quality of a gashed collander, they managed to create a recipe to bring the very best out of their new centre-forward.

In Terry Paine and John Sydenham they had two orthodox wingers whose very strength was their ability to cross the ball with precision. Alongside Davies they used a home-product, Martin Chivers, who had a deft touch on the ground for a big man. Between them Davies and Chivers managed enough goals to give Southampton a creditable score in what was their first year as a First Division club.

In their second season together, Davies hammered in another 28 goals to retain his title as the Football League's leading scorer— sharing the honour with Manchester United's George Best. However, in 1968, Spurs persuaded Chivers to leave his native Southampton, and the partnership was broken. Chivers has affectionate memories of his playing colleague. 'It was marvellous playing with "Big Ron". Whoever we were playing against we always felt we had a good chance of scoring—despite the tightness of First Division defences.'

Naturally enough, Davies regretted losing such a talented colleague, who had proved so complementary to his own skills and, for a time, grew restless. Manchester United and Arsenal were just two of many clubs reputed to be willing to write out a cheque for £200,000 for his services.

But by 1971, he was content enough to say that he would stay with the 'Saints' as long as his manager, Ted Bates, thought he was good enough to keep his place.

His success at Southampton turned him into a new commodity for his country. From one of several big forwards, all fighting to gain one or two places, he became the focal point of the Wales attack. In May 1969, he really established himself as a striker of true international worth with three outrageously spectacular headers in the Home International tournament. Twice against Scotland he rattled the back of the net with devastating power, and he gave Wales a fighting even if vain chance of beating England at Wembley. He steepled above Jack Charlton—no slouch in the air—to nod the ball down past Gordon Banks and give Wales a 1-0 lead.

'I think he's one of the greatest in Europe—his record speaks for itself'

For Dave Bowen, the Wales team-manager, Davies' improvement was like a manna from heaven. 'There's not much better than Ron. He'd always be my centre-forward. I think he's one of the greatest in Europe—his record speaks for itself.'

By 1971, at the peak of his career, Davies had relaxed at Southampton. 'The social life here is very good. I've got six or seven good mates in the team, and we spend a lot of time together.' He appeared to have overcome his early shyness, and he obviously enjoyed involving himself in the life of his adopted town.

Like many footballers since the abolition of the maximum wage, he made sure that he used the big money, that was now coming his way, wisely.

He admitted candidly, 'I have no real desire to go into football when I finish. I'm far too soft to become a manager. I'd never be able to tell all my players to be in bed at half-past ten on Friday night. I wouldn't mind doing some coaching, but I'm not fanatical about it—like Jimmy Gabriel for instance—and I haven't got any qualifications for it.

'I'm hoping to invest my money wisely so that when I finish playing I shall be in a comfortable position to look around and see what I want to do next.'

He had been wisely advised. He invested in

COLORSPORT

p left Leaping higher than the Manchester City *...ence*, Ron Davies flicks the ball towards the goal. *...w* would doubt that Davies is one of the greatest *...ders* in football today.
...ft In this match against Liverpool he is almost *...mbing* over the defence while fellow-Welsh *...ernational* John Toshack looks on enviously.
...p centre In the same match, he once again

towers over his opponents, a vital asset for any side.
Top right Davies is an accomplished cartoonist, and this is how he sees himself.
Above Concentration shows on Davies' face as he yet again soars above his opponents, this time, at Leicester City. Early training at Chester leaping over hurdles wearing heavy army boots may have been the reason for Davies' rise to fame.

be scoring himself. I think that it was this ...atiable appetite that kept him scoring wherever ...played.'

...That second season produced only 14 goals, the ...rd four more—as Norwich struggled to free ...mselves from being an average Second Division ...e. Unhappy, Davies asked for a transfer: 'I got ...up with us not winning anything. Norwich was a ...ely place to be, but I had begun to feel that ...uld perhaps cope with First Division football.

...For weeks it looked certain that he would get ... wish at St James' Park, Newcastle. Joe Harvey, ... Newcastle manager had him watched frequently and even contacted Norwich, but seemed ...uctant to commit himself to an expensive

player who had scored a lot of goals—but none of them in the First Division. (Later he was to reverse this policy, when he signed Malcolm Macdonald for £180,000 at the end of the 1970-71 season, a player who had never scored a First Division goal.) Newcastle bought Wyn Davies from Bolton Wanderers instead, but Ron Ashman has always maintained that 'they bought the wrong Davies!'

Finally after years of slogging slowly through an apprenticeship in League football, an apprenticeship more arduous than any a steelworks could have offered him, Davies found the success that had eluded him—and it was an extravagant success.

137

ANGLING TIMES LTD

Though sea-fishing is his hobby, Davies has turned it into a business, taking out visitors in his own boat.

wife in the later stages of her first pregnan
back to the homeland—to qualify a son for Wal
But Sylvia gave birth to a daughter, Karen. I
the time their second child was expected, he h
become anglicized enough not to send Sylv
away again. But any hopes of the arrival of
potential England centre-forward were doused I
the birth of Nicola.

Had Davies been an Englishman, his ski
would have undoubtedly been of interest to t
national selectors. But he was sceptical as
whether he would have capitalized on a
chances they might have given him. 'I would ha
made more money if I had been successful, but
would have been so much harder to get into t
national side. And if I had played for Engla
as badly as I have on some occasions for Wal
they'd never have considered me again.'

Headwork that could be
compared with the greate
—Dean and Lawton

It is the unfulfilled and unfulfillable potenti
that makes Ron Davies such a fascinating playe
As a Welshman his talents could never be put
the critical test at World Cup level, yet the
talents were so expansive in the late sixties a
early seventies that experts would nearly alwa
pick him as the centre-forward in a mythic
Great Britain side.

Had he been blessed with success at club level-
apart from his Welsh caps, he had won no oth
honours by 1971—his imperious headwo
might have placed him on the pedestal occupi
by Dixie Dean and Tommy Lawton. Only wh
Southampton enjoyed a brief run in the Fai
Cup in 1969 did he battle against European cl
defences. And even then they were dismissed fro
the competition by a fellow English club, Ne
castle United.

Even more intriguingly, he admitted th
amongst the clubs he had served he had rare
been trained by a strict disciplinarian. T
toughest was Chester's ex-sergeant-major, B
Lambton, the man who had the coltish Davi
leaping over hurdles in Army boots and sudden
developing in him a talent for heading the ba
Who knows what other skills he might ha
developed with another Lambton somewhe
else?

But the fact that at 29 the standards of h
success—more and more goals and caps—f
easily to him suited his aimiable personali
And in the light of his eight-year struggle throu
the Minor Counties of Cheshire, Bedfordsh
and Norfolk to First-class Hampshire he cou
be excused if he felt satisfied with what he ha
accomplished.

In 1973, he and Southampton finally fell ou
and he moved along the coast to Portsmou
There he settled in happily, under his former coa
at The Dell, John Mortimore, and the blond m
continued to direct in the goals.

And in retirement the prospects all indicat
that the Davies family would live in comfo
from their business ventures. For 'Big Ron' the
would be time to draw, time to fish and time f
a quiet drink. More than most men, he wou
appreciate that.

property, and became the landlord of a block of
eight luxury flats. That alone ensured a sound
future for his family.

In his other businesses he has injected more
of his own personality. He developed a talent for
drawing cartoons—although he would be the first
to deny it. 'The best thing about my drawing is
that it gives me an excuse to be moody. Sometimes my friends accuse me of being a bit tempera-
mental—but now I can pass it off as artistic
temperament.' His cartoons, particularly cari-
catures of his team-mates, sold in their own right,
and in 1971 he was negotiating to sell sets of
cartoons, printed on metal, through garage chains.
He became involved in a discotheque in the town,
originally an idea to draw the crowds by using
his name—but the atmosphere had its own appeal
for him.

But perhaps the business venture that best
summed up the Welsh striker was a fishing-boat
concern. As he said: 'Ever since I was a little lad,
I've always enjoyed fishing as a hobby. I used to fish
trout when I was at home in North Wales. When I
went to Norwich I went coarse fishing on the
Broads, especially for pike. Then when I came
down here I got the taste for sea-fishing.'

In 1970 he bought a boat—a spacious, 30-foot,
petrol-engined craft. He used it simply to take out
his family and friends—'just to get away from the
pressures of football', before realizing its potential
as a post-football investment. The following year
he entered into partnership with a friend, who
became the boat's full-time skipper. Whenever

possible Davies accompanies the fishermen who
hire the boat. Sitting out at sea fishing, with a
couple of bottles of lager beside him—and the
knowledge that the trip was both earning him
some money and giving him some relaxation, Ron
Davies felt at peace with the world.

A genial, affable man, he kept his outbursts of
'artistic temperament' off the field of play. It
took 11 years before he retaliated to the batterings
and bruisings every successful striker has to
endure. Then, in 1971, he suffered a savage
mauling from the Chelsea defence and finally
reacted.

'One tackle from Ron Harris had already
sliced open my shin-pad. Then he whacked me
again, ages after I had got rid of the ball. I just
turned and wellied him. The linesman saw it,
and I got booked. But I was lucky not to be sent
off.'

He never remembered the goals he scored, but
worried about always needing help from other
players to score them. 'Someone's got to keep
crossing the ball for me to score, but there just
aren't that many good crossers about.'

At 29 and an established First Division and
international performer, he still sensed that he
could improve. 'I would like to be better at turning
with the ball and taking defenders on, but you so
rarely get the time. So I just play the ball off most
of the time. Anyway, at Southampton the midfield
players are always screaming to be given the ball,
so I have to lay it off.'

Like many exiled footballers he despatched his

Ron DAVIES

Club	Season	League		Int'nls	
		Mtchs	Gls	Mtchs	Gls
Chester	1959-60	8	1		
	1960-61	39	23		
	1961-62	38	13		
	1962-63	9	7		
Luton Town	1962-63	29	21		
	1963-64	3			
Norwich City	1963-64	38	27	1	1
	1964-65	35	14	1	
	1965-66	40	18	3	1
Southampton	1966-67	41	37	3	2
	1967-68	40	28	3	2
	1968-69	38	20	5	3
	1969-70	29	12	4	
	1970-71	40	17	4	1
	1971-72	27	11	4	
	1972-73	25	9		
Total		479	258	28	10

GERRY CRANHAM

THE GOALSCORERS

Martin Chivers —no longer the too gentle giant

Martin Chivers of Spurs moves forward confidently, despite the threatening presence of Crystal Palace defender John McCormick. While at Southampton, Chivers had formed a perfect goalscoring partnership with Ron Davies but after his move to London he had missed his partner. Bought for the then record fee of £125,000 by Spurs manager Bill Nicholson, he found it difficult to recover his true form in a side living with the memory of the double, and dominated by the magic of Greaves. But after Greaves had left and Chivers had recovered from a crippling leg injury, Nicholson bullied and shamed his centre-forward to the sort of form that eventually made him an England regular.

uring the early seventies, if Bill Nicholson had ephoned the Press Association and announced at he was about to place Martin Chivers on the ansfer list, the size of the ensuing bids ould have caused questions to be asked in the ouse.

By the time Nicholson had slipped on his mbre, conservatively-cut jacket and climbed to his executive Rover, the bids of £300,000 ould have started coming in.

The measure of Chivers' status in the game d of his value to Spurs is that the bid, imaginable though it may be, would have cer- nly been turned down. Despite his aggravating ndencies not to use his magnificent skills to the

full, the tall, muscular striker is unarguably in a class of his own when in the mood.

It was not always like that, of course. Time was when the Tottenham loyalists would gladly have seen Chivers depart for the price of the bus fare to Highbury, but times and people have changed and Chivers himself has changed most of all.

His physique, however, is unaltered: thirteen stones spread across a six foot one and a half inch frame and spread as if the architect had an England striker in mind with strong legs topped by heavily muscled thighs, a massively powerful chest and the shoulders of a heavyweight contender. When you have those kind of physical

credentials, and pace to match, then you have a head start on the rest. Stripped of all its theory, football is essentially about a fast, powerful man driving a ball into a net and exciting people with the controlled violence of his action. And that is how it works out when the ball is coming through conveniently and the defenders are acquiescent and the shooting is accurate.

But when the passes are awkward; when the defence is harsh and determined and the shooting hurried and wayward—that is when the big man can look absurd and clumsy and the crowd, who have not paid to watch clumsy absurdities, can then become cruelly contemptuous.

Chivers had his clumsy days even at Southampton, the club he joined straight from the local school and with whom he took his first steps in League football during the 1962-63 season.

But he learned to adjust, to enjoy the good times and work through the awkward patches, and his ability helped bring Southampton promotion to the First Division in 1966—for the first time in the history of the Hampshire club. At the same time, it won for him the first of what was to become a record run of 17 England Under-23 caps.

Both he and Southampton were fortunate in having their efforts to establish themselves in the highest class sustained by the acquisition of Ron Davies, who was himself quickly recognized as one of the most accomplished forwards in the modern game.

Davies was a craftsman whose work in the air had the nostalgic and the middle-aged recalling Lawton with reverence and relish. Chivers' strength, for all his height, lay principally on the ground and his own gifts prefectly complemented the more spectacular Davies.

But Southampton were Southampton and the real issues were being debated in places like Manchester, Liverpool and London and so, from motives which will be appreciated only outside Hampshire, Chivers asked for a transfer a few days before Christmas 1967.

Southampton replied by offering him for sale at £125,000. It was something of an each-way bet for them; on the one hand they had Mike Channon, a player of similar style, tender years and enormous potential, developing satisfactorily —and on the other they had the comfortable knowledge that the price they were asking for Chivers exceeded the then British transfer record by some £15,000.

'I wasn't really looking for Chivers. My real need was for a defender'

Within a month they had found a buyer and— due regard having been paid to the cloak and dagger convention which attends deals of this size—Chivers signed for Tottenham in a small hotel in Winchester, Frank Saul moving to Southampton as a £45,000 part of the transaction.

Nicholson, who thus became the first manager in British football history to have poured a million pounds into the transfer market, chose the occasion to offer an admirable rationalization of the manager's role in that market.

'I wasn't really looking for Chivers. My real need was for a defender, but because you are looking for one type of player it doesn't mean you can look away when another kind comes on the market. There are so few available that the chance might not come again.

'I go about it like this: I look at any good player who is offered, ask myself if he would improve my team and if, like Chivers, I think he would, then I try to buy him.

'As far as the money goes, you have to pay the current market price whether you like it or not. The value of a player is in what he can do for you, not what he costs.'

Nicholson's logic was beyond reproach. The onus was now on Chivers to prove that he could make Spurs a better team and demonstrate that £125,000 was a reasonable outlay for his talents. He attempted these objectives in a side which had yet to emerge from the shadow of the double-winning Spurs and before a crowd whose expectations traditionally exceeded their charity. For a man who was still some years from a full international cap, it was a daunting task.

The presence of Jimmy Greaves didn't help the big fellow's chances of acceptance. Jimmy, the peerless and inimitable, had long since proved himself at every level. Moreover he was quick, quicker than anyone in the game. Anybody playing regularly alongside Greaves had to look sluggish by comparison unless they were of a totally different style, that of a Bobby Smith,

perhaps, bullish and invulnerable, scoring goals while scorning finesse.

Chivers wasn't that kind of player. He wanted to reveal his skill, to use the ability which had prompted the enormous cheque, but the critical crowd and the pressure which Greaves' genius unwittingly exerted were inhibiting factors. However he worked at his game to the extent that by the time he took the field against Nottingham Forest on 21 September 1968 he had scored ten goals in only 28 League matches for Spurs—the fact that only four of them were at White Hart Lane is a revealing statistic.

Things started to happen for Chivers and for Spurs on that September afternoon. They were playing well, with flair and confidence. Chivers was moving fluently alongside Greaves and even the hyper-critical were starting to revise opinions.

Then, in the 63rd minute, Chivers and Bob McKinlay—the big, gentle Forest centre-half—disputed a ball which had been played up from around half way. The Spurs man fell awkwardly and stayed down. 'Come on,' said Greaves. 'Get up, Big Fella. Your leg can't just go like that.' But Chivers left White Hart Lane on a stretcher that day, the ligament behind his left knee completely severed. Chivers' season was over and for a time his very career was in doubt. 'I'm told it could take six months to mend,' he said. In

fact, it took nearly ten.

But significantly, the fans had given him ovation when they wheeled him away.

He came back, by courtesy of surgical sk and intense therapy, for the start of the 196 70 season. And his troubles returned with him.

He worried about the knee, fiercely a naturally. Every tackle, every challenge was threat to his career. The mental scar was a de one and needed time and patience, but the si were not playing well and Nicholson's patier was wearing thin.

'Watch everything Hurst does, because that's the way I want you to play'

He took to pulling his striker off the pitch disgust, occasionally substituting a defenc up front: 'It happened so often I was scared look towards the touchline,' recalls Chivers.

Then he was dropped for the derby mat with West Ham, with Nicholson sprinkling s in the wound by instructing Chivers to sit the directors' box to watch Geoff Hurst pl 'Watch everything he does,' said Nicholse 'Because that's the way I want you to play f us.'

On reflection, Chivers believes that the mc

he remembers with relish.

'We're playing Stoke and I go for this ball right out on the left touchline. Denis Smith comes with me and challenges and instead of being knocked off the ball—as I would have been once—I've suddenly got the confidence to charge him off before starting a run.

'Then Banks comes out to meet me and I'm feeling good enough to check, change feet and bend the ball right round him into the far corner. I really enjoyed that one.' One can never really appreciate the satisfaction of a forward who has done his job superbly, but the memory of the world's finest goalkeeper doing everything right yet being made to look inadequate by the striker's judgement provides a strong clue to Chivers' state of mind.

Goals of this kind were pushing Spurs up the League and into the final of the Football League Cup; they also had the effect of bringing Chivers his long-awaited first cap. It was won in February 1971 on a dust heap in Valletta and while he didn't manage a goal against the Maltese he retained his place and scored in the match against Greece, scored two more in the return with Malta and finally began to look every inch an England player with two goals in the home international against Scotland, one of them struck with stunning and dramatic power.

There was a physical edge to his game which had never been there before. He wasn't Bobby Smith or anything like him, but to his ball skills and speed he had added a new toughness, a determination not to come off worse in a physical challenge. It was what Nicholson and the Spurs staff had always demanded of him.

The only British forward who can compare with the great Luigi Riva

His ability was now acquiring international appreciation. From Italy, the manager of Cagliari, Manilo Scopigno, paid him Italian football's ultimate compliment: 'He is the only British forward', said Scopigno, 'who can compare with Luigi Riva.' Then, after a brilliant game and goal in a Nations Cup match in Switzerland, Chivers was showered with compliments for Europe's finest centre-forward.

There is something in Bill Nicholson's character which distrusts the easy label—particularly when it is being applied to one of his own players. So, with the benefit of hindsight, it is perhaps not too surprising that, just one week after the Swiss match, Nicholson was castigating Chivers for a 'diabolical' display in a EUFA Cup tie in France.

'He was too cocky and I hope he realizes it,' said Nicholson. Chivers replied that the criticism had hurt him: 'It's taken me too long to make my mark in the game to get carried away suddenly,' he said. 'I'll admit I'm more confident now than I've ever been, but that's because it's only in the last twelve months that I've realized I'm a good footballer.'

Both men had made their point and honour was satisfied, but the incident and its aftermath served to reveal the respect for his own ability that Chivers had developed.

Once he had convinced himself that the skills were there and that the knee would no longer represent an impediment, Martin Chivers had become something approaching a great player; a player of flair and strength and balance. Yet he left himself open to intense criticism with a lifeless, almost disinterested performance for England in their vital World Cup tie with Poland—a game in which he was pulled off near the end.

If injury avoids him and he puts his mind to the task there is still virtually no limit to what Chivers can achieve in the game, both at club and international level.

It is to Nicholson's credit that he saw the potential and backed his judgement with £125,000. 'The value of a player is in what he can do for you, not what he costs' . . . . It makes sense.

ED LACEY

ght have been useful, but at the time—when neral opinion insisted that Nicholson had ught himself a £125,000 novice—he was dly hurt.

Desperately needing a decent break at this ge, Chivers found it in a reserve match at rthampton. Assistant manager Eddie Baily d stressed the importance of the match, of the nefits which could blossom from a flood of als—and Chivers provided five of the most portant goals he has ever scored.

The £200,000 deal which brought Martin ters to Tottenham and sent Greaves to West m in March 1970 was to prove of critical portance to Chivers' development. With eaves gone, Chivers was the focal point of ttenham's attack, the man the team and, imately, the fans looked to for important als. And the character of the big fellow, the nfidence bordering on a kind of unconscious 'ogance which is part of his make-up, relished responsibility and the rewards.

Peters helped draw the best from Chivers, as I the simple direct service supplied by young ve Perryman. He began to score consistently d excitingly; he began the 1970-71 season with burst of goals which promised high times :ad and he secured, in the October of that son, the complete acceptance of his White rt Lane critics with a goal whose every detail

Left In a match against Northern Ireland, England centre-forward Martin Chivers leaps for a cross. As his confidence and form began to flood back in season 1970-71 he received his first, long-awaited full cap in February 1971, against Malta.
Top Fighting off a challenge from Bobby Moncur of Scotland, Chivers continues his run with the ball. During his first days with Spurs, he seemed incapable of taking such challenges in his stride.
Above Lurking in the goalmouth, Chivers waits for a header from Mike England. In season 1970-71 he scored 21 goals in the League alone. And in 1971-72 he continued to find the back of the net.

Martin CHIVERS

Honours: League Cup winners medal, 1971, 1973; UEFA Cup winners medal, 1972

Club	Season	League		Int'nls	
		Mtchs	Gls	Mtchs	Gls
Southampton	1962-63	3	1		
	1963-64	27	21		
	1964-65	39	18		
	1965-66	39	30		
	1966-67	42	14		
	1967-68	24	13		
Tottenham	1967-68	18	7		
Hotspur	1968-69	10	3		
	1969-70	31	11		
	1970-71	42	21	5	5
	1971-72	39	25	7	2
	1972-73	38	17	10	5
Total		352	181	22	12

The King

The imperishable compliment 'all time great' has been bestowed upon Denis Law by Sir Matt Busby, so long his manager and mentor at Manchester United.

It can also be said of Law that he is a veritable Peter Pan of football, side-stepping the call of time which usually comes early to players who have suffered wear and tear as strikers.

Law, a trawlerman's son born in Aberdeen in February 1940, knows enough of treatment tables, hospitals, doctors, specialists and X-ray apparatus to be qualified in physiotherapy.

Often the victim of his own abrasive temperament on the field, he came close to having his United career wrecked by knee injury and dressing-room clashes in the late sixties.

The short reign of Wilf McGuinness as Old Trafford team manager was almost negative in Law's playing life and he was eventually put on offer for transfer at £60,000 by United—seemingly discarded by the club of which he felt he had become a permanent part.

Stoke City and Hamilton Academicals held an instant if cautious interest but the reaction of the majority of clubs was reflected in the comment of Glasgow Rangers manager Willie Waddell: 'The news does not excite me.'

Pele's display in Mexico helped Law to make his come-back

Law, still one of the highest paid players in Britain at the time, replied with self-inflicted punishment in a Spartan one-man training course during the summer; and he returned to challenge once more for the status given him by many United fans over other stars like George Best and Bobby Charlton: 'The King'.

He willingly turned it into the greatest challenge of his career. It became a kind of solitary confinement with hard labour—'I trained like a lunatic for almost four months'—and probably no player has ever sentenced himself to such a tough close season.

It was Pele, playing in the 1970 World Cup, who had partly been the inspiration that lifted Law out of his injury and depression. 'I was moping about the house all day feeling sorry for myself,' he explains. 'Pele played brilliantly despite taking a lot of punishment. I realized that, like me, he'd been taking it for years, was still going well after some set-backs, and that I needed to pull myself together.'

Perhaps Law's greatest reward came two seasons later when, almost four years after the last of his 44 caps, he was named for the Scotland squad to play in Brazil in the 1972 international tournament there.

And after a lean season in 1972-3 followed by a free transfer back to his former club Manchester City, it was Law who led the Scotland charge to Munich. After some wholehearted displays and spectacular goals for City, Willy Ormond called on him for the vital international against Czechoslovakia at Hampden Park, and he was outstanding in the win that took them into the finals.

The emotional and sometimes explosive Stretford End at Old Trafford had long since recrowned their 'king' and football had re-accepted one of it's most original characters: a player who had so often embraced the emotions of his profession.

Aptly named, Law has usually made his own laws wherever he has been, a temperamental warrior who occasionally had to be brought into line by the tolerant Busby.

The most notable occasion was at the end of his first long contract with United, when he ill-advisedly made public his demands for even better terms and showed a reluctance to re-sign with a veiled threat of a transfer request.

Busby, with an untypical but equally public rejoinder, immediately placed Law on the transfer list with the explanation that 'no one threatens Manchester United'.

Law vowed never to do so again, apologized both privately and through the press, and renewed what has generally been a happy relationship with the club he has liked more than any other.

The entertainer who has had an intimate hold on crowds at Huddersfield, Turin, Manchester and Glasgow is far removed from the individualist who, away from his stage, prefers to hold the rest of the world at arm's length.

But, throughout his long career, Denis Law has been nothing if not a violent contradiction, an enigma whose riddle he found difficult explaining himself.

Law is often and justifiably referred to as a 'loner'. Yet for all his puzzles he has had five consistencies which have seldom deserted his side: a passion for winning and bettering the next man; a grasp of the game's commercial values (as a 17 year old at Huddersfield he precociously and vainly asked a Sunday newspaper for over £2,000 for a series they wanted to publish); an inseparable family life founded on an understanding wife and four sons; a genius for scoring the most unlikely goals; and an unquenchable sense of comedy.

Law's humorous repartee is well known. But if there was ever a time which threatened to be devoid of humour, it was in the 1967-68 season when his knee trouble was slowly poisoning his love of football and rushing his decline from public standing.

When United became the first English club to win the European Cup beating Benfica at Wembley at the end of that season, Law was in hospital with only a television link to comfort him.

'It took a lot of guts for Denis to even play at First Division level'

His friends had become fewer. Some United fans had started to turn against him and, perhaps more humiliating, players began to sympathize.

Allan Clarke, the Leeds United striker, who had idolized Law when he was at Walsall, Fulham and Leicester, recalls: 'It was pathetic to hear some of the United crowd getting on to Denis after all he had done there. If only they'd have realized how hard he was trying at half fitness. If he turned or twisted he was obviously in agony. It took a lot of guts even to make an effort to play at First Division level.'

Law himself says: 'Every game I played was labelled a come-back.'

For all his sporadic appearances he was still big enough to cause other players to ape his style. Clarke copies his theatrical, one-handed salute after scoring; Rodney Marsh, another member of the Law fan club, admitted to wearing

his shirts out of his shorts 'like Denis Law' and trying to play 'like Denis Law'—until he saw himself on television one day. Then he dropped the act because he felt he looked 'ridiculous' copying another player. John Fitzpatrick, a United team-mate, imitated Law's passing technique—with body and head over the ball and arms outstretched to give balance and impact. Law, seeking perfection, always made this action so pronounced that onlookers were tempted to see him as orthodox.

Only in his distribution can he ever be accused of such normality. For the rest, he is unchained tiger, snarling competitor, wisecracking actor using referees and linesmen for his props and, most of all, he is the undying professional.

The professional and pride in Law has meant never surrendering to an opponent, to a setback or to a scoring chance that would look lost to others.

Busby offers £10,000 for Law—and ends up paying £115,000

It was the latter which made him a genius in turning the simple half-chance into the spectacular goal.

'I've never in my life seen goals to equal those scored by Law for bravery or sheer unexpectancy,' says Busby—a man who once failed to buy Law, later didn't want to when he had the chance, and finally paid a British record £115,000 to bring him back from Turin to Manchester.

Law's goals in first-class football have totalled over 300 and, while this falls short of the massive hauls of Arthur Rowley or Jimmy Greaves, he is the highest post-War scorer in the FA Cup (41 by the end of the 1971-72 season) and for Scotland (29).

He claims over 200 Football League goals, in the European Cup (including nine in 1965-6), six in the Cup Winners Cup, and nine in the Fairs Cup a season later.

Many of Law's goals have come from nothing. Like Greaves, he enjoyed tidying up the penalty area to score goals that looked simple. But the creation had come from deep reading, razor-sharp anticipation and, most of all, willingness Law would often chase a lost cause and turn it into a winning one.

The one Busby remembers most was in a First Division match at Everton. Charlton took a corner on the left, driving the ball towards the near post. The left boot of an Everton defender was swung in a high back lift to clear; before the foot could come through, Law dived like a spear, heading the ball into the near corner of the net. Busby, sitting in the stand, mentally recorded it as 'the most courageous goal I'd ever seen'.

From his goal records, Law appears to be most a big occasion player. This is misleading; seldom has he appeared to hold back in an ordinary game.

Busby's failure to sign Law came in the late fifties when his famous 'Babes' were at their pre-Munich peak. 'I first saw Denis at Heckmondwike in Yorkshire one night when he was playing for Huddersfield against us in a youth match,' he recalls. 'When we were losing 2-0 at half time, I wondered who was taking us apart. Then I realized it was a little will o' the wisp called Law, who had also scored both goals.

'After the match I offered £10,000 for him but Huddersfield wouldn't listen, even though that was a high figure for such a young player in those days.'

Unknown to Busby, Law slipped away to the Huddersfield coach that night wearing his chrome-rimmed spectacles. His eyes were so weak that when he had arrived at Huddersfield not long before to have a trial with another player, they thought the skinny, squinting Scottish lad was just there as a friend.

'Anyone less like a footballer I'd never seen,' reflects Andy Beattie, then manager at Leeds

Above *Denis Law puts Scotland ahead at Wembley in 1967. The goal, saluted in characteristic fashion by the scorer (far left) was the platform for a 3-2 win over the world champions.*
Left *Law as a 16 year old with Huddersfield. In March 1960 Bill Shankly sold him to Manchester City for a British record £55,000. Then in 1962, after a season in Italy, he again moved to Manchester—this time to United for £115,000. Both figures were British records.*

Denis LAW

Honours: League Championship medal 1964-65, 1966-67
FA Cup winners medal 1963
European Footballer of the Year 1964

Club	Season	League		Int'nls	
		Mtchs	Gls	Mtchs	Gls
Huddersfield Town	1956-57	13	2		
	1957-58	18	5		
	1958-59	26	2	4	1
	1959-60	24	7	2	
Manchester City	1959-60	7	2	3	
	1960-61	37	19	2	1
(Torino)	1961-62			3	2
Manchester United	1962-63	38	23	7	11
	1963-64	30	30	4	5
	1964-65	36	28	7	3
	1965-66	33	15	3	1
	1966-67	36	23	3	2
	1967-68	23	7	1	
	1968-69	30	14	3	1
	1969-70	11	2		
	1970-71	28	15		
	1971-72	33	13	7	2
	1972-73	11	1		
Total		434	208	49	29

Road. 'But once I watched him kick the ball I realized he had it in him to be truly great.'

Law was in Huddersfield's first team at 16, and his precocity seemed to amount to cockiness as he strutted around the Second Division grounds. His impudence, industry and skills contrived to outwit West Ham on a skating rink at Upton Park one mid-week. Questioning London eyes were looking upon the youthful invader from the North, some for the first time. Law won the match for Huddersfield, and London beamed over his gifted performance in the most treacherous conditions.

'The Turin public had never seen anyone as quick-thinking as Denis'

Law was 18 years and 7 months old when he made his debut for Scotland, against Wales in October 1958. He was introduced to the international arena by Busby (who had taken over his country's team) and the fact he was Scotland's youngest ever player did not seem to worry the United manager.

In Law's second game Busby employed him in midfield to puncture the poise of Northern Ireland captain Danny Blanchflower. The eager pupil followed the instructions implicitly, and Blanchflower clearly did not approve.

As Hampden Park's crowd, who were occasionally to deride their new young hero in the future, were rejoicing over Law's tenacity, Danny was shaking his head and offering a meaningful 'tut, tut'.

'He could have done with more experience,' claims Blanchflower. 'Nearly every tackle was a foul. But he wasn't kicking me so much as always coming in late.

'I knew he had ability or he wouldn't have been in a Scotland team. He wasn't a tough player, but he had strength and vital energy and was direct and determined.

'When I came out of the dressing-room Bill Shankly, the successor to Beattie as Huddersfield manager, was standing there saying what a great player Denis was. I decided not to argue and walked away. I wasn't bitter. Did Denis become great? Well, greatness to me spans a lot of time.

'Peter Doherty was great. So was di Stefano. Denis had the capabilities to become great but perhaps his serious injuries stopped him just short of that. For a skinny kid with a squint to develop into a magnificent blond striker who was fast and fierce was like growing from a toad to a prince. It was a tribute to his determination.'

Busby had the second chance of signing Law when Shankly left Huddersfield to take charge at Liverpool. Shankly, Beattie's loquacious assistant when Law arrived at Huddersfield, called the Aberdonian 'the greatest thing on two feet,' and refused all bids for Law before leaving for Merseyside. Then, when Town decided to sell, Busby had no room for Law at Old Trafford.

'The team were going too well,' he says. 'Denis Viollet and Bobby Charlton were very effective. I didn't need Denis then.'

Arsenal, however, did have room, and manager George Swindin sent off assistant Ron Greenwood to sign Law when the bidding opened.

The London club didn't get him, and all too soon the theory was advanced that Law was put off by Swindin's own absence.

Greenwood disputes this. 'The deal fell through because Huddersfield wanted a little more

Above left Explosive, theatrical and expressive, Law has proved to be one of the great football entertainers of the post-War period.

Above Among his many assets is a prodigious leap, one that has brought him a host of goals.

Top right Law lies prostrate after a typical, vain, diving header. He has never shrunk from taking any chance, no matter how slight.

Middle right A volatile temperament has often led Law into trouble with authority, though his strong personality has made him loved or hated.

Bottom right An ecstatic Denis Law after a goal against Crystal Palace in September 1971. He scored twice that day to reinforce the feeling that, this time, he was back at the top to stay.

than our bid,' he explains. 'And when I phoned Highbury the board wouldn't raise it.'

Another factor was that Law did not want to live in London—and never has since. So, in March 1960, Law signed for a British record of £55,000 for Manchester City.

'He reminds me of the pre-War Raich Carter,' said Les McDowell, City's manager. 'He never stops running and is always dangerous.'

To reach Old Trafford, which might always have been his final destination if he had been able to choose, Law had to go via Italy.

This was an unsatisfactory chapter for Law and his travel companion, Joe Baker, an England international who left Scottish club Hibs to sign for Torino with him. There were big headlines about a crash in Baker's Alfa Romeo and a later punch-up with an Italian photographer.

But there were also many fine games for Torino who were still, a decade later, attempting to rebuild following the Superga air crash of 1949, when their whole team was killed. Gigi Peronace, who signed Law and Baker, recalls

'They cost around £100,000 each, big money for Britain in those days, and they convinced the Turin public that their old great team was back. The speed and technical brilliance of Law reminded them of their former hero, Valentino Mazzola. They had never seen anyone quite as quick-thinking as Denis. He was always two or three moves ahead. It was a pity he stayed only a year.'

Law's motives for going to Italy had been largely material. And he was tempted back to England for the same reasons—plus the desire to play for United.

After frustrating delays at the Turin end, Busby flew from a club tour in Majorca to make his most expensive capture—£115,000. His private talk with Law lasted nearly two hours, and Law drove a hard bargain to become the highest paid player in Britain. His new boss summed up the negotiations: 'There's a lad who knows his own value.'

Law, however, made a poor start at Old Trafford. He had always preferred 'do-it-yourself' football and wanted to be involved in almost everything on the field except the goal-keeping. He even ran up to his own team mates and dispossessed them in order to take charge of a move from midfield or defensive positions.

Though United were injected by his spirit and will, they did not benefit enough from his skills. Eventually Busby and his assistant, Jimmy Murphy, had to change it all by playing him upfield as a striker. Law didn't like it, especially when he was ordered by Busby not to come back behind the half-way line, but it proved effective: he finished the season with 23 League goals and scored in the FA Cup win over Leicester City at Wembley.

The next year he averaged a goal a game in 30 League matches, and in 1964-65, while scoring a record nine goals in the Fairs Cup, he helped United to the League title with 28. Two seasons later he won a second Championship medal after scoring 23.

Although he is Scotland's leading scorer, Law cannot claim a really distinguished or worldwide international career. As Blanchflower sympathized: 'He was unlucky that none of the Scottish sides of his best days got far in World Cups and he wasn't seen around the world too much.'

Law scored seven goals— and still finished on the losing side

Law seemed to reserve his ambition and agression for the games with England. He played in the fixture on eight consecutive occasions from 1960—and only twice finished on the losing side. He was as upset as any self-respecting Scot was when England won the World Cup—he was playing golf at the time—but was brilliantly instrumental in producing the first defeat for the world champions the following year, scoring the first goal in a 3-2 win.

Though Law had quietened down a lot by 1967, he still retained his essential, explosive character. Some opponents admired him. Ron Harris, the Chelsea captain, said: 'Denis Law is the most honest player. You can kick him and he kicks you back. Never complains.'

Law was sent off in a First Division match at Blackpool for using a four-letter word to York referee Peter Rhodes and was suspended appropriately, if harshly, for four weeks. He got marching orders again against Aston Villa for

going through the motions of kicking an opponent, although he didn't actually make contact. The intent was his crime.

Law's flare-ups with opponents were mostly retaliatory—and he never repented. 'When I get kicked I'm supposed to count to ten and then walk away. I can't. If a player deliberately kicks me I'll kick him back.'

In many ways, not least in brilliance and rebellion, Law was superseded by George Best. 'A great player who can do everything needed in a game,' says Law. 'And he would become even greater if he paid a little more heed to team work.'

Of all Law's memorable goals two gave him complete satisfaction—and six gave him no satisfaction at all.

The six, all scored for Manchester City at Luton in an FA Cup tie in January 1961, didn't count. With City leading 6-2, the match was abandoned through heavy rain. Law even got City's only goal when the tie was replayed, but Luton won 3-1 to go through. He had scored seven goals—and finished on the losing side.

The two were both in 1963 at Wembley. The first helped United to the Cup Final win over Leicester when he and Pat Crerand, a friend and favourite player, were in devastating form.

The second was the only goal for the Rest of the World, beaten 2-1 by England in the FA Centenary match, when he walked as an equal alongside men like di Stefano, Puskas, Yashin, Masopust, Schnellinger, Kopa, Gento, Eusebio—and outshone them all as midfield general, defence organizer and striker.

In a stuttered combination of Portuguese and English, the Brazilian star Djalma Santos, asked who had been the best player at Wembley, said: 'Number ten. Law. Buenos. Muchos.' Anyone who has seen Law at his peak knows what he means.

145

Geoff Hurst: a self-made legend

Geoff Hurst may be best described as the exception which proved the rule 'nice guys finish last'. No man in football has achieved a more certain place in the history of the game whilst so lacking in the qualities allegedly necessary to win fame.

For a start he was not born with the exceptional skills that invite the description 'star'; nor, despite a dedication to self-improvement that bordered on the masochistic, was he ever able to acquire them. His game lacked the inventiveness of the genius, the blind courage of the true hero, while his temperament was without the streak of non-conformity that provides the 'character', the arrogance that supports the 'idol'.

It would be fatally easy, in fact, to regard him as a lucky man who somehow, on a sunny and portentous afternoon in July 1966, had stumbled into the right place at the right moment three times, and scored three goals for England against West Germany in the World Cup final. One writer's description of that occasion—'Geoff Hurst may have proved that in football this is the age of the common man, just so long as he can do something as uncommon as scoring three goals in the final'—suggests that the temptation to dismiss the feat and the man was strong.

Not just 'the man who scored three goals in a World Cup final'

But too many factors mitigate against the 'lucky man' theory. For one thing, how was it that Hurst was playing in the match at all when, had a vote been taken on team selection, England would have voted 52 million to one to give the number ten shirt to Jimmy Greaves, a true genius and star by any standards.

It is clear now that Alf Ramsey, the man whose one vote counted, had seen in Hurst the man for the hour, had trusted in abilities that most were not to recognize until much later—and that some were never to appreciate at all.

Again, if Hurst's only claim to fame was the staggering consequence of one afternoon's happy incidents, then how was it that a full two years later he was the subject of the first ever £200,000 transfer bid (Manchester United made the bid, and West Ham rejected it in a one-word telegram 'No') at a time when half that amount was considered the ceiling for the best?

Yet again, even the euphoria of 'The Day the World Cup was Won' could not explain how, six years later, Hurst was still disrupting traffic in provincial market towns when making personal appearances in connection with his sports-goods business, nor disguise the fact that from him grew a whole generation of attackers goaded through long hot afternoons of instruction with the command 'no, no . . . think of what Hurstie would do'. It is a fact that soon after paying a record £125,000 for Martin Chivers, Spurs manager Bill Nicholson bought a ticket in a West Ham stand for his signing and told him: 'Sit there and watch the big fellow . . . that's how I want you to play.'

Hurst's physical attributes were not startling. He had two good strong shooting feet (the left better than the right) and a sense of timing and direction that made him a dangerously accurate header of the ball. Other men have boasted as much. He was strong and tall, his massive thighs giving him strength and balance to resist rivals'

challenges and the stamina to persist with his own; but he was seldom the biggest or toughest man on the pitch in any game he played.

Hurst had enough instinctive ball control to be more than competent schoolboy footballer (for Chelmsford) and later a promising young professional (he won six youth international caps in 1959). Careful application honed those skills to enable him to subsequently match tricks against all but the very best. He had, in total, the playing equipment of an unexceptional pro. It was the extra element, the *thinking* application of those skills, that eventually sent him to the peak of the international game.

The process began in 1961, when Ron Greenwood became the West Ham manager and struck an immediate spark off Hurst with his lectures. Hurst, until this time, had been a dogged wing-half and little more. Indeed, he had become so disillusioned with his lack of progress (he made only eight first team appearances in two seasons) that he was ready for a change of club. The rivalry with men like John Smith, Bobby Moore and the young Martin Peters for the same positions put Hurst way down the list for promotion.

But Greenwood saw in Hurst the strength of character and the eagerness to learn that he needed for the tactical revolution he was about to press. Until this moment centre-forwards were of a type and their duties were simple: big men, they were asked to battle with centre-halves from halfway to the goalmouth in a sort of ritual, and there patiently await the service of passes and centres that other forwards would eventually provide.

Greenwood wanted more, much more. He wanted a forward with the brains and vision to be a mobile target for passes from defence, to be an elusive, unpredictable 'wall' off whom attacks could be built in the opponents' half, and then to be the unfindable, unmarkable late-arriving finisher who would sweep in on goal to deliver the ultimate shot.

Greenwood converts Hurst from reserve wing-half to dangerous striker

Hurst threw himself into the task of learning the role from scratch. He had no example to follow; he was the first, the original. And slowly, painfully acquiring his own precepts, he became magnificently gifted at proving Greenwood's theory.

When West Ham were under attack, Hurst was never still: moving a few paces this way, checking, then turning to sprint in another direction, stopping again to retrace his path, then sliding off on another angled run. It all seemed so pointless, like the meanderings of a man too nervous to keep still. But Hurst knew precisely what he was doing; with a skill that amounted to intuition he was placing himself where he could always be seen, and reached, by a pass the moment one of his defensive team-mates gained possession.

And when those passes came arcing out to him, with a consistency only the observant could have seen, Hurst's second task had to be done. With the care that hours of training over months had made possible, he would place the ball with foot, head or chest, precisely down into space, ready for collection by one of the advancing body of midfield men. Now Hurst's job was to disappear.

He found it easier than seems likely. N rivals' eyes were glued to the swift movemen the ball and the men involved in the second ph of West Ham's play. Defenders found little worry them in the sight of Hurst wander off with apparent disinterest to a part of pitch that seemed to have little connection w the move now building up elsewhere. And the n time they noticed him was often too late—for would be halfway to the corner-flag salutin goal struck on the run through a defence n preoccupied with the inquest 'Where the l did *he* come from? . . . why didn't *you* pick h up? . . . why *me*? . . . didn't *you* see him? . where? . . . when? . . . how?'

For Hurst had learned how to become a dif ent sort of scorer. There were the famous who their many goals with the force of their shoot or heading . . . Dean, Lawton, Lofthouse, Cha ton. There were those who wrecked defences improbable feats of dribbling . . . James, Greav Best. Those who took their goals through sh agility, like Law; or pace, like Baker; or coura like Bobby Smith.

Few people appreciated Hurst's role — but one of them was Alf Ramsey

Hurst was different. He became, simply, 'man who wasn't there'. Until he scored. 'Y can't mark someone who is moving,' he explai 'You can't impede someone who isn't there, y can't save a shot until it's made, you can't tac a man who hasn't got the ball. My game was keep away, keep out of it, out of the goalmou out of sight, until the ball was halfway towar the goalkeeper's hands. Then beat him to it.' that is what he did, better than anyone has do before or since—racing from deep positions edge his forehead to the ball an inch before 'keeper's grab, a toe-cap in front of the full-bac clearance.

One move in particular became his tradema —the near-post goal. He made it famous, a was made famous by its effects. In the ye before Hurst, centre-forwards by traini instinct, habit and instruction, always mov to the far side of goal to meet centres; the thec being that by waiting at the far post for pas they gave themselves the entire goal to aim Greenwood reasoned that the 'bad centr apparently dropped too short, caused go keepers and defenders to relax and left them the mercy of forwards arriving late from positic behind them and out of vision. Hurst proved theory accurate.

A large proportion of the goals he struck those learning years (from 1963 to 1966) ca from this move. Greenwood, uncharacteristical was once moved to gloat: 'Hurstie has been doi this for three seasons, and rivals still have worked out what he's doing. They reckon it' fluke . . . that happens week after week.'

But if the rivals were slow on the up-ta the fans, even West Ham's own, were hard more perceptive. For Hurst was few people's id of a good player; most of the praise for t successes of West Ham in the early sixties we to his extravagantly skilled team-mate, Johnn Byrne, and as late as January 1966 Hurst w still being barracked as 'that great cart-hors by the Upton Park following.

One important man, however, shared Gree wood's perception: Alf Ramsey. In the 1965– season Hurst was selected for the England squ for the first time—to the astonishment of mo including Hurst himself. 'I suppose I'd rath come to accept most people's verdict on myself— a willing trier,' he said later. 'I felt I was doing good job for West Ham. But England? It nev seemed likely. I was terrified of mixing with all t big names of the game.'

Hurst's modesty put him in trouble wi Ramsey right at the start. At the first Englan training session he made a point of keeping ou of the limelight, backing hurriedly into the bac ground, contributing nothing to discussions, ar

only an orthodox minimum to practice matches. 'I wasn't getting the passes as I needed them and I was too shy to say so. I mean, how could I start rucking people like Bobby Charlton.' Ramsey, as ever shrewdly alert to the nuances, spotted Hurst's problems and called him to one side. 'Listen here,' he said. 'I picked you in this squad because you're good enough to play for England. But I can't make you an international player. You've got to do that yourself. If you don't believe in yourself, there's nothing I can do. All the players in this squad are equals. You're here on merit. So for God's sake stop hiding yourself and start taking part.'

A few days later Hurst exploded at the lack of perceptive passes he was receiving from England colleagues and began rucking everyone in sight. 'It just came naturally. If I'd stopped to think I would never have dared do it. But the point is they all took it naturally, as though I was, in fact, their equal. From that moment on my problems just fell away.'

Hurst sat through 'the longest hours of my life' waiting for the decision

Well, not quite. Hurst, after making his debut against West Germany and holding his place against Scotland and Yugoslavia, still had to suffer a terrible pre-World Cup tour to Scandinavia, when his own play was appalling and Ramsey's faith was tested to the limit. And he still had to suffer the torment of sitting on the sidelines to watch England struggle through the first three matches of the finals without him.

It was after the third game, when Hurst returned to the hotel to find Greaves nursing a vicious gash in his shin, that he sensed he might after all have a part to play in England's greatest test. Hurst came into the team, scored the only goal against Argentina with a text-book copy of that West Ham near post play (Peters made the pass), helped England beat Portugal in the finest match of the series by making a goal for Charlton —and then sat down to wait to discover whether he or the now fit Greaves would be chosen for the final. 'The longest hours of my life,' Hurst has said of those pre-decision days. 'I knew Jimmy was getting better, but I didn't know how *much* better. I was afraid to even ask him how he felt —because he was a friend of mine and if he'd answered "fine" I would have hated him.'

History records that, finally, it was Hurst who got the vote, Hurst who got the goals, and England who won the trophy. What history does not say is the effect that afternoon's work had on the player and the man.

He knew within hours that his life would change. Suddenly he was 'someone' in the game. 'Before the final I used to ring up this posh restaurant for a booking, and tell them I was a friend of Bobby Moore's to make sure I got a table. Now I was able to ring up and give my own name. That's one thing that showed the difference.' There were soon to be many more changes.

Within days every post and every phone call brought an invitation or an offer; everyone wanted to meet, or to use, the man who had scored three in the final. Hurst, obviously, was in a position to capitalize on his fame. He was going places. The question was: did he need an 'image' to extract the full value from the commercial overtures?

Hurst and two journalists, friends who had been asked to help, debated the problem for hours. Perhaps he should grow his hair long (in 1966 that would have been a gimmick)... perhaps he should be 'coached' to pungent comments... perhaps he should start adopting mannerisms on the pitch that would stamp him a personality... perhaps he should begin sensationalizing his lifestyle. At every suggestion the two journalists looked at Hurst—and shook their heads. Nothing so contrived seemed to fit the man. Finally one blurted out, 'For God's sake, this is nonsense. What we have here is a straight, natural nice

Above *Geoff Hurst, as usual, chasing everything, harrying everyone—this time West Germany's Fichtel during England's defeat in the Mexico World Cup. The same fixture four years earlier had been so different for the West Ham player: his hat-trick had made him a world figure overnight.*
Above right *Hurst with Billy Bonds. He has always enjoyed his football, even when the marking became tighter and the tackling harder after his success in 1966.*
Right *Hurst has had to pick himself up mentally as well as physically. As the epitome of Alf Ramsey's 'old guard', he was accused of keeping his England place on sentiment rather than merit.*
Bottom *Hurst is beaten by Iam McFaul of Newcastle.*

Geoff HURST

Honours: World Cup winners medal 1966
European Cup Winners Cup medal 1965
FA Cup winners medal 1964
League Cup runners-up medal 1966

Club	Season	League		Int'nls	
		Mtchs	Gls	Mtchs	Gls
West Ham United	1959-60	3			
	1960-61	5			
	1961-62	24	1		
	1962-63	28	13		
	1963-64	37	14		
	1964-65	42	18		
	1965-66	39	23	8	5
	1966-67	41	29	6	3
	1967-68	38	19	7	2
	1968-69	41	25	9	8
	1969-70	39	16	11	3
	1970-71	39	14	4	1
	1971-72	34	8	4	2
Stoke City	1972-73	38	10		
Total		448	190	49	24

guy. Why not let him be himself and leave it at that?'

So it was decided. And in the next few years Hurst wrote columns for newspapers, appeared on television and radio, made speeches, opened stores, endorsed products and continued to play football in a manner that came naturally. The 'image' grew of its own accord: this was the son parents would have chosen for themselves, the boy the favourite daughter brought home to tea, the friend men would have liked to have had, the nice lad from next door, the star with the common touch, the idol with his feet on the ground.

On the pitch Hurst's image was different and, in a way, greater still. He went back to club football after Wembley bursting with confidence: 'I felt ten feet tall, and I found myself playing in a way I had thought only those others, the stars, would have dared.' A new dimension was added to his game overnight, as the unselfish maker of space for others started to turn with

ment in the following seasons. He became, in fact, a symbol—of the uncomplaining victim of a regime of defensive ruthlessness that went on unchecked until the 'referees revolution' of 1971-72. 'The crunchers are getting away with murder—look at what they are doing to Hurst' became the slogan of the swelling voice of the reformers.

Hurst's equanimity during these punishing years bordered on the miraculous. Fouled a dozen times a match, limping at the end of most, he never retaliated or lost his temper. Except once. And Greenwood still recalls that incident as his definition of professionalism. 'Geoff had been kicked in the back about ten times by this bloke and when it happened again something seemed to snap. He grabbed the ball, I could see his face white with rage, and rushed at the offender. I thought he was going to smash the ball in his face, and I could have understood and forgiven him if he had, it had been so blatant. Instead, Geoff got a grip on himself after about three strides, and while still running he put the ball down, took the kick and was sprinting for the return pass as this other bloke stood there petrified with his hands up to protect himself. *That* was professionalism.'

Two other stories illustrate Hurst's attitude to his chosen calling. In 1967, towards the end of his first and only discussion with West Ham about wages (he had been paid since 1966 at his old pre-World Cup rate), he signed a new contract that would tie him to the club for six years—with the spaces for the pay and bonuses still left blank. 'Ron Greenwood asked me to trust him, and I did. I knew I'd done my bit for the club, so why should they try and cheat me?'

A transfer request in 1969 —but he stays at West Ham for three years

The other story dates from 1969, when Hurst became dissatisfied with his game and talked himself into believing that a change of club would lift him out of a rut. He asked for a transfer—only to discover to his horror that England team-mate Martin Peters had made precisely the same request 20 minutes earlier. 'I couldn't do that to the club, not the two of us on one day,' says Geoff. 'How would it have looked to outsiders? So I walked back in and withdrew my request. It seemed the only decent thing to do.' While Peters soon left for Spurs in British football's first £200,000 deal, Hurst settled loyally back into the 'rut' with West Ham—though he knew Manchester United would have made him rich had he persisted with his demand.

Hurst was to remain a West Ham player for another three years. He also remained an England regular, though the criticism of his continued selection at international level grew steadily—along with that of Ramsey. He became the symbol of the manager's loyalty to the 'old guard' of 1966. As it was none of his rivals for the job—unless Martin Chivers is counted among that number (the two played several times together)—could match Hurst's consistency and, despite some unnecessarily cruel and often illogical, shallow attacks, he maintained both his contribution to the side and his place in it.

Hurst certainly did well from the game. By 1972 he, his wife Judith and two small daughters were living in a house in Chigwell worth perhaps twice the £20,000 it cost him, he drove a Mercedes and was sufficiently established in a sportsgoods business to think briefly about a £7,500-a-year offer to give up the game and concentrate on selling football boots.

That offer came at a moment of rare despair. Hurst had just been dropped from the England squad for the return match with West Germany in the European Championship—the news coming all the harder in that he heard it second-hand and not directly from Ramsey. Two days of hard thinking persuaded him that, while he could live without the money from football, he was not ready to live without the game.

But he felt he *had* to leave West Ham. 'It's been a great club to me, and I like to think I've been a good servant. But you can be too long in one place. The very familiarity of the place, driving along the same road every day for 15 years to hang your coat on the same hook, gets you in a rut. It will be better for all of us if I go.' So, reluctantly, Hurst asked for permission to leave a team which he had been instrumental in building—but which had relied too heavily on him and its other stars, Moore and Peters, to have realized its potential.

England's poor displays persuade Hurst to stay in the First Division

An offer to move to Bournemouth, a sort of semi-retirement in effect despite the Third Division club's ambitions, tempted him for a while. What finally turned him against the idea were the performances of England in the Home Championship after the defeat by West Germany: 'Had someone come into my place and played great, I would have said "that's it, they'll never need me again." Well, frankly, I don't think that quite happened. Watching those games I felt that even at 30 I might still do a bit more for the team. But I couldn't get back if I went to Bournemouth, so when First Division Stoke came in with a bid I said "that's me".'

Hurst joined Stoke, the latest in a line of senior players other clubs had discarded prematurely to be signed by Tony Waddington, before the start of the 1972-73 season. 'I want to get goals for Stoke,' he said at the time. 'At West Ham, although people thought of me as a scorer, it never mattered to me who got them as long as we were successful. But I see now that it's goals by which people judge you. For the first time in years I suddenly have something to prove, and goalscoring is the way to prove it.'

Hurst, valued at £80,000, started well at Stoke, and those goals arrived—including one in a 5-1 defeat of Manchester City. But a red and white striped shirt was not the only strange thing about Geoff Hurst in the early weeks of the season: on 16 September, in a niggling game at Ipswich, he was sent off for the first time in his career—for arguing. It was an ironic dismissal for a man whose placid temperament had enabled him to avoid retaliation, and thus the likelihood of a similar fate, for so many years.

Thus Hurst embarked, somewhat belatedly, on a second playing career. It would be to the benefit of Stoke and England if he succeeded. But the man who was born near Manchester, the son of a competent Third Division centre-half, Charlie Hurst, the youngster whose first football headline came when he was fined £1.50 for playing football in the streets, the self-made player who became an example to an entire football generation, did not *need* to succeed to preserve his place in any hall of fame.

Two tributes paid to him towards the end of his first career emphasize the point. Nobby Stiles said of his old England team-mate: 'Watching Hurst at first, casually, you see nothing. Studying him carefully you start noticing qualities in his play that surprise you. Then when you play against him you realize he's a bit special. He must be the game's most solid ghost. You can't pin him down or keep him out. But it's when you play *with* him that you really know. He's got an instinct for being in the right place at the only right time, and he chases so hard it's almost impossible to give him a bad ball.'

One journalist wrote, at the time of a testimonial dinner to Hurst: 'A few have played more often for England, some may have scored more League goals. There may have been players who have shown equal courage, similar determination, introduced to tactics as much thought, or taken greater punishment with less complaint. But it is the total claim of the man that makes it clear that the bitter remark "Fame, somehow, seems too precious to be wasted on the famous" was *not* directed at Geoff Hurst.'

the ball and destroy defences with a deliberate-looking but oddly effective dribbling style.

This was a new and infinitely more dangerous Hurst—he scored 29 League goals in the post-World Cup season and six in one game against Sunderland in October 1968—and it was now a talent that even the least aware of fans were forced to appreciate. Hurst recalls: 'The greatest encouragement of all was to notice the difference in attitude of rival players. Now I could hear them calling each other for help—"for chris-sake don't leave me alone with this bloke. Get back quick." It did wonders for my confidence.'

But there was a price to be paid. Now Hurst had a shadow behind him in every match, and many of them were not particular how they chose to meet this new and greater threat. Hurst's speciality, arriving quickly to play that first ball back to midfield colleagues, left him particularly vulnerable to the deliberate late tackle from behind. The backs of his legs and, eventually, his spinal muscles, were to take terrible punish-

Gerd Muller—the man with the Golden Boots

With a twist of his thick torso, Gerd Muller hoisted himself off the ground and volleyed the ball into the top of the England net. Bayern Munich and West Germany's 'King of the Penalty Box' had pricked the bubble of England's 1970 World Cup hopes and gained adequate revenge for the previous World Cup final.

When Lohr headed back across the face of the England goal, Muller at once saw that Labone could not reach it to head clear. While most players would have challenged Labone in an aerial duel, Muller moved away from him into free space and hooked the dropping ball past Bonetti. But it was more than one goal—even as famous a goal as this—that makes Muller worth examination as a player of rare quality.

Up to 1971 Muller had scored 33 goals in 29 internationals, and 152 in six League seasons. In the 1970 World Cup he was top scorer with ten goals. In the 1969-70 season he was top scorer in Europe with 38 goals, which won him the annual Golden Boots award. It was Muller's prolific rate of scoring alone that earned him the distinction of twice becoming German Footballer of the Year and once European Footballer of the Year. The term 'striker' could have been invented for Gerd Muller.

The Germany of 1945, even in the comparatively remote Bavarian village of Zinsen, was not the ideal place to bring up a future European Footballer of the Year. But in the November of that year Frau Muller gave birth to a fourth child, a son, Gerhard.

He was only 15 when his father died and the young Muller was sent out to work in the weaving trade, because his mother could no longer afford to keep him at school. Football became strictly a Sunday affair. Muller joined the local club, TSV 1861 Nordlingen, where he gave some indication of his talents by scoring 46 goals for them in two seasons. His marksmanship soon came to the attention of the more senior sides.

Nordlingen's coach, Conny Kraft, a professional with Nuremberg in the 1950s, intended Gerd to sign for his old club. There were others in the market as well—among them Stuttgart Kickers, Augsburg, and Munich 1860—but they were all upstaged by Bayern Munich's sudden and decisive interest.

Wilhelm Neudecker, president of Bayern, sent his two best men to persuade Frau Muller that her son's future lay in joining the clu[b].

The deal had not been complete[d] when the rush to sign Mul[ler] reached its peak. There was [a] barrage of telephone calls fro[m] interested parties and even th[e] Mayor of Nordlingen called on th[e] Mullers, requesting Gerd not [to] leave the local club. But Mull[er] said simply 'I have given my word[d]' and moved to Munich in th[e] summer of 1963.

Despite Muller's record, on[e] man at Bayern was not immediate[ly] impressed by the new prodig[y]. The club coach, Yugoslav inte[r]national 'Tshik' Cajkovski, i[n]dignantly asked Neudecker 'Do yo[u] want me to put a bear among m[y] racehorses?' Within a year Mull[er] had dispelled all doubts by scorin[g] 35 goals in the Regional Leagu[e] South and helping Bayern to wi[n] promotion to the national divisio[n] the Bundesliga.

Physically Muller's build is no[t] unlike that of a bear; stocky, wit[h] thick thighs and short legs. Pe[r]haps an agile bear, with Muller['s] reflexes and coordination, woul[d] make an excellent striker. It [is] tempting to regard Muller's flair f[or] goalscoring as the product of shee[r] instinct, as a skill impossible [to] analyse, like that of a grea[t] musician or painter.

He himself admits that he's n[ot] sure how he does it—'Somehow something inside tells me "Gerd g[o]

COLOUR BY EMIL PERAUER

SVEN SIMON

Far left Gerd Muller was top scorer in the Mexico World Cup, but long after all the other goals are forgotten, his winner against England will be remembered. The expression of shocked disbelief on Brian Labone's face tells the story, as Muller calmly hooks the ball high into the England net.

Left Like other top players, Muller has many offers from advertising firms. But when he posed with this model for one of Germany's more spicy magazines his club, Bayern Munich, considered he had gone too far.

Below Muller comes in close and lifts the ball clear of Dusseldorf keeper Woyke, to give Bayern a 1-0 win. Muller's supreme anticipation and lightning reflexes, his coolness under pressure and his ability to take the knocks of the modern game make him Europe's most feared striker.

his way, Gerd go that way, Gerd move up"—and the ball is coming over and I score. I know that's not a very satisfactory answer, but I can't explain it any better than that. After all, if I don't know how to do it, no one can find out how to stop me.'

But in fact Muller is a great exploiter of free space, playing the percentages so that should the ball escape the defence, it falls prey to his deadly finishing. Muller has such rare powers of concentration and anticipation that he can assess situation instantly without moving his head to betray his intentions to an opponent.

If someone were to sit down at a drawing board and attempt to design the ultimate striker for the crowded penalty boxes of today's tight-marking game, the chances are he would come up with something like Gerd Muller. Stocky, about 5ft 8in (small enough to weave his way through the crush but not so small that he can be pushed easily off the ball), short thick legs, giving him a low centre of gravity which enables him to keep his balance in the tightest of turns. Add to these his sense of anticipation and concentration plus his excellent coordination and you have the ideal modern striker.

Muller is at his most dangerous in the physical challenge, for the strength of his hips and thighs

enables him to evade opponents, jockeying for position in a swift twisting movement that can often bring him clear through to goal. He showed this in the World Cup semi-final against Italy, when Poletti, screening the ball on the assumption that Muller was directly behind him, suddenly found the German wriggling through to beat Albertosi, Italy's goalkeeper, with the merest, stretching touch.

Some centre-halves have countered this trick of Muller's by holding off their tackle until the last possible moment, but in doing so they take an enormous risk. The centre-forward showed his stunning speed on the turn against Scotland's Ron McKinnon—no raw recruit—when, during a 1969 World Cup qualifying match in Glasgow, Muller left him like a bale of straw and shot the ball sweetly past Lawrence for West Germany's only goal of the match.

Muller's short, stocky legs give him a sense of balance far beyond that of the average player. In this way he can produce a shot out of a fall or a stumble, at precisely the moment when a defender or goalkeeper may have begun to relax.

It has been argued that Muller's heading ability is comparatively ordinary, but some of his goals suggest otherwise. Against Cyprus in Essen he turned a fast shot going

wide into a goal via a remarkable gliding header that required precision timing and perfect placing.

Muller is undoubtedly the best out-and-out striker in Europe, although there are others who excel in aspects of play where he is noticeably deficient. For example, Muller is not two-footed, and tends to favour the left for first-time shooting; a shrewd opponent can sometimes risk an early tackle, knowing which way Muller is likely to go.

Nor can one expect much of Muller when he is a long way from goal without support; he likes to lay the ball off and make his approach run for the return. Muller lacks the ability to take on opponent after opponent in meandering dribbles. This tends to make him a somewhat less attractive player to watch than, say, Cruyff of Barcelona who has that perfect mixture of genius and adventure, coupled with superb control.

Essentially, Muller does the simple things extremely well: he is not to be found trying to flight or chip the ball into goal by stroking it with the outside of his foot in the manner of Real Madrid's Pirri. Although Muller is an exciting player, it is an austere excitement engendered by physical endeavour: there is none of that instinctive artistry that one sometimes sees in other top players. Perhaps Muller

is a mechanic rather than a craftsman.

Muller played a subordinate role in his first season (1965-66) in top-class football, scoring just 14 goals and appearing in the Bayern side that won the German Cup, but it was in the following season that he began to confirm his true ability.

Muller's tally of goals in Bayern's 1966-67 season encouraged the West German team manager, Helmut Schoen, to give him a chance in the national side. Muller did not score in his first game, against Turkey in October 1966, but he justified himself with a vengeance by scoring four in his second appearance, albeit against Albania. In doing so, Muller became the first German player to score four goals in an international since 1942.

In the 1966-67 season, Muller, still only 21, had helped Bayern take both the German Cup and the Cup Winners' Cup, scoring 47 goals altogether (28 in the League, eight in the Cup Winners' Cup, seven in the German Cup and four in the international against Albania). He went on to win the Footballer of the Year award by 417 votes to team-mate Franz Beckenbauer's 60.

The goals continued to come for both club and country. In 1968-69 Muller helped Bayern to a League and Cup double and was once

Above *Simeonov, the Bulgarian goalkeeper, almost does a backward somersault as Muller scores from the penalty-spot. It was West Germany's third goal and Muller's second in a 5-2 win over Bulgaria in Mexico. Muller scored a third goal to complete the first hat-trick of the tournament. He repeated the performance against Peru.*

Left *Despite his extraordinary talent for scoring goals, Muller has never made his mark in other departments of the game. His kingdom is the penalty-box where his uncanny sense of position, his speed on the turn and his deadly accuracy make him one of the most feared strikers in Europe.*

again voted Footballer of the Year. The silver cannon, the top-scorer's trophy, and the golden ball, the Footballer of the Year trophy, were both presented to him before Bayern's opening match of the 1969-70 season, against Rot-Weiss Essen. Gerd responded appropriately by scoring a hat-trick.

In the World Cup qualifying competition, only Muller's ability seemed to stand between West Germany and complete disaster. In the games against Austria, Scotland and Cyprus he scored in every game, totalling nine goals from six matches.

Though West Germany managed to qualify for the 1970 World Cup, the team was far from settled, and Muller himself was unhappy with some of the experiments made by their manager Schoen. Following the second match against Austria, in which Germany snatched two points thanks only to Muller's goal two minutes from the end, he complained to reporters that his style simply did not fit in with certain members of the team, and either they would have to go, or he would. In the heat of the moment, Muller replied to a question, 'Yes, that even applies to Uwe Seeler.' From such small beginnings came a series of headlines about a Muller-Seeler feud. Muller and Seeler may not have been exactly life-long friends, but they always had the sense to put the team's interests above their own personal rivalries. The rumours were finally quashed only when Schoen cleverly made them share a room together for five weeks in their Mexican World Cup headquarters.

In the 1970 close season Bayern inexplicably allowed one of Muller's colleagues, Rainer Olhauser, to sign for the Swiss club, Grasshoppers of Zurich. Olhauser had played a vital part in Bayern's string of success, providing much of the ammunition for the Muller cannon. Without him Muller had to go looking for the ball more than he liked; in a match against Rot-Weiss Essen, he played so deep that he found himself handling in his own penalty area to prevent a certain goal.

The perpetual television flashbacks to Mexico provided opponents with a rare opportunity to study Muller's style: every telltale twitch, every mannerism became another footnote in the 'Stop Muller Textbook'. If it were possible, he found himself more closely marked than ever, and by defenders who had studied his every move.

Inevitably, his prolific scoring rate declined; only eleven goals in his first 20 league matches, only 22 in the 1970-71 season. He was less carefully marked in the European Fairs Cup, where he scored eight out of 14 goals in the first six games. It was unfortunate for Bayern that when they met Liverpool in the quarter finals Muller was below his peak form—still feeling the effects of a week in bed with flu. They lost 3-0 at Anfield, and could only manage a draw at home.

Bayern qualified for the 1971 German Cup final against Cologne, and Muller was lucky to play in the match. In January of that year he had been sent off in distant Lima, against Universitario, in what was euphemistically described as a friendly match. In Germany, sendings-off abroad are treated more sternly than in England, and although Bayern tried to keep the case out of the hands of the disciplinary committee, it came up a fortnight before the end of the League season. Muller received a two-month suspension, which should have kept him out of the cup final, but after an appeal by his club, the German FA relented and allowed him to play.

At this point the League title still hung in the balance, and even without Muller, Bayern actually managed to overtake Borussia Moenchengladbach at the top by one goal—in Germany, when teams are level on points, goal difference is used instead of goal average to decide their placings. But Borussia won their final match, while Bayern lost at Duisburg, after missing several chances that Muller would almost certainly have put away.

Because Bayern Munich—like a lot of German clubs—have financial problems, Muller's earnings fall a long way short of the enormou salaries paid to such as George Be and Luigi Riva. He does ha business interests, although aga not on the same sort of scale Best. Apart from the usual offe for advertising and sponsorsh Muller has a successful insuran agency in Nordlingen. In 1970 moved into a large new house Strasslach—a smart Munic suburb—and in that year he nette a clear £8,300 from his busine interests alone. However h earnings from football are hard comparable with those available a top Italian club.

Muller's rise to fame has no gone to his head. He still has tim for a friendly word with thos who were kind to him when he wa an unknown youngster, men lil 73-year-old Sepp Renn, wh spends 12 hours a day lookin after the Bayern player's boots.

But then Muller is essentially a easy going fellow who, despite tw suspensions, lacks the callousnes on the field that some stars fin essential for success. Off the fiel too, he is hardly what one woul call a hard-headed businessma He tends to agree to advertisin offers indiscriminately, and on got into trouble with his club f posing with a nude model for on of Germany's more spicy magazine

He also fights a constant battl between his stomach and h professional common sense. H weakness for food has given hi weight problems—his colleague play on his sensitivity by callin him 'Der Dicker', 'The Fat Fellow Unfortunately his shy wife Ursul or 'Uschi' as she's known, ha constant fears of him wastin away, and likes nothing better tha to heap platefuls of potato salad i front of him.

Up until 1974 Gerd Muller ha shown himself to be nothing othe than an out-and-out goal-getter However, he is only mortal: ag will eventually dull his concentra tion and reflexes, and when tha happens what will Gerd do then Other top strikers, such as Deni Law and Alfredo Di Stefano hav been able to drop back and mak their mark as creators rather tha finishers, but their styles wer inherently different from Muller's they were footballers who had flair for scoring goals. Muller i unique in that he is purely a goal scoring machine. If the machin continues to function efficientl Muller could become Germany' most prolific scorer ever, but if breaks down his fall from th pinnacle could be fast and final.

Gerhardt MULLER

Honours: European Cup Winners Cup winners medal 1967;
German League Championship medal 1968-69, 1971-72, 1972-73;
German Cup winners medal 1966, 1967, 1969, 1971;
European Footballer of the Year 1970;
German Footballer of the Year 1967, 1969

Club	Season	League		Int'nls	
		Mtchs	Gls	Mtchs	Gls
Bayern Munich	1965-66	33	15		
	1966-67	32	28	3	4
	1967-68	34	19	2	2
	1968-69	20	30	7	8
	1969-70	33	38	13	13
	1970-71	32	22	4	6
	1971-72	34	40	9	15
	1972-73	33	36	2	6
Total		251	228	40	54

Johan Cruyff— the finishing touch

umber 14 is dead' read the head-e in a Dutch newspaper, as it scribed Johan Cruyff's transfer m Ajax to CF Barcelona in ptember 1973.

Cruyff, the brilliantly gifted ward who for the previous three ars had superstitiously clung to shirt once worn successfully as substitute, had outgrown Dutch otball.

His speed, ball skills and ruthless ishing ability had been both ife and club in a series of suc-sses that had brought Ajax a t-trick of European Cup triumphs. The fee commanded by such a ent was of unique proportions. rcelona wrote a cheque for

around £460,000, a new record for a player's services. But their invest-ment did not end there. Cruyff received a similar sum, and there could be no doubt that the man who was arguably the best footballer of his generation was certainly the best financially placed.

When it came to talking business Cruyff left everything to his father-in-law Cor Coster. He admitted: 'If I'd had to conduct my own negotiations, I would be facing men of twice my age and experience. Negotiating-wise I'd be a walk-over for them. My father-in-law screws them for as much as he can because he can talk to them on the same level.'

In arranging the transfer Coster surpassed himself. In 1971 he had used the threat of a move abroad to secure Cruyff a marvellous con-tract with Ajax. It made him the first guilder millionaire footballer in Holland, guaranteeing him a sum of 1.5 million guilders (then £177,000) over a period of seven years.

The contract was never com-pleted. In the summer of 1973, Barcelona asked for Cruyff, and this time it seemed certain the deal would be on. At the eleventh hour, Ajax's superstar issued a communi-que: 'I won't go. I'm staying.'

It was left to Coster to give the reasons. His wife, Johan's mother-

Ajax have just beaten the Greek side Panathinaikos 2-0 at Wembley.

in-law, could not bear to see him leave Amsterdam. 'I told him leav-ing for Spain would break her heart. We really thought she was dying. She was unconscious and I had to send for the doctor when I told her about the transfer.'

Exactly what happened a week later is not clear except that Cruyff —and presumably Mr and Mrs Coster—was happy enough for the transfer to go through. And though the Dutch FA made an initial ban on him playing league football in Spain it was lifted within weeks of his move.

To many Dutchmen this high pressure negotiating was distasteful and tarnished Cruyff's popularity a little. He was undismayed.

Cruyff, no fool, realized just how short a footballer's life is: 'Our problem is that we are earning a lot of money while still young. But we are unable to prepare our-selves for the life after. I don't want to fall back once my playing days are over. I am used to a good life. So are my wife and my children and I want this to continue.'

Cruyff made his debut for Ajax

in the 1965-66 season and quickly started to amass goals. In fact he scored in his first match. In 1966, at the age of 19 he was capped for Holland, but in his first international season he ran into trouble. Against Czechoslovakia, he was provoked by a defender, he retaliated and was sent off. That episode earned him a year's suspension from international football.

In the 1966-67 season he tore the Liverpool defence to pieces with three goals—two of them at Anfield —in Ajax's 7-3 win in the European Cup. Two years later, again in the European Cup, Cruyff played a

Bar the final, Cruyff scored in every round of the Cup

major part. Though Ajax lost in the final to AC Milan, Cruyff scored in every round up to then. In the quarter-final against Benfica, with the score from the first two legs 4-4 on aggregate, Cruyff scored two in Ajax's 3-0 win in the play-off in Lisbon. An injury towards the end of that season slowed him down and consequently impaired the effectiveness of the team.

Off the field, Johan Cruyff is definitely no 'high life' fan. He is a quiet family man who is happy when he can take his attractive blonde wife Danny out for dinner after a Sunday league match.

Cruyff explained 'It is quite easy to get involved in the hectic life. But it affects your form. As a professional footballer I have to take care that I have the sort of relaxing home life that enables me to give my best on the field.'

These sort of thoughts are typical of Cruyff. He is a 100 per cent footballer whose first love and duty is to the game.

Ajax's former coach Stephan Kovacs, once trainer of the Rumanian national team and Rumanian champion Steaua, discovered this after only two months with Ajax.

'Johan loves football,' he enthused. 'You see this from the way he trains. He is more like a schoolboy who loves showing off what he can do with a ball. All the time he is trying to perfect his control, to try out new moves, flicks, shots and dribbles.'

When Ajax played Celtic in the 1970 European Cup quarter-finals, they were lodged at Troon. Cruyff, being told that this was on the coast, moaned 'Oh hell, that means miles

and miles of walking and running.'

Kovacs smiled 'I know. That's why I permitted him to do all his pre-season and present training with a ball. It suits him much better and he runs more with it than he ever does without.'

All of his training done with a ball— to make him run

Cruyff's love for the game started at an early age.

He watched the Ajax elite of that time train and eagerly copied their skills. At 15 he joined Ajax, and his talents were quickly spotted.

The lithe youngster packed a lot of power in his right foot but was physically underdeveloped and had a weak left foot. Youth trainer Jany van der Veen made Cruyff train with weights attached to his legs.

Cruyff matured quickly. He developed a powerful shot and the ability to score from all angles. Yet this was not his greatest asset.

His phenomenal speed, coupled with his superb ball control, made him stand out. He evaded tackles with the ease and grace of a leaping gazelle, leaving fullbacks flat on

their faces.

When younger he used to enjoy tormenting defenders, but after a couple of injuries he stopped that and concentrated on using his guile and his skill to crack open defence and create the easiest of chance for his fellow forwards.

Like the great Real Madrid players, Di Stefano and Puskas, the Dutch star had mastered variation of pace which bewildered defenders.

Rinus Israel, captain of Feyenoord and the Dutch national team, and undoubtedly one of the best centra defenders on the continent, knew just what it was like to be left by Cruyff: 'Of course you can sto Cruyff,' said Rinus. 'You can sto any player. But his variations a so many, his skill so bewilderin that many a time you don't kno what he is going to do next. You on know when he has gone.'

In the 1971 season, possibly because of the extra-close attention he received from opponents in the middle and also because of team tactics, Cruyff started to wander more to the left-wing. Piet Keizer normal outside-left and ear mentor to his friend Cruyff, fe back to link in midfield and fi openings.

op Cruyff lets fly at goal in a Euro-an match against AC Milan.

bove England's Hunter keeps a close atch on Cruyff at Wembley.

ight Cruyff trains in Hyde Park fore an Arsenal-Ajax Fairs Cup tie.

eft Cruyff in full cry.

Consequently Cruyff scored fewer *als but created twice as many. ccording to Kovacs, 'Cruyff going own the wing, drawing at least /o defenders towards him then ipping them contemptuously is* thal.

'From the bye-line he sends over *rving crosses with his right foot— e ball dropping just behind the fence. Goalkeepers frequently mis- dge these crosses and that's when e goals come.'

How great a player is Johan* ruyff? Surprisingly enough there is *me discussion in Holland about his ents. Most Dutchmen think he is e greatest player their country* s ever produced.

If he's good, he's rilliant—when he's ad, he's atrocious

But Abe Lenstra, Holland's most nerated inside-left, who could win *ternationals on his own and some- mes did, has his doubts. In an terview he once said 'Cruyff's ouble is that when he is good he very good. When he has a bad game e is atrocious.'

In his opinion there are several *hers, notably Piet Keizer, who e better players and are more con- stent.*

Nevertheless he has nearly always earned glowing tributes from football experts wherever he has played abroad. One always feels something extraordinary is going to happen once he fastens on a ball.

To many it seemed strange that Cruyff should have tied himself to one club for so long in his career before picking up valuable experience with a Spanish or Italian club. But he chose to remain in Holland as a large fish in a small pool.

His style seemed particularly suited to the Latin type of football. The hard competition in those countries seems likely to bring out fully all the talents he was so richly endowed with. Provided of course that he remains able to absorb the tough discipline in southern European football.

Kovacs had little doubt that Cruyff would easily succeed in adapting to Latin conditions. 'He has a Latin temperament,' he emphasized.

It was just this temperament which got Cruyff into trouble in the early stages of his career. When only 19 he was sent off in an international against Yugoslavia, because World Cup final referee Rudi Glockner claimed he had been hit by Cruyff. Nobody saw the blow, though everyone in the Amsterdam Olympic Stadium saw Cruyff kicking an opponent.

At the start of the 1971-72 season he became the first Dutch player to be hauled before the Dutch FA's disciplinary committee under a new rule. Though the referee had not booked Cruyff for a blatant foul in

a league match, an FA observer had reported him after the match and after shots of the match had been shown on Dutch television.

Cruyff was acquitted however because the committee could not find enough evidence to support the observer's charge.

Considering how many defenders both in Holland and abroad in European Cup matches 'had a go at him', Cruyff's remark 'I always try to control myself no matter what provocation' seemed largely true. There were very few marks against his name in the Dutch FA blackbook.

It is essentially because Johan Cruyff wanted to get on with the game. 'Football is his life,' said Kovacs. 'I can always feel it when we are training. He is one of that small band of footballers who understand instinctively what I mean even though they cannot always translate my sort of German. Training with Cruyff makes me feel young again,' he said.

In 1971 Ajax won the European Cup after beating the Greek side Panathinaikos 2-0 at Wembley. For Ajax it was not a particularly good game, they were complacent and never really controlled the play as they could have done. Cruyff too had—by his own high standards—a poor game. Even so, three times in 15 minutes he came down the left flank and had the Greek defence in disorder.

He was brilliant even by his own standards in the 1972 final against Inter-Milan when his two second-half goals won the game. And his skills stood out in a drab 1973 final in which Juventus fell victims to Ajax. Characteristically he left the Dutch club with a flourish early in the 1973-74 season with a magical solo goal in his last game.

After being initially confined to friendlies at Barcelona, he celebrated his first Spanish League game with two goals. Even without the number 14, the genius remained.

Johan CRUYFF

Honours: European Cup winners medal 1971, 1972, 1973
European Cup runners-up medal 1969
Dutch League winners medal 1966, 1967, 1968, 1970, 1972, 1973
Dutch Cup winners medal 1967, 1970, 1971, 1972

Club	Season	League Gls	Intls Mtchs	Gls
Ajax	1964-65	4		
	1965-66	16		
	1966-67	33	2	1
	1967-68	25	4	1
	1968-69	24	1	1
	1969-70	23	3	
	1970-71	21	2	4
	1971-72	25	5	6
	1972-73	16	4	5
Total		187	21	18

George Best— last of the superstars?

*George Best smiles for the cameras—his is a pu...
life. This montage gives an impression of the press
which turned him away from football for a ti...
He earns a lot of money and enjoys spending it,...
drives fast cars and takes out beautiful women.
engagement to the Danish girl, Eva Haraldsted, ...
front-page news from start to finish. He's met a pr...
minister, been sued for breach of promise, been...
before the disciplinary committee of the FA more th...
once, and built himself an expensive new house. Bu...
this the real George Best? Is there more to this son ...
Belfast shipyard worker than his public face? For t...
son of the good life has gone on record saying...
don't really need other people.'*

Whether or not George Best is one of the finest British players of all time, he is far and away the most symbolic of his age, with his life style, his earnings, his appearance, his sad misadventures, as much as his electric skills.

A comparison with Stanley Matthews is interesting. For decades, Matthews was the wayward star of British football, by general consent the most astonishingly gifted, the most revered and celebrated abroad. But Matthews, whose long career spanned the Depression, the Second World War and the post-War years, never became the household word that Best did, never began to exercise the same appeal on girls and women. Matthews' 'image', however enigmatic on the field, was that of a sober family man who put his light out early and trained with phenomenal dedication.

Best, who lives in a football world much tougher than Matthews', one in which hard work and superior physical conditioning plays a much more important part, is renowned as a creature of night clubs, boutiques and all the trappings of the easy rich life. His dramatic departure from football in 1972, reeling under these pressures was as inevitable as it was sensational.

'If you think about getting hurt for a minute, you're a loser'

Indeed, perhaps the most astonishing thing about Best is that he was able to perform such magical feats under such extreme pressure for so long when the game has never been so ruthless. He was an immensely courageous player, who simply refused to be intimidated even by the most severe treatment. 'I know six players in the First Division', he has said, 'who are going to trip and kick me. They're told to do it, usually. Some of them laugh about it, they think it's clever. With these players you have to watch two things; the ball, and someone coming to chop you. There aren't many cowards in football. If you think about getting hurt, you're a loser before you start out.' He has also said that there are two full-backs in the First Division who have deliberately set out to break his leg, adding sombrely, 'I think you have got to say that I hate these men.'

The comparison between Best and Matthews as players should not be pushed too far. Matthews, though he once scored three goals in an international match from inside-right with his left foot, was essentially a right-winger, relying on his incredible body swerve outside the back. Best began as an outside-right but prefers to be in the middle of the park, directing play, and looking for chances to score. He has Matthews' swerve right enough, but he is a smaller, quicker, more galvanic man with a wider repertory altogether. Often he will beat a man simply with a sudden and remarkable turn, as he did when he ran through to score a vital goal for Manchester United early in extra time in the European Cup final of 1968 against Benfica, at Wembley.

Two years later, on the same ground but down the other end, a similar, extraordinary pivot took him round his United colleague Nobby Stiles, to score a memorable goal against England. That was four days after he had been sent off the field at Windsor Park for throwing mud at the referee and spitting during an international against Scotland. This, too, distinguishes him from Matthews, who scarcely ever had even a free kick

There is more to football than the game on Saturdays. The struggle to regain peak fitness was George Best's greatest problem when he returned to Manchester United in September 1973.

RAY GREEN

given against him.

Though he does everything much more sharply and suddenly, Best, like Matthews, owes much of his success to perfect balance. It is very hard to knock him off the ball, though he is only 5 feet 8½ inches and weighs merely 10 stone 3 pounds. At the same time, this amazing balance allows him to beat men and score goals in ways which other players would never dream of. Once at Chelsea, for example, he took a wall pass from David Sadler in the penalty area, seemed to have no chance of shooting before he was tackled, then promptly proceeded to score with the 'wrong' foot, while seemingly off balance.

He is surprisingly good with his head, too, jumping remarkable heights and making good use of a powerful neck; but his virtuosity becomes obvious when looking at so many of his spectacular goals. Sometimes the goal may follow a dazzling individual run around player after player, sometimes it can be impertinently lobbed—like one against Spurs at Old Trafford, early in 1971— sometimes it is whipped in on the turn with one foot, after a tightly marking player has been beaten with the other. There is no end to Best's originality, his cool cheek. And with all this, he

has a footballing brain, and can distribute the b... with subtle accuracy.

His quarrel with referees has been a bitter o... which has led to such incidents as the one ... Belfast, when Best threw mud at the referee a... spat hard on the ground, and to a two-month s... pension which followed a piece of unnecessa... petulance after a televised floodlit game agai... Manchester City; Best knocked the ball out ... the referee's hands.

'Do they seriously think I don't want to change? Of course I do!'

'Do they seriously think I don't want ... change?' he has cried. 'Of course I do! But I ca... change. I know myself well enough to realiz... can't promise to change. I can only try and go ... trying. I can get whacked from the back or ... when the ball has gone past 28 times in a row a... do nothing or say nothing. I don't know why... should boil, the 29th time, which has been... different. It just happens.'

'I've met only two referees I've any time fc... he remarked on another occasion. 'How can y... respect anybody who doesn't do his job properly...

At the beginning of the 1971-72 season, B... was in trouble with the referees again. He w... one of the first victims of the surprise hard li... they took on the interpretation of the laws whi... shook footballers and managers alike. Refer... Norman Burtenshaw had no hesitation in sendi... him off the field in the match against Chelsea f... 'dissent', after protesting at a Chelsea go... Just before he renounced the game in 1972 ... was sent off once again while playing for ... country against Bulgaria.

Best was brought up in one of the ugly, r... brick streets of Belfast, born in that city ... 22 May 1946, the son of a shipyard worker. ... obviously has a very close bond with his moth... whom he physically resembles. And he has pa... tribute to his father in these words: 'I might ha... missed everything I'm enjoying now if my fath... had not pointed me in the right direction. But th... he had me kicking a ball from the time I cou... toddle, before I can even remember.'

It was his father, too, who insisted that ... return to Old Trafford when, as a homesick ... year-old, he left Manchester to return home... Belfast within 48 hours of starting his n... career, after a trial there with another gift... Irish player, McMordie, who later moved ... Middlesbrough. This time Best settled dow... thanks largely to a kindly landlady. At 17 he w... in the Manchester United League team, despite ... fragility. He had weighed just seven and a h... stone on his arrival in Manchester, and it w... only the insistence of United's Irish scout whi... took him there in the first place, after others h... passed him over—a familiar enough story in fo... ball.

His keenness on the game had led him to give ... the chance of going to a grammar school, becau... he wanted to go on playing soccer. Football, rath... than the Protestantism in which he was broug... up, was his virtual 'religion'; and he has alwa... been amiably free from bias. 'Even when I wa... kid', he has said, 'religion didn't bother me. I w... a Protestant and I went to school in a Catho... district, and when I was walking home t... Catholics would start fighting, so I've got as goo...

reason as any to hate them, but I don't.'

Among the first to marvel at his talents at Old Trafford was a fellow Ulsterman, Harry Gregg, then the international goalkeeper. Gregg had been injured, and took part in a practice game with the juniors. 'Well, this kid from Belfast came at me with the ball,' he has said. 'I went out to meet him; and he done me! In those days, I could usually dictate what League players should do, never mind youngsters. But with this boy, I'd gone one way and the ball the other. For the sake of my ego, I tried to believe that I'd sold myself, but it happened again shortly afterwards.'

'But George must have had cotton wool in his ears. He didn't hear'

At Old Trafford, too, Best came under the benign, paternalist influence of United's manager, Matt Busby, the most significant figure in his career. Busby was always one who let his gifted players play, rather than put them in a tactical straightjacket, which had been greatly to Best's advantage; though Busby himself was often exasperated at times. He speaks, particularly, of one of Best's most brilliant performances; a quarter-final away tie in the European Cup, in 1966 against Benfica, in Lisbon. 'We planned to contain them for the opening 20 minutes or so, let them come at us, hold them, then strike back suddenly. That was the plan.

'But George must have had cotton wool in his ears. He didn't hear. Within the first quarter of an hour he destroyed them on his own with two goals and another made for Connelly. It was fantastic, and I was almost angry with them.'

Billy Bingham, Northern Ireland's former manager, has also spoken with some grief of Best's attitude in team conferences. 'He contributes nothing . . . Nothing at all. He sits and never utters a word. At team talks most players want to get involved, but when I bring George into

the discussion he'll only say yes or no . . . I don't know why, because he's an intelligent boy.'

Best can exasperate his fellow players, too. One of the most illustrious of them, Scotland and Manchester City's Denis Law, once observed, 'He's one of the finest footballers I've ever seen, but would be twice as good and would score twice as many goals if he got it into his head that there are other players to pass to and that he'll get the ball back.'

This was complemented by the remark of another United player when Best, in sensational circumstances, dropped out of the team to play Chelsea in London early in 1971, and United, after a long, bad run, won the game. 'The reason we went so well today was that George wasn't there hogging the ball. We all got a chance to play with it.'

Which was basically unfair since Best, all that season, had been taking risks and knocks, going it alone, precisely because he was getting so little support; though he himself has admitted that his besetting fault is to hang on so long. Didn't Matthews?

This Chelsea episode was in some sense the turning point of Best's career, the incident which showed just how astonishingly prominent a national figure he had become. Never before had so much newspaper space and television time been devoted to the escapades of a professional footballer.

Best, who had been missing more and more trains to London, and who had recently obliged Busby to eat humble pie after turning up late for a meeting of a disciplinary committee at the Football Association, now missed another train. United arrived in London on the Friday without him, and although Best followed them down, he went to ground in the Islington flat of a talented young actress called Sinead Cusack.

The flat was besieged by television and newspaper reporters, and there was buzzing speculation as to whether the immense pressures of Best's life, on the field, where he was maltreated, and off

In action against a Blackpool defender who has been sent completely off-balance, George Best demonstrates the ball-control and body-swerve which have made him famous all over the world. In addition, he showed the courage to face any challenge modern football could throw at him, a quality demonstrated in the left inset where Best and Dave Mackay

it, where he lived in an illuminated goldfish bowl, had finally proved too much.

The following Monday, Busby, 'the Boss', waited in his office at Old Trafford for Best to come to see him. Best didn't come. Sympathy swung away from him. But soon come he did, apologizing, promising to be good, and receiving a light two-week suspension. The liaison with Miss Cusack came, like so many of Best's much publicized amours, to a quick conclusion, and Best, on his return, lobbed that spectacular goal against Tottenham.

No player in the history of British football has ever been such a centre of attraction as Best, has ever had to cope with so much attention and publicity. With his long hair, his beard, the fashionable clothes he wears, models and endorses, his expensive sports cars, the £36,000 house he built for himself outside Manchester, the reputed £30,000 a year from all sources he earns, he is essentially the product, and emblem, of the years which followed the abolition of soccer's £20 maximum wage, in 1961. He himself has been described by his mother as a home-loving boy who will often sit quietly for hours in the house. But there is still the paradox of Best's frenetic social life, where he so often appears as the still centre of a whirling activity, not happy to be there, but not able to tear himself away, to be without it.

'If there are three or four people I can regard as real friends', he has admitted, 'that's the lot. I don't find it easy to get really close to people, or maybe I should say I don't find it easy to let them get really close to me. A lot of the other people I come in contact with I've learned to suspect,

fight for a high ball. But because he pushed himself and was being pushed to the limit, the situation would flare up at any time. Best has said that he can control his temper only for so long, then he explodes. The result can be seen in the right inset. In the green shirt of Ireland, he dejectedly leaves the field, sent off in an international against Scotland in 1970.

because I know how little their friendship means. But I'm not suggesting that's the full explanation of why I can count my friends on one hand. The thing is I don't really need other people all that much. I don't have to lean on them emotionally. In fact when I feel I'm getting involved it makes me uneasy.'

In this connection, a revealing anecdote concerns the girl Best was once seeing in London, one whom, originally, he had long cherished from afar. One morning, in Best's words, 'She was coming round to pick me up at the place where I was staying, but suddenly I got out of bed, packed and took off for Manchester. I left a note on the door for her. It said, "Nobody knows me".'

'I'm not a machine, you know. I have feelings like everyone else'

In this context Best's character seems to be a compound of loneliness and immaturity; yet how many young men could, with so sketchy an educational and worldly background, at so early an age, have coped with such adulation? Best has complained of the negative attention he often has to put up with. 'I can take stick,' he says, 'I don't mind that. I know when I'm not playing well and I don't care who tells me so. But sometimes, the pressures of it all can become just too much, particularly when it's criticism all the way. I'm not a machine, you know; I have feelings like everyone else. I don't always show them, but they are there. What upsets me is the way people can say what they like about me, and I can say

nothing back . . . I would be lying if I said I didn't like all the fuss when I first started—I did. In the beginning, I liked it. Then suddenly it all started to go sour. Suddenly I could go nowhere, do nothing, without people staring, trying to pick fights, or telling me how to do my job. Men would come up and try to pick a fight because a friend of a friend has told them that I was looking at their wife in some club or another. They will jostle me in bars and then accuse me of trying to cause trouble. They come and look at my house and say it looks like a public lavatory ... They wait for me to make a mistake on the field and they start. My God, do they start.'

The first signs that the pressure was really beginning to tell came in January 1972, two months after he was forced to withdraw from an international in Belfast because of death threats.

On 7 January it was announced from Old Trafford that Best had gone missing, that he had not reported for training for a week. He was consequently dropped from the Saturday match against Wolverhampton Wanderers.

United were by now being managed by Frank O'Farrell. Busby had assumed the stature of a father figure at Old Trafford. On the following Monday Best was interviewed by O'Farrell and the upshot was that the prodigal was ordered to leave his luxury bachelor home and move back into digs for the rest of the season. He was also fined two weeks wages and told to report for extra training, morning and afternoons, to get fit in time for a forthcoming Cup tie.

The match was at Southampton and United drew, their goal coming from a Bobby Charlton shot after a magical Best dummy had set up the chance. In the replay at Old Trafford, Best gave a virtuoso performance to win the game in extra time.

He saw out the season to finish at the top of the club's scoring lists, but in May he failed to report to the Northern Ireland training camp for the Home International Championship. He

was reported to be holidaying in Spain. Understandably the team manager Terry Neill had to drop Best from the squad, and while the team are losing 2-0 at Hampden Park, their reluctant star is preparing a sensational announcement.

On 20 May George Best proclaimed that he was retiring from football: 'I am a physical and mental wreck,' he explained. 'I have been drinking too much because of the pressures particularly over the last four months.' At the news Terry Neill generously offered to take Best back into the international squad, but he refused to talk to anybody—even his past mentor Matt Busby.

But Busby was a significant figure in eventually persuading Best to retract, and he lined up for the first match of the new season. But it was an uneasy peace, not only for Best but also for Frank O'Farrell and the rest of the United players, who were far from happy with the tolerant attitude shown to Best's aberrations by the board of directors.

On the field the tension within the club began to show. The Best affair could not be solely blamed for the fact that United were bottom

George BEST

Honours: European Cup winner's medal 1967-68; League Championship medal 1964-65, 1966-67; Footballer of the Year 1967-68; European Footballer of the Year 1968

Club	Season	League		Int'nls	
		Mtchs	Gls	Mtchs	Gls
Manchester United	1963-64	17	4	2	
	1964-65	41	10	7	3
	1965-66	31	9	3	
	1966-67	42	10	1	
	1967-68	41	28	1	
	1968-69	41	19	4	1
	1969-70	37	15	4	1
	1970-71	40	18	6	4
	1971-72	40	18	2	
	1972-73	19	4	1	
Total		349	135	31	9

Three days later, O'Farrell, his coach Malco[lm] Musgrove and chief scout John Aston w[ere] sacked. 'The team is bottom of the table,' [was] O'Farrell's only reason as he explained his [dis]missal to the Press. The same day a letter arri[ved] at Old Trafford from George Best in which [he] once more stated that he was retiring from fo[ot]ball. It was a sorry epitaph to O'Farrell's s[tay] with United. During his period in charge he [had] rarely shown publicly that he could control B[est]. Or even if he had been able to do so, the event[s at] board room level had impaired his control.

The managerial chair went to Tom[my] Docherty, who imported Scottish internation[als] in large enough numbers to keep United in [the] First Division. Best flitted around the wor[ld] refusing an offer to play in North Ameri[ca] turning his back on football. To his critics [it] was an irresponsible joy-ride. To his support[ers] it was a detailed, detached period of s[elf] analysis.

The events of the summer of 1973 illustr[ate] the complexities and the contradictions of [the] man. Television personality and sports journa[list] Michael Parkinson had approached Best ab[out] compiling a book telling the story of his fi[rst] disenchantment with football. It was to be [a] serious work, unlike so many of the chea[p,] contrived souvenirs that typified much of [the] Best image propagated by the hangers-on t[hat] had surrounded him in droves.

Best accepted the offer, and in close collabo[ra]tion much of the book was written. Suddenly l[ate] in the summer, with the season a couple [of] matches old, a press conference was called [at] Old Trafford. George Best had been forgi[ven] once more; he was back.

The news came as a surprise to Parkinson w[ho] had dined with Best an evening or two earl[ier]. He had told him not to let the work stand [in] his way if he seriously wanted to return [to] football. All Parkinson asked, a reasona[ble] request, was a quick telephone call to put h[im] in the picture before the story broke. As [he] admitted with some humility he is still waiti[ng] for that call.

Best returned a stone overweight, an alm[ost] chubby caricature of himself. But with Uni[ted] again in the grips of a fight for survival, the[re] was a premium on a quick return—provid[ing] the magic remained.

Two testimonial appearances, one for De[nis] Law against Ajax, only emphasised the physi[cal] problems he faced. But within two months [of] his return he won a place in the League si[de]. The saga had taken yet another twist.

Best's position in the British game is capa[ble] of exhaustive analysis. At the time of his '[re]tirement' he was clearly the only crowd-pul[ler] left. For all the reputations built by the likes [of] Charlton and Moore, or the histrionics of [the] Charlie Georges and Peter Osgoods, Best w[as] the only man capable of adding 10,000 to a ga[te]. With him gone, the game was in dire danger [of] losing the little magic it had left at the st[art] of a disillusioned decade.

Again, just why Best should be so special h[as] never been defined. Many 15-year-olds must ha[ve] had that ball control, that balance, that burst [of] speed and even those perceptions about t[he] game. But where were they five years later? P[er]haps the closest guess came from a colleag[ue]. 'What made George so different was that [he] came back. If he was kicked he didn't mind, [he] didn't hide. He just set out to prove that [the] other guy was a fool, that he wasn't fit to be [on] the same field as George Best. He wanted [to] prove that he was the best there was.'

It is not easy to apportion the blame f[or] Best's downfall. His excesses at times were [in]excusable, but how much should those who rev[el]led in his character—the officials and players [at] United, the hangers-on, the press and the age[nts] —be regarded as accomplices. Best was the fi[rst] of the new superstars, and perhaps the last.

---

of the First Division, without a win until their tenth League match, but their failure was relevant.

Best lasted until 25 November 1972 when United beat Southampton to lift themselves to 19th in the table, but the following week he missed further training sessions. O'Farrell, already under immense pressure, dropped him and after talks Best not only walked out on United but on Manchester itself, without the club's permission. The most persistent of London journalists located him in a London night club.

The following day United and O'Farrell took a stand, and George Best, for so long the hottest property in British football, was put on the transfer list. It was a testimony to the extent of Best's unreliability that only one manager, Brian Clough of Derby County, expressed any interest in purchasing him.

Ten days later came a staggering announcement from Old Trafford that Best would start training again, and that presumably he would not be available for transfer. But the news did not come from Frank O'Farrell but from the United chairman Louis Edwards.

What the players thought of the apparent total reprieve of a man who had from their point of view abandoned the club in a crisis never reached beyond the dressing-room door. What Frank O'Farrell thought about the matter being taken out of his hands he was too gentlemanly to reveal.

But the performance of the team in their next fixture spoke volumes about the state of morale. United, away to fellow strugglers Crystal Palace, were not only beaten, they were totally destroyed as the Palace players, unable to believe their good fortune, scored five times without the hint of a reply.